and Economic Change

Social Stratification and Economic Change

Edited by David Rose

Sociology Editor Howard Newby

Hutchinson
London Melbourne Auckland Johannesburg

Hutchinson Education

An imprint of Century Hutchinson Ltd

62–65 Chandos Place, London WC2N 4NW

Century Hutchinson Australia Pty Ltd
PO Box 496, 16–22 Church Street, Hawthorn,
Victoria 3122, Australia

Century Hutchinson New Zealand Ltd
PO Box 40–086, Glenfield, Auckland 10,
New Zealand

Century Hutchinson South Africa (Pty) Ltd
PO Box 337, Bergvlei 2012, South Africa

First published 1988

British Library Cataloguing in Publication Data
Social stratification and economic change.
   1. Great Britain. Social stratification.
   Economic aspects
   I. Rose, David
   305′.0941

   ISBN 0-916469-1-X

Set in 10/12pt Times

Printed and bound in Great Britain by
Anchor Brendon Ltd, Tiptree, Essex

SB 39926 (1) £8.95. 11.88

Contents

List of contributors

Frank Bechhofer is Director of the Research Centre for Social Sciences, University of Edinburgh. He is joint author of *The Affluent Worker* and joint editor of *The Petite Bourgeoisie*. In addition he has written numerous papers on both social stratification and sociological methods. He was the original convenor of the SSRC Social Stratification Seminar.

Bob Blackburn is Head of Sociological Research in the Department of Applied Economics at Cambridge and a Fellow of Clare College. He has been a Nuffield Foundation Fellow at the University of Lausanne and Fellow at the Netherlands Institute of Advanced Study. He is author of *Union Character and Social Class* and joint author of *Perceptions of Work*, *The Working Class in the Labour Market*, *Social Stratification and Occupations*, *White Collar Work* and *White Collar Unionism*.

Brian Elliott was until recently Senior Lecturer in Sociology, University of Edinburgh but now teaches in Canada. He has published extensively in the fields of urban sociology, political sociology and social stratification and is joint author of *Property and Power in the City* and *The Petite Bourgeoisie*.

Robert Goffee is Lecturer in Organisational Behaviour at the London Business School. He has published numerous articles on small business and is joint author of *The Real World of the Small Business Owner*, *The Entrepreneurial Middle Class* and *Women in Charge*.

John H. Goldthorpe is an Official Fellow of Nuffield College, Oxford. He is joint author of *The Affluent Worker* studies and author of *Social Mobility and Class Structure*. In addition he has written numerous articles on aspects of social stratification and is currently involved in an international project on social mobility.

Chris Harris has published chiefly in the fields of the sociology of the family, social theory and religion. His best known works are *The Family* and *The Family and Industrial Society*. He is currently Professor of Sociology and Anthropology at University College, Swansea.

Raymond M. Lee is Senior Lecturer in Sociology at St Mary's College, Twickenham. He was previously Senior Research Officer in Sociology at University College, Swansea, where he did research on redundant steelworkers. He has also done research on Northern Ireland and on the sociology of religion.

David Lockwood is Professor of Sociology, University of Essex and a Fellow of the British Academy. His books include *The Blackcoated Worker*, *The Affluent Worker* and *Solidarity and Schism*. In addition he has published widely in the areas of social stratification and sociological theory.

Gordon Marshall is Lecturer in Sociology, University of Essex. He is author of *Presbyteries and Profits* and *In Search of the Spirit of Capitalism* and joint author of *Social Class in Modern Britain*. He has published articles on a wide range of sociological topics from Durkheim to behaviour in a licensed restaurant.

David McCrone is Lecturer in Sociology, University of Edinburgh. He has undertaken research on the *petit bourgeoisie*, urban sociology and Scottish society and politics. His publications include *The City: Patterns of Domination and Conflict* and *Property and Power in a City*, both written with Brian Elliott.

Howard Newby is Professor of Sociology, University of Essex and Director of the ESRC Data Archive. His books include *The Deferential Worker*, *Green and Pleasant Land* and *Country Life*. He has co-authored and co-edited a number of other studies including *Doing Sociological Research*, *The Problem of Sociology*, *Property, Paternalism and Power* and *Social Class in Modern Britain*.

Iain Noble is Research Fellow in the Department of Sociological Studies, University of Sheffield. Previously worked at the Universities of Reading and Manchester and for the Office of Population Censuses and Surveys. Joint author of *After Redundancy*.

Ray Pahl is Research Professor of Sociology, University of Kent. He has done empirical research on commuter villages, British managers and directors and unemployed workers. His many publications include *Whose City?*, *Patterns of Urban Life* and *Divisions of Labour*. He has been a member of the Social Studies Sub-Committee of UGC since 1979.

David Rose is Lecturer in Sociology, University of Essex. He is joint author of *Property, Paternalism and Power* and *Social Class in Modern Britain*. He has written articles in the areas of social stratification, rural and community sociology and sociological methods. He was convenor of the ESRC Social Stratification Seminar from 1980–5.

Richard Scase is Professor of Sociology, University of Kent. His publications include *Social Democracy in Capitalist Society* and his three books with Robert Goffee, *The Real World of the Small Business Owner*, *The Entrepreneurial Middle Class* and *Women in Charge*. He is a broadcaster and director of a local radio station.

Carolyn Vogler is Research Officer on the ESRC 'Social Change and Economic Life' initiative at Nuffield College, Oxford. She is author of *The Nation State* and joint author of *Social Class in Modern Britain*.

Alan Walker is Professor of Social Policy, University of Sheffield. His publications include *Unqualified and Unemployed*, *Public Expenditure and Social Policy* and *Social Planning*. He is joint author of *After Redundancy*.

Claire Wallace is Lecturer in Sociology at Plymouth Polytechnic and Secretary of the British Sociological Association. She worked with Ray Pahl on the study of Sheppey and has written articles on the sociology of youth. She is author of *For Richer, For Poorer: Growing up in and out of Work*.

John Westergaard is Professor of Sociological Studies, University of Sheffield. He has written widely on aspects of class structure, urban development and land use planning. He is author of *Class in a Capitalist Society* and joint author of *After Redundancy*.

Acknowledgements

This volume has been far too long in gestation for a variety of reasons. It is therefore particularly important that I thank all the contributors, as well as Claire L'Enfant of Hutchinson, for their forbearance. The SSRC/ESRC financed the Social Stratification Seminar for twelve years and the contributors are grateful for this support. I am also very grateful to the Nuffield Foundation for the award of a Social Science Research Fellowship which was spent in part on work for this text, although mainly in work on the Essex class project. A. H. Halsey and Duncan Gallie made very helpful suggestions about this book at an early stage in its development. Sandra Dyson, Gilly Burrell, Carole Allington and Mary Girling (as well as the editor) typed and retyped what follows. Richard Curtin prepared the bibliography. But, most importantly, my colleague and friend Gordon Marshall never let me forget that I had to get this to the publishers. Without his support during difficult times, and that of Ted Benton, Shelley Pennington, Penny Rickman, Howard Newby, Ray Pahl, Lynne Foweraker, Gladis Garcia, Everard Longland, Annie Menzies, Brigitte Preissl and Carolyn Yates, I would have taken even longer to get this volume finished. '

For permission to reproduce copyright material I wish to record my thanks to the Department of Sociology, University of Essex for *Intellectuals and the Working Class in Modern Britain*; JAI Press for *The Weakest Link in the Chain*; and the Editorial Board of *Politics and Society* and their publishers Geron-X for *Some Remarks on the Study of Working-Class Consciousness*.

David Rose
Colchester
1987

1 Introduction

David Rose

The contributors to this volume were all members of the Economic and Social Research Council Social Stratification Seminar in the years between 1973 and 1985. This group had a somewhat elitist, anti-feminist, exclusivist reputation in British sociology which, if understandable in terms of the development of British sociology in the 1970s, was undeserved. It began life as a result of an SSRC conference at Durham in 1972 (see Bulmer, 1975 (ed.), for the proceedings of this conference). One of the participants, Frank Bechhofer, persuaded the Sociology Committee of SSRC to finance a seminar to continue the type of discussions which the Durham conference had instigated. The initial membership of the seminar was provided by those sociologists who, in 1973, were in receipt of SSRC grants to study aspects of social stratification in Britain. The seminar was designed to provide an informal forum for the discussion of the common interests of its members. Over the years old members dropped out and new ones attended, with the new members being invited on the basis of the changing nature of stratification research. Towards the end of its life the seminar attracted funds from ESRC to widen its discussions by holding colloquia on particular themes. One of these, on gender and stratification, led to the publication of some of its proceedings (Crompton and Mann, 1986). With a change of policy at ESRC the decision was made to withdraw the regular funding of such seminars. This volume was conceived in the wake of that decision. It was not conceived as a summary of the discussions which had taken place over the years, however, but more as some kind of memorial to the seminar's erstwhile existence.

The first three chapters in Part One have all been published previously but are reproduced here because they are important theoretical statements and because they were initially published in rather obscure places and deserve a more accessible outlet. The remainder of the papers are all new and reflect the empirical work which was being conducted by members of the Economic and Social Research Council Social Stratification Seminar at the time of its demise. Since this work all has some bearing on economic decline and the social, political and economic changes induced during the life of the Thatcher administration, the title *Social Stratification and Economic Change* seemed appropriate. However, it was never the intention to produce a comprehensive review of economic change, still less of social stratification. What this volume is designed to do is to introduce students in particular to some of the important recent debates in social stratification, as well as to some of the more significant empirical studies of the 1980s in this area. Other recently

11

published volumes complement the purposes of this one (for example, Roberts *et al.* (eds), 1985) and can usefully be used in conjunction with this to obtain a broader overview of the field.

Because this is primarily a student text, and given the difficulties which some of the chapters will present students, this introduction attempts some exegesis of what follows. It also tries to place the various contributions in a wider context, as well as drawing out some of the relationships between the chapters. Part One presents four complementary, largely theoretical papers. The main theme which unites them is that of anti-historicism, although they all make statements which go beyond this common denominator. Part Two offers a variety of empirical papers covering unemployment, political and work ideologies in a variety of local and national contexts. If this introduction and the papers which follow serve to awaken students to the importance of social stratification as the central element of macro-sociology, the book will have served an important purpose.

*   *   *

The chapters in Part One all raise central theoretical and empirical issues for the study of social stratification. Goldthorpe criticizes three approaches to the study of the working class which, while different in their analyses and prognostications, nevertheless share one thing in common. Each projects its own socio-political goals on to the working class through its particular brand of historicism. One of these approaches is Marxism and it is recent Marxist class analysis which is the subject of Lockwood's chapter. In a penetrating critique of the most important Marxist contributions on class of the 1970s, Lockwood demonstrates, *inter alia*, Marxism's inability to cope satisfactorily with the non-rational elements of social action. Whereas Goldthorpe and Lockwood are critical of perspectives with which they are out of sympathy, Marshall takes issue with much of the empirical work on working-class consciousness which Goldthorpe and Lockwood's earlier work had stimulated. Marshall's incisive review lays bare the inadequacies of both 'instrumentalism' and 'ambivalence' as interpretations of the available evidence on working-class consciousness and argues for new research strategies which relate consciousness to action. Finally, Pahl and Wallace critically examine the concept of cultural privatization which to an extent informs the empirical work of Goldthorpe and Lockwood, and Marshall, Newby and Rose. While readers must judge for themselves the merits of the arguments presented in these four chapters, this introduction attempts both to provide some explanation of crucial issues and to place the various authors' work in their context.

John H. Goldthorpe has been a persistent and influential critic of liberal and Marxist accounts of social stratification throughout his career (see, for example, Goldthorpe, 1964, 1971, 1972, 1983a and 1986; Goldthorpe and Lockwood, 1963; Goldthorpe *et al.*, 1969). In the essay reproduced here he criticizes each of these approaches to studies of the working class and extends his critique to 'organicist' writers in the literary tradition of F. R. Leavis. *Intellectuals and the Working Class in Modern Britain* was originally written for the 1979 Fuller Lecture in the Department of Sociology, University of Essex, and as such deals only with developments to the end of the 1970s. The themes contained in the essay have continued to inform Goldthorpe's more recent work (see, for example, Goldthorpe, 1983a and 1986), but this essay was selected for inclusion in this volume both because it deserves wider publication than it has hitherto received, and because the issues it raises are of continuing importance for the debate on the working class. Indeed, they are explicitly referred to in some of the subsequent chapters in this book.

As Newby has observed, studies of the working class have tended to predominate in British social stratification research, not least because of 'the value commitments of sociologists, ranging from a desire to promote ameliorative social engineering to a historicist concern with the working class as a purveyor of political and social revolution' (1981, p. 9). And it is historicism, of whatever theoretical or political persuasion, which is Goldthorpe's main target in Chapter 2. Perhaps because of the influence of Popper (1945 and 1957) many people have come to equate historicism with Marxism alone. However, the fact is that Marxists are not alone in producing such accounts. Indeed one of Goldthorpe's continuing preoccupations has been the historicism of avowedly anti-Marxist American social scientists such as Kerr, Bell and Lipset – the liberal theorists whom he discusses in relation to the work of Anthony Crosland (see, for example, Goldthorpe 1965, 1971, 1986). In *Intellectuals and the Working Class in Modern Britain* he extends his critique to a third group of writers whom he calls the 'organicists'. In their work, as well as that of social democrats such as Crosland and Marxists such as Perry Anderson, Goldthorpe finds examples of 'wishful, rather than critical, thinking' about the working class. Ultimately this is because each group has considered the working class 'as the crucial social agency for the achievement of *their own* social and political goals'. In so doing each has tended to ignore the niceties of the empirical evidence in favour of arguments concerning immanent tendencies and supposedly long-term historical trends. A brief examination of Goldthorpe's claims in relation to liberal and Marxist theories might help to elucidate his essay further.

In the 1950s certain American social scientists began to develop a distinctive 'theory of industrial society' (compare Badham, 1984, Giddens, 1982 and Kumar, 1978). Typically this theory stressed the beneficial aspects of industrial societies as equalizers of opportunities, the institutionalization of class conflict through the extension of citizenship, the accompanying rise of the liberal-democratic state, and a 'logic of industrialism' such that as societies industrialize so they become more similar and converge in a common process of development. Much evidence was adduced for this view. For example, high rates of social mobility were taken as evidence of equalization and openness in society, as was the contraction of the 'traditional' (i.e. manual) working class and the growth of white-collar and service occupations. This latter trend was seen to involve a reskilling or upgrading of work in advanced industrial societies. Work would generally become both less alienating and less likely to be the source of class conflict. This development would be reinforced by another – the managerial revolution in which people-motivated rather than profit-motivated managers would take control of industry. Indeed some writers hailed the coming of 'post-industrial society' with its promise of greater wealth and less effort for all.

Unfortunately the social scientists who advocated such a view had misread their tea-leaves. As I have commented elsewhere, the promise of the post-industrial society has given way to the less comfortable realities of the deindustrializing society (see Rose *et al.*, 1984). While industrial society theorists were correct to identify as important the contraction in the traditional working class and the expansion of white-collar work, they did not anticipate that this could lead to wider rather than narrower social and economic inequalities – especially in a context such as that experienced in Britain since the mid 1960s. Both the instrumental collectivism of the late 1960s and early 1970s, consequent upon the fuller participation of the working class in society, and the current reality of high levels of unemployment, along with the increasing tendency towards less secure forms of employment, have emphasized the extent to which liberal analyses of class structure and class processes are wanting.

These weaknesses of liberal theories have been made even more apparent by Goldthorpe's work on social mobility and class formation (1980; 1986). For example, liberals had assumed that high levels of social *mobility* such as those found in western societies could be equated with high levels of social *fluidity* or openness in society. However, research by Goldthorpe and others has demonstrated that while the shape of the class structure has changed to produce higher levels of *absolute* mobility, nevertheless the relationship between class origins and class destinations has remained *relatively* the same. In other words, to take one example, the chances of a child of working-class parents achieving a secure position in the middle class have hardly changed at all in recent decades, once changes in the shape of the class structure (due to the decline in the numbers of 'blue-collar' workers and the increase in the number of 'white-collar' workers) are accounted for (see Goldthorpe, 1982; 1983; and 1986; Goldthorpe and Payne, 1986). Mobility and openness are not the same phenomenon. Hence, if class is relatively less important in late twentieth-century western societies, as liberals have claimed, it is certainly not because their class structures are more open. In so far as class may be somewhat muted in its significance in the 1980s, this is more likely to be the result of high levels of unemployment, insecure forms of employment and other similar divisions which principally affect the working class and its political and industrial organizations. However, it is by no means certain that class is as muted as some have claimed. A recent study of class in modern Britain has concluded both that class remains by far the most important form of social identity and that the death of social class has been much exaggerated (see Marshall *et al.*, 1988).

Goldthorpe finds Marxist accounts equally as implausible as their liberal counterparts. Whereas liberal theorists of industrial and post-industrial society emphasized the incorporation of the working class and the embourgeoisement of society, Marxists have argued the opposite; namely the continuing hegemonic sway of capitalism over the working class, and the complementary thesis of proletarianization. In the essay reproduced in this volume, Goldthorpe focuses on those Marxist writers who have concentrated their attention on what might be termed the 'false consciousness' of the working class and the need to overcome this via '"the penetration of reason, of rationality into [the] closed affective universe" of the working class'. The problems involved here for Marxist theory are precisely those raised in Chapter 3 by David Lockwood and are discussed in more detail below. At this point we need only note the historicist elements in Marxist accounts to which Goldthorpe rightly objects.

Unlike their liberal opponents, Marxist writers see the extent to which the growth of an affluent consumer society could (and did) lead to greater class conflict – at least in the form of distributional struggles (Marshall *et al.*, 1985). But, as Goldthorpe observes, Marxism requires more than mere distributional struggle of the working class; it requires socialist revolution. The whole Marxist argument regarding the hegemony of capitalism and the higher order rationality of a revolutionary proletariat to overcome it only makes sense if the working class is seen as having an 'historically appointed affinity' with socialism rather than a merely contingent support for it. This problem is compounded by a more practical one which confronts neo-Marxists – the decline in the magnitude of the working class. This is a problem which has taxed, among others, Wright (1978 and 1985) and Poulantzas (1979). It also accounts for the salience of the so-called 'boundary debate', about what, precisely, constitutes the working class in modern capitalist societies (see Parkin, 1979).

We have already seen that for liberal theorists the decline of manual employment and the rise of white-collar work represents an embourgeoisement of society. For Marxists, it means the opposite – proletarianization. It is argued that much of the new white-collar employment is, in fact, routine, degraded, lacking in autonomy and not dissimilar from the blue-collar work it has displaced (see, for example, Braverman, 1974). Hence the traditionally defined working class (male, manual and muscular) may have declined in numerical importance, but in objective terms much white-collar work is essentially proletarianized and working class in character. In effect, this allows Marxists to deny the charge that the increasingly differentiated nature of class structures has reduced the size of its revolutionary class.

Once again, however, what empirical evidence we have casts doubt on all forms of the proletarianization thesis. For example, the greatest expansion in nonmanual employment is not among routine white-collar workers, but in what Goldthorpe terms the 'service class' of managerial, administrative and professional occupations. Even if this evidence is ignored, it is not the case that routine white-collar workers form a monolithic, proletarianized group. Indeed they are every bit as internally divided as the working class itself. A crucial distinction which must be made in class analysis, and one which causes many problems, is that between persons and positions. Many different kinds of *person* occupy routine white-collar *positions*. Some persons will be at the start of a career which will take them to the service class; others may be at the end of a career in which clerical work represents the high point after years of manual work (see Stewart *et al.*, 1980). In short the clerical work-force is much more differentiated than it would appear to be at first glance, with all sorts of consequences for the socio-political class formation of white-collar workers (see Marshall *et al.*, 1988, Chapter 5, for more detail).

Thus Marxists and liberals alike have either ignored or misread crucial empirical evidence. Goldthorpe's contention in Chapter 2, and in other of his essays (see 1971; 1972; 1986), is that this misreading is directly related to the historicism of the authors. As he has argued recently, liberal and Marxist theories

stem from an ultimate ambition of achieving some cognitive grasp on the course of historical development which can then be used for normative and political purposes: that is to say, to show that certain political beliefs, values and commitments have an 'objective' superiority in being those that the movement of history favours, while others can be 'correctly' dismissed as historically outmoded (1986, p. 27).

In the final paragraph of this essay it can be seen why Goldthorpe objects so strongly to such historicist perspectives – they leave out people; or, to put the matter more technically, they have weak micro-sociological foundations. People become 'bearers' of historical forces, agents in a process over which they have no control, rather than conscious actors 'making their own history' but not of their own free will (Marx, 1973b, p. 146). As Goldthorpe once remarked in another context, when confronting historical situations, rather than intellectual problems, we

don't know how it will work out. I'm a good Popperian: I don't believe in historicist predictions about what's going to happen in the future, or in developmental laws of society – that's why I'm not a Marxist. We have an open political situation. I don't know what's going to happen, and I don't see any point in pretending that I do (Goldthorpe, 1978, p. 216).

David Lockwood is another 'good Popperian' and in Chapter 3 we find some of the points concerning historicism made by Goldthorpe being analysed in minute detail for the case of Marxism. 'The weakest link in the chain . . . ' is probably the most sustained and demanding critique of Marxist class theory ever published. And, just as Goldthorpe's essay reveals some of his most abiding concerns in sociological analysis, so it is with Lockwood's essay on Marxism. Lockwood is regarded as a neo-Weberian sociologist but, perhaps more accurately, his writings demonstrate, as Halsey has observed, an attempt to combine 'Parsons' abstractions of value with Marx's abstractions of material circumstances' (1985, p. 160). This concern is expressed early in Lockwood's career (see, for example, Lockwood, 1956) and appears clearly in the action frame of reference which he developed with Goldthorpe for research on the Affluent Worker Project in the 1960s. In a more theoretical form it is found in the classic essay on 'Social integration and system integration' (1964) which has a direct bearing on his chapter in this volume as well as his forthcoming text *Solidarity and Schism*.

System integration refers to the relations, whether of order or conflict, between the *parts* of a social system; *social integration* refers to the (orderly or conflictful) relations between *actors* in a social system (see Lockwood, 1964, p. 245 and *passim*). Parsons' work (and that of other 'normative functionalists') tends to concentrate wholly on the problem of system integration, where socially binding values are of central importance; whereas the so-called 'conflict theorists' (for example Dahrendorf, 1959; Rex, 1964) tend towards an exclusive concern for social integration, where material circumstances, including class relations, are to the fore. Marx, on the other hand, attempts to relate the two in his social analyses by arguing that class conflict (social integration aspect) arises out of contradictions in the economic system between the institutions of property (class relations) and the forces of production (system integration aspect). For Marx, therefore, social integration and system integration are analytically separate but equally necessary for his theory of social change. In 'The weakest link . . .', Lockwood seeks to demonstrate the problems posed for Marxist theories of class as a result of the way in which Marx theorized the social integration/system integration relationship. In so doing, Lockwood argues that Marx's theory of action is essentially utilitarian and, therefore, shares the flaws of all such theories of action.

Utilitarianism argues that society is the product of its participants following their own rational, self-seeking actions. However, as both Durkheim and Parsons observed, this fails to explain the source of that rationality because it has no conception of *values*, i.e. of an independent moral realm in society. Hence, utilitarianism could potentially explain the social action of the stockbroker while working in the City, but would have difficulty explaining that same person's devotions in church on a Sunday. Rational action can be explained but non-rational action cannot. When analysed, Marx's theory, because of its utilitarian roots, shares the same problem – the failure to take account of non-rational action, or the extent to which social actors behave in ways which relate to 'ultimate values' (Parsons, 1935 and 1937).

But how can Marxism be a utilitarian theory? After all, utilitarianism is the theory and ideology of capitalism (and, it might be argued, Thatcherism). Moreover, it is a theory which Marx specifically *rejected* because of its assumptions of a universalistic human nature. However, Lockwood argues that while Marx explains the action of the capitalist as the product of specific social conditions, nevertheless that capitalist is utilitarian in character. That is, Marx essentially presents us with a capitalist who is a rational class egoist, as someone whose ends are determined by a class position. Of course, the actions of capitalists are seen as self-defeating because, by pursuing their rational class interests, they produce what is, from their viewpoint, an irrational result – the conditions for proletarian revolution.

Marx's proletarians are also, at least initially, rational class egoists. Their immediate interest is in the maximization of wages but, just as capitalists are forced into an irrational competition for their position in the class structure, so it is for workers in terms of wages competition. However, Marx endows the workers with the capacity of 'reason' as well as rationality. Workers come to realize that to enter into a wages competition is self-defeating and that their real interests lie in the abolition of the capitalist system itself. As Lockwood terms it, for the proletariat there is an 'end-shift' from the struggle over wages as the end to be pursued to the struggle over the system itself. The capitalists, via their competition, produce the conditions under which the proletariat can make a revolution, *but* the proletariat must be able to see beyond the immediate ends of rational action in order to realize this. They must exercise their reason. Hence, where capitalists are merely rational, proletarians are 'super-rational'.

At this point Lockwood returns to the problem of non-rational or irrational action. It has already been stated that one of the major problems for utilitarianism is its inability to account for non-rational forms of action. One way in whch this could be achieved would be to ascribe to actors an ignorance of the necessary facts or an error in their interpretation of them – quite simply, faulty reasoning. This is precisely what Marx did. Utilitarianism's ignorance or error becomes Marxism's 'false consciousness'. However, if utilitarianism (and, by extension, Marxism) had a developed theory of the moral realm, 'irrational' action could be reinterpreted and explained as being non-rational action, i.e. as action which is not the result of ignorance, error or false consciousness, but which arises out of a commitment to 'ultimate values'. This raises the Parsonsian problem of the extent to which values integrate the ends which actors pursue, of how far values condition action, and of the extent to which different values are held by people differently placed in the social structure; or, as Lockwood terms it, 'variations in the institutionalization of values'. Whereas Lockwood has frequently criticized Parsons and the normative functionalists for their tendency to overemphasize the extent of the institutionalization of values (see 1956; 1964), in 'The weakest link . . .' Marxists are accused of the opposite fault, hence the reference earlier to Halsey's comment on the roots of Lockwood's sociology. For the suggestion which Lockwood makes is that, by failing to make any clear distinction between *irrational* action (arising from ignorance or error) and *non-rational* action (arising from value commitments), Marxism effectively ignores the problem of the institutionalization of values. Moreover this problem is in-built to Marx's account of the conditions making for proletarian revolution.

Lockwood draws attention to three elements in Marx's overall arguments. First, there is an economic argument: the relative deprivation of the working class in capitalist societies. Second, there is a sociological argument: the way in which workers develop their 'reason' through engaging in political activity – *praxis*. Finally there is a philosophical argument: the working class is revolutionary because it is alienated. Each of these arguments contains, on close examination, undertheorized normative components. For example, to talk of *relative* deprivation is to admit a normative element. Indeed, Marx himself recognized that wages contained a 'traditional', non-economic component. This effectively introduces values into the Marxist explanation of action, since one impulse towards revolution is the realization on the part of workers that their standard of living is relatively poorer than that of capitalists. In other words, there is a challenge to the traditional *status order* which defines the traditional standard of living of each class. However, because of the *ad hoc* way in which Marx introduces this status element, it is never properly integrated to his class theory. Hence, no allowance can be made for the way in which (*pace* Weber) subscription to a status order might actually inhibit class action.

Similarly, Marx ignores those normative factors which might inhibit *praxis*. For example, he saw trade union action as fundamental to the consciousness-raising process of the proletariat. When trade union activity became arrested at the level of so-called 'trade union consciousness', Marxists attributed this to ignorance and error. Workers were constrained ideologically by the legal order of citizenship (see Marshall, 1950 and Lockwood, 1974) which served to integrate and incorporate workers and their trades unions into capitalist societies. Again this is a statement of the ways in which the status order inhibits class action, yet it remains implicit rather than explicit in the theory. As Lockwood notes 'status has no place in [the Marxist] theory of social integration'. Moreover, it is not the fact of workers' ideological constraint which accounts for trade union consciousness, but the fact that trades unions had first to gain a legal status in order to exist. Workers had to struggle for trade union rights. Once granted a status within the legal order, trades unions were less likely to challenge the order of which they had become a part. To struggle for recognition within the existing order involves some kind of intrinsic rather than merely instrumental acceptance of that order's moral elements. Of course, Lockwood's argument does not require subscription to eternalism. The working class need not remain forever incorporated, nor can class conflict ever be assumed to be finally institutionalized. However, Lockwood is concerned to cast doubts on a theory which fails to examine the extent to which people can make a positive commitment to non-rational forms of action.

Marxists might argue that a prime role *is* given in their theory to the non-rational aspects of social action. There is, after all, a developed Marxist theory of ideology which moves well beyond the crude incantation that the ideas of the ruling class are the ruling ideas of society. But here, too, Lockwood detects elements of utilitarianism. Moreover, underlying all Marxist accounts of ideology – including those of commodity fetishism and the Gramscian notion of hegemony – lies the same problem to which Goldthorpe draws attention in Chapter 2: 'the unquestioned postulate of eventual proletarian revolution'. While Marxists are unlikely to abandon this postulate, Lockwood argues that they could still profit from abandoning their current theory of action for one which is more voluntaristic. Such a theory would involve a recognition of the actual situations in which people act and how those situations are socially defined. It is, of course, the type of theory employed by Goldthorpe and Lockwood for their own empirical work (Goldthorpe *et al.*, 1968a; 1968b; and 1969) and would, therefore, bring Marxist and non-Marxist class theory closer together. Indeed, there is some evidence in the latest work of the American neo-Marxist, Erik Wright, that this is beginning to happen (see Wright, 1985 and Rose and Marshall, 1986). However, Lockwood found no such evidence in Wright's earlier work, nor in that of the other Marxist theorists of class whose work he examines in the second half of Chapter 3. Instead, he finds much discussion of the boundary problem, especially in terms of the 'correct' definition of the working class, and a rejection of the problem of relating class structure to class action.

The 'correct' definition of the working class is, of course, the subject of the debate between Wright (1978) and Poulantzas (1979). In part this debate is a further example of Marxism's subjugation of sociological concerns to essentially political ones, for it relates to the problem of proletarian revolution; but equally it is an attempt to address the changes which have taken place in the class structures of advanced capitalist societies as manual work has declined relative to nonmanual work. Hence the importance of the boundaries between classes and of whether, for example, routine white-collar workers should be regarded as part of the working class. But while there has been a continuing discussion about how to categorize positions which are neither capitalist nor proletarian, Marxists have paid little heed to the actual structure of the working class itself, again because of its unquestioned role in history.

At the end of Chapter 3, Lockwood returns to his overall theme – the problems of the Marxist theory of action and its failure to take account of developments in the status order as part of a wider theory of social integration. The constituents of social action involve not only 'the means and conditions of action . . . but also . . . the determination of the ends of actors and of the standards by which they relate means to ends. It is in the latter respect that the status order plays a central role. . .'.

From his earliest work (see Lockwood, 1958) to that produced here and subsequently (for example, 1986), Lockwood has consistently argued for the crucial role of the status order within any theory of social integration. Action is not only a question of an actor's objective situation but it also has normative determinants. Marxism has never satisfactorily included such normative elements within its theory of action and hence views people's ends solely in terms of their class interests and sees the means–ends relation only in terms of rationality. Given such a limited definition of action it is small wonder that writers such as Braverman and Wright have avoided the question of the relationship between class structure, class consciousness and class action, or that Poulantzas was forced to acknowledge the need for detailed empirical analyses, and still less that Hirst (1977) and his associates should abandon the idea of the objective interests of classes entirely.

Gordon Marshall's essay focuses attention on one of the major problems discussed by Lockwood in relation to Marxism, class consciousness, and specifically examines various attempts made by sociologists to explain why the proletariat has not become a revolutionary class in capitalist societies. His thesis, echoing that of Goldthorpe in Chapter 2, is that research on the working class has reached an impasse. This is partly for technical, methodological reasons, and partly results from 'a stalemate between theories of working-class instrumentalism and working-class ambivalence'.

In broad terms, explanations of working-class passivity have been of two kinds (compare Hill, 1981, chapter 10). There are those like Lockwood who have stressed the *heterogeneity* of the working class, i.e., who have examined intra-working class divisions such as those between skilled and unskilled workers, and more particularly have used the market, work and status situations model to explain the segmentation, and therefore lack of revolutionary consciousness, of the working class (see Lockwood, 1958 and Bulmer (ed.), 1975). Marshall suggests that Marxists such as Wright (1978) have similarly produced explanations in terms of heterogeneity. This could be said to be even more true of Wright's most recent work (1985; and Rose and Marshall, 1986). For while, as Lockwood notes in his chapter, Wright fails to examine the internal structure of the working class in *Class, Crisis and the State*, it is nevertheless true that there are heterogeneous elements in his initial and more recent models of contradictory class locations. These are most apparent in the approach to the boundary debate, the relation between the new middle classes and the traditional working class and in Wright's arguments concerning the conflict between the immediate and fundamental interests of the working class and its socio-political consequences.

The alternative model, provided by writers such as Parkin (1972), is *incorporationist*, i.e., stresses outside influences on working-class consciousness such as dominant value systems and hegemonic ideologies which result in working-class accommodation to the social order, an acceptance of the status quo and the place of the working class within it. In fact, Lockwood's emphasis on the role of the status order, and especially the citizenship order, of modern societies would also fit here (see, for example, Lockwood's comments on trade union consciousness in Chapter 3). By the same token, both heterogeneity and incorporation are examples of what Lockwood terms theories of social integration.

Precisely because there is no clear dividing line between heterogeneous and incorporationist accounts of working-class passivity, Marshall suggests that the distinction must be misleading. More helpful is the distinction between accounts of working-class consciousness which see it as *ambivalent* and those which see it as *instrumentalist*. The thesis of working-class ambivalence has been used to account for the lack of clear 'images of society' (Bulmer, 1975) among groups as disparate as male farm workers in Suffolk (Newby, 1979) and female tobacco workers in Bristol (Pollert, 1981). Mann (1970) has even suggested that only those with a direct interest in the retention or overthrow of the status quo actually *need* coherent images of society.

Instrumentalist accounts emphasize the pecuniary motives of workers. The foremost advocate of this approach is Goldthorpe (1978) who argues that a demographically mature working class (one which reproduces itself across generations), freed from the constraints of traditional status orders and strengthened by the extension of the new status order of citizenship, develops an instrumental view of society and a pragmatic view of politics. Put crudely, it sees what society has to offer and demands its share.

However, even if a contrast between ambivalence and instrumentalism provides a more helpful distinction than that between heterogeneity and incorporationism, Marshall still believes that the varying accounts of working-class consciousness have generated more heat than light. While there is no shortage of critiques of the various approaches, there is little that points in the direction of novel approaches. This is partly because the critiques which have been made are lacking in penetration. In this respect, Marshall suggests that insufficient attention has been paid to the role of individual actors or the model of consciousness employed. Moreover, *pace* Goldthorpe and Lockwood, too much historicism and too little detailed historical analysis of class processes is evident.

Of course, the problem of the individual actor is particularly stark in the work of various structurally inclined Marxist accounts. Individuals come to be defined as the *bearers* of class relations rather than their embodiment as active subjects. In this respect Marshall approaches some of Lockwood's arguments in Chapter 3. Even where Marxists have adopted the alternative, Gramscian strategy which stresses the ideological constraints on the working class, their accounts have been more concerned with the medium and the message rather than with their alleged effects on the individuals who are supposed to be subject to them and constrained ideologically by them. For example, the *Sun* may be accused of poisoning the minds of the working class, of trivializing women, of distorting politics, of excessive and overweaning support for Thatcherism and many other similar sins – yet one third of its readership actually think it is a Labour inclined newspaper.

Instrumentalist accounts such as those of Goldthorpe can be equally guilty of losing contact with the subject. The fact that workers often stress the financial aspects of work is less important, Marshall argues, than the *meaning* of such orientations. In a capitalist society people do tend to think in monetary terms, but does such evidence necessarily mean that workers are simply rational economic egoists? This question cannot be answered unless and until the *context* of instrumentalism is examined. Those who argue for the ambivalence or volatility of working-class belief systems, on the other hand, have failed to make their case. Here, Marshall detects the ecological fallacy in much of the survey-based research conducted in the 1970s. The inconsistent values and beliefs of *groups* have been taken to indicate inconsistency on the part of the *individuals* who comprise the groups, but inconsistency at the individual level is not proven to be present. The ecological (group level) correlations between social classes and a range of contradictory belief systems tell us nothing about the attitudes or beliefs of any individual class member. Workers may be ambivalent, but the studies Marshall analyses do not prove this.

In sum, whether the analysts in question are Marxists or 'bourgeois' sociologists, and regardless of the model of consciousness being employed, the actors seem strangely uni-dimensional, cardboard figures against the backdrop of history. So what of the conceptualization of consciousness itself? Marshall suggests that many analysts of the working class have adopted a rather crude version of the relationship between consciousness and action. While there is a general subscription to the view that consciousness needs to be understood in terms of everyday experiences and practices, nevertheless in their analyses many sociologists have detached consciousness from action. In short, whereas consciousness is abstractly conceived in relational terms (as a property of social relations), most empirical work fails to do justice to such a conception. What remains is a more or less crude dualism of objective structure/subjective consciousness.

One way to avoid such a trap would be to consider consciousness in relation to the dynamics of social reality, since consciousness relates to individuals' biographies and their historical contexts. Increasingly, sociologists and Marxists have become proponents of such a trajectory view of class, which might be expected to have produced more refined conceptualizations of consciousness. However, this has not been the result. In the case of Marxists such as Wright this is largely because of a preference for historicism over a greater sensitivity to actual historical processes. But Marxists are not alone in this regard. Despite their strictures against historicism in the work of others, sociologists such as Lockwood, Goldthorpe, Mann, Newby and Parkin are all accused by Marshall of a different kind of violence to history. Their work is seen as in some respects *ahistorical*. In following Weber's prescription concerning the need for sociologists to produce ahistorical ideal types, neo-Weberian sociologists tended to restrict themselves to a narrow range of variables wnich might explain consciousness. For example, Lockwood (1966) tried to explain variations in working-class consciousness by reference to work, family and community variables, but any questions relating to how these might change over time or how they might relate to an individual's past experiences or current expectations were ignored for conceptual or methodological reasons. Conceptually the crude dualism of opposing family, community and work structures to images of society (consciousness) prevented any serious consideration of action and experience. Methodologically the survey method was too crude and inadequate to explore the complexities of action and experience. Hence, in Marshall's view, working-class 'ambivalence' is as likely to be the product of faulty theories and methods as it is alleged to be the consequence of diverse (but undocumented) experiences. People were assumed to have contradictory consciousness because they had contradictory experiences, yet the experiences were neither considered in the theoretical models nor could they be adequately explored in the survey method. Ultimately neo-Weberians became guilty of the very historicism they condemned in others since their analyses detached class consciousness from both action and historical/biographical processes.

In his conclusion Marshall makes constructive comments designed to remedy the malaise he has diagnosed. First, social action should be brought to centre stage and be related to consciousness. Consciousness is not separate from action but a part of it and should, therefore, be studied *contextually*. Secondly, class consciousness should not be viewed as if it were only related to the goals of socialism. Here, Marshall agrees with Goldthorpe that there is no elective affinity between the working class and socialism, and by implication with Lockwood's views concerning the importance of understanding non-rational action. Finally, he advocates new techniques for studying consciousness and action and in particular recommends ethnographic methods as likely to produce richer information than surveys. Ultimately, however, Marshall's aim is similar to both Goldthorpe's and Lockwood's; that is, the production of an historically sensitive sociology.

It might be thought somewhat ironic that after his critique of those using the survey method, and his comments on the need for more ethnographic work, Marshall has subsequently studied social class in modern Britain using survey techniques (Marshall, *et al.*, 1988). However, this is not so contradictory as it might appear, since Marshall was not arguing that surveys were of no value in studying class consciousness, but that the conclusions drawn from them were often not substantiated by the results. When, as was the case in the national study of class conducted by Marshall and his colleagues at Essex University, the initial evidence required is extensive rather than intensive, a survey is the only reliable means of obtaining the necessary information. It was always intended that the Essex survey would be followed by ethnographic work on class of the type advocated by Marshall in Chapter 4. Nevertheless, in the process of analysing and reflecting upon data drawn from the Essex survey, Marshall was led to modify some of his criticisms, and to rethink the analysis of consciousness. These revisions will be discussed below in relation to the chapter by Pahl and Wallace.

Goldthorpe and Lockwood, through the affluent worker studies, and Marshall, through his work with Newby, Vogler and Rose, are each associated with the use of the concept of privatization in order to explain certain aspects of working-class consciousness and action. The authors of the final chapter in Part One, Ray Pahl and Claire Wallace, whilst generally sympathetic to the neo-Weberian approach, critically examine privatization and find the concept inadequate to carry the explanatory power ascribed to it.

Initially it was David Lockwood who argued that the privatized worker was prototypical of the post-war working class (see Lockwood, 1960). This argument was developed in his work with Goldthorpe (Goldthorpe and Lockwood, 1963) and in a further seminal paper written during the time of their collaboration on the affluent worker study (Lockwood, 1966 and 1975). The concept of privatization played a major explanatory role in that study and more recently has been used by the Essex group – Marshall, Newby and Rose – in their discussion of working-class consciousness and action in the 1980s (Newby *et al.*, 1985).

The privatized worker was originally described by Goldthorpe and Lockwood as the worker who holds a pecuniary model of society which reflects an instrumental attachment to work and a socially isolated or privatized community life. This description of privatization (sometimes now referred to as privatism or cultural privatization, to distinguish it from the denationalizing practices of the Thatcher government) when applied to communal life was drawn in contrast to the life of the traditional working-class community as described in the 1950s by writers such as Wilmott and Young (1957) and Dennis *et al.* (1956). Thus the privatized worker is the resident of 'Greenleigh' rather than Bethnal Green (Wilmott and Young, 1957). Whereas in the 1950s privatized workers were typically seen as the residents of the new, post-war council estates, by the 1980s they would more generally be expected to be owner-occupiers on private estates. Often such workers are geographically mobile and are said to have broken from the ascriptive ties of more traditional working-class communities or never to have experienced these. They live a socially isolated, home-centred existence. According to Goldthorpe and Lockwood it is precisely the social isolation of the privatized worker which leads to the adoption of a pecuniary model of society rather than either the power model of the traditional proletarian worker or the status model of the traditional deferential worker.

Of course, in subsequent analyses of working-class consciousness and action, the claims of Goldthorpe and Lockwood have been extensively criticized (see, for example, Westergaard, 1970; Mackenzie, 1974; and Bulmer (ed.), 1975). Moreover the structural, normative and relational character of class has changed in the period since privatization was first referred to in the sociological literature. Whether these changes have led to an intensification of privatization, as might be expected on the basis of the earlier claims of Goldthorpe and Lockwood, or whether privatization is really as novel a process as they claimed, have both been subjects of much debate. To some extent these issues have been revived by the Essex group's attempt to understand working-class politics in the 1980s through a broader historical analysis of privatization (Newby *et al.*, 1985; Marshall *et al.*, 1987 and 1988). It is this latest attempt to revive the concept which Pahl and Wallace criticize in Chapter 5. Moreover, their critique neatly poses some of the dilemmas which have to be faced if we are to take the conclusions of the chapters by Goldthorpe, Lockwood and Marshall seriously, since, in their different ways, all the authors in Part One raise fundamental problems concerning the model of structure, consciousness and action used in so many class analyses in the last twenty-five years.

Pahl and Wallace first present their own view of the impasse which class analysis has reached. In so doing they point to recent research by specialists in areas of sociology other than mainstream social stratification – gender studies, race, urban and political sociology – which offer new insights into the discussion of social consciousness. These alternative approaches point both to social divisions other than those of class and raise issues about the class concept as traditionally defined in terms of the occupation of male heads of household. In particular they review theories of state dependency, gender relations and sectoral cleavage in terms of the explanation of social

25

consciousness. However, the particular focus of their critique is the Essex group and its adherence to the concept of cultural privatization as a possible explanation for some aspects of working-class consciousness.

In formulating their ideas for a major study of social class in modern Britain, Marshall, Newby, Rose and Vogler attempted to assimilate many of the more recent developments referred to by Pahl and Wallace. Further, they accepted as a working hypothesis what was becoming the conventional wisdom, the demise of class as the single, crucial aspect of social integration, and did so in part by reference to the process of privatization. It is here that Pahl and Wallace are dissatisfied with the initial Essex model. Ironically, given Marshall's warnings in Chapter 4, they detect a lack of historical sensitivity in the Essex approach.

Each of the papers in Part One raises the issue of the relationship between sociology and history, and in particular of the historical basis of sociological theories of class. In this particular context it is necessary to consider the extent to which cultural privatization is a phenomenon of the post-war period which could, therefore, legitimately be used to account for other recent social changes, including the declining salience of class in shaping people's social consciousness. How far have the Essex group fallen into the same trap that Lockwood's critics detected; namely, that of creating an ahistorical and inaccurate model of the traditional working class, in order to make a comparison with a supposedly new form of privatized working class? Pahl and Wallace examine this question by reference to their recent empirical research in the Isle of Sheppey (Pahl, 1984) and the conclusions they had drawn concerning how people construct their social identities. This is, of course, the crucial issue since, at root, questions of class consciousness and action are questions concerning the extent to which people have identities which derive from their class position as objectively defined. The work of sociologists studying the family, gender, race, consumption and production cleavages and so on in part asks how far these other factors are a basis for the construction of social identity and a motivator of social action.

The research which Pahl and Wallace conducted convinced them of the complex ways in which social identities are constructed and, especially, that social identity does not have a single-stranded character shaped by people's employment and, therefore, their class experiences. On the contrary, they wish to emphasize 'the multi-faceted sources of social consciousness [and] the complex mosaic of social experience out of which people construct their social identities'. In making this emphasis, Pahl and Wallace are not claiming that class analysis is redundant but are reminding us of the other differentiations and identities which exist in class societies.

In fact the Essex group did not intend to argue that privatization was a novel process and would accept the claim by Pahl and Wallace that, rather than retreating into domesticity in recent times, the working class has always been there. Not only has domesticity always been an essential element of working-class life, and the goal of much collective working-class action, but it is also, Pahl and Wallace suggest, the domestic sphere which is crucial to the generation of social identity. In their initial work on privatization, the Essex group sought precisely to bring the domestic sphere into the consideration of the formation of social identity, in much the same way as Pahl and Wallace, and attempted to offer a somewhat different account of the phenomenon of privatization than that produced in the 1950s and 1960s. In particular they wished to explore the links between structural privatization, as analysed historically, and cultural privatization as analysed sociologically. Both in a subsequent paper and their book on social class (Marshall *et al.*, 1987 and 1988) they have taken their analysis further and, in the process, have revised their views on the problem of social consciousness in ways relevant to the previous discussion in this Introduction.

Pahl and Wallace are, of course, quite correct to emphasize that the type of domesticity implied by privatization is not a new phenomenon. Apart from the historical analyses to which they refer, there is other historical scholarship which has largely undermined Lockwood's claims concerning the supposedly prototypical nature of the privatized instrumental worker possessed of a pecuniary image of society which is displacing the world-views of traditional deferentials and proletarians. Research on the working class in the nineteenth century suggests that the three images of society identified by Lockwood have co-existed for more than a century. Moreover, they have been equally capable of producing collective action of both class and status forms. People are not and never have been particularly clear and consistent in the views they hold about society in general or social class in particular. They do not interpret the world in terms of a coherent package of underlying values and principles. Such an observation raises a crucial question, however. If subjective factors have remained relatively unchanged, yet the scope and intensity of class action has varied historically, how can this seeming paradox be explained?

Reflecting on these issues led Marshall and his colleagues to advocate a new approach to the whole problem of social consciousness. Whereas so many studies have treated class consciousness as an attribute of individuals, the Essex group suggest that it should be seen as an attribute of *collective* actors. The class practices organized by parties, trades unions and other class organizations become the central issue rather than the subjectivity of individual class members. Class consciousness cannot be seen simply in terms of people's beliefs, attitudes and values explicable by reference to structural locations, however defined. Consciousness is not a spiritual reflection of social location. Instead, Marshall *et al.* argue that those who

. . . reason directly from shifts in the social or occupational structure to swings in values or electoral behaviour oversimplify the relationship between the distributional order of society itself, and the specific forms of distributional conflict evident at any particular time. To do so is to neglect the lesson taught by Michels: namely that organizations count. Between the shared consciousness of commonly held values or beliefs, and joint pursuit of these in co-ordinated action, lies the necessity of collective organization. But the dynamics of organization itself intervenes between the shared experience or consciousness and the collective actions of particular members (1987, p. 67).

Once class consciousness is seen in terms of organizations rather than individuals, it also becomes possible to see the lack of moral order in capitalist societies, to which Pahl and Wallace refer at the end of their chapter, in a different light. Rather than agreeing with their conclusion that 'if what is needed is a new sense of moral purpose then it may be that political parties have outlived their usefulness as agents of change', the Essex group would argue the opposite. As they put it,

what is important . . . is the ability of class organizations to mobilize members behind centrally organized initiatives on behalf of class rather than particular interests; and, once mobilized, to hold in check groups who would 'free ride' or pursue sectional gains at the expense of the collectivity as a whole (1987, p. 68).

Nevertheless, with much else that Pahl and Wallace argue, Marshall and his colleagues would agree. Privatized instrumentalism, domesticity and the ideology of familism can be consistent with both collective action based on class consciousness and sectionalism. In societies like Sweden, where corporatist solutions to problems of distributional dissent have been pursued, classes have been organized into the political arena and trades unions have achieved real advances on behalf of their members. But in Britain under the Thatcher administration class organizations, and especially those of the working class, have been excluded and undermined and sectional identities have been encouraged (see Goldthorpe, 1984). Hence the irony noted by Marshall *et al.* that

it is not lack of capitalist *Sittlichkeit* that poses the greater threat to pluralist democracies, but its achievement, since corporatist arrangements tend . . . both progressively to undermine the free play of the capitalist labour market, and to reinforce class-based as opposed to sectional identities (1987, p. 69).

In whichever way we choose to examine the problems discussed in this Introduction, one issue stands out as a lesson from recent research. It is raised explicitly by Pahl and Wallace when they argue that the conventional model of *structure* → *consciousness* → *action* is highly problematic and needs to be 'unpacked and each part scrutinized carefully'. They make a sound case for a differentiated approach to consciousness and action, and, moreover, one which recognizes that such features as familism and individualism are not incompatible with analyses in terms of class. Indeed all those who have contributed to this volume are seeking in their different ways to understand the relationship between identities based on class and other identities, and they are by no means alone in this endeavour. A considerable amount of effort has and is being expended in trying to break the impasse identified in the chapters in Part One. If this Introduction makes that impasse clearer in its outline, it has fulfilled its main purpose.

Part Two of this book presents a selection of more empirically based studies of unemployment, work ideologies, female self-employment and, finally, the relationship between the *petit bourgeoisie* and the New Right. Unemployment is, of course, the major social, economic and political issue of the 1980s. Few social scientists, political commentators or politicians would ever have believed that a government which presided over unemployment levels of 13+per cent could have been re-elected once, let alone twice. Prior to the 1980s the conventional wisdom was that high and persistent levels of unemployment would not simply be disastrous for the government in office but might even lead to a major breakdown of social order. Indeed, Prime Minister Edward Heath was so concerned by rising unemployment that he undertook his famous U-turn in economic policy in 1972–3. Throughout most of the last fifteen years, in poll after poll, more people have nominated unemployment as the major issue facing Britain than any other, and yet Margaret Thatcher has had two landslide victories in 1983 and 1987. How has this been possible? To some extent, of course, she has been lucky. Divisions in the Labour Party and the splitting of the anti-Thatcher vote between Labour and the Alliance partly account for the Tories' electoral success. We should not forget, even if Mrs Thatcher tends to, that the present government had the support of only 42 per cent of those who voted in 1987. Even so, it remains the case that the Conservatives have survived in power despite record post-war levels of unemployment. The chapters by Westergaard, Harris, Marshall and their colleagues allow us to see some of the reasons why this has happened.

In the late 1970s both John Westergaard and Chris Harris received grants from the ESRC to study the effects of redundancy among steelworkers, a supposedly traditional proletarian group, in Sheffield and South Wales respectively, supposedly traditional proletarian occupational communities. The story which Westergaard, Noble and Walker tell of the experience of redundancy and unemployment among their sample is vivid and starkly depressing. As they observe, the objective inequalities of class are well demonstrated by their findings. However, the experience of unemployment did not further radicalize what was already an overwhelmingly Labour supporting group. Indeed, on the contrary, after 1979 many of the Sheffield sample switched their allegiance away from Labour to the Conservatives and Alliance. Of course, many had found new employment, especially those with higher qualifications. It was also the case that these higher qualified, skilled workers were more likely to defect from Labour, thus following the national trend. But even the less skilled workers who remained unemployed after redundancy were not radicalized by their direct experience of recession. They might have lived in a strongly pro-Labour area, in the 'Socialist Republic of South Yorkshire', but this did not prevent them from experiencing unemployment in the way that most people do, as a profoundly socially isolating experience rather than one which encourages the kind of collective response required for radicalism. Indeed, Westergaard and his colleagues specifically refer to the experience of many of their sample as 'privatization in recession' precisely because so many exhibited the pattern of social isolation which Lockwood described as typical of privatized workers. When we add to this the

29

evidence provided by the Sheffield study of a rejection of some of the policies and the image of Labour on the part, especially, of skilled workers, we are once again reminded that the objective realities of class map very uneasily on to the socio-political consciousness of human subjects.

The study by Harris and Lee complements the Sheffield study while posing somewhat different questions. Harris and Lee concentrate on the redundancy process as a key element in understanding both how people respond to being made redundant and their subsequent experiences. In the case of the Port Talbot steelworkers, the fact that redundancies were largely the consequence of a change in the labour process – the way steel was made – and were selective, i.e. involved the shedding of older and less healthy employees, is seen as crucial to people's subsequent labour market experiences. This insight is then used both to describe and explain the experiences of those redundant workers whose post-British Steel work histories have been 'chequered' in the sense of involving alternating periods of short-term employment and unemployment.

In explaining chequered work histories, Harris and Lee draw a distinction between understanding local labour markets in conventional and narrow economic terms, and understanding such markets in sociological terms as social structures. They argue that a person's position in the market seen in the latter sense is a determinant of their position on the market in the former sense. This is especially the case where unemployment is high, as in South Wales. In this situation, employers will hire workers on the basis of their social location, and often by informal means. Thus a person's position in the market conceived as a local social structure will affect their ability to obtain employment in the market as more narrowly conceived. The chequered category of workers were on the whole younger, less skilled, and had more experience of unemployment. In Marxist terms their class position was akin to that of what Marx really meant by the proletariat, i.e. people with access to jobs but no property rights in them in the sense of being denied or excluded from the full rights of industrial citizenship. However, this form of proletarianization does not lead to the development of any proletarian consciousness, partly because of their situation of competition with other workers for jobs, but partly because Marxian class categories do not allow us to understand how real individuals relate to one another. It is only possible to do this, Harris and Lee suggest, if local labour markets are conceived as social classes in T. H. Marshall's sense, as groups with shared norms and ways of life which arise from the way people have responded to past experiences and transformations in the market.

In this way Harris and Lee suggest one reason why some among their sample of workers who became unemployed nevertheless remained politically quiescent. The paper by Marshall, Rose, Newby and Vogler uses data from a national survey of class processes in contemporary Britain to pose the same question. In particular they examine how far their data support the conclusions of recent American research on this issue by Schlozman and Verba which suggests that political mobilization of the unemployed is inhibited by a continuing support on their part for the core values of American society.

Not surprisingly, and as with their counterparts in the USA, the unemployed in Britain are both relatively deprived and relatively dissatisfied. However, they are not so committed to the type of individualistic ideologies which are held by Schlozman and Verba to inhibit the development of collective identities and action in the USA. Hence, in Britain, the government is held more responsible both for the overall economic situation which produces unemployment and for failing to create more jobs. Equally class consciousness is more pronounced among the unemployed in Britain. Consequently there is a shared collective identity, that of class, of a kind which Schlozman and Verba have argued as one necessary precondition for a political response on the part of the unemployed to their situation. A second precondition for such a response, the perception that unemployment results from social forces rather than individual weakness, is also met in the British case, as is the further perception that government action is required to remedy the problem. However, the unemployed in Britain are no different from the employed in terms of general economic and social policy preferences, voting patterns and political make-up. In other words such perceptions do not seem to change as a result of becoming unemployed.

Of course, as in the USA, the unemployed have not taken concerted political action as a group. Indeed, the Essex survey showed them to be somewhat less likely than the employed to take part in any kind of political activity, a further confirmation of Pahl's (1984) finding concerning the isolating effects of unemployment generally. Unemployment would appear to induce quiescence rather than mobilization. Thus the British data appear to confirm Schlozman and Verba's findings but to undermine their explanatory model since the preconditions for mobilization which are absent in America are present in Britain but the end result, political quiescence, is the same. In discussion, Marshall and his colleagues relate their findings more generally to the issue of explaining social consciousness referred to earlier in this chapter. They see Schlozman and Verba as having provided yet another example of the mechanical linking of structure, consciousness and action without reference to the conditions of action, including the failure of collective organizations such as trades unions and political parties to convince the unemployed that collective action is a potential solution to their plight.

Blackburn's discussion of ideologies of work offers further insights into such issues as the political quiescence of the unemployed. He examines work ideologies as part of a social process which sustains and reproduces the socio-economic structure and its associated inequalities. In so doing he provides a sophisticated account of why the disadvantaged tend to accept their social situation rather than seeking to change it.

Ideologies are both general and individual. The analysis of general ideologies of work, while important, does not explain the acceptance of the inequalities which such ideologies serve to justify. Explanations of this kind require the sociologist to locate ideologies in terms of people's concrete

31

experiences. In particular, it calls for a consideration of social identity, for which work is an extremely important source. As Blackburn notes 'the right to work is a right to a significant social identity'. Additionally it is necessary to consider how experience is constrained by social location if we are to explain how individuals come to accept an ideology which maintains inequality. The most constrained are those at the bottom of the social hierarchy. They are also those who are likely to have least sense of competence to alter their circumstances and, therefore, less basis to make critical judgements of social arrangements which disadvantage them. Of course, circumstances could always emerge which might generate a more critical response, but for most people for most of the time individual ideologies of work correspond to the more general ideology. Blackburn assesses this argument against data collected among unskilled workers in Peterborough and discovers that it is largely borne out. It was the workers with the most constrained experience who also had least belief in their ability to improve their situation. It is when Blackburn reflects more widely on this analysis that the relation between his chapter and those on unemployment becomes most obvious. Unemployment does not radicalize people, but rather reinforces their experience of constraint, especially when so many others share the experience of unemployment. Moreover, unemployment involves a loss of the social identity which work provides, and a concomitant sense of loss of control. But beyond this Blackburn's argument also provides a link to the chapters in Part One by providing an additional approach to understanding constraints to the development of an oppositional working-class consciousness.

British research in social stratification has often been criticized for concentrating too much attention on the male working class (compare Newby, 1982). However, in recent years, there has been an increasing concern both to bring women into class analysis and to examine the class situations of nonmanual employees, often in conjunction (see, for example, Crompton and Jones, 1984; Marshall *et al.*, 1988; and Crompton and Mann, 1986). There have also been increasing numbers of studies of the self-employed and among the most notable of these are those undertaken by Richard Scase and Robert Goffee (1980; 1982; 1985). In their contribution to this volume they discuss self-employment among females as one strategy for escaping subordination. Moreover, they examine how far the appeal and meaning of self-employment is different, first for women compared with men and, second, for being adopted during a period of recession.

Self-employment as a form of self-help strategy during a period of high unemployment has been much emphasized by the Thatcher government. Various incentives, such as the Enterprise Allowance Scheme, have been offered to the unemployed to set up their own businesses, and local enterprise agencies, financed and operated under the aegis of large companies, have appeared in their hundreds to offer advice and help to potential entrepreneurs. Scase and Goffee suggest that, for women in particular, self-employment may often be the only feasible path out of subordination and may be a more viable individual strategy than the pursuit of an occupational career. This reflects the overall class situation of women. They are overwhelmingly concentrated either in situations which do not offer chances for career mobility or, where this is not necessarily the case, in situations where men are more likely to be promoted than women (see Marshall *et al.*, *ibid*, chapter 4; Crompton and Jones, 1984; Crompton and Mann, 1986. Just as business proprietorship offers an escape from subordination for other groups who are discriminated against by the various inclusionary and exclusionary devices of the market, so it is for women. Moreover, proprietorship may offer a radical potential for women who reject the exploitative nature of capitalism and the traditionally defined gender roles which accompany it. While this is not true for all female proprietors, it is certainly true for some, as Scase and Goffee demonstrate. Hence, there are women in their sample for whom the major objective of proprietorship is not the pursuit of personal advancement, but rather of catering for those needs of women which are not met by either the private or public sectors. In some cases an attempt is made to create an alternative feminist reality through a proprietorship which minimizes contacts with men.

However, precisely because such businesses still have to be profitable to survive, there is sometimes a tension between this and a commitment to a non-exploitative feminism. Conscious strategies are often developed to reduce this tension but these can have inhibiting effects on the growth potential of the business. Despite such problems, Scase and Goffee point to the political potential of female self-employment and they argue that more women may turn in this direction so long as the overall position of women in our society remains one of subordination in the family and the economy.

The issues discussed in Part Two – the growth of unemployment and its consequences; the increasing sense of labour as alienating and the experience of powerlessness in work and outside of it – can be related to the policies and ideology of the Thatcher administration. The revival of the right in British politics and the overthrow of the political consensus of the period from 1945 to 1979 are interconnected phenomena which require sociological explanation. After three electoral successes the New Right is now claiming that it has produced a new consensus based on its ideas and moral precepts. Elliott, McCrone and Bechhofer, in a continuation of their earlier work on the *petit bourgeoisie*, examine the rise of the New Right and the extent of its political success. In particular they investigate the growth of small business organizations, the anxieties and ambitions which gave rise to them, and the influence that they have exerted on the New Right in the last decade.

First, Elliott and his colleagues chart the sudden growth in associations for the self-employed in the mid 1970s, and the resource which these represented for the Conservative opposition under Margaret Thatcher. While these new associations were not incorporated by either the Tory Party or other New Right groups, they did serve to add something to the New Right critique of 'social-democratic-welfarism-corporatism' as well as providing new vehicles for the dissemination of that critique. However, it was not simply the traditional concerns of the small business sector which gave rise to the new associations. Beneath this, Elliott *et al.* detect factors relating to the changing

33

class structure and especially the declining importance of the *petit bourgeoisie*. Put bluntly, the *petit bourgeoisie* felt insecure and relatively deprived socially, economically and politically compared with other classes. It seemed that government policies had eroded their position, the final straw being the employment protection legislation of the 1974–9 Labour government. Such an example of class rule required them to mobilize their own class interests. Moreover, the *petit bourgeoisie* felt as threatened by the new middle class of bureaucrats, professionals and technicians as they were by the working class. Not only did the power of the unions need to be curbed: so did that of the new middle class.

The *petit bourgeoisie* also felt materially threatened by inflation. The developing New Right attachment to monetarism found ready support among the associations of the self-employed, both as a means of reducing inflation, and as a justification of economic inequality. In this area, and in that of reducing state regulation of the economy, the interests of big and small business coincided. Beyond these economic concerns there also developed a form of social conservatism which questioned the 'permissive' social reforms of the 1960s and 1970s. What was required was the restoration of bourgeois values and society and in Margaret Thatcher they found their champion. Nevertheless, Elliott and his colleagues question the extent to which the policies of the Thatcher government have or could generate the kind of entrepreneurial revolution called for by the small business associations. Even the growth in self-employment since 1979 is as much an indicator of economic decline as of regeneration. As was argued previously, much of this growth is accounted for by attempts on the part of the unemployed to provide themselves with work. Up to 80 per cent of such ventures quickly end in failure. The real beneficiaries of the Thatcher years have been the City and big business – not the corner shop.

If anything beyond what has been discussed already unites the various chapters in Part Two of this book, it is the way in which they demonstrate sociology's ability to penetrate the appearances and ideologies of society, to uncover a different reality. In a period of social, political and economic change such as that currently being witnessed, there will be many victims. It is equally certain that the victims will be blamed for their own circumstances and that there will be those who question the extent to which victims really suffer. However, the studies of unemployment and employment offered here show, among many other things, that, for example, the unemployed and sub-employed are the least likely groups to engage in the informal economy, the least likely to be able to organize to defend themselves, and the most likely to be forced into forms of self-employment or casual employment which offer no real hope of an escape from poverty and constraint. The unemployed are not fiddling, scrounging and cheating, nor are they in the vanguard of the socialist revolution. Rather they demonstrate the continuing harsh realities of life at the wrong end of a class-based society. The current rhetoric of the New Right may be one of freedom, but the freedom of the market economy requires that one had better not be unemployed, nor, for that matter, sick, or poorly qualified, or black, or dependent on the state. It was precisely the recognition of such realities, in a society based upon a philosophy of unbridled capitalism, which gave early sociology much of its moral force and intellectual rationale. The chapters in this book reflect a continuation of that moral and intellectual critique of society, and also the continuing need for it.

Further Reading

John H. Goldthorpe and Philippa Bevan, 'The study of social stratification in Great Britain: 1946–1976', *Social Science Information*, **16**, no. 3/4, 1976, pp. 279–334.

Gordon Marshall, David Rose, Howard Newby and Carolyn Vogler, *Social Class in Modern Britain*, London: Hutchinson, 1988.

Howard Newby, *The State of Social Stratification Research in Great Britain*, London: SSRC, 1982.

Bryan Roberts, Ruth Finnegan and Duncan Gallie (eds), *New Approaches to Economic Life*, Manchester: Manchester University Press, 1985.

Part One

Theoretical Issues

2   Intellectuals and the working class in modern Britain

John H. Goldthorpe

In all western societies over the last hundred years or more the working class has been the subject of continuous, and often passionate, debate among intellectuals. By 'the working class' I mean the collectivity of men and women who live by selling their labour to employers on the basis of worktime or output. By 'intellectuals' I mean thinkers and writers who feel a close personal concern with questions of the human condition, and who aim to treat such questions in more than a purely scientific or scholarly manner: in particular, by 'situating' them, as they arise in a specific place and period, within some wider context of meaning in order to bring out their significance beyond the immediate experience and interests of the individuals directly involved. And in turn, one could say, intellectuals typically endeavour to communicate their concern and their understanding to others in such a way as to exert not merely a cognitive influence, but a moral and a political influence also.

That the working class has been a focal point of attention and engagement among intellectuals is the evident fact from which I start. *Why* this should have been so is a question to which, I would hope, an answer may be suggested by the end of this chapter, at least for the case of modern Britain up to the end of the 1970s.

In thus concentrating my attention, I am, I realize, retreating within somewhat arbitrary limits. None the less, the arguments that I shall have to consider are still wide in range and their interrelationships complex. In the British case, it is worth noting, the debate on the working class has never been entirely reducible, as in some continental European countries, to what is, in effect, a 'debate with Marx' – although, as will be seen, the work of Marx and of his followers still figures prominently. Indeed, even my chosen ground is too extensive for me to cover here in any detail and I shall be forced to indulge in some rather drastic simplification.

With this being understood, I propose to distinguish three major intellectual standpoints from which the debate on the working class has been carried on: that is, the standpoints of those whom I shall call 'the liberals', 'the organicists' and 'the left'. I shall review arguments advanced from each of these positions in turn, and I shall note certain obvious divergences and conflicts. However, my chief aim is a critical rather than an expository one. It is to show how, in each case alike, an attempt has been made to give an interpretation of the historical, and emergent, significance of the British working class – that is, of its economic and social situation, its culture, its modes of industrial and political action; but how, again in each case, the attempt has failed, and most clearly in simply being refuted by events. It will in fact quite often be possible to discover acknowledgements of such failure made implicitly by participants in the debate in the course of adapting, revising or abandoning arguments that they had initially offered.

There is thus one further issue which must be addressed. As well as wishing to know why intellectuals have shown such concern with the working class, we shall be led to ask also why they have been so uniformly unsuccessful in their analyses and prognoses, and why therefore the debate on the working class has at the present time reached a serious impasse.

Liberal views on the British working class derive from the reception in this country of more general interpretations – mainly American in provenance – of the 'developmental logic' of modern industrial society. These interpretations, which claimed the emergence in the West of a new, stabilized, prosperous and welfare-oriented capitalism, originated in the period of intense Cold War and were, quite evidently, ones intended to rival and oppose those available from Marxist sources. Their authors, to no less an extent than their Marxist adversaries, could be regarded as engaged not only in an intellectual argument but further in a political strategy.

Liberal intellectuals recognized that within the system of classical Marxism the role of the working class was crucial: that it was the working class that provided the link between theory and practice as the historical agency through which the two would be actually united and the transition from capitalism to socialism achieved. Thus writers such as Edward Shils, Daniel Bell, Clark Kerr and S. M. Lipset attempted to undermine the Marxist position by arguing that in the newly developed form of western society the working class was no longer a revolutionary force – was no longer capable (if indeed it ever has been) of the historic mission which Marxism assigned to it. Equally, therefore, it was the aim of these writers to create an intellectual atmosphere in which the working-class movements of western European nations might be more readily induced to abandon revolutionary, or indeed any kind of radical socialist objectives, in favour of 'social democracy'; and to cease in effect to be social *movements* in favour of participating in a kind of politics more appropriate to modern societies. That is, a 'civic' politics of an essentially non-ideological, pragmatic and, as far as possible, consensual kind.

In the British case, efforts to this end were most prominent in the late 1950s and early 1960s, in the propitious circumstances created by a period of rapidly rising living standards and of electoral failure for the Labour Party. Within the British labour movement traditions of moderation and 'gradualism' had, of course, always been powerful, if not dominant. But the new ideas crossing the Atlantic were still highly attractive to many adherents of these native traditions in offering them a far more impressive rationale for their political stance than they had hitherto possessed, and one on which they could effectively draw in urging an explicit 'revision' of the character and orientations of the Labour Party as the prerequisite for its survival in the modern era. The arguments that are of interest here are thus ones presented by exponents of the revisionist case within the labour movement – but speaking essentially in the voices of their liberal mentors. The key figure was undoubtedly Anthony Crosland; and the key texts made their appearance sometimes as Fabian Society publications but, more often, in the pages of *Encounter*.[1]* It is in these latter writings of Crosland, rather than his *Future of Socialism* (1956) that the influence of American liberalism becomes prominent (see Crosland, 1959; 1960a, b, c; 1961).

In the arguments in question, the political message was presented as following directly from a sociological analysis. So far as the latter was concerned, three major themes could be distinguished. First, it was held that, contrary to Marxist expectations, the development of western industrialism had not been accompanied by growing working-class consciousness and alienation but, rather, by the progressive integration of the working class into the evolving social structure of liberal democracy. This tendency has been encouraged by the benign influence of economic growth, but had also resulted from major institutional changes, especially within the political and industrial orders, that had enabled conflicts originating in class relations to be effectively contained and regulated (see Crosland 1959, 1960a, b, c; see also Kerr *er al.*, 1960; Shils, 1958 and 1960).

Second, it was claimed that as a modern society reached the stage of economic development of Britain in the 1950s, the working class would, in any event, begin to decompose. In the sense of a collectivity with its own distinctive economic situation, social milieux and life-styles, it became progressively eroded by the main currents of social change: for example, by the 'homogenization' of consumption standards, by advanced forms of industrial technology and organization, by new patterns of residence and community life, by the widening of educational opportunities and growing social mobility. The emergent society of the West was one of an essentially 'middle-class' character or, at least, one characterized by an amorphous 'middle mass' that comprised the large majority of the population (see Crosland, 1960c; Hinden, 1960).

Third, then, this structural transition from 'class' to 'mass' society was seen as paralleled on the cultural plane by the growth of 'mass' culture which acted as a powerful solvent of all 'particularisms', whether based on class or on region, religion or ethnicity. Although in certain respects mass culture might appear aesthetically repellent, to view it in an entirely negative light was seriously mistaken. Dismissive criticism from conservative quarters was often based on fallacious notions of some previous 'golden age' of popular or folk culture from which a supposed decline was traced; while on the left such criticism stemmed largely from the anguish felt at the working-class preference for mass culture over revolutionary praxis. The positive aspects of mass society and its culture were in fact rather more evident. A sense of 'moral equalitarianism' was encouraged among the population at large and, in

---

* Superior figures refer to the Notes and references section following each chapter.

place of more or less discrete subcultural configurations, there was created a broad commonality of values and goals. In particular, the working class was helped to see beyond the restricted horizons of its traditional way of life, lost the 'wantlessness' of the truly poor and oppressed, and joined together with other groups and strata in the pursuit of higher material standards – a pursuit which, Crosland maintained, reflected 'a basic human desire for choice, leisure, comfort, privacy and a more spacious family life' (1962, p. 4; compare Shils, 1957 and 1960, whom Crosland acknowledges as a major influence; see also Bell, 1960).

Politically, therefore, the course indicated for the Labour Party was clear. It must, the revisionists argued, seek to reduce its dependence on its historical, but now crumbling, base in the working class, and to widen its electoral appeal in order to win over the bulk of the expanding middle mass. This would require that Labour rid itself of its 'cloth cap' image and present itself as a national rather than as a class party. But, more fundamentally, Labour would need also to reorientate its political and policy concerns. In a social context in which the 'economic class struggle' had become 'heavily muted' (Crosland, 1960b, p. 5) it was important to de-emphasize issues which were closely linked with that struggle – such as ones of ownership, control and authority in industry – and to give greater prominence to ones which, to quote Crosland again,

make not a narrow class or sectional appeal, but a wide, radical appeal to broad sections of the population, including the newly emerging social groups; for example, such issues as educational provision, town planning and the environment, and consumer protection (1960c, p. 19; see also Hinden, 1960).

In sum, the argument was that a focus on the politics of class – and hence on issues of social power located primarily in the sphere of production – was outmoded, and in electoral terms increasingly irrelevant; and that attention needed rather to be centred on issues in the – broadly defined – sphere of consumption in which social-democratic objectives could be defined in essentially 'redistributive' terms.

It is not my concern here to trace out what exactly was achieved by, or followed from, revisionist efforts within the Labour Party. What is relevant to my purpose is rather to note, on the one hand, that these efforts embodied the major intellectual initiative taken within the party during the post-war period; but that, on the other hand, the analyses offered were by the end of the 1970s revealed as gravely inadequate and as in large part irrelevant to the current British economic and political situation – so that in fact to speak of the 'crisis of British social democracy' became commonplace.

Most obviously, the problems that emerged as politically crucial, whether from an electoral or a governmental standpoint, were the interlinked ones of industrial relations, industrial productivity and inflation. While conventionally defined as 'economic', these are problems generated by social action within labour market and work situations – or, in other words, are problems of class. And what their persistence and their frequent expression in social conflict betokened was that the supposed institutional containment and regulation of the disruptive potential of class relations had rather seriously broken down. Moreover, while the problems and conflicts in question involved to a greater or lesser extent all groups and strata in society, it was evident that the part played by the working class on the current socio-political scene was by no means diminishing but was rather one of a distinctive importance.

At around the same time as proponents of revisionism were proclaiming the decomposition of the working class, a major development in working-class organization was in fact first becoming apparent: that is, the growth among manual employees of the extent and strength of their workplace organization. By the 1970s, this had resulted in a substantial involvement of shop stewards in processes of collective bargaining and of job regulation generally across large areas of British industry, and in a corresponding limitation of managerial prerogatives and power. Over the same period, labour militancy showed a tendency to increase, in the sense that claims in regard to wages and conditions of service were advanced, and pressed, with far less inhibition than previously. Different groups of workers came to realize more fully – and to exploit more thoroughly – their strategic bargaining possibilities and their capacity for organized action in support of their demands. It is against this background, it may be argued, that the distinctive problems of British political economy in the 1980s must in large part be understood (compare Goldthorpe 1984; 1985).

Where, it would seem, liberal analysts went most crucially astray was in failing to see that in so far as members of the working class were becoming assimilated into mass society, this was primarily in their acceptance of its ethos of continuing material advancement rather than through any radical change in their class situation *per se*, and that this process could not in fact be taken as essentially integrative in its implications. On the contrary, the freeing of manual workers and their families from traditional restraints on their wants and aspirations and their entry into 'consumerism' had the effect chiefly of intensifying the struggle for relative shares and the sharpness of distributional dissent. And furthermore, since workers did, of course, pursue their expanding material ambitions on the basis of their growing organized power in the workplace, the heightened conflict was inevitably extended back into the sphere of production, which liberals believed had been effectively 'pacified'.[2]

It is not then surprising that in later versions of liberal evolutionism one finds that the tone of Panglossian blandness, characteristic of the 1950s, has quite disappeared, and that in its place were doubt, pessimism and spleen. Professor Bell, for example, anxiously explored 'the cultural contradictions of capitalism': the appetites and expectations stimulated among the masses by the very success of capitalism threaten, he feared, both its economic and its political viability (Bell, 1976; 1978). In similar vein, in the pages of *Encounter* celebrations of the new affluence, moral equalitarianism and civil politics gave way to jeremiads on the extent of class envy and antagonism, on the lack of true *civitas* on the part of trade unionists, and on the disasters that must generally ensue once the spirit of acquisition is no longer confined to the minority with whom it could be trusted (see, for example, Mishan 1974, 1976; Hartley, 1975; Worsthorne, 1976; Toulmin, 1978; Sinai, 1979).

Liberal, or social-democratic, views on the British working class were, I have argued, largely shaped by American influences. In contrast, the views of those whom I have labelled 'organicists' – to which I now turn – may be situated in an indigenous intellectual tradition. Furthermore, the major concern of the creators of this tradition has in fact been to call directly into question a claim central to all liberal interpretations of modern industrialism, at least in their more innocent and optimistic versions: that is, the claim that material and cultural advance have, in general, proceeded togcther. The tradition to which I refer can be traced back at least as far as the earlier nineteenth century – via, for example, the critiques offered by Arnold, Ruskin, Carlyle and Coleridge of the liberal theories of progress of their own day. However, for present purposes, an appropriate starting point will be found with the outstanding figure in the tradition in the middle decades of the twentieth century, namely, F. R. Leavis.

It is not too much to say that the primary theme of Leavis's social criticism – and quite often of his literary criticism too – is the extent of the cultural *loss* which, in the modern world, has been the concomitant of material gain. Thus, already in the 1930s Leavis sought to show how a grave – and now irrecoverable – cost of industrialism and of urban growth had been the destruction of the 'organic community': that is, of the kind of small-scale, relatively self-sufficient community that was typical of the pre-industrial village or township. For with the disappearance of the organic community, he argued, there disappeared too a way of life that allowed a full expression of human nature and a full satisfaction of basic human needs – above all, of the need for stable, expressive relationships with one's fellows (Leavis, 1932; Leavis and Thompson, 1933).

Moreover, in Leavis's later writing during the years of rising affluence of the 1950s and 1960s his emphasis on cultural decline and deprivation became even more marked – and especially so with regard to the working class. The relative prosperity and leisure that some of its members had come to enjoy, Leavis held, represented a 'felicity . . . [that] cannot be regarded by a fully human mind as a matter for happy contemplation'. This was so because the whole context of life of industrial workers constrained them to regard real living as being reserved for leisure, but then to use their leisure time in essentially passive and trivial ways. The working class had been betrayed – left 'to enjoy a "high standard of living" in a vacuum of disinheritance' (Leavis, 1972, pp. 59 and 79).

However, over the same period in which Leavis was thus lapsing into ever deeper cultural despair, the organicist challenge to the prevailing liberalism was in fact being given new impetus and direction in a rather surprising manner. That was by the 'rediscovery' of the organic community, or at all events of a surrogate for it, in the very heart of urban Britain and, precisely, in the working-class communities that survived as 'urban villages' within the great industrial towns and cities. While recognizing that the future of such class enclaves was indeed menaced by processes of social change in the direction of mass society, a number of influential writers of the 1950s and 1960s sought, none the less, to invest the urban working-class community with major socio-cultural significance. First of all, it was taken as demonstrating that a way of life based on kinship and neighbourhood, and capable of inspiring a deep sense of rootedness, continuity and belonging, *could* exist within an urban–industrial context. But second, and more importantly, the working-class community was seen as constituting historically a source of moral, and in turn of social, values that could stand as a corrective, if not indeed as a total alternative, to those of the mass society and of its economic base.

For example, in *The Uses of Literacy* (1957) Richard Hoggart sought to bring out the distinctiveness of the culture of the traditional working-class 'district' in both form and content. It was, he argued, a culture genuinely 'of the people' in that it arose out of, and was specific to, a particular social milieu – in contrast with the anonymous, 'faceless' mass culture that increasingly threatened it. The working-class emphasis on the personal and concrete, on the importance of primary group ties and hence of communal solidarity all directly reflected the conditions of traditional working-class life; and these values must be seen, Hoggart went on, as forming a vital component of, so to speak, the moral stock of the society as a whole (see also Hoggart, 1960 and 1970). Similarly, Brian Jackson in his book, *Working Class Community* (1968) posed the question directly of what were 'the main qualities that a civilised society should try to take over from working-class life' (p. 159); and the answer he gave was one which in effect represented the working class as the main locus of a 'counter-culture' within contemporary British society. Against the dominant middle-class, or middle-mass, individualism, as expressed in economic competitiveness, status rivalry and a privatized domestic life, could be set working-class collectivism – the 'deeply grained' habits of co-operativeness and mutuality and the 'constant reaching out for the communal' (p. 147).

However, of major significance in this revival and reorientation of the organicist tradition was the work of Raymond Williams which, somewhat paradoxically, showed the most obvious line of descent from the social criticism of Leavis and yet the sharpest departure from it – in the direction of the left. Williams in fact breaks with the argument that would associate industrialism with cultural decline, and sees in the organicist critique of industrialism a distortion of what was really required – namely a critique of *capitalism* (Williams, 1958 and 1973a). His own interpretation of modern British history, at least as presented in his earlier studies, is encapsulated in the title of the most important of these, *The Long Revolution* (2nd edition, 1965) and has an undoubtedly optimistic, indeed progressivist, character. The industrial revolution, in complex interaction with the democratic revolution, in turn engendered a third, cultural revolution – as expressed in the expansion of literacy, skills and education and in the widening network of communications.

This process, Williams maintains, calls basically for assent: the critical task is to see the ways in which the enormous potentialities of the long revolution can be realized beyond the limitations set by its historical matrix, the capitalist economy and society. And it is, then, in this respect, Williams argues, that the major achievement of the working class may be recognized. This lies, ultimately, not in the qualities expressed in its community life but, rather, in the *social institutions* that grew out of the core working-class values of equality, solidarity and collective endeavour, and which formed the basis of the labour movement: the friendly and co-operative societies, the trade unions, and then the Labour Party itself. It is through the creation of these institutions that the working class has made its great contribution to the building of a future, socialist society: it has provided an alternative model of social organization to the individualistic, competitive and hierarchical model of the established bourgeois order.

Thus, while in liberal interpretations the historical development of the working class tends towards its assimilation into the socio-cultural uniformity of mass society, organicist interpretations entail an emphasis on the socio-cultural distinctiveness of the working class, and on its continuing significance as the bearer of 'oppositional' values. And even perhaps, in Marxisant fashion, the working class appears as the inspiration and potential agency, if not of revolution in the classical sense, then at all events of a moral reconstitution of society. However, one must here again ask: how far are these arguments ones that proved capable of maintaining their plausibility? And merely to pose this question is, I believe, to incite a negative answer.

It is, first of all, worth noting the very variable confidence that the organicists themselves displayed over whether what they saw as historical potential would in fact be realized. For example, Hoggart's *The Uses of Literacy* is in large part taken up with regretful accounts, in Leavisite vein, of the 'dilution' of working-class culture already evident as a result of the influence of the mass media and mass markets; and Jackson directly echoes many of Hoggart's fears. Again, in the closing chapter of *The Long Revolution*, which is devoted to the state of contemporary Britain, Williams makes an abrupt, and largely unexplained, shift from the optimistic perspectives of his historical analyses. The actual achievement of socialism is represented as being now highly problematic in that the labour movement is in 'visible moral decline': the unions have become increasingly sectionalist in outlook; the co-operatives are reduced to no more than trading organizations; the Labour Party is content to be merely an alternative government within the existing socio-political system; and the working class itself displays a 'serious diminution of consciousness' and thus a weakening response to socialist ideas and politics.[3]

Moreover, underlying these doubts and uncertainties, one may detect in all the authors in question some barely suppressed awareness of what is in fact the inherent weakness of the organicist position. If, as is claimed, distinctly working-class values are grounded in the conditions of traditional working-class life, then this would in itself tend to tell against the possibility of the working class continuing to adhere to these values under changed conditions; and, still more, against that of working-class values being extended into society at large. It is, in other words, precisely *because* of their intimate relationship with the constraints and exigencies of working-class life that the values in which organicists see a universal, moral significance should rather be viewed as being to an important extent of a particularistic and instrumental character.[4] And it would therefore follow that working-class traditions of mutuality, solidarity and collective action generally are especially likely to be abandoned, or modified, in response to changes in the context of their use; and to be retained, or extended to other groups, only in so far as they continue to serve other values that are of a more 'final' kind.

It would be difficult to maintain that the conflicts that broke out in British society during the 1970s derived from some basic clash between the value systems of different classes. On the contrary, they may far more readily be seen, as I earlier suggested, as reflecting a heightened dissent over distributional, and, in turn industrial relations issues – which presupposed ultimate goals that were largely held in common: for example, those listed by Crosland of 'choice, leisure, comfort, privacy and a more spacious family life', plus, I would want to say, greater control over one's destiny in working life. These are, moreover, goals that imply an individualistic, or privatized, rather than a communal frame of reference. The one major respect in which a commitment to collectivism clearly persisted among the working class – and did indeed become a model for other groups – was, significantly, that of trade unionism, seen as a powerful *means* of defending and advancing collective positions within the struggle for relative advantage in market and work situations (compare Goldthorpe and Lockwood, 1963; Goldthorpe, 1978).

The liberals, one could say, anticipated working-class acceptance of the ethos of the mass society, and were then disappointed in that this did not lead to greater social integration but rather to intensified conflict. The organicists, on the other hand, anticipated conflict, and were disappointed in that this has found expression not in the opposition of values but rather in the rivalry of interests.

Finally, then, I come to interpretations of the working class in post-war Britain that have been advanced from the left. Williams' work could, of course, be seen as falling under this head, as well as representing the main development of the period within the organicist tradition. But what one must also recognize are the further analyses and arguments, involving direct criticism of Williams, which, from the early 1960s onwards, were presented from more decisively Marxist positions. Here in fact one has the source of a fierce controversy between the founders of the post 1956 New Left in Britain, notably Williams and E. P. Thompson, and a succeeding generation, determinedly 'European' in its intellectual proclivities.

The 'new' New Left offensive was launched in two essays by Perry Anderson and Tom Nairn which appeared in the *New Left Review* in 1964. Basically their objection to Williams' interpretation of the development of the working class in Britain was that this was not set within a sufficiently

47

'totalizing' historical account. Once even the outlines of such an account were provided, it became evident that the seeming 'moral decline' of the labour movement and the lack of working-class response to socialism were 'not accidental'. The British working class was created within a capitalist society which had not, however, emerged from a true bourgeois revolution, and whose ruling class was in fact an amalgam of the new industrial bourgeoisie and the old aristocracy. This class had thus the capacity to exert a uniquely powerful 'hegemony' over the society as a whole: that is, as Anderson put it in paraphrase of Gramsci, a dominance over other groups and strata 'not simply by means of force or wealth, but by a social authority whose ultimate sanction and expression is a profound cultural supremacy' (1964, p. 39). In turn, then, the cultural, including the ideological, development of the working class was inevitably stunted; the capitalist hegemony did not merely set external limits to the aims and actions of the working class but internal ones also, 'imposing contingent historical facts as the necessary co-ordinates of social life itself' (p. 39).

It is, Anderson argues, indeed the case that 'the real historical content of the working-class movement has not in the main been articulated ideologically at all, but institutionally'. However, he goes on, what William fails to see in applauding the institution-building achievements of the working class, is that these were such as to usurp its aspirations to be itself a hegemonic – or, in other words, a revolutionary – class, and condemned it to remain rather a 'corporate' class, securely accommodated within the capitalist order. Anderson writes,

If a hegemonic class can be defined as one which imposes its own ends and own vision on a society as a whole, a corporate class is conversely one which pursues its own ends within a social totality whose global determination lies outside it.

Williams may have accurately characterized working-class culture and the institutions that have grown from it; but the difficulty is that 'the will to universalise [this culture], to make it the general model of society, which [Williams] tacitly assumes to be a concomitant, has only rarely existed'.[5]

In this new perspective, then, neither the distinctiveness of working-class culture, nor the actual content of the values it embodies, nor yet the institutions that it has nurtured, can be regarded as having a radically oppositional significance; they do not give rise to a decisive negation of the existing form of society. On the contrary, they are seen as having severely restricted the political range of working-class action; and, more seriously still, as being reflected in a social consciousness that is in the end profoundly conservative in the resistance that it offers to the general, critical ideas of socialist theory – 'a carapace of dead matter', to quote now from Nairn, '. . . the product of generations of the static, vegetative culture of working-class "apartheid", with all its parochialism and elements of mimesis' (1964, p. 56).

Thus, in the view of the 'new' New Left, the British working class is 'one of the enigmas of modern history'; while charged with great revolutionary potential – in respect of its size and capacity for solidary action – this is a potential that can be realized only to the extent that the social consciousness of its members is transformed. Moreover, though, it follows from the analysis offered that such a transformation will not be achieved 'merely', as Nairn puts it, 'by the annunciation of Marxist ideas'. What will also be required is that the sway of capitalist hegemony over the working class is in some way weakened, so that it becomes possible for the relevance of these ideas to be perceived (Nairn, pp. 56–7). And indeed it could be said that from the time of their initial *prise de position* onwards, a leading concern of Anderson and Nairn, and of their associates on the left, has been to try to discern socio-political trends or conjunctures of a kind that might thus prove emancipatory: that is, which could serve to release the working class from the ideological limitations at present imposed on it, and to create among its members a new receptivity to the theory which is essential for any class that seeks to raise a hegemonic challenge.[6]

For example, in a further essay, Anderson saw promise in the very growth among the working class of 'instrumental collectivism'. This signified, he argued, 'for the first time the penetration of *reason*, of rationality into [the] closed affective universe' of the working class. There was danger in the fact that the rationality in question was the egoistic, market rationality of capitalism; but this was none the less destructive of 'the mystical values of deference' and of 'the ideology of stupefied traditionalism' that had held the working class in thrall, and could thus help open the way to the acceptance of an alternative rationality, that of socialism. Nor would much of value be lost if the merely communal forms of working-class solidarity and consciousness were undermined in the process. As Anderson proclaimed,

The incursion of rationalism into the hermetic world of the English working class is a necessary stage in its emancipation – however limited or confusing its initial manifestations. . . . The battle for the working class can . . . only be won on the plane of ideology. The new rationalism may be preparing the conditions for a real victory (1965, p. 265).

However, by the end of the 1960s, the hopes of the left had in fact shifted rather radically from developments occurring within the working class itself to the revolutionary significance that was perceived in the activities of another group – the students. While the latter, it was acknowledged, could never usurp the historic role of the working class in the overthrow of capitalism, they could be seen as a vanguard force, 'the petrels of a future general uprising'. Moreover, in the British case specifically, student radicalism was poised to make a quite crucial contribution: that is, in actually demonstrating, in the struggle within *academe*, the unity of theory and practice as yet unappreciated by the working class, and in thus helping to overcome, as Stedman-Jones saw it, 'this long-standing barrier to the emergence of an insurgent working-class movement' (1969, p. 53. And see also Cockburn, 1969). Once more, Anderson himself announced a new dawn: the creation of a truly revolutionary culture in Britain might still be some way off 'but a revolutionary practice within culture is still possible and necessary today. The student struggle is its initial form' (1968, p. 57).

Finally, though, as student radicalism faded away in the 1970s – having achieved no impact whatever on the labour movement – the left was forced to move on yet again in its quest for the catalyst that would produce the further required revolutionary reaction. While signs of some theoretical disarray were by now apparent, one further recourse was actually proposed, notably by Nairn, which was more surprising perhaps than any previous – that to ethno-nationalism. Typically, nationalism has been treated as a countervailing force to the growth of class consciousness or, by Marxists, as merely an ephiphenomenon of deeper class antagonisms. However, in Nairn's agonized reappraisal, it was only nationalism that could provide the basis for any new political mobilization of a relatively large-scale and radical character: the theory of uneven development must, for some time ahead, take precedence over that of class conflict as the key to the understanding of the dynamics of British history. It was the resurgence of nationalist movements on the Celtic fringe that were creating a situation in which the break-up of the British state was imminent, and in which at the same time a serious threat was posed to the hegemony that had sustained it for more than a century. But such a situation did then give rise to the hope that the tradition of untheoretical, populist socialism, as fostered by the 'old' New Left, could take on new life and significance: that is, as no less than the expression of an *English* cultural nationalism, in which form it could thus, after all, hold out emancipatory promise. Nairn tells us,

To those who care for England and strive to see her free of the old harness, this hope is critical. It means there is a romanticism not infallibly Tory in its results, and a national-populism distinguishable from the habit of authority and the sink of deference . . . it may one day serve as a cultural bond between sectarian Marxism and a wider popular movement (1977, p. 304. See also Gellner, 1978).

Now simply to review this succession of 'hopes' for the future of a revolutionary socialism achieved via working-class action is, I believe, to indicate an increasing *desperation* on the left. And furthermore, the fact that these hopes have always remained, to say the least, at some distance from fulfilment must call into doubt the underlying analysis.

To an extent, the view taken of the working class from the left is compatible with that offered by the Cold War liberals. In both cases, the working class is seen as effectively integrated into the existing socio-political order and as constituting no serious threat to its stability. The difference is that while for the liberals this state of affairs had come about as part of the inherent logic of the development of democratic industrialism and was destined to continue, for the left it testified to the considerable repressive powers of capitalism which were, however, destined at some point to be overcome. For this reason, the left was certainly better placed than the liberals to account for the major role played by working-class militancy in the general heightening of social conflict evident in Britain from the mid 1960s onwards. Further it must be acknowledged that Anderson recognized what the liberals, and also the organicists, overlooked: that is, the disruptive, destabilizing potential of the decline of working-class particularism and of the more complete acceptance by members of the working class of the values and orientations characteristic of modern capitalism. But what led the 'new' New Left into its grave difficulties was its initial need to perceive some way through in which, under these conditions of greater instability, there could develop a conscious, theoretically-directed drive by the working class, *leading beyond mere militancy* to the achievement of a socialist society. Or, one could say, its difficulties stemmed from the insistence of its adherents on still interpreting Marxism as not only a theory of the internal contradictions of capitalism but further of proletarian revolution (see, for example, Robin Blackburn, 1977). For this interpretation demands of them a crucial assumption: that underlying, and occluded by, all the manifestations of capitalist hegemony, there exists, so to speak, a historically appointed affinity between the working class and socialism. And it is, then, this assumption that energizes the unremitting search for the key to the 'enigma' of the working class: the key that will allow this affinity to emerge and to realize itself.

However, for those who see no reason to suppose any such affinity, and who would regard working-class support for socialism – even if it should one day prove powerful – as being always contingent, the terms of the left's search must appear quite mistaken, and the problems, empirical and theoretical, to which it gives rise as essentially 'degenerate' ones. Arguments concerning hegemony and the means whereby it might be overcome are made necessary *only* by the assumption of a potentially revolutionary working class; and they have in fact no other *raison d'être* than to protect this assumption.[7]

The first question to which, I hoped, I could provide an answer by the end of this chapter was that of why intellectuals in modern Britain should have shown such concern with the working class. The answer is, I believe, now fairly apparent. It is that the working class has been seen by each of the three groups of intellectuals that I have considered as the crucial social agency for the achievement of *their own* socio-political goals.

This is most evident in the case of the left – and not surprisingly so; for the nature of the relationship between intellectuals and the working class that I am here suggesting is that actually proposed by Marx when he spoke, not only of the proletariat finding its intellectual weapons in philosophy, but of philosophy at the same time finding its material weapons in the proletariat (Marx, 1964, p. 59). Although the Marxist left in modern Britain has been much troubled by the reluctance of the working class to take over its philosophy, it none the less continues to regard the working class as the only agency through which the unity of revolutionary theory and practice might be effected. However, what must also be recognized is that this perception of the working class as the essential means to the realization of a philosophy has not been confined to the left. For the organicists, for example, the working class appeared, as we have seen, as the last carriers of a culture that is 'of the people', and as the one remaining living source of organic conceptions of social life – from which might then be developed real alternatives to the individualistic values of middle-class, or middle-mass, society, and even

51

perhaps an entirely new moral order. And then again for the liberals, one could say, the historic role to be played by the working class was, in effect, the reverse of that which was envisaged by the left. In this case, the working class was to ensure the long-term stability of capitalism by quietly fading away – by ceasing to exist as a distinctive economic and cultural entity encamped within capitalist society like an alien force, and by thus bringing to an end the disruption of class conflict and the threat of ideological – that is to say, of socialist – politics.

The second question which, I suggested, would eventually need consideration was that of why the interpretations offered by these rival groups of intellectuals of, as I put it, 'the historical and emergent significance' of the working class should have proved to be so uniformly unsuccessful. For example, one could now more specifically ask: why did the liberals fail to recognize that as the working class came increasingly to accept the normative standards of mass society this could well, in itself, lead to its members displaying greater rather than less distributional dissent, and thus to the intensification of class-based conflict? Why did the organicists not see the extent to which the values of the traditional working-class community were in fact instrumental ones rather than implying some ultimate commitment to communal as opposed to individual and privatized concerns? Why did the left seek first to postulate the subordination of the working class to a capitalist hegemony, but then to pursue a series of possibilities for its emancipation requiring socio-political developments of an increasingly implausible kind?

The answer that must be given here is, I believe, already indicated in part by that provided to the first question. Because these different, and contending, groups of intellectuals all saw in the working class the agency through which their own goals might be attained, the interpretations they offered of its significance could scarcely be ones conceived and advanced in an attitude of detachment. A pressure towards wishful, rather than critical, thinking was almost inevitably set up, and one that was perhaps most often expressed in a tendency to assert that what was desired was already historically in train.

Moreover, related to this, one can identify a further serious source of error: that is, the propensity among the intellectuals I have considered to interpret the present situation of the working class in the context of relatively long-term historical trends, which they believe they had discerned, rather than on the basis of direct and detailed investigation of this situation itself. Thus, for example, the liberals grounded their claim that the British working class was in process of decomposition chiefly in the supposed logic of the evolution of modern industrial society, and quite failed to show – or even to inquire – exactly how, and how far, this process was in fact occurring (see Goldthorpe and Lockwood, 1963; and Lockwood, 1960). The organicists represented the working class as the key source of alternative values to those of the prevailing social order by constructing a new version of British cultural history to replace the conservative and pessimistic one of Leavis – its fullest expression being found in Williams' account of 'the long revolution'. But no systematic and critical assessment was made of the extent to which, or of the conditions under which, the values that were attributed to the working class were in fact those held by its members, let alone were ones capable of being 'universalized' (compare, for example, the accounts given in Roberts, 1971; Kerr, 1958; Dennis *et al.*, 1956; Currie, 1979). The left sought to demonstrate the power of capitalist hegemony in Britain and the corporate character of the working class through presenting a 'totalizing' history of British society extending back to the imperfect nature of the bourgeois revolution of the seventeenth century. At no point, though, does one find any account of how precisely – through what social and psychological processes – hegemonic power is actually exerted over the working class and shapes the consciousness of its members, nor thus of just what would be entailed in the breaking of this power (compare, for example, Gray, 1976).

In sum, then, the conclusion to which I am led is the following: that each of the major intellectual efforts at comprehending the British working class that I have reviewed rests to a large extent on what might be described as a half-hearted, usually covert, and ultimately defeated historicism. In each case, the working class has been assigned a crucial role within a historical scenario leading to a desired socio-political outcome – although the scenarios have not for the most part been expressed in the language of a strict historical determinism but rather, and somewhat cloudily, in that of historical 'process', 'logic' or 'tendency'. In so far as patterns of social change might be seen as consistent with such a scenario, they have been seized upon with enthusiasm by its proponents – but with little inquiry into how in fact they were generated. When, on the other hand, apparently favourable trends or conjunctures have disappeared, and have perhaps been succeeded by unfavourable ones, then confidence has waned and the scenario has been either simply abandoned or subjected to some more or less radical *ad hoc* modification.

That the historicism in question should have been generally muted or implicit is not difficult to appreciate: an open acceptance of a historicist position has become increasingly regarded as a methodological embarrassment. None the less, for intellectuals, historicist thinking still retains a powerful attraction. As I suggested at the outset, intellectuals seek to exert not only a cognitive, but also a moral and a political influence; and what historicism offers them is in effect a tempting short-cut from the one to the other. To the extent that intellectuals can lay claim to possess some cognitive hold on the 'movement' of history, then they are, of course, at once in a position to draw out moral and political implications of a forceful kind. In particular, they can seek to show the alignment of their own values and ideas with this historical movement, rather than having to make the case for them on their intrinsic merits or to defend them against rational criticism. And, more generally, they can represent the connection between the fate of 'philosophies' and of the groups and strata that serve as their social vehicles as being ultimately one of historical appointment – and revelation – rather than as one of a contingent nature and dependent, among other things, on argument, persuasion and political leadership.

For these very reasons, then, historicist thinking has been regarded – and, I believe, rightly – as not only mistaken but further as morally and politically deleterious: that is, in encouraging irrationalism and denying choice. And from this standpoint, therefore, it is possible to view with considerable satisfaction the refusal of the British working class to become peaceably integrated into capitalist society, *or* to perpetuate organicism, *or* to make a Marxist revolution: in other words, its refusal to fit in with any of the attempts at historicist, or crypto-historicist, pattern-making that intellectuals have sought to impose upon it. For the latter, this recalcitrance of the working class is evidently the cause of much disillusion and disappointment. It is rather for those of us who would always wish to see such pattern-making discredited in practice as well as in principle that the working class appears as a resolute and effective ally.

Notes and references

1   The political significance of *Encounter* is a matter which would repay further inquiry. As is well known, it emerged in 1967 that between 1953 and 1964 *Encounter* had been in part supported by United States Central Intelligence Agency funds – passed via the Fairfield Foundation (a CIA 'front' organization) to the Congress of Cultural Freedom for the purpose of publishing the journal, and similar ones, in other western European countries. What would however be of further interest is to know the exact nature of the CIA's objectives and, perhaps, directives. Remarks made at the time of the 1967 disclosure by Mr T. W. Braden, from 1951 to 1954 head of the CIA's Division of International Organisations, suggest that to promote 'revisionism' among western European labour movements was a current CIA concern.

2   Compare the excellent analysis presented in Fred Hirsch, *Social Limits to Growth*, Harvard University Press, 1976, ch. 12. Crosland, one may add, did in fact recognize at an early stage the growth in the power of industrial labour via the extension of shop-floor organization and collective bargaining (see, for example, the discussion in 'What does the worker want?'); but at the same time he appears not to have appreciated the disruptive implications of this development when in conjunction with the expansion of working-class wants and aspirations that he welcomed.

3   *The Long Revolution* (2nd edn), pp. 328–9, 352. In so far as Williams seeks to account for the declining prospects of socialism in terms of a weakening working-class consciousness – and indeed of 'traditional definitions' of class being broken down – his interpretation does of course come close to that of the liberals. He appears, however, to wish to differentiate it by referring ultimately to the effects not of affluence or changing conditions of work, residence, etc., but rather to cultural

influences and in particular to those associated with the fact that most of the country's cultural apparatus is directly or indirectly under capitalist control. See also on this, Williams (1962).

4 Compare further on this point Wollheim (1961), which is probably the most sophisticated and effective critique of organicist views from a liberal or social-democratic position. Jackson seems partly to recognize the problem of universalizing the values of community when he observes that among the working class

Community ends very sharply, and if we are ever to develop its qualities for our whole society, we have to know not only whether it can exist apart from the cramped and unequal conditions that bred it, but whether it can be opened up to new experiences (1968, p. 160).

This still, however, neglects the issue of how an *inherently* particularistic value, such as that of solidarity, can in principle be universalized: the practice of solidarity would seem to require both an 'in-group' *and* an 'out-group'. Williams has remarked more generally (in a recorded conversation with Hoggart) that 'The most difficult bit of theory . . . is what relation there is between kinds of community that we call working-class and the high working-class tradition leading to democracy, solidarity in the unions, socialism.'

5 Anderson, 1964, pp. 44–5. Compare also the criticism of Williams advanced by another luminary of the 'new' New Left, Terry Eagleton:

The idealist epistemology, organicist aesthetics, and corporatist sociology of *The Long Revolution* went logically together. . . . The form of all three was a Romantic populism. Williams' political gradualism rested upon a deep-seated trust in the capacity of individuals to create 'new meanings and values' *now* – meanings and values which will extend (at some infinite point in the future?) to socialism. The creation of new values which is in fact only *enabled* by revolutionary rupture was read back by him as a description of the present. . . . Williams often manoeuvred himself into the contradictory position of opposing a crippling hegemony whose power he had simultaneously to deny, because not to do so would have suggested that 'ordinary people' were not, after all, the true creators of 'meanings and values' (Eagleton, 1978, pp. 27–8; emphases in original).

6 Anderson has also rehearsed his and Nairn's initial position in the course of polemics with E. P. Thompson. In a critique of their 1964 articles, Thompson argued, *inter alia*, and in apparent defence of Williams, that the distinction between a corporate and a hegemonic class was of doubtful value.

The antithesis to the hegemony of a [dominant] class would appear to be, not the corporateness of a class but a state of naked dictatorship by a class which does not have the cultural resources and the intellectual maturity, to hold power in any other way. . .'

And moreover, then, the theoretical coherence of the idea of a hegemonic *working* class becomes highly questionable: 'Strictly, the concept [of hegemony] can only be related to that of State power, and is inapplicable to a subordinate class which by the nature of its situation cannot dominate the ethos of a society.' Thus, not only may the new account lead one to suppose 'that some radically new explanation has been offered whereas these are simply new ways of describing a long familiar set of facts', but further it fails to give adequate weight to the real achievements of the British working class through its own institutions and organizations and to its future potential, even if following reformist tactics (Thompson, 1965, p. 346). Anderson's reply, while going little way to meet these points, does serve to bring out still more clearly than before the very low valuation that the 'new' New Left would set on both the British labour movement and the quality of the intellectual support with which it has been provided by its supporters among the 'old' New Left. The obverse of the latter's neglect of the importance of theory – both sociological and socialist – is found in a pervasive *populism*: serious analysis is relinquished for 'a perpetual, sententious invocation of "the people".' See Anderson, 1966; compare also Nairn, 1964.

7 I have taken this point somewhat further elsewhere (see Goldthorpe, 1972). It is of interest to note that an aspect of what has been described as Williams' 'growing rapprochement with Marxism' (Eagleton, 1978, p. 41) has been the acceptance of the concept of hegemony in his more recent social analysis (see, for example, Williams, 1973b). This development has enabled Williams to meet, to some extent, the demand of the 'new' New Left that his pessimism over the socialist potential of the working class, as expressed in the final chapter of *The Long Revolution*, should be given an appropriate theoretical basis. But the implication, inevitably, is an a priori exclusion of the possibility of any 'authentic' working-class rejection of socialism – whether in principle or out of doubts about the specific proposals being made for its realization. It is then easy to see why dogmatists of Eagleton's stamp feared the idea which they found in Williams' earlier work that members of the working class had the capacity to create new values and meanings for themselves in an essentially independent and autonomous fashion.

Further reading

Perry Anderson, 'Origins of the Present Crisis', *New Left Review*, **23**, 1964.

C. A. R. Crosland, *The Conservative Enemy*, London: Cape, 1962.

John H. Goldthorpe, 'Class Status and Party in Modern Britain', *Archives Europeennes de Sociologie*, **13**, 1972.

Tom Nairn, 'The English Working Class', *New Left Review*, **24**, 1964.

Edward Shils, *The Intellectuals and the Powers*, Chicago: Chicago University Press, 1972.

Raymond Williams, *The Long Revolution*, London: Chatto and Windus, 1961.

3   The weakest link in the chain? Some comments on the Marxist theory of action

David Lockwood

On the face of it, it seems improbable that there is any such thing as the Marxist theory of action. Marxists have, of course, always laid claim to a uniquely privileged understanding of society through their possession of a body of theory which, by its singular unity, transcends the artificial specialisms of 'bourgeois' social science. But this claim is surely invalid. It is simply that Marxism is now in such a state of epistemological disarray that some of its illuminati can deny the very possibility of one of the two subjects in which Marxist scholarship has traditionally excelled, namely, history. It is also that, in practice, Marxism ehibits very much the selfsame division of intellectual labour as that of 'bourgeois' social science. Economic theorists go their several ways without paying much attention to the problems of class formation and class consciousness (for example, Sweezy, 1949; Baran and Sweezy, 1966; Mandel, 1975). On the other hand, students of the political sociology of class do not as a matter of course relate their work to Marxist economic theory in any systematic way, if at all (for example, Miliband, 1969; Poulantzas, 1973). Finally, there is a quite distinctive school of 'philosophical anthropology' which centres on the concept of alienation (see, for example, Meszaros, 1970; Ollman, 1971; Heller, 1974). Writings on this subject have only the most tenuous connection with the substance of Marxist economic theory, and the majority of leading Marxist political sociologists find the whole notion of alienation of small relevance, if not downright heretical.

Given that contemporary Marxism exhibits such a heterogeneity of persuasion, is it reasonable to suppose that underlying this diversity there is a coherent theory of class action? This is not a question that can be answered within the confines of the present chapter without a drastic simplication of the way it is posed. But it may be that there is some advantage to be gained from pursuing this matter without too much subtlety, and even with a certain bluntness, since no small part of the discussion that complicates the subject appears, in however sophisticated a manner, to fudge the basic issues.

From a sociological viewpoint, the most crucial aspect of the problem is the conceptual link between system integration and social integration (Lockwood, 1964); and in Marxism there is only one such link that is at all well forged. What is at stake is quite simply the attempt to relate the economic theory of capitalist accumulation to the political sociology, or the philosophical anthropology, of proletarian revolution. The elucidation of this connection has always been, and still is, the most problematic feature of Marxist theory.[1] The argument that follows has a twofold purpose. The first is to show that the main link between system and social integration has been established by means of a basically 'utilitarian' concept of action that leads to unstable and contradictory explanations of conflict and order. The second aim is to show how the most influential exponents of contemporary class theory have 'solved' the problems arising from this concept of action either by avoiding them or by rejecting the entire classical Marxist formulation of system and social integration.

The generally accepted view that, in working out his 'law of motion' of the capitalist mode of production, Marx was more indebted to Ricardo than to Hegel is the starting point of the discussion. In particular, the extent to which the Marxian theory of class action represents a modification of what Parsons has called the utilitarian scheme of action will be of prime concern (Parsons, 1937; see also Lindsay, 1925). The two chief distinguishing characteristics of the classical utilitarian position are first, the assumption that the ends of actors are 'random', and second, the assumption that in adapting their means to their given ends, actors are governed by the standard of 'rationality'. By the time of Malthus and Ricardo, however, the concept of the actor as a rational individual egoist, a view that Parsons attributes to Hobbes, had been replaced by the notion of rational class egoists whose ends are determined by their position within specific relations of production. By this time also the post-Hobbesian solution of the problem of order, which took the form of a political or economic theory of a natural identity of interests, had been replaced by a theory of a natural identity of interests (Halevy, 1955, p. 319). The assumption that the ends of actors are random because they are purely idiosyncratic and not subject to a social determination had therefore been abandoned. But the idea that ends are random in the sense that they lack moral integration through a common value system is one that persisted, at least implicitly. The problem of moral integration was peripheral to the type of theory that centred increasingly on the antagonisms of interest between capitalists, labourers, and landlords. Moreover, the key assumption that class actors pursued their given interests according to the standard of rationality precluded systematic consideration of the normative determination of action.

Marx may be said to have modified this reconstituted utilitarian framework in two main ways, both of which are related to his claim that his predecessors in political economy treated the modes of action typical of capitalist society as universally valid instead of seeing them as historically relative. First of all, Marx postulates an asymmetry between the ends of capitalists and proletarians in that he ascribes to the latter class the extrasystemic end of its self-abolition. Second, this 'end-shift' of the proletariat is integrally bound up with Marx's revision of the rationality assumption of the utilitarian action scheme. Corresponding to the asymmetry of the ends of capitalists and proletarians is the assumption of differential class rationality. The distinction between rationality, in the sense of a technologically, or economically, rational adaptation of means to given ends, and 'reason', in the sense of a capacity to understand that rational action as just defined can be self-defeating, is a notion already present in the work of Locke (Parsons, 1937, p. 96), who attributed this higher-order rationality to the propertied classes (MacPherson, 1977, pp. 221–38). By contrast, Marx endows the proletariat with this same kind of reason, and it is, indeed, through its exercise, under conditions created by capitalist accumulation, that the end-shift of the proletariat occurs. These rather compressed introductory remarks on the asymmetry of the ends of class actors and on the distinction between rationality and reason will now be developed in such a way as to bring out the basic source of instability in Marxist explanations of the relationship between system contradiction and proletarian revolution.

Marx's view of the capitalist class is epitomized by his description of the 'rational miser' whose 'subjective aim' and 'sole motive' is the 'restless, never-ending process of profit making alone' (1906, pp. 130–1). The rational pursuit of capital accumulation is determined by two conditions. The first draws on the distinction between production aimed at use value and production based on exchange value. In the former case, 'surplus-labour will be limited to a given set of wants which may be greater or less' and 'no boundless thirst for surplus-labour arises from the nature of production itself' (1906, p. 219). Production is 'kept within bounds by the very object it aims at, namely, consumption or the satisfaction of definite wants, an aim that lies altogether outside the sphere of circulation' (1906, p. 128). In a capitalist system, however, 'the circulation of money as capital is, on the contrary, an end in itself. The circulation of capital has therefore no limits' (1906, p. 129). The second condition is the competition between capitalists.

That which in the miser is a mere idiosyncrasy, is, in the capitalist, the effect of the social mechanism of which he is but one of the wheels. Moreover, the development of capitalist production makes it constantly necessary to keep increasing the amount of capital laid out in a given undertaking, and competition makes the immanent laws of capitalist production to be felt by each individual capitalist, as external coercive laws (1906, p. 603; see also p. 305).

Marx's rational miser is thus not the product of fixed human nature but of specific social conditions. Nevertheless, the question of whether Marx was correct in accusing his forerunners in political economy of conflating this distinction is unimportant, because his concept of the capitalist as a rational accumulator is, in effect, just as utilitarian in character as his theory that individual capitalists, in rationally pursuing their given ends, unintendedly produce conditions that are irrational from the viewpoint of the capitalist class as a whole. He presents the capitalist only as the 'personification of an economic category', but his construct of the rational miser does not differ in its essentials from the concept of the actor which is to be found in theories of the natural identity or divergence of interests put forward by previous writers within the utilitarian tradition. Without this postulate of the capitalist as a rational class egoist Marx's system cannot work. Each capitalist finds himself in a situation whose logic dictates that capital accumulation becomes his ultimate end, and, as a result of his rationally pursuing it, rational knowledge in the form of technology becomes progressively incorporated into the means of production as the chief method of obtaining relative surplus value. And this rising organic composition of capital not only provides the key to Marx's theory of system contradiction but serves to explain how capitalism creates all the major conditions conducive to proletarian revolt.

In turning to the concept of proletarian action the picture becomes more complicated. Like capitalists, proletarians are assumed to act rationally in pursuit of an end that is immediately given by the existing system of production. This is the wage that is necessary for maintaining and producing labour at a level of existence that is either purely physical or one that involves some 'traditional' standard of life. And like the class situation of capitalists, that of the proletariat is characterized, initially at least, by competition among workers. But, unlike the capitalist class,[2] the proletariat possesses a higher-order rationality, or faculty of reason, which enables it to acquire an understanding that the rational pursuit of its immediate ends is self-defeating, and that it has an ultimate end, which can only be realized through the abolition of the capitalist system. The nature of this postulated end-shift is identified by the distinction between a struggle over the level of wages and a struggle over the 'wages system' itself. The first goal is determined simply by a zero-sum conflict between capitalist and proletarian, 'a continuous struggle between capital and labour, the capitalist constantly tending to reduce wages to their physical minimum, and to extend the working day to its physical maximum, while the working man constantly presses in the opposite direction' (Marx and Engels, 1950, p. 402). From the viewpoint of Marx's theory of human nature, this goal represents the alienated need engendered by capitalist relations of production: 'The need for money is, therefore, the real need created by the modern economic system, and the only need which it creates' (1964, p. 168). By contrast, the extrasystemic end of the proletariat is the unalienated condition of

socialised man, the associated producers, rationally regulating their interchange with Nature, bringing it under their common control, instead of being ruled by it as by the blind forces of Nature; and achieving this with the least expenditure of energy and under the conditions most favourable to, and worthy of, their human nature (Marx, 1972, p. 820).

According to Marx, this end is not simply an ideal standard but a state of affairs that is already prefigured in the existing society.

The working class ought not to forget that they are fighting with effects but not with the causes of these effects . . . they ought to understand that, with all the miseries it imposes on them, the present system simultaneously engenders the material conditions and the social forms necessary for an economic reconstruction of society (Marx and Engels, 1950, p. 404).

The conditions that make this extrasystemic end of the proletariat attainable are produced by capitalists rationally pursuing their intrasystemic end. The increasing concentration and centralization of capital, the progressive socialization of labour and the growing material and moral misery of the working class are all consequences of the general tendency of capitalist accumulation. But the mediating factor between these conditions and revolutionary action is the proletariat's faculty of reason, its ability to grasp the connection between its immediate and fundamental interests (Ollman, 1971, pp. 112–15, 122–4, 238–9).

This is brought out very clearly by Wright when he says that

Class interests, therefore, are in a sense hypotheses about the objectives of struggles which would occur if the actors in the struggle had a scientifically correct understanding of their situations. To make the claim that socialism is in the 'interests' of the working class is not simply to make a historical, moralistic claim that workers ought to be in favour of socialism nor to make a normative claim that they would be 'better off' in a socialist society, but rather to claim that if workers had a scientific understanding of the contradictions of capitalism, they would in fact engage in struggles for socialism (1978, p. 89).

Marx did expect that workers would be able to come close to such an understanding, and mainly as a result of their own experience and powers of ratiocination. Indeed, this revolutionary consciousness of the proletariat would be a necessary condition of the success of genuine socialist revolution. His assumption that the proletariat could achieve its historically ascribed end-shift through the exercise of its faculty of reason is a view of action in which the utilitarian source of Marxian thinking merges into the Hegelian. Unlike previous revolutionary classes, the proletariat cannot simply pursue its immediate interests and entrust the consequences of its action to the 'cunning of reason'. As Lukacs puts it, 'the dialectical relationship between immediate interests and objective impact on the whole of society is located in the consciousness of the proletariat itself' (1971, p. 71). The fusion of immediate and fundamental interests comes about, so it is argued, through the process of revolutionary practice in which the proletariat's unfolding power of reason plays a crucial role. As it stands, however, the famous formula that the changing of people goes hand in hand with the changing of their circumstances possesses no more cogency than an incantation. To grasp its concrete meaning requires a specification of the nature of the people and circumstances in question. But before turning to consider what these are, it is necessary to deal with one final issue that arises from the assumption that action is governed by the standard of scientific rationality. This is the explanation of 'irrational' action.

Marx's belief that history would vindicate his theory is inseparable from his belief that his theory would prove to be a real historical force in just the same way as the reason of the proletariat with which it had an assignation. But this does not alter the fact that his theory *qua* theory only works by attributing rationality and reason to the actors it creates, and must therefore also be able to account for irrational action. Moreover, it can hardly be said that history has been backward in providing cause for treating this problem very seriously. In general, social theory has found only two main ways of explaining deviations from rational action. The first, an integral part of utilitarian thinking, relies heavily on the concepts of 'ignorance' and 'error'. In other words, irrational action is seen to be due either to the actor's inadequate knowledge of the facts of the situation or to his imperfect understanding of the most efficient, that is, scientifically rational, means of attaining his ends. This type of explanation has always been central to Marxist theory, and it has figured more prominently as the problem of accounting for the aberration of the proletariat has become more exigent. What is referred to here is the analytical promotion of the concept of capitalist ideological domination, and, by implication, that of the false consciousness of the proletariat. This concept has taken different forms, but, as will be seen in due course, the general use to which it has been put has had the effect of creating a high degree of instability in the theory of proletarian action.

The second way of explaining deviation from rational action does not play a systematic role in either utilitarian or Marxist thought. It rests on the distinction between irrational and nonrational action (Parsons, 1937, pp. 712–13). Whereas the former is defined negatively by the actor's 'failure' to conform to the standard of scientific rationality in adapting his means to his ends, the latter is defined positively by the actor's conformity to rules or norms that he or she regards as obligatory because they embody some ultimate end or value. This type of action, which finds its limiting case in Durkheim's notion of religious ritual, is, therefore, nonrational only in the sense that it is finally inexplicable in terms of ignorance or error. Although some norms may be partly justified as the most appropriate means of attaining proximate ends, and thus capable of being judged according to criteria of scientific rationality, progression up the means–end chain sooner or later reaches a point where the rationale of the rule is grounded in an end that is ultimate in that it is scientifically irrefutable. It is true that ultimate values are still open to rational scrutiny; but, at the same time, it is unlikely that a society made up entirely of moral philosophers would be at all durable. Nevertheless, the fact that most people do not acquire, and seldom change, their ultimate ends purely as a result of logical reflection does not imply that they are simply socialized into an unquestioning conformity to the rules that these values underpin. The view of action now being considered merely serves to bring into focus questions that the utilitarian scheme leaves obscure. The most basic of these is the extent to which the ultimate ends of actors are integrated with one another through a system of common values. This then concentrates attention on the factors that determine the extent to which values and norms defining the ends and means appropriate to different classes of actors come to constitute conditions of their action in the form of internal, rather than external, constraints. From this perspective, the central problem is no longer that of accounting for deviations from scientifically rational action but rather that of explaining variations in the institutionalization of values.

The position of values and norms within the Marxist theory of class action is very uncertain. Recognition of their significance grows as the evident weaknesses of explanations of ideologically induced ignorance and error call for a much more explicit treatment of the 'cultural', as opposed to the 'cognitive', obstacles to revolutionary consciousness. In general, however, these cultural factors have been incorporated into the category of ideology.

The main reason for this is the lack of a clear distinction between irrational and nonrational action, which rules out the possibility of the rigorous analysis and empirical study of the conditions determining the institutionalization of values. In default of this, the tendency is to resort to an 'over-socialized' concept of man, which only accentuates the instability of the theory of class action by encouraging 'idealistic' forms of explanation closely resembling those of normative functionalism.

Before examining the way in which Marxism has sought to explain the absence of revolutionary class consciousness by reference to ideological and cultural barriers to proletarian reason, it may be worthwhile to at least indicate how the problem of dealing with normative factors arises directly from Marx's account of the conditions making for proletarian revolt. For the purposes of exposition, it is convenient to separate out three main strands of his argument. First, there is an 'economic' theory, which centres on the absolute or relative impoverishment of the working class. Second, there is a 'sociological' theory, which sees revolution as the outcome of a process of proletarian self-education or praxis And, third, there is the 'philosophical anthropology' of alienation, which locates the revolutionary impulse of the proletariat in the degradation of its species-being.

The most basic question about any past, present, or future material impoverishment of the working class concerns the concept of action that links this condition with working-class revolt. As De Man puts it,

Of what use is it to prove that economic crises have assumed other forms than those foreseen by Marx? What matters to us is whether there really is, as Marx believed, a necessary connection between economic crises and the social revolution (1928, p. 23).

Impoverishment is, of course, only one aspect of this connection. The other is the way in which recurrent crises that plunge the proletariat into poverty also provide the conditions of proletarian self-education. It may be thought, therefore, that it is factitious to separate the discussion of these two aspects of the problem. But this procedure is not entirely unwarranted, because it is still a common, albeit implicit assumption of Marxist writers that impoverishment, or affluence, *per se*, does have a direct and immediate effect on working-class consciousness. Moreover, as will be seen in due course, this assumption is made less rather than more plausible by the introduction of the notion of self-education, since the latter does not usually take into account the importance of the distinction between human and organizational life spans, and thus confuses the learning embodied in the tradition of a corporate group with the learning of its individual members.

The question of whether Marx predicted an absolute or a relative immiseration of the proletariat is a matter of no great importance in the present context, however controversial it might be from other points of view (Bober, 1948, pp. 213–21 is still the best short account). The main point is that the hypothesis that impoverishment leads to radicalism, or conversely that affluence results in conservatism, is neither empirically supportable nor logically sound. It is not the case that the most impoverished and economically insecure workers are invariably, or even usually, the most radical or that periods of falling real wages and high unemployment are invariably those of working-class radicalism. What is of equal significance is that Marx himself provides the reasons for doubting that there should be a simple and direct relation between the economic condition and the class consciousness of the proletariat. First of all, like Ricardo before him, Marx recognized the needs of labourers, and hence the value of labour, were variable, determined not only by the conditions of sheer physical subsistence but also by 'a traditional standard of life', that is, by 'a historical and moral element' (for an extended discussion of this point see Browder, 1959). This means that there is introduced into the very notion of impoverishment a concept of the relativity of deprivation, and that the effects of economic circumstances on class consciousness are mediated by the variability of 'moral' factors. Most significantly, in the last analysis, the concept of a 'traditional standard of life' involves reference to the phenomenon of status group stratification. Thus, quite apart from the possibility noted by Durkheim that poverty can just as easily lead to fatalism as to revolt because 'actual possessions are partly the criterion of those aspired to' (1952, p. 254) – a consideration that should have entered into Marx's thinking about working-class consciousness from his reading of factory inspectors' reports (Ollman, 1972, p. 9) – the notion of 'tradition' introduces into the Marxian concept of action a normative element of fundamental importance, but one that remains analytically residual.

The systematic nature of this 'moral element' becomes more evident if it is accepted that Marx predicted not the absolute, but only the relative, impoverishment of the working class. Whatever the merits of this interpretation, it has far-reaching sociological implications. For unless it is held that it means no more than a purely objective divergence of profits and wages, both of which increase in absolute terms, then the explanation of the feeling of unjust deprivation associated with relative impoverishment must involve reference to the normative interrelationship of the ends of capitalists and proletarians. In other words, the sense of deprivation on the part of the proletariat results not from a comparison of their means relative to their traditionally defined standard of living, but rather from a comparison of their standard of living with that of the capitalist class. If the idea of relative impoverishment does not refer to this kind of comparison, then it is a purely statistical notion with no implications for the action of the proletariat. But if it does have this connotation, then it entails the concept of a status order. If the standard of living of a class contains a moral element, then the relationship between the standard of living of one class and that of another must imply a moral relationship; that is, a status hierarchy which defines the ends, or standards of living, to which different classes may legitimately aspire. Although Marx and Engels were not oblivious of the fact that class solidarity could be impaired by status differentiation, the concept of status entered into their explanation of class action in an entirely *ad hoc* fashion. This has remained characteristic of subsequent Marxist theory; and, as will be seen shortly, the failure to differentiate the institutionalization of status from the general category of the ideological is a main reason why Marxism exhibits a marked tendency to oscillate between two equally untenable schemes of action: at the one extreme, the 'positivistic' (of which the impoverishment thesis is archetypal); and, at the other, what can only be called – though in a necessarily limited sense – the 'idealistic'.[3] At this stage, however, it simply needs to be emphasized that the foregoing criticisms of the impoverishment thesis apply with equal force to the opposite kind of argument which seeks to explain working-class acquiescence or conservatism in terms of relative affluence. Lenin's theory of the 'labour aristocracy' is the most striking example of this type of explanation. His idea that proletarian revolution was averted by leading sections of the working class being 'bribed' or bought off by their sharing in imperialist 'super-profits' is based on the familiar positivistic assumption that reduces the determination of ends to changes in material conditions. Subsequent research has demonstrated the inadequacy of this theory (Moorehouse, 1978). It has also shown that, far from being 'bourgeoisified' or indoctrinated with ruling-class ideology, the labour aristocracy constituted itself as a status group – and hence as a reference group for other sections of the working class – through the creation of its own distinctive values and beliefs, which stood at some distance from those of the bourgeoisie (Crossick, 1976; Gray, 1973).

In turning to the second line of argument, namely that which seeks to explain working-class revolt as a process of proletarian self-education, the same kinds of problems arise. The basic weakness of the theory of revolutionary praxis is its neglect of the obstacles placed in the path of proletarian reason by 'moral elements' and 'tradition'. Of particular importance here are first the status incorporation of the working-class movement, and second, the tradition or ritual of the movement itself. In seeking to demonstrate their significance, it is convenient to begin by noting that the concrete meaning of the statement that 'In revolutionary activity, the changing of oneself coincides with the changing of circumstances' is to be found in the great importance Marx attached to trade union action as a means of both enhancing proletarian solidarity and altering conditions in such a way as to intensify class conflict. The escalation of trade union action from the level of particular economic struggles to the fight to pass legislation that would generalize the conflict between classes was something he set great store by. Trade unions were the 'schools of socialism', the primary mode of praxis through which the end-shift of the proletariat would be realized.

The fact that Marx's theory was not borne out is uncontroversial. When Kautsky coined the phrase *Nur Gewerkschaftlerei* he wrote the epitaph to proletarian reason. And Lenin drove home the point that from then on philosophy would have to work much harder to find its material weapon in the proletariat. To account for this short-circuiting of proletarian praxis, for its fixation at the level of 'trade union consciousness', Marxism has had to rely increasingly on explanations that emphasize the role of ideological obfuscation, which results either from a purposive ruling-class indoctrination of the

65

proletariat or from the false consciousness that is generated by capitalist relations of production themselves and affects both capitalists and proletarians alike. In other words, the main recourse has been to the notions of ignorance and error, which, in the utilitarian scheme, are the basic categories for explaining deviations from rational action. The way in which this resort to explanations of class action by reference to ideological constraint introduces a chronic instability into Marxist theory is a matter that will be taken up in the next section. For the moment, interest attaches to a particular aspect of this more general problem: namely, the attempt to account for the arrestment of proletarian praxis at the level of trade union consciousness by reference to the ideological effects of the peculiar civil and political relations of capitalist society. For this kind of argument once again brings into prominence the uncertain position within Marxist theory of the nature of status stratification.

The political and civil relations of capitalist society are held to prevent the emergence of a revolutionary proletariat because they serve to atomize society into a mass of juridically separate individuals and thereby disguise the real nature of class relations and class exploitation. As one writer puts it, 'The fundamental form of the Western Parliamentary State – the juridicial sum of its citizenry – is itself the hub of the ideological apparatuses of capitalism' (Anderson, 1976/7, p. 29; see also Poulantzas, 1973, pp. 123–37, 210–21; Wright, 1978, p. 241). And, corresponding to this individualization of political relations, the institutions of private property and free contract have always been regarded by Marxism as having the effect of obscuring the class structure of civil society in an essentially similar manner. Now what is abundantly clear is that these arguments refer to the legal aspect of the status order. Citizenship is no less a part of the status system because it has to do with the equality of civil, political, and social status. On the contrary, it is the foundation of the modern status order, on which are superimposed what Weber refers to as 'conventional' status inequalities. In stressing the socially integrative, or at least stabilizing effect of citizenship, then, Marxist theories of the abortion of proletarian revolution are brought into a fairly close approximation to those of 'bourgeois' sociology; and in particular to studies that have focused on the consequences for class action of the institutionalization of civil, political, and social citizenship (for example, Marshall, 1950; Bendix, 1964). But Marxism lacks a clear conception of the interrelationship between class and status structures. This is because the analysis of the institutionalization of status has no place in its theory of social integration. The entire problem of status is lost sight of in highly general and essentially functionalist conceptions of ideological domination.

One reason for this neglect is the erroneous view that status consists of purely 'subjective' judgements of prestige, which are amorphous, vacillating, and simply ideological products; a view that precludes the study of status groups whose boundaries are maintained through acts of social acceptance, deference, and derogation. But the neglect is also partly attributable to the, again mistaken, idea that, since status implies inequality of social standing, the status of legal equality cannot be part of a status order. On the first count, then, status is regarded as 'trivial' and its consequences for class action are assumed to be somehow less 'real' than those of the economic structure. And, on the second count, the core, that is, the legal, element of any status relationship is not included in the status system of capitalist society at all. The full implications of this double misconception cannot be gone into here;[4] but it is important, if only briefly, to indicate its bearing on the explanation of 'trade union consciousness'.

The first point that needs to be made about the supposedly atomizing effects of the political and civil relations of capitalist society is that firm evidence in support of this thesis has still to be adduced. The second point is that there is much evidence that casts doubt upon the thesis. For if workers had really conceived of themselves as juridically discrete and isolated individuals how could they have joined together to form trades unions in the first place? And if workers could overcome this initial ideological obstacle to their collective action what is it that prevents proletarian reason from making the further breakthrough that would shift the interests of the working class from intrasystemic to extrasystemic ends? The formula of trade union consciousness does not provide an answer. Either it merely redescribes the problem, or else it seeks to account for it in a manner that would also fail to explain trade union consciousness itself.

With the benefit of hindsight, it is easy to see why Marx's expectation that the pursuit by trades unions of political goals would have revolutionary consequences was mistaken. And the reason why he was mistaken is very significant. For, in fact, the main end that trades unions have sought to attain through legislative action is that of securing and legitimating their own corporate status: namely, what Marshall refers to as 'a secondary system of industrial citizenship parallel with and supplementary to the system of political citizenship' (1950, p. 44). To dismiss this as mere trade union consciousness may be all very well from the point of view of socialist eschatology. But it is usually the case that the ends of newly formed economic groups, whose position in the status order is anomalous, are in the first instance heavily influenced by an interest in negotiating a definite position within the existing hierarchy of authority and status. It is only when there are no institutionalized means of accommodating this interest that the legitimacy of the status order as a whole is brought into question. This general observation does not imply that the 'civic incorporation' of the working class represents an historical end-state, or that the 'institutionalization of class conflict' is the final word on the dynamics of class formation in capitalist societies. Its significance lies rather in the problems it poses for the concept of action underlying the theory that praxis is the midwife of proletarian reason.

For one way of defining trade union consciousness is to say that it is a rational, but not a reasonable, response to the situation in which the working class finds itself. This is tantamount to saying that securing the legal rights legitimating the corporate status of trade unions is a rational means of attaining the immediate ends of the working class, but an unreasonable means of attaining its fundamental ends. But this formulation rests on a concept of action that reduces all normative elements in the situation to external means and conditions that rational actors have to take account of. It is, of course, possible to postulate a proletarian actor for whom the acquisition of status rights is purely a means of obtaining other ends. For example, Marx actually did envisage the possibility that an enfranchised working class could vote itself into socialism. The basic flaw in this type of argument, however, is its inability to cope with the 'historical and moral element'. In particular, it cannot admit that, since the struggle to acquire status rights involves an orientation to 'moral elements' legitimating the status order as a whole, the acquisition of these rights results in their having an intrinsic, and not merely an instrumental, value for the actors concerned. This implies, for example, that the institutionalization of 'free collective bargaining' is not only a rational means of workers pursuing their immediate interests, but also a mode of action that inevitably takes on a traditional or ritual character by virtue of its having developed within, and at the same time having changed, a status order based on the 'moral elements' of citizenship. To dismiss such action as an expression of trade union consciousness, the result of ruling-class indoctrination, and thus by implication as irrational, is not just to take a condescending view of the working-class struggle itself; it also ignores the extent to which such action is nonrational in the sense that it involves a positive commitment to normative standards (status rights) which legitimate the immediate means–end relationship, and thus in some degree to the ultimate values from which this legitimation is derived.

The ritual accretions of proletarian practice obstruct the exercise of proletarian reason in two other ways as well. First, there is the familiar tendency towards oligarchy in working-class organizations, which results in goal-displacement. This transformation of organizational means into ends in themselves – a process not unconnected with the interests of leaders in their status within and outside the organization – is the paradigm case of ritual action (Merton, 1957, p. 149–53). Second, adherence to working-class, as to any other, organizations involves a ritual element in so far as there is a disparity between the life span of the organization and that of the member of it. In this disparity lies another main weakness of the thesis of praxis, which tends to confuse the self-education, or learning through experience, of an individual with that of an organization whose capacity to learn is in part a function of its tradition, which is in turn the residue of the experiences and learning of past generations of individuals. It is through the tradition of an organization that a ritual element inevitably enters into the determination of what is rational action for the individuals who compose its present membership. Tradition, status, and ritual signify modes of action which Marxism, like the utilitarian tradition in which it is rooted, is constrained to treat as irrational. While their particular relevance may be very well appreciated (see, for example, Hobsbawm, 1959), they are not factors that occupy a central analytical place within the Marxist theory of action.

The third main type of explanation of working-class consciousness, which centres on the idea of alienation, merits only brief consideration as a theory of proletarian revolt. But it is important to begin by noting that, while the concept of alienation is used chiefly to account for working-class acquiescence, it is also capable of yielding an explanation of working-class revolt. Thus, whatever value it may be thought to have as a dialectical safeguard against every contingency of the class struggle, the fact that contradictory conclusions can be derived from it hardly commends it as a rigorous explanation of class action. The root of the difficulty is to be found in the ambiguity of the two basic terms that enter into its formulation; on the one hand, the concept of 'human nature', and, on the other, that of the conditions making for alienation.

As regards the former, it is well known that Marx refers to 'human nature in general' as well as to 'human nature as modified in each historical epoch'. The major difficulty, however, is that the relative importance of these two elements for the action of the proletariat remains highly indeterminate. Fromm expresses this well when he writes

Marx argues against two points of view here: the ahistorical, which postulates the nature of man as a substance existing since the beginning of history, as well as the relativistic, which endows the nature of man with none of its own properties but considers it the reflection of social conditions. However, he never formulated conclusively his own theory of the nature of man to transcend both the ahistorical and the relativistic points of view. For this reason the interpretations of his theory are so variant and contradictory (1962, p. 31).

As far as the theory of proletarian action is concerned, what is essentially at stake is the extent to which socially determined and false needs inhibit the emergence of the essential need to engage in that 'free, conscious activity' which is 'the species-character of human beings'. Depending on which of these two aspects of need-formation is emphasized, the reaction to alienating conditions can be either passive or active. There is no doubt that Marx laid great stress on the latter response. He writes

. . . the class of the proletariat is abased and indignant at that debasement, an indignation to which it is necessarily driven by the contradiction between its human nature and its condition of life, which is the outright, decisive and comprehensive negation of that nature (McLellan, 1971, p. 113).

And again

From the start, the worker is superior to the capitalist in that the capitalist is rooted in his process of alienation and is completely content therein, whereas the worker who is its victim finds himself from the beginning in a state of rebellion against it and experiences the process as one of enslavement (p. 119).

Yet, at the same time, there is ample evidence in Marx's writings to support the opposite interpretation, which has become prominent in subsequent Marxist literature, and which lays much greater stress on the more passive response to alienating conditions, and thereby on the power of these conditions to induce false wants.

Corresponding to the ambiguity of the conception of 'human nature', and further confounding the whole issue of the dynamics of alienation in capitalist society, is the problem of whether the conditions making for alienation are to be understood as variable or invariable. If, as is usually the case, the source of alienation is located in capitalist relations of production *per se*, then alienation is global, affecting both capitalists and proletarians alike. Yet it is also possible to argue that, although all workers are alienated, some workers are more alienated than others. The warrant for this is to be found in the passage in *Capital* where Marx writes that 'in proportion as capital accumulates, the lot of the labourer, be his payment high or low, must grow worse' and goes on to claim that 'all methods for raising the social productiveness of labour' result in increasingly alienating conditions of work (Marx, 1906, p. 771). Since these methods are technological, and since it is a fact that technologies of production differ in the extent to which they diminish the autonomy of the worker, this introduces an important element of variability into the conditions of proletarian alienation.

Of the theoretical permutations permitted by the conceptual ambiguities just referred to, it is necessary to mention only two. These are the hypotheses about proletarian action that are most frequently to be met with, and which, in their contradictory conclusions, best demonstrate the incoherence of the idea of alienation. The first may be simply stated without comment since it is a strand in the safety-net thesis of the ideological repression of proletarian reason, the discussion of which will shortly follow. It is an argument designed to account for the lack of a working-class revolution in advanced capitalist societies and the unlikelihood of such an event in the foreseeable future. This type of explanation emphasizes the plasticity of the ends of the proletariat and the global character of the conditions making for alienation. In some versions of the argument the extinction of the capacity of the working class to exercise its reason and to comprehend its essential needs is apparently complete; in others, this capacity is regarded as inextinguishable, but too enfeebled to assert itself save by the intervention of an external agency. In marked contrast to this pessimistic view of alienated proletarian passivity, there is a second theory which ingeniously inverts the alternative Marxian thesis that the working class will revolt under conditions of increasing alienation. This interpretation assumes that the essential needs of the proletariat, far from being expunged or deeply repressed, grow more imperative as the nature of work becomes objectively less alienating. It is in the latter respect that ingenuity enters. For, contrary to Marx's expectations, the most dehumanizing conditions of production result in, at most, fractious accommodation on the part of workers; and the longer workers are exposed to such conditions the more pathologically inured to them they become (Argyris, 1957). It is therefore a dialectical *tour de force* to discover that the most radical workers are those who work under the objectively least alienating conditions. Moreover, since these conditions are also associated with the most advanced 'forces of production', the theory of 'the new working class' (Mallet, 1975) has at least one straw of orthodoxy to clutch at. This is Marx's belief – though one that is hard to square with his view of the tendency of technological development within capitalist relations of production – that human powers and needs would unfold with people's increasing command over nature through progressively socialized production. Underlying the thesis of 'the new working class', then, is a concept of 'human nature', which postulates some inbuilt hierarchy of needs. It is because workers in advanced technological industries are relatively well paid and secure in their jobs that they are capable of developing wants of a qualitatively different kind from those of other workers: demands for worker control and self-management as opposed to merely 'economist', ones. These interests, which pose the most fundamental threat to capitalist production relations, are also promoted by the nature of the workers' integration into the enterprise. Unlike the passively alienated workers in mass-production industries, the new working class are in a situation where individual labour loses all meaning, where workers' knowledge, skills, and collective involvement in production not only give them a high disruptive capacity but also make them aware of the contradiction between the socialized character of the labour process and the private character of its control. In pursuing their goals, the trade unions of the new working class are able to use new strike methods and are self-educated into making demands that encroach increasingly upon the prerogatives of management, even in areas of financial decision-making.

The merit of this argument, which distinguishes it from other theories of alienation, is that it can be refuted; and it has been (Gallie, 1978). It is wrong because it assumes a technological determination of class action which is unable to account for marked national differences in the attitudes and behaviour of workers employed in technologically identical plants. These differences have to be explained by reference to the wider system of industrial and political relations, and in large part by the particular modes of the 'civic integration' of the working class. In this respect, the deficiency of the thesis of the alienation of the 'new working class' brings to the fore once again the significance for class action of the status order in which class relations are embedded.

This brief survey of the three main kinds of explanations entering into the theory of proletarian revolution shows that, while they comprise a very versatile set of arguments, all have the same flaw. This is to be found in the assumption that, through their power of reason, workers will be quick to learn from their experience of capitalist relations of production that their ends can only be realized by the abolition of these relations. Moreover, the fact that material and moral impoverishment, and self-education through collective action, have not led to proletarian revolution in the most advanced capitalist societies now suggests, and not least to many Marxists, that the assumption of proletarian reason is faulty. By according the standard of rationality such a central role in explaining the means–end relationship, Marxism shares the same weakness as utilitarian theory in that it excludes from its purview systematic consideration of nonrational action. In contrast with irrational action, which can always be explained in terms of ignorance and error, nonrational action can only be understood by reference to the normative

71

integration of ends. At the outset, it was stated that the utilitarian scheme treats the ends of actors as 'random' in the sense that the question of their interrelationship lies outside the scope of the theory. It was also claimed that the same tendency is characteristic of Marxism. This is now in need of qualification.

At first sight, the concept of ideology would seem to explain why ends are not random and thus demolish the argument that Marxism is a version of a basically utilitarian theory of action. But in order to understand exactly the extent to which this is the case, it is necessary to say something about the main variants of the Marxist concept of ideology. And in doing this, special note must be taken of the way in which the notion of ideology undergoes not only an analytical promotion, but also a qualitative change. Both aspects may be considered as responses to the problem of explaining the lack of proletarian revolution, and hence the failure of proletarian reason.

What might be called the vulgar version of ideologically induced false consciousness originates in certain passages of *The German Ideology* and finds its most extreme formulation in *What Is To Be Done*? It has the following, characteristically utilitarian components. Control over the production of ideas, and thus the ability to inculcate in the proletariat a false consciousness of its position, is one of the means by which the capitalist class rationally pursues its intrasystemic end. This is possible because the ruling class possesses overwhelmingly superior resources for the creation and dissemination of its ideas. In fact, in this theory of social integration, the power attributed to bourgeois ideology is equivalent to the coercive power of Hobbes' *Leviathan*. As far as the subjugated class is concerned, dominant ideas constitute a, presumably internalized, condition of its action, so that it remains ignorant of the means–ends chain that would lead it to recognize its extrasystemic end. With Lenin, what constituted an auxiliary Marxian hypothesis about proletarian action becomes central and axiomatic. Proletarian ignorance is equated with trade union consciousness, and the means of 'correcting' this ignorance are conceived of in typically utilitarian terms. It is by systematic 'arraignment' and 'exposure' that the proletariat can be informed of their real situation; and, as a result of their enlightenment by the revolutionary party in which proletarian reason is enshrined, they will be able to achieve a 'socialist' consciousness and embark on their historical mission. What distinguishes this first interpretation of ideology is that, far from raising the problem of the institutionalization of values, it concentrates attention on the cognitive obstacles to revolutionary consciousness and, equally, on the cognitive means by which these obstacles can be removed.

This emphasis on the cognitive element of ideological domination is also characteristic of the second theory of ideology, which has its origin in the concept of commodity fetishism, and which, by contrast with the first, may be termed 'sophisticated'. But this theory too has very definite underpinnings in the utilitarian theory of action. Most obviously, commodity fetishism is a form of false consciousness which is a 'system effect', a consequence of market exchanges. Unlike the vulgar theory of ideology, the fetishism of commodities does not refer to the means by which one class imposes its ideas upon another in order rationally to attain its ends. It denotes the unintended ideological effect produced by the interaction of rational egoists, who, in mediating their relationships through the exchange of commodities, purportedly come to think of their relations with one another as the relations between entities (especially the values attaching to commodities) that possess a life of their own. Individuals are ruled by forces that have the same properties of externality, constraint, and ineluctability which Durkheim, in his phase of sociological positivism, attributed to social facts in general. Marx's theory of commodity fetishism deserves to be called sophisticated for two main reasons. First of all, by contrast with the vulgar theory, it refers to an ideological effect that affects capitalists and proletarians alike. This effect is the unanticipated outcome of a myriad of individual, rational actions, and, like Adam Smith's 'invisible hand' of the market, it has socially integrative consequences. Second, these consequences are considered to be much more deeply ideological in their nature than any resulting from the attempt of one class to impose its beliefs upon another. This is because commodity fetishism is constitutive of actual class relations and not just an abstract and external justification of them. As such, commodity fetishism is a much more intractable obstacle to the end-shift of the proletariat. It binds the working class into the same system of ideological compulsion to that which the capitalist class is subject. The real illusion of commodity fetishism is not that 'the direct social relations between individuals at work' take on the character of 'material relations between persons and social relations between things' but rather that this condition – which is real – is regarded as inexorable (Lichtman, 1975, p. 67).

The theory of 'systemic' ideology is one whose truth appears to have been regarded as so self-evident among those Marxists who have espoused it that it has been thought necessary only to reiterate the theory instead of proving it. The fact that it is not a theory that finds favour with Marxist historians is particularly unfortunate, since it is premised on the existence of market relations which, if they ever existed, are now defunct. Nevertheless, its basic assumption that ideology is effective through its embodiment in everyday class relations is one that has found a new expression in some recent Marxist accounts of proletarian passivity; and most extravagantly in the concept of 'ideological state apparatuses'. The latter is noteworthy mainly for the fact that, by its indiscriminate attribution of ideological repressiveness to every social institution of contemporary capitalist societies (save for, perhaps, their communist parties), it manages to transform the vulgar theory of ideology into something closely resembling the naive sociological functionalism of the 1950s. From the point of view of Marxism, however, the most objectionable aspect of the rag-bag concept of ideological state apparatuses consists in the damage it does to Gramsci's notion of 'hegemony', which has good reason to be treated as the third main variant of the Marxist theory of ideology.

Fragmentary though it is, Gramsci's account of hegemony provides Marxism with the basis of a sophisticated theory of ideology which avoids the positivistic tendencies of the vulgar version. In contrast with the latter, the concept of hegemony places much less emphasis on control over the production of dissemination of ideas as a means by which the ruling class manipulates proletarian consciousness in order to attain its own ends. This view of ideology is due in part to Gramsci's much more subtle and elaborate conception of the functions of intellectuals. But it is due principally to his appreciation of the need for a precise study of how the 'grounding' or institutionalization of values and beliefs succeeds in generating a spontaneous, but necessarily imperfect, moral and intellectual consensus. A major consequence of this shift in emphasis is that ideological domination is no longer understood as an easily identifiable, basically cognitive, obstacle to proletarian revolution. False consciousness cannot be equated with a state of ignorance and error that is readily corrigible by the Leninist strategy of an 'all-embracing political arrangement' of ruling-class oppression. The very definition of what counts as 'common sense' is, as Gramsci puts it, 'determined not by reason but by faith', that is by the individual's attachment to social groups; and, as such, it is not easily alterable by exposure to scientific knowledge. Revolutionary ascendency therefore presupposes a long and arduous struggle to establish a proletarian hegemony which can compete on equal cultural terms with that of the ruling class. This much is evident from Williams's definition of hegemony as

an order in which a certain way of life and thought is dominant, in which one concept of reality is diffused throughout society in all its institutional and private manifestations, informing with its spirit all taste, morality, customs, religious and political principles, and all social relations, particularly in their intellectual and moral connotations (1960, p. 587).

It is easy to see why this view of ideology should have such a powerful appeal to contemporary Marxism. For what it does is to modify out of all recognition the utilitarian action scheme underlying the vulgar theory of ideology, and, at the same time, it provides a general, sociological formulation of the notion, deriving from the concept of commodity fetishism, that the effectiveness of ideology consists in its systematic nature, in the manner in which dominant values and beliefs are embodied in everyday social relations.

The highly general scope of the concept of hegemony is, however, the source of its main weakness. Gramsci provided the outline of a theory of ideology, the detailed working out of which would have to include a systematic consideration of precisely those moral or normative elements that have remained analytically inchoate within the Marxist scheme of action, and whose effects have been relegated to the category of the irrational. To give the idea of hegemony a cutting edge requires a specification of the modes of institutionalization of values and beliefs, and, more importantly, of the conditions under which such processes are more or less successful in producing a consensual social integration. Gramsci's notion of 'contradictory consciousness' might well be the starting point of this investigation (Femia, 1975). But the task has hardly begun. Gramsci's ideas have been incorporated into Marxism in a highly generalized way, with the result that explanations of class action based on them veer towards a form of cultural determinism. It would not be too much to say that Gramsci is the Durkheim of modern Marxism. In most major respects, the concept of hegemony is scarcely distinguishable from Durkheim's concept of the 'diffuse' collective conscience which he contrasts with the more specific 'government consciousness' (Durkheim, 1957, p. 79). And just as Durkheim's concept of the collective conscience allowed his successors to construct a sociology that was characterized by an over-integrated view of society and an over-socialized view of man, so Gramsci's concept of hegemony has tempted many Marxist theorists concerned with explaining the lack of proletarian revolution to espouse an equally questionable view of global ideological domination. As one leading Marxist frankly admits, 'What is involved is an overstatement of the ideological predominance of the "ruling class", or of the effectiveness of their predominance' (Miliband, 1977, p. 53). Miliband draws attention to

the dearth of sustained Marxist work analyzing and exposing the meanings and messages purveyed in the cultural output produced for mass consumption in, say, the thirty-odd years since the end of World War II – not to speak of the virtual absence of such work in the years preceding it (1977, p. 49).

But it is one thing to show that 'the cultural output' is heavily biased towards the maintenance of the status quo, which is what Miliband attempts to show in his earlier work (1969, especially chapters 7 and 8), and quite another thing to demonstrate that this output does have the effects that are claimed for it. In the absence of such evidence, the whole argument of ideological domination, whichever form it takes, necessarily totters on the brink of circularity. For the answer to the question of why the working class does not revolt is that it has a false consciousness of its position due to its subjection to ruling-class ideology; and the answer to the question of what evidence can be adduced to show that the working class is in this state of ideological subordination is that the working class lacks a revolutionary consciousness. Of course, theories of ideological domination never descend to quite this crass level. But, on the other hand, they seldom rise far above it, consisting mostly of plausible but unsubstantiated arguments about the effects of ideology on this or that aspect of working-class attitudes or behaviour. Most importantly, all theories of the ideological obstacles to proletarian reason have their *raison d'être* in the unquestioned postulate of eventual proletarian revolution. If the general course of proletarian action were not thus prescribed, it would be unnecessary to invent such equally general explanations of the proletariat's deflection from the pursuit of its ultimate goal. In this regard, modern Marxism merely renews and updates the comprehensive insurance policy that Marx himself took out. For within the space of thirty pages of the first volume of *Capital*, he claims first that 'The advance of capitalist production develops a working class, which by education, tradition, habit, looks upon the conditions of that mode of production as self-evident laws of nature', and second, that 'with this too grows the revolt of the working class, a class always increasing in

75

numbers, and disciplined, united, organised by the very mechanisms of capitalist production itself' (1906, pp. 761 and 789).

The instability of the Marxist theory of action is manifested by the tendency to shuttle back and forth between positivistic and idealistic explanations of working-class radicalism and acquiescence. The positivistic type of explanation makes it possible, for example, to hold to the belief that the next economic crisis will provide the occasion for the leap in consciousness that fuses the immediate and fundamental interests of the proletariat. At the same time, the idealistic reaction to this utilitarian conspectus can lead to the opposite, pessimistic theory that the working class is sunk in a chronic and almost irremediable false consciousness. Depending on which of these two views is preferred, the role of the party differs. In the first case, the party serves as little more than a catalyst of the end-shift of the proletariat. In the second case, revolution being a remote eventuality; it is only through a prolonged ideological struggle that the party, in which proletarian reason is for the time being displaced, can hope to convert the working class to socialism. This oscillation between one conception of the condition of the proletariat and the other is perfectly well understandable if the foregoing account of the instability of the Marxist scheme of action is correct. It is, moreover, not just an abstract, theoretical problem; it has practical, political consequences. For example, writers referring to the same society at the same point in time can arrive at widely discrepant estimates of the radical potential of the working class, as may readily be seen from a comparison of the prognoses of Miliband (1969, pp. 275–6) and Glyn and Sutcliffe (1972, pp. 208–16).

The only remedy of this unsatisfactory state of affairs involves abandoning the assumption that the proletariat *in toto* is identifiable by either a capacity for reasoning that will imminently be actualized or a susceptibility to ideological indoctrination that there is little prospect of alleviating. Positively, this would involve the replacement of global explanations of class consciousness and class action by a much more precise conception of the way in which class interests are, as Parsons put it, 'a function of the realistic situations in which people act and of the "definitions" of those situations which are institutionalized in the society' (1949, p. 313). By moving towards such a 'voluntaristic' concept of action Marxism would perhaps only be making explicit at the level of its general theory what is normally recognized to be the case by serious Marxist students of particular, historical instances of class formation. It is, of course, unlikely that any such change in theoretical direction would be accompanied by the abandonment of the belief in the revolutionary capacity of the working class. But until proletarian reason manifests itself, it is difficult to believe that forthright Marxist theorists of class action will not sooner or later be constrained to adopt a mode of analysis which, notwithstanding some natural 'commodity differentiation', does not differ substantially from that of their 'bourgeois' counterparts. In other words, due recognition will have to be given to the fact that the situations in which proletarian rationality operates include normative elements that exhibit great variability in respect of both their content and the extent to which they become internalized conditions of action. Once again, this is not merely an abstract, academic point. It is one that is prerequisite to any attempt to understand which sections of the proletariat are more or less likely to be subject to 'bourgeois indoctrination' or open to socialist initiatives.

Surprisingly enough, recent Marxist writings on the class structure of capitalist societies show little sign of the theoretical reorientation just referred to; or even of the recognition of the need for it. The writings in question have two chief characteristics. The first is that they reveal a deep controversy over what are the correct Marxist criteria by means of which definitions of the objective 'places' or 'locations' of classes are to be reached. The second is that they virtually reject the problem of the relationship between class structure and class consciousness/class conflict, either by trying to legislate it out of existence or, and in the end this amounts to the same thing, by treating it as highly indeterminate. As things stand, then, there is on the one hand much conflict over the concept of class, and, on the other, not much in the way of a theory of class conflict.

As regards the definition of class, the anarchy of Marxist analysis is well exemplified by a comparison of the work of Poulantzas and Wright. Of fundamental importance is their disagreement over the relevance of the distinction between productive and unproductive labour, since this is really the only possible conceptual means of establishing a direct link between the economic theory of system contradiction and the political sociology of class conflict. For Poulantzas productive labour is the basic 'economic' criterion of the working class. Wright is of the completely opposite opinion, and for three reasons. The first is that Poulantzas's restriction of the notion of productive labour to productive labour involved in material production is totally at odds with Marx's definition of it. The second is that, for the purposes of defining class boundaries, the concept is deficient because it is extremely difficult to establish where productive labour ends and unproductive labour begins. Third, and perhaps most importantly, Wright holds to the view that 'It is hard to see where a fundamental divergence of economic interests emerges from positions of unproductive and productive labour in capitalist relations of production. Certainly Poulantzas has not demonstrated that such a divergence exists' (1979, p. 50). In this, Wright has the support of Braverman who writes that 'Although technically distinct . . . the two masses of labour are not otherwise in striking contrast . . . they form a continuous mass of employment which . . . has everything in common' (1974, p. 423). And in what is perhaps the most notable study of economic divisions within the working class, the productive/unproductive labour concept plays no major role (O'Conner, 1973). In this respect, then, the most elementary notion of what constitutes the economic definition of class is in grave dispute. But this is not the only aspect of Poulantzas's analysis to which Wright takes exception. In what Poulantzas calls the 'ideological' criterion of class determination, that is, the distinction between manual and nonmanual labour, the sociologist may perceive some faltering recognition of the significance of status differentiation (1979, pp. 258–9). For Wright, however, such a distinction is completely

77

unacceptable because it means abandoning the tenet of 'the primacy of economic relations in the definition of class' (1978, pp. 51). For Poulantzas's third principle of class placement, the 'political', which is basically the distinction between supervisory and nonsupervisory labour, Wright has some sympathy, because it approximates to his own criterion of class location, which refers to control over both what is produced and its method of production. He is, however, loath to accept the label of 'political' to signify this distinction, which he prefers to regard 'as one aspect of the structural dissociation between economic ownership and possession at the economic level itself' (1978, p. 52).

To anyone not absorbed in it, this debate might appear as no more than a futile logomarchy. But this would not explain why the definition of classes is such an important issue for contemporary Marxism and why it should give rise to so much conceptual discord. The answer to the first question is that the definition of class is not simply a sociological exercise but a matter of vital political concern. From the latter point of view, the problem of utmost significance is that of the size of the proletariat, a magnitude that can vary dramatically depending on whether, for example, the productive/unproductive labour distinction (and which particular interpretation of it) is deemed relevant to the determination of class boundaries. Wright calculates that the size of the American proletariat more than doubles if it is estimated according to his criteria (all nonsupervisory employees) rather than by those of Poulantzas, who defines this class more stringently as productive, non-supervisory, manual labour (1979, pp. 57 and 86). In fact, Poulantzas's criteria could reduce the American working class to hardly 20 per cent of the economically active population. And for Wright this is a bitter pill to swallow, because, as he puts it, 'It is hard to imagine a viable socialist movement developing in an advanced capitalist society in which less than one in five people are workers' (1976, p. 23). This is not to imply, however, that Marxist theorists simply tailor their definitions of classes to suit their political needs. Their conceptual disagreement has a real foundation in the fact that the development of capitalism is associated with the declining importance of manual, or blue-collar, workers relative to nonmanual, or white-collar, workers. When the latter threaten to outnumber the former, this raises the crucial question of how to conceptualize the class position of a vast number of heterogeneous functions that cannot easily be identified as either capitalist or proletarian. Politically, it is a question of how many of these white-collar workers can be enlisted in the ranks of the proletariat or counted as its immediate allies. But traditional Marxist categories provide no easy answers. The axiom that within any mode of production there are only two basic class positions and interests requires substantial qualification. This is achieved, for example, by Poulantzas's invention of 'political' and 'ideological' criteria of class determination and, more generally, by the emphasis that is now placed on 'relations of possession', and not just on 'economic ownership' (both real and juridical). Through such notions as 'political' criteria, 'relations of possession', and the 'global functions of capital', Marx's observations on 'the transformation of the actually functioning capitalist into a mere manager' and on 'the double nature' of the 'labour of supervision and management' (1971, pp. 436 and 383) have come to acquire a central and systematic importance in the definition of class structure. As a result, recent Marxist writings on the class location of white-collar workers employ concepts that are fairly familiar to 'bourgeois' social scientists whose work on the formation of the middle classes and on the structure of industrial bureaucracy has been in part a reaction to, and a critique of, an earlier phase of relatively crude Marxist theorizing. And it is not just that these writings use different terms to describe the same phenomena that have for some time past been of interest to 'bourgeois' social scientists; it is also mainly on the basis of the research carried out by the latter (into such problems as 'white-collar proletarianization' and 'the separation of ownership and control') that recent contributions to Marxist class analysis enjoy whatever empirical credibility they possess. This is, after all, not very surprising, since, while both groups of scholars are grappling with the same highly complicated set of problems, those committed to a Marxist approach are not only fewer in number but usually less concerned with collecting new evidence than with establishing which brand of concepts is most genuinely Marxian in its derivation.

The final point about these discussions of class structure which needs to be brought out is that the whole exercise of defining class 'places' and 'locations' is of small relevance to the most important problem of the Marxist theory of action: namely, the explanation of the end-shift of the proletariat. Indeed, the most striking feature of the writings under consideration is not that their treatment of the placement of white-collar workers exhibits such a profound conceptual disarray, but rather that they have practically nothing to say about the structure of the core of the working class or proletariat, both of which terms are used interchangeably. While its boundary alters according to the particular definition preferred, the proletariat remains a mysterious entity. Poulantzas is strict in awarding the privilege of proletarian status, but he ends up with a class that is broadly equivalent to the whole of the industrial, manual labour force. Nevertheless, having defined the proletariat to his satisfaction, he finds it unnecessary to investigate its composition. It is as if in his theatre of structural determination the chief actor never takes to the stage but remains hidden in the left wing. Wright is hardly more informative. He states baldly that 'the working class (i.e., nonsupervisory, nonautonomous employees) in the United States consists of between 41 and 54 per cent of the economically active population' (1978, p. 87). This massive aggregate is not subjected to further analysis. It is true that in considering briefly the relation between class structure and class struggle he acknowledges that proletarians differ in their 'structural and organizational capacities'. Class structure 'sets limits of variation on the forms of class capacities', that is on 'the ways in which social relations are formed among positions within the class structure' (1978, pp. 105–6). But this determination is very broad: it means that 'bourgeois positions, for example, cannot be organized into working-class trade unions or revolutionary socialist parties'.

Nevertheless, the factors accounting for variations in structural capacity within the limits set by the class structure overall might be thought to be of central importance to the explanation of working-class action. And Wright certainly accepts this in principle. 'Class capacities', he writes, 'constitute one of the most decisive selection determinations of class struggle. The underlying structural capacities of classes and the specific organizational forms shaped by these structural capacities have a tremendous impact on forms of class struggle' (1978, p. 103). In view of this, his discussion of the factors explaining variations in the structural capacity of the proletariat is surprisingly short and unsystematic. He mentions four by way of illustration: the concentration of workers in large factories and thus the emergence of 'the collective worker'; attempts by capitalists to undermine working-class solidarity through 'the creation of job hierarchies, structures of privileges and promotions', the degree to which workers are involved in occupational communities; and the extent to which 'ethnic solidarity' reinforces 'the class-based social relations within the community' (1978, pp. 99–100). This list of factors is *ad hoc* and plainly inadequate for a thoroughgoing study of variations in the structural capacity of the proletariat. Moreover, these social conditions play no part in the definition of the location of the proletariat in the class structure, which rests simply on the two criteria mentioned above (nonsupervisory, non-autonomous employees). Why is this? It cannot be that the kind of factors Wright refers to are so heterogeneous that they defy systematic analysis; after all, there is an extensive literature on the subject which shows that this is not the case. Yet for Wright, no less than Poulantzas, the proletariat remains conceptually inviolate. The only conclusion that can be drawn from this is that the structure of the working class is not a matter of ultimate importance because the question of whether the proletariat has a fundamental interest in socialism is considered to be just as unproblematic as that of whether it will eventually realize this interest. In the last analysis, then, it is the objective interest ascribed to the working class as a whole which guarantees its potential unity and makes the detailed analysis of its structure otiose. This does not mean that the diversity of the working class and of its immediate interests is not real, but rather that it is somehow less real than the underlying unity of its basic class location and fundamental interest, which the class struggle will eventually reveal. It is, in other words, still the proletariat of *The Holy Family*.

Remarkably enough, Braverman's study is almost equally uninformative when it comes to elucidating the structure of the working class, which is the task he sets himself (1974, p. 25). His main concern, however, as is indicated by the subtitle of the book, is to document the moral and material impoverishment of the working class, or as he says its 'degradation'. His study must be seen, then, as the latest version of the alienation thesis, and in pursuing it he takes a fairly broad-ranging view of the structure of the working class. For Braverman, the latter consists in the relationship between three sections of the working class: the traditional blue-collar working class of industrial manual workers; the 'growing working-class occupations' of clerical, sales, and service workers; and the 'reserve army' of the unemployed (or subemployed). His argument is that the process of capital accumulation results in an increasing moral impoverishment (i.e., loss of control over the labour process) and/or material impoverishment (i.e., relatively low incomes) among the first two sections of the working class, each one of which is roughly equivalent in size. The mechanization of blue-collar work results in its dehumanization and in displacement of industrial labour, most of which is absorbed into the clerical, sales, and service sector of employment, though some of it is jettisoned into the reserve army of labour. Moreover, even though the extraction, and especially the realization, of surplus value leads to an expansion of employment in the clerical, sales, and service sector, these workers are also subject to increasing degradation as a result of the rationalization and mechanization of their work (particularly clerical employees) and the lowering of their incomes through the pressure on the labour market of the reserve army of the unemployed. If this last section of the working class is defined as including the subemployed, then it overlaps very considerably with the employed working class, and especially with the retail and service sector of employment.

Braverman's view of the working class is very much the same as Wright's. Both reject the productive/unproductive labour distinction as a significant line of intraclass demarcation. Both define the working class as a whole by reference to loss of control over the labour process. And although Braverman's working class appears to have some structure to it in the sense that he distinguishes between factory workers, clerical workers, retail, and service workers, this is more apparent than real because he claims that all these sections of the working class are becoming less and less distinct. As he says

The giant mass of workers who are relatively homogeneous as to lack of developed skill, low pay, and interchangeability of person and function (although heterogeneous in such particulars as the site and nature of work they perform) is not limited to offices and factories. Another huge concentration is to be found in the so-called service occupations and in retail trade (1974, p. 359).

Thus, having set out to investigate the structure of the working class, Braverman ends up with the now familiar picture of a vast proletarian mass. He and Wright reach the same conclusion, but by different methods. For Wright, it is the fundamental, socialist interest he ascribes to the proletariat which secures its unity, despite intraclass differences in structural and organizational capacity and the short-sightedness of its immediate interests. For Braverman, however, the basic common interest of the working class is demonstrated by the fact of its increasing homogeneity and shared degradation.

But has Braverman really demonstrated that the working class has become practically homogeneous in its work and market situation? And are these the only criteria that are relevant to the study of the structure of the working class? As regards the first question, the evidence Braverman adduces in support of his thesis is not very substantial. In his foreword to the book,

81

Sweezy observes that 'there is hardly an occupation or any other aspect of the labour process which would not repay a great deal more detailed historical and analytical investigation than are accorded to it in this broad survey' (1974, p. xii). Broad survey indeed it is. In fact, the greater part of the book is not even a broad survey of the American working class. It is rather a potted history of 'scientific management' and technological innovation based on familiar secondary sources which in the majority of instances are concerned less with describing how factory and clerical work is actually organized than with prescribing how it could and should be organized. While Braverman makes good illustrative use of these materials in his account of the 'degradation of work', this does not alter the fact that much of his argument proceeds by conflation and by assuming what has to be shown to be the case; it is, in consequence, highly schematic and tendentious. For example, to the basic question posed by his own thesis, of exactly to what degree which sections of the manual and nonmanual labour force are subject to the dehumanizing conditions of work that he describes so graphically in general terms, Braverman has scarcely the beginnings of a definite answer.

Quite apart from this, in so far as the analysis of the situation of the working class is intended to provide a basis for explaining class action, there is no inherent reason why the organization of the work process should be the exclusive focus of investigation. If 'what is needed first of all is a picture of the working class as it exists' (Braverman, 1974, p. 27), then this must emerge from a much more detailed study of the way in which what Wright refers to as 'structural capacities' of the working class differ as a result of not only the organization of work but also the interdependence of work and community relationships. This is brought out very well, for example, in a book that was published in the same year as Braverman's: Kornblum's account of the steel workers in South Chicago (1974). There, in the late 1960s and early 1970s at least, the working class did not take on the shape of a vast homogeneous mass. On the contrary, it was composed of a dense network of primary groups which both segregated and aggregated workers whose status differed according to their jobs, ethnicity, and place of residence. And, as Kornblum shows, this infrastructure of primary groups is of vital importance in understanding the dynamics of local union and political organization. More directly relevant to Braverman's particular thesis is the fact that, in the production process, groups of workers differed markedly in respect of the status that attached to different tasks as well as in their autonomy in carrying out these tasks. Now it might be said that Kornblum presents a picture of the working class that is atypical, and that in focusing too closely on the sources of differentiation within the working class, he loses sight of its basic unity. As regards the first point, Kornblum recognizes that his study cannot be presented as a '"typical" working-class community'. But at the same time he holds that 'South Chicago's diverse population of blue-collar ethnic groups and its range of community institutions are representative of a rather widespread pattern of working-class community organizations in the United States' (1974, p. 2). In any case, what is regarded as typical or representative of the working class is a question that presupposes a systematic analysis of its structure as a whole; and Marxists such as Braverman, Wright and Poulantzas have not provided this. For them, the proletariat is characterized by its homogeneity; and from this point of view one section of the working class must be just as typical as another. The second point raises questions of a similar kind, since, in the absence of a frame of reference by which it is possible to establish what is of particular rather than of general significance in the study of the structure of the working class, on what basis is it possible to decide which perspective is the more valid: Kornblum's worm's-eye view, which is vertical within its limited range; or Braverman's bird's-eye view, which is the favourite vantage point of the Marxist wishful thinker?

There is, however, one sense in which Braverman's perspective on the working class is insufficiently broad in its scope. This appertains to a point made by Mackenzie who, after referring to 'Braverman's failure to consider the uniqueness of the United States', goes on to argue that 'any analysis of changes in the structure and composition of the American working class should make explicit recognition of the unique as well as the general structural features of that society' (1977, pp. 250–1). Mackenzie's strictures on Braverman apply with equal force to the conceptionalization of class structure advanced by Wright and Poulantzas, even though Poulantzas's distinctive concern with the 'petty bourgeoisie' might be thought to reflect something especially characteristic of his own society. For they likewise deny the proletariat any national identity; and thus, in possessing neither a structure nor a history, the proletariat truly acquires the nature of a 'universal' class. What is basically at stake here is not so much the uniqueness of this or that society, but rather those aspects of its historical development that can be grasped, through comparative study, in more general terms. Perhaps the most important single point of reference in this respect is the one referred to earlier on in the chapter: namely, the status structure of civil, political, industrial, and social citizenship. The mode of the civic incorporation of the working class is a factor of major significance in explaining national differences in class formation. But once again this involves reference to a 'moral and historical' element which has no definite place in Marxist theory; and, in the writings being discussed, this means that the analysis of the status system can play no part in the definition of the position of the working class. The result is that the conceptual sanitation of the proletariat is complete.

This suggests that these modern theories of class structure are still based, at least implicitly, on the classical Marxist action scheme. For in so far as the definition of class structure is intended to elucidate the variability of the class struggle, it must involve some idea of the constituents of social action. That is, it must take account not only of the means and conditions of action (such as control over the labour process) but also of the determination of the ends of actors and of the standards by which they relate means to ends. It is in the latter respect that the status order plays a central role in both the differentiation and integration of ends and the legitimation of means. It must be repeated that this does not entail the assumption that an actor's status

83

situation is an internalized condition of his or her action. The extent to which an actor regards its legitimation of his or her ends and means as binding is variable and is affected by, among other things, changes in his or her class situation. On the other hand, the status situation cannot be reduced to the category of those external means and conditions that actors relate to in a purely instrumental manner. In Marxism, however, this problem of the institutionalization of status does not arise. Yet just because the concept of status plays no systematic role in its theory of action, the effects of status can only be taken into account by treating them in an *ad hoc* fashion or by subsuming them under the catch-all concept of ideology. The former alternative is evident in the work of contemporary class theorists.

For example, when Braverman characterizes loss of control over the labour process as 'degradation', he resorts to some idea of socially invariable and hence completely unproblematic ends akin to Marx's notion of authentic human needs, and it is only by making this assumption that he can infer the potential of working-class revolt from changes in the conditions of class action (1974, pp. 139 and 151). But, quite apart from the fact that this conclusion sits uneasily, though familiarly, with his discussion of the 'habituation' of the worker to alienated conditions of work, Braverman's explanations of both degradation and habituation take no account of the way in which the status system inculcates different levels of expectation of autonomy in work. Once again, this is not to suggest that variations in these expectations provide a sufficient explanation of action; the problem is rather to understand how action is jointly determined by both realistic and normative elements, and particularly by the way in which changes in these elements are mutually interdependent. In Wright's work also there are traces of the resort to an arbitrary notion of status. For example, when he writes that 'job hierarchies, structures of privileges and promotions' can operate to 'weaken the social relations among workers within production' (1978, p. 100), his argument relies on the general assumption that status differentiation can shape ends in a way that is inimical to class solidarity. But there is no reason why effects of this kind should be seen as restricted to 'workers within production'. So what is glimpsed here is but the tip of a conceptual iceberg which could appear anywhere on the chart of class locations. Finally, as was noted above, Poulantzas's treatment of the ideological division between manual and nonmanual labour involves a fairly explicit reference to what anyone but a Marxist would term a line of status demarcation. But again, why should status manifest itself only at this level of the class structure, and not, for instance, as Wright suggests, within the working class itself? The answer is that it is the consequence of Poulantzas's decision that the ideological criterion of class relates exclusively to the distinction between manual and nonmanual labour. And to make things worse, it is a decision that has no clear Marxian warrant.

From this rather lengthy discussion of recent Marxist definitions of class structure, three main conclusions can be drawn. The first is that, while the criteria for placing or locating classes are in deep dispute, the one that there is least disagreement about in principle – namely, the significance of 'relations of possession' – raises conceptual and empirical issues of a basically similar kind to those that have occupied the attention of 'bourgeois' social scientists in their studies of the bureaucratization of industrial organization. The second notable feature of Marxist class definition is that the classical conception of the proletariat as a unitary class actor survives intact. The working class retains its essential identity either by the ascription to it of a unifying fundamental interest or by the attempt to demonstrate its homogeneity. Third, by concentrating on the means and conditions of action, these definitions of class structure perpetuate a conception of action whose chief defect has always been its failure to take account of the nature and variability of normative elements in the determination of ends and of the means–ends relationship. At the structural level, the most striking consequence of this omission is the abstraction of class relations from the context of the status system of a society. By ignoring these factors, modern Marxism implicitly falls back on a notion of action in which the only significant ends are the given or fundamental interests of class actors, the only norm for relating means to ends is that of rationality, and the only way of explaining deviation from rational action is by reference to ideologically induced ignorance or error.

In raising this last issue, the discussion of the definition of class structure has already engaged with the second main problem it set out to raise: namely, the question of the relation between class structure on the one hand, and class consciousness and class conflict on the other. It is now time to face this problem directly.

Within classical Marxism, the crucial problem of the end-shift of the proletariat centered on the distinction between a class-in-itself and a class-for-itself. This is a distinction between a class that has objectively defined interests by virtue of its position within the class structure and a class that is an ideologically united and politically organized entity, acting in pursuit of its interests against those of another class. In general, modern Marxism continues to accept this distinction. That is to say, the purpose of the analysis of class structure is to provide an explanation of class consciousness and class conflict. As Wright puts it,

It is all very well and good to clarify the structure of positions defined by social relations of production and to link these to other positions in the social structure. Marxism, however, is not primarily a theory of class structure; it is above all a theory of class struggle (1978, pp. 97–8).

How, then, is the relationship between class structure and class conflict understood?

The first approach to this problem, which is fairly characteristic of writers whose work is almost exclusively concerned with the definition of classes, is in one way or another to avoid it. Braverman, for example, excludes the analysis of class conflict and class consciousness from his discussion altogether.

No attempt will be made to deal with the modern working class on the level of its consciousness, organization, or activities. This is a book about the working class in

85

itself, not as a class for itself. I realize that to many readers it will appear that I have omitted the most urgent part of the subject matter (1974, p. 27).

He goes on to say it is not his purpose 'to deprecate the importance of the study of the state of consciousness of the working class, since it is only through consciousness that a class becomes an actor on the historic stage' (1974, p. 29). But the only indication he gives of how this study might proceed is by distinguishing between the 'absolute expression' of class consciousness ('a pervasive and durable attitude on the part of a class toward its position in society'), its 'long-term relative expression' ('found in the slowly changing traditions, experiences, education, and organization of the class'), and its 'short-term relative expression' ('a dynamic complex of moods and sentiments affected by circumstances and changing with them, sometimes, in periods of stress and conflict, almost from day to day') (1974, pp. 29–30). Virtually the same position is taken up by Crompton and Gubbay, whose study is almost entirely given over to the analysis of class position. In asking how 'the location in the class structure is reflected in the consciousness of particular groups', their general answer is that there are

no easy answers: the particular structure of the labour market, the dominant ideology, and short-term historical circumstances will all tend to act as intervening variables in the description and explanation of objective location in the class structure and the consciousness, attitudes and behaviour of the groups so located (1977, pp. 97–8).

This list of intervening variables is presented simply to indicate the complexity of the problem and not as a basis for the systematic analysis of it. And in the section of the book where they attempt to discuss class consciousness in rather more detail, their treatment of it relies on an equally *ad hoc* reference to adventitious 'secondary structural factors' (differentiation of function, bureaucracy, market and status factors), which, 'far from determining the class structure of contemporary capitalist societies', must nevertheless 'be systematically taken into account in the detailed empirical analysis of the class structure of any particular society' (1977, p. 196). Finally, Wright, who gives primacy to the study of class struggle, provides no more than a highly schematic account of how such a study might proceed. This involves a distinction between class structure (which defines the potential objectives of the potential actors in the class struggle), class formation (which refers to the structural and organizational capacities of classes), and class struggle itself, conceived as 'the complex social processes which dialectically link class interests to class capacities' (1978, p. 102). Wright provides brief illustrations of the 'dialectical' relationships between these three elements. But the exposition is entirely illustrative of how the schema might be applied. Its 'central message' is that

An adequate political understanding of the possibilities and constraints present in a given social formation depends upon showing the ways in which class structure establishes limits on class struggle and class formation, the ways in which class struggle transforms both class structure and class formation, and the ways in which class struggle mediates the relationship between class structure and class formation (1978, p. 108).

One definition of 'message' given by *The Concise Oxford Dictionary* is a 'prophet's, writer's, preacher's inspired communication'. Until Wright demonstrates how his schema can provide a systematic analysis of the relation between class structure and class struggle in a given social formation, his advocacy of its usefulness for this purpose must be considered as no more than a message in the sense just defined.

The work of Poulantzas belongs in a different category because it begins by attempting to abolish the distinction between a class-in-itself and a class-for-itself. For him, 'classes have existence only in the class struggle', and the latter is not something that is to be treated separately from the analysis of class structure. 'Classes do not firstly exist as such and then only enter into the class struggle' (1979, p. 14). By this he means that classes are not purely economically determined entities which then become transformed into classes-for-themselves at the political and ideological level of class consciousness and organization. According to Poulantzas, this misleading distinction derives from an Hegelian interpretation of Marx, which he foists on Lukacs. The purpose of saddling Lukacs with this error and absolving Marx from it is all too transparent and requires no further comment. What is important about Poulantzas's argument is first that his rejection of the Hegelian 'problematic' leads to ambiguity in his concepts of the 'political', the 'ideological', and the 'class struggle', and, second, that the resolution of this ambiguity results in the resurgence of the 'problematic' he attempts to dispose of.

To say that classes cannot be defined outside of the class struggle is all very well in so far as it means that class relations are inherently an arena of class struggle and that this class struggle does not necessarily involve class consciousness and class struggle in the traditional sense of a class-for-itself. Moreover, there is nothing objectionable about Poulantzas's argument that class structure is to be defined by reference to 'political' and 'ideological' (as well as economic) criteria as long as it is remembered that these refer to the supervisory and nonmanual functions which are focal points of class struggle in the social division of labour. So far, so good. The difficulty arises not from this special meaning of political and ideological class struggle being constitutive of class structure but from the fact that class struggle and class consciousness are empirically variable. Granted that in Poulantzas's terms production relations contain a political and ideological dimension, it is nevertheless the case that this refers to a different order of fact than the political organization and ideology through which the objectively determined interests of a class are expressed or represented at the societal level of the class struggle. Poulantzas is forced to recognize this distinction.

This structural determination of classes, which thus exists only as the class struggle, must however be distinguished from class position in each specific conjuncture – the focal point of the always unique historic individuality of a social formation, in other words the concrete situation of the class struggle (1979, p. 14).

To exemplify this distinction, take, for example, the working class. Its structural place is determined by reference to aspects of class struggle that constitute class structure: that is by the economic aspect (productive labour), the political aspect (subjection to supervision), and the ideological aspect (manual labour excluded from the 'secret knowledge' of the production process). Its 'class position', however, refers to '"Class consciousness" and autonomous political organization, i.e., as far as the working class is concerned, a revolutionary proletarian ideology and an autonomous party of class struggle, refer to the terrain of class positions and the conjuncture' (1979, p. 17).

What this means is that there is a latent class struggle and a manifest class struggle. There is the political and ideological class struggle that determines the structure of classes, and there is the political and ideological class struggle that is manifested in the forms of class consciousness and political organization specific to class 'positions' in the 'conjuncture'. In other words, by distinguishing between a structural and a conjunctural class struggle, Poulantzas conjures up in a different form the Hegelian spectre of the class-in-itself/class-for-itself that he set out to exorcise. Moreover, his conception of the relationship between the structural determination of classes and class positions in the conjuncture is no less vague. On the one hand, 'A social class, or fraction or stratum of a class, may take up a class position that does not correspond to its interests, which are defined by the class determination that fixes the horizon of the class's struggle' (1979, p. 15). Yet, on the other hand, 'structural class determination involves economic, political, and ideological class struggle, and these struggles are all expressed in the form of class positions in the conjuncture' (p. 16). The problem here is basically that, while Poulantzas admits that classes may not take up positions in the conjunctural class struggle that correspond to their interests, which are determined by their place in the class structure, this discrepancy can only be explained by a systematic study of the specific political and ideological factors affecting 'the concrete situation of the class struggle'. Since he does not undertake this kind of analysis it is difficult to disagree with the conclusion of one Marxist critic who argues that 'Poulantzas's class determination/class position distinction is incoherent and unstable' because the concept of class position in the conjuncture is 'not theorized. It is merely a means of hedging any bets made on the basis of class determination' (Hirst, 1977, p. 133).

In the present context, however, what is most important about Poulantzas's theory of class structure and class consciousness is that the place, interest, and position of the proletariat appears to be entirely unproblematic. It has already been noted that his definition of the class place of the proletariat is such that it constitutes a clear-cut entity: it is at once economically exploited, politically subjected, and ideologically excluded, i.e., productive, nonsupervisory manual labour. Beyond this, Poulantzas has very little to say about the working class. It is excluded from his purview at the outset. But its role in his theory of classes is as crucial as its socialist class 'position' is indisputable. As he says, although 'these essays do not deal directly with the working class, this class is constantly present'; and it is always present as 'the class that is situated beneath the exploitation which the bourgeoisie imposes on the popular masses, and the class to which the leadership of the revolutionary process falls' (Poulantzas, 1979, p. 9). It has already been observed that he equates the 'position' of the working class with 'a revolutionary proletarian ideology', and elsewhere he refers to 'The long-term interests of the working class itself, which is the only class that is revolutionary to the end' (p. 204). Only occasionally is there a glimpse of doubt: for example, 'certain ideological elements specific to the petty bourgeoisie may themselves have their effects on the working class's ideology' and 'this is even the main danger that permanently threatens the working class' (p. 289). But his basic assumption is that the interests and position of the proletariat are beyond question.

The class struggle in a social formation takes place within the basic context of a polarization of various classes in relation to the two basic classes, those of the dominant mode of production, whose relationship constitutes the principal contradiction of that formation (p. 200).

These basic classes are naturally 'the bourgeoisie and the proletariat; the only real class ideologies, in the strong sense of this term, are those of these two basic classes, which are in fundamental political opposition' (p. 287).

The problem of the relationship between the class place and class position of the proletariat – the problem of its end-shift – is therefore solved by fiat. This 'solution' has most unfortunate consequences for his analysis of the new *petit bourgeoisie*, a subject to which Poulantzas devotes a great deal of attention. Given his general theory of class struggle, the new *petit bourgeoisie* can have no real class position of its own that is independent of 'the bourgeois way and the proletarian (the socialist) way' (1979, p. 297). Its class place is distinguished from those of the two basic classes by reference to the economic, political, and ideological criteria of class determination, and particularly by its intermediate location in bureaucratic structures of authority. Much of what Poulantzas has to say on this score is sociologically commonplace and some of it ungraciously derived; compare, for example, his remarks on 'the stupidity of the bourgeois problematic of social mobility' with his subsequent observations on the effects of mobility chances on the consciousness of the new *petit bourgeoisie* (1979, pp. 33, 280, 284). It is, however, on the basis of this analysis of the structural place of the new *petit bourgeoisie* that he seeks to identify its class position. As he says, the 'structural determination of the new *petit bourgeoisie* in the social division of labour has certain effects on the ideology of its agents, which directly influences its class positions' (p. 287). The chief features of this ideology, which unites the new and the traditional *petit bourgeoisie* at the ideological level, are as follows: it is anticapitalist, reformist, individualistic, and conceives of the state as a neutral arbiter of class interests. But the new *petit bourgeoisie* is not a homogeneous body. By reference to several broad changes affecting the *petit bourgeoisie* in general (its feminization, the narrowing of wage differentials between nonmanual and manual labour, the rationalization and mechanization of office work, etc.), Poulantzas seeks to identify three 'fractions' of the class that 'display the most favourable objective conditions for a quite specific alliance with the working class and under its leadership' (p. 314). His discussion of the internal differentiation of the new *petit bourgeoisie* is much more acute than Braverman's treatment of the subject, and not least because Poulantzas's is empirically and sociologically more discriminating. The result is a novel and challenging Marxist interpretation of class structure, which identifies precisely the potential allies of the working class.

But it is at this point that Poulantzas's argument begins to break down. For the class position of those 'fractions' of the new *petit bourgeoisie* whose place in the class structure most closely approximates that of the proletariat depends ultimately on the strategy of the latter class. It is not to be assumed that 'an objective proletarian polarization of class determination must necessarily lead in time to a polarization of class positions' (1979, p. 334). And in fact

the objective polarization which, together with current transformations, marks the class determination of these petty-bourgeois fractions, has not till now been accompanied by a polarization of their class positions. In other words, no alliance has yet materialized between the major sections of these fractions and the working class, based on the specific objectives of a socialist revolution (p. 333).

Whether this alliance takes place depends entirely on 'the strategy of the working class and its organizations of class struggle' (p. 334). In the last analysis, then, everything depends on the proletariat, the class actor to whom he assigns a 'socialist position' *ex cathedra*. That is, until one reaches the penultimate page of his book. For there Poulantzas admits that the problem of how the working class can attempt to establish its 'hegemony' over the proletarianized 'fractions' of the new *petit bourgeoisie* presupposes a study of the working class that he has not even begun to make. 'For this', he writes,

it would have been necessary, among other things, to undertake a study of the history and experience of the workers' and international revolutionary movement in this respect – of its organizations, of its theories, and the changes in them, on the question of the revolutionary process, of organization (party and trade unions), and of alliances, and finally to understand in more detail the significance of social-democratic ideology and social-democratic tendencies, and their real basis (p. 335).

In other words, it would be necessary to consider how working-class consciousness is formed not only by the place of the proletariat in the class structure but also by the specific political organizations and ideologies that represent its objective interest. Most importantly, the latter would involve a comparative study of the formation of the working class that took account of 'the unique historical individuality of a social formation' and of the cumulative effect on the political organization of the working class of the outcomes of successive 'concrete situations of the class struggle'.

In conclusion, then, whatever the merits of Poulantzas's analysis of the class place of the bourgeoisie and the *petit bourgeoisie*, his theory of social classes provides no systematic explanation of class action and does not even begin to deal with the chronic and intractable problem of the end-shift of the proletariat. His belated recognition that the study of specific working-class organizations and their ideologies is essential to an understanding of the way in which the interest of the proletariat is represented in the concrete, conjunctural class struggle introduces a quite abrupt and damaging qualification of his general thesis that the relation between the structural place and the position of the proletariat is unproblematic: that the 'long-term interests' of the working class ensure that it is 'the only class that is revolutionary to the end'. Like most of his fellow theorists of class structure, Poulantzas holds to a fundamentalist conception of the proletariat. Absolutely basic to this idea is the assumption that the proletariat has an objective, long-run, and, however long that run may be, an imperative interest in socialism. The action of the class may deviate from the pursuit of this interest because of a variety of particular social and economic circumstances that influence the course of the concrete class struggle. But, given that its socialist interest is known to be the only 'reasonable' end that it can pursue, deviations from this goal must be misrepresentations of its interest and are explicable finally in terms of ignorance or error. This is brought out nicely in Poulantzas's interpretation of the rise of fascism, a conjuncture in which neither social democracy nor communism served the interest of the working class: the former was an 'ideological state apparatus' whose role was 'to mislead the masses and hold back the revolution', while the latter was itself misled by its 'incorrect strategy' based on the theory of social fascism (1974, pp. 147–65).

The demolition of this whole orthodox framework is the aim of the last version of Marxist class theory to be considered here. Its most forceful exponent is Hirst (1977). The crux of his argument is that Marxism is forced to choose between some form of economism, which conceives of the political and ideological struggle as ultimately the expression or representation of class interests that are objectively given by the economic structure, and what he calls 'necessary noncorrespondence', which means that there are no such objective interests, but only the interests that are constituted by specific political and ideological forces. Classes as such do not have interests and are not actors, and the basic misconception of economism is its assumption that the real actors in the class struggle, namely political organizations in a broad sense, must necessarily, in the long run, represent objective class interests. Economism is shown to be deficient because the divergence between political representation and objective class interest is all too apparent. One solution of this problem is to accord the political a 'relative autonomy', a device that is, in effect, identical with Poulantzas's notion of class position in the conjuncture. But this is merely a sophisticated, but none the less theoretically unstable, version of economism.

Once any degree of autonomous action is accorded to political forces as a means of representation vis-à-vis classes of economic agents, then there is no necessary correspondence between the forces that appear in the political (and what they 'represent') and economic classes (Hirst, 1977, p. 130).

Given the idea of relative autonomy, there can be no guarantee that the political means of representation can be constrained in such a way that they do represent class interests, unless the relativeness of the autonomy is restricted to economism: 'it asserts the primacy of the economy while affirming that politics and ideology cannot simply be reduced to its effects' (Cutler, *et al.*, 1977, pp. 235–6). Moreover, like economism in general, it can provide no satisfactory theory of the 'specificity of the political'. This has already been shown to be a major weakness of Poulantzas's theory of classes in which the conjunctural class struggle finally emerges as a zone of particularity and contingency. At best, the systematization of the relative autonomy of the political results in a functionalist form of economism, typified by the concept of 'ideological state apparatuses' (Hirst, 1977, pp. 131–2; Cutler, *et al.*, 1977, pp. 200–2).

Hirst and his colleagues realize that in rejecting the concept of objective class interest and in espousing the idea of necessary noncorrespondence they adopt a position that 'shatters the classical conception of classes' (Cutler, *et al.*, p. 236). If their argument is accepted – and it is a very cogent one – then many of the most intractable problems of the Marxist theory of class action just disappear. But what of Marxism remains? The broadest statement of intent is that the

connections between social relations, institutions, and practices must be conceived of not in terms of any relations of determination, 'in the last instance' or otherwise, but rather in terms of conditions of existence. This means that while specific social relations and practices always presuppose definite social conditions of existence, they neither secure these conditions through their own action nor do they determine the form in which they will be secured. Thus, while a set of relations of production can be shown to have definite legal, political, and cultural conditions of existence these conditions are in no way determined or secured by the action of the economy (Cutler, *et al.*, p. 314).

What might seem to be involved, then, is replacing the quasi-Parsonsian functionalism of Althusser[5] with a form of Marxism that begins where Weber left off.

* * *

Contemporary Marxist theories of social class are in a poor state. There are no doubt reasons why this is the case, other than those advanced above. Nevertheless, it might be useful to recapitulate the latter, however much a simplification and exaggeration of certain tendencies of the Marxist corpus they represent. The burden of this essay is that the main weakness of the link between Marxist theories of system and social integration is to be found in the persistence of a basically utilitarian action scheme. One reason why the latter should have been so predominant is that it is fundamental to the economic theory of capitalist development, which is by far the most powerfully developed branch of the subject. Furthermore, in seeking to demonstrate that the proletariat has an objective, scientifically guaranteed interest in socialism, Marxist economic theory has provided the terms of reference for the analysis of social integration. It has set the 'norm' against which the rationality of proletarian action must be measured. This, together with the assumption that the proletariat possesses a power of reason commensurate with the task of realizing its fundamental interest, has meant that, from the outset, explanations of conflict and order have taken on a characteristically utilitarian form. The standard of rationality is the major reference point for understanding how capitalists and proletarians adapt their means to their respectively given, intrasystemic, ends, just as the higher-order rationality of reason is indispensable to explaining the transmogrification, or end-shift, of the proletariat. Finally, in the absence of a clear distinction between action that is simply irrational, and nonrational action oriented to the alternative standard of ultimate values, there is no other way of accounting for ostensible lapses from rationality and reason save by recourse to some version of the classical utilitarian notions of ignorance and error.

This theory of action has two basic defects. First, it precludes systematic analysis of the factors determining the extent to which the values and norms defining the legitimate ends and means of actors become internalized conditions of action. The whole problem of the institutionalization of values is inadmissible. Most crucially, this denies Marxism an adequate conception of the status order, the primary focus of the integration of the ends of class actors. The tendency to dismiss both hierarchical and egalitarian aspects of status as ideological reflections of the class structure is not only far too crude to grasp the complicated ways in which the legitimation of status relationships is both contingent upon, and constitutive of, class interests; it is also symptomatic of the second major defect. In so far as normative elements enter into Marxist explanations of action, they do so either in an implicit, *ad hoc* way, or, as is more usually the case, through their incorporation into the general category of ideology. This is to be expected. By according the standard of rationality such a central place in its explanatory system, and by collapsing the distinction between irrational and nonrational action, Marxism is constantly tempted to lump together as ideologically determined all kinds of apparently irrational behaviour. The concept of 'ideological state apparatuses' is only the most egregious example of this. Ideology thus serves an analytical function analogous to that performed by the concepts of ignorance and error in utilitarian theorizing. Even though it locates the sources of irrationality in society rather than in the individual, the theory of ideology has been formulated at a highly abstract level, which befits its chief purpose of providing global explanations of social order. Indeed, in the course of its promotion to account for the absence of proletarian revolution in the most advanced capitalist societies, its conceptual scope has widened to cover ever more disparate phenomena, including not only systems of beliefs and values, but most major social institutions and corporate groups, all of which are seen in some way to be performing ideological functions. At the same time, the precise manner in which, and therefore the effectiveness with which,

93

ideological factors enter into the determination of social action has remained extremely problematic. For these reasons, ideology comes close to being a residual category, resort to which has the theoretically destabilizing effect of introducing into the basic, strongly positivistic, framework of Marxism a type of explanation that approaches the opposite pole of the idealistic scheme of action.

These inherent defects of the theory may help to explain why contemporary studies of class concentrate so heavily on the analysis of class structure and avoid the problem of class action. But this is putting the cart before the horse, because the identification of significant structural factors presupposes an explicit and well-founded theory of action. This is most strikingly evident in the way that these studies deal, or rather fail to deal, with the structure of the working class. By reducing to the very minimum the elements that define the basic conditions of the proletarian class situation, it is then discovered that the working class still possesses the homogeneity and potential solidarity requisite to the attainment of its ultimate interest in socialism. But the question of how, under these conditions, the working class will act to realize its final goal, receives no serious attention. To provide an adequate answer would require nothing less than the reconstitution of the classical Marxist theory of action. But far from attending to this task, contemporary class theorists appear to have no clear concept of action whatsoever. So now it is no longer just the case that explanations of the relationship between class structure and class struggle are bound to be unstable and contradictory: the relationship is completely indeterminate.

Notes and references

1 It has become increasingly fashionable to argue that Marx did not expect, and that his work provides no grounds for thinking, that socialist revolutions would occur in the most advanced capitalist societies (there is even in circulation an analytical blank cheque called 'over-determination', which guarantees that revolutions will occur whenever and wherever the sufficient conditions of their occurrence exist). This view is not in the least convincing. To be sure, during his own lifetime, Marx believed that revolution was imminent on several occasions and in different places. But unless the relation between his theory of system and social integration is held to be a purely contingent one, then the whole logic of his major work points to one and only one conclusion: that the conditions of proletarian revolution will be found in the most advanced, and the most capitalist of capitalist societies. What he has to say on this score in the famous 'Preface' to the *Critique of Political Economy* finds identical expression in the *Grundrisse*: 'If we did not find concealed in society as it is the material conditions of production and the corresponding relations of exchange prerequisite for a classless society, then all attempts to explode it would be quixotic' (1973, p. 159). And *Capital* is replete with similar statements. For example:

. . . in theory, it is assumed that the laws of capitalist production operate in their pure form. In reality there exists only approximation; but this approximation is the greater, the more developed the capitalist mode of production and the less it is adulterated and amalgamated with survivals of former economic conditions (1972, p. 175).

From this standpoint, the United States has always been the chief embarrassment. To the naming of the factors making for American 'exceptionalism' there is hardly any end. But in that case, at what point does one admit that the sociological law of motion of capitalist society has ground to a halt in the sands of historical particularity?

2   It is not altogether clear why capitalists should lack 'reason' and be unable to understand that the rational pursuit of their immediate individual ends is detrimental to their fundamental interest as a class. As Elster points out, Marx's account of the introduction of factory legislation sees the process as

partly the result of the political activity of the workers and partly as the defence of the capitalist class against its own members, the idea being that the over-exploitation of the workers might threaten their physical reproduction and thus capitalism itself. The latter explanation either requires the collective interests of capitalists to overcome their individual interests or their long-term interest to overcome their short-term interest. Both ideas, however, are hard to square with what Marx says elsewhere about the possibility of solidarity between capitalists (1978, p. 139).

While Lukacs seems to suggest that capitalists cannot comprehend the unintended irrationality of their individual rational actions, and, somewhat unnecessarily, that, even if they could, they could do nothing in the way of correcting this outcome that would not further undermine the capitalist system (1971, pp. 61–4), the main solution of the problem is to be found in the role of the state. As Sweezy puts it, 'it is not inconsistent to say that State action may run counter to the immediate interests of some or even all of the capitalists provided only that the overriding aim of preserving the system intact is promoted' (1949, p. 248). And the greater the emphasis on the 'relative autonomy' of the state's socially stabilizing function, the more the state acquires the role of 'the cunning of reason' as far as the capitalist class is concerned.

3   For the sense in which the concepts 'positivistic' and 'idealistic' are used in this essay, see Parsons (1937, chapter II). In brief,

Just as positivism eliminates the creative, voluntaristic character of action by dispensing with the analytical significance of values, and the other normative elements by making them epiphenomena, so idealism has the same effect for the opposite reason – idealism eliminates the reality of the obstacles to the realization of values (Parsons, 1937, p. 446).

It is only proper to point out that the instability of Marxist explanations of class action has its source in a very general problem which also gives rise to intractable difficulties in 'bourgeois' social theory. Despite Parsons's

95

ecumenical notion of 'the voluntaristic theory of action', explanations based on the competing concepts of 'rational' and 'socialised' man appear to be irreconcilable (Barry, 1970; Heath, 1976). In Marxism, this problem is merely magnified because the attempt to provide a unified theory of system and social integration brings out any inadequacy of the underlying action scheme in a much more dramatic fashion than is the case in theories of less ambitious scope.

4 When Lukacs writes that 'status consciousness – a real historical factor – masks class consciousness; in fact it prevents it from emerging at all', he limits his observation to precapitalist societies on the ground that in these, in contrast with capitalism, 'the structuring of society into castes and estates means that economic elements are inextricably joined to political and religious factors' and 'legal institutions intervene substantively in the interplay of economic forces' (1971, pp. 58, 55, 57). But this contrast is exaggerated and represents an over-simplification of Weber's view of the interdependence of class and status formation. While he recognized that societies can be differentiated according to whether class or status relationships are predominant, he did not thereby suppose that in either type of society life chances and life experiences are determined exclusively by either class or status situations. Class relationships are always determined in part by a specific framework of status, and Avineri draws attention to this when he writes that

for Marx the heyday of unfettered capitalism, when economic activity, at least in England, was not encumbered by any limitation at all, pre- or post-capitalist, was short: from the Repeal of the Corn Laws to the introduction of the Ten Hours Bill (1968, p. 161).

But what this fails to bring out is that, even then, capitalism was not 'unfettered' and economic activity was not without 'limitation'. Vital to the understanding of both the basis of, and the limits to, the 'free play' of economic forces is 'the fact that the core of citizenship at this stage was composed of civil rights' (Marshall, 1950, p. 33). Conversely, even the most rigidly status-ordered societies were never able to establish more than a very imperfect 'fit' between the economic prerogatives of different status groups and the actual disposition of economic power. The status order can no more completely immobilize economic forces through legal sanctions than, at the other extreme, class relations, class interests, and class conflicts can wholly break loose from the moral confines of the status system in which they are embedded. This interdependence of class and status relations at the structural level is no less evident at the situational one – even in evolutionary situations, as is strikingly exemplified by the Lemmgen incident in Berlin in January 1919 (Ryder, 1967, p. 201).

5 The similarity between Parsons' later system of normative functionalism and the covert functionalism of Althusserian Marxism (Cutler, et al., 1977, pp. 201–2) is, on the surface, fairly obvious. Even though the latter cannot stand comparison with the former in terms of analytical development,

there is, nevertheless, a striking correspondence between Parsons' concept of the 'cybernetic hierarchy' of action, in which values have the 'ultimately determining' role, and Althusser's notion of a social totality, which is composed of 'relatively autonomous' levels or instances, and which obtains its structural unity through 'determination in the last instance' by the 'economy' of which of the levels plays the 'dominant' role. Marxism has been transformed into a more clearly functionalist form by Habermas (1976), who makes free use of terms such as 'functional necessities' and 'functional equivalents' and concentrates on certain substantive problems which have long been of central interest to sociological functionalism and 'political systems' theory. Although his work is highly tentative and schematic, its most novel feature is the discussion of 'legitimation' and 'motivation' crises. What Habermas does not seem to appreciate, however, is how closely his general approach to this problem resembles Parsons' theory of 'power deflation'.

Further Reading

David Lockwood, 'Social integration and system integration' in G. K. Zollschan and W. Hirsch (eds), *Explorations in Social Change*, London: RKP, 1964, pp. 244–57

Ted Benton, *The Rise and Fall of Structural Marxism*, Basingstoke: Macmillan, 1984

G. Marshall *et al.*, *Social Class in Modern Britain*, London: Hutchinson, 1988

F. Parkin, *Marxism and Class Theory: A Bourgeois Critique*, London: Tavistock, 1979

4 Some remarks on the study of working-class consciousness

Gordon Marshall

Why, in advanced capitalist societies, have working classes not become revolutionary classes? In addressing this question, commentators have focused attention increasingly upon elements of the collusion between the rulers and the ruled that has long been recognized to coexist alongside the possibility of outright coercion. Machiavelli, for example, advised princes to practice deceit as well as force since the lessons of history suggested that force, by itself, was insufficient to obtain or maintain power whereas 'instances can easily be found in which fraud alone has sufficed' (Walker (ed.), 1975, pp. 244, 364, 392–3). Even Hobbes did not advance the alternative thesis – that the powerful could simply coerce the powerless into a constant submission: not only force but also religious, legal, and political 'wiles' were necessary in order to keep the common people from 'discontent, murmuring, and commotion against the State' (Hobbes, 1949, pp. 59–60, 63–4, 107–9). The road from Hobbes' several deceptions to the normative consensus secured by Parsons' ultimate value system or to the conditions for class domination reproduced by Louis Althusser's ideological state apparatuses is both long and winding, but it is recognizably the same route (Parsons, 1935; Althusser, 1971). It is the principal thesis of this chapter that, as theorists have come increasingly to employ concepts of ideology in order to explain why the working class has not become a revolutionary class, empirical research offering an understanding of the nature of working-class consciousness has reached an impasse. Theories of working-class consciousness seem to have advanced beyond their empirical foundations and beyond the ability of the methodologies upon which these are conventionally erected to provide suitable justification for them. More particularly, I shall argue that research into working-class consciousness has reached a stalemate between theories of working-class instrumentalism and working-class ambivalence. I then suggest that neither of these interpretations is in any way enlightening and that both may well be false. Certainly it can readily be shown that they are not substantiated by the survey and attitudinal data from which each has been derived. In my conclusion, I draw attention to an alternative though perhaps unfashionable research strategy, one that facilitates analyses that do not share the limitations evident in the two current strategies.

Theories of ambivalence and instrumentalism

It is standard practice among sociologists reviewing the literature on class consciousness to distinguish two broad explanations of workers' passivity, one emphasizing the 'heterogeneity' and the other the 'incorporation' of the working class. David Lockwood's categorization of workers as traditional proletarians, traditional deferentialists, or privatized instrumentalists, and the various American and French theories of working-class segmentation, are generally held to represent the emphasis on working-class heterogeneity. Here, consciousness is linked directly to social structural factors and to personal attributes. Since labour is divided into segments with different market and work situations, and hence with different life-experiences, the absence of a unified class consciousness can readily be explained by the rise of labour aristocracies, by the division between new and traditional working classes, by the cleavages created by discrimination against minority groups, by the operation of dual or segmented labour markets, and so on (see, for example, Lockwood, 1975).

The most recent examples of this approach are to be found in discussions, largely Marxist, about the so-called boundary problem in the demarcation of social classes and of capital and labour generally. The ideal-typical proletarian in Marx's *Capital* is, of course, a fully employed, male, class-conscious factory worker. Certain prominent features of the class structures of advanced capitalist societies, such as the disproportionate growth of routine nonmanual occupations, the rapid expansion of the service sector of the economy, the increased though highly particularized participation of women in the formal labour-market, the volatility of voting habits, and the growth of white-collar unions, therefore pose a theoretical and a political problem for historical materialists. How does one conceptualize within a Marxist framework the diversity of work and market situations currently embraced by that stratum of society referred to generically as 'the working class'? And what are the consequences of this diversity for class consciousness and action? In short, who now will make the Revolution?

The major contributors to this debate – Nicos Poulantzas (1979), G. Carchedi (1977) and Erik Olin Wright (1978) – have attempted to 'theorize' these changes while remaining true to the axioms of Marxist analysis. Their central concepts of relative autonomy, contradictory class locations, and overdetermination, though allegedly descriptive of the real world, have in fact been subjected only to limited empirical scrutiny, and there are significant disagreements within Marxism as to the explanatory and political usefulness of the various analyses. Specific differences aside, however, the general thrust of these analyses is consistent with the claim of working-class heterogeneity. The most sophisticated and empirically well-grounded analysis concludes that

defining the working class matters because it helps to specify the extent to which the task of building a viable socialist movement hinges on drawing contradictory locations within class relations into working class organizations. The contradictory locations around the boundary of the working class represent positions which do have a real interest in socialism, yet simultaneously gain certain real privileges directly from capitalist relations of production. . . . When such contradictory locations are formed

99

into the working class, the contradictory quality of their underlying class interests does not disappear. This implies that to the extent that contradictory locations are mapped into working class organizational capacities, those organizations will have to contend with potential conflicts of interests, and not simply conflicts of immediate interests but of fundamental interests as well. . . . Part of the impressive durability of capitalist systems can be attributed to the capacity of capitalism to displace conflicts from the fundamental to the immediate level, and one of the central tasks of any serious socialist movement is to reorient those conflicts back towards fundamental interests (Wright, 1978, pp. 108–9).

The task for socialists is here clearly identified as one of unifying a heterogeneous labouring class, divided by conflicting fundamental and immediate interests and by a fragmented consciousness, into a single entity capable of realizing its structural and organizational capacities as a revolutionary force.

Incorporationists emphasize the present unity of working-class culture or consciousness. By one means or another, however, this consciousness is profoundly shaped by values that originate outside the working class. Frank Parkin's description of the dominant, subordinate, and radical value systems in society exemplifies this approach, as do Marxist accounts of hegemonic dominant ideologies. Here, the working class endorses the fundamental institutional order of the society as legitimized in the dominant ideology, but it transforms certain dominant values, and adds a few of its own, such that greater equality can be fought for within the rules of the established order and without destroying the system. Unlike the genuinely oppositional values present in radical meaning systems, those of subordinate value systems represent a compromise with the existing order. To quote Parkin:

In so far as it is possible to characterise a complex set of normative arrangements by a single term, the subordinate value system could be said to be essentially *accommodative*; that is to say its representation of the class structure and inequality emphasizes various modes of adaptation, rather than either full endorsement of, or opposition to, the *status quo* (1972, p. 88).

Or, to take an example from the Marxist tradition, the ruling capitalist classes exercise power by means of political and cultural hegemony. The central institutions of capitalist societies – educational, political, legal, trades unions, the media – act in concert 'to raise the great mass of the population to a particular cultural and moral level (or type) which corresponds to the needs of the productive forces for development, and hence to the interests of the ruling class' (Gramsci, 1980, p. 258).

As a means of characterizing the current state of the debate about working-class consciousness, the conventional distinction between heterogenists and incorporationists is misleading. In reality most accounts contain elements of both.[1] Lockwood himself, generally identified as one of the doyens of heterogeneity, seems also to argue a version of incorporatism when he holds that privatized instrumentalists (who are incorporated workers *par excellence*) are prototypical of workers in general in advanced capitalist societies (Lockwood, 1975 and 1960). Similarly, the incorporationist stance of Parkin's early writings sits uneasily alongside his more recent descriptions of the mechanisms of social closure, of the practices of exclusion and inclusion in social class formation, and of the existence of intraclass cleavages around a variety of obvious and not so obvious dividing lines (Parkin, 1972 and 1979). The alleged dualism of the two models seems no less artificial when applied to many Marxist accounts. Allen's contribution to the boundary debate, for example, is simultaneously heterogenist and incorporationist in that he argues that the segmentation of labour markets, which fragments sellers of labour power and which creates friction and contradictions between them, is ideologically determined. Intra-working-class divisions are therefore the material consequences of 'bourgeois categories' that act as 'instruments of social control' and that maintain the dominance of the ruling ideology (Allen, 1978).

More importantly, however, I wish to argue that recent studies of working-class consciousness actually fall into two quite different camps. One claims that working-class consciousness is, quite simply, 'ambivalent'; the other that workers are 'instrumentally oriented' and interested in little beyond straightforward pecuniary gain.

The argument for the ambivalence of working-class consciousness comes in several versions. Parkin's account of subordinate meaning-systems itself implies that these are ambiguous in their implications for class action, since they accept the existing framework of rules specified by the dominant value system but, in their limited challenge to the morality of the distributive system and the inequalities generated by it, contain an unfocused or latent possibility for developing class consciousness and class action. Indeed Parkin explicitly describes the negotiated version of the dominant values encompassed by the subordinate value system as generating a form of 'normative ambivalence' among its adherents. Drawing on Hyman Rodman's formulation of the 'lower class value stretch' he concludes that:

Rodman's formulation draws attention to the fact that the subordinate class has two distinct levels of normative reference; the dominant value system and a 'stretched' or 'negotiated' version of it. We can perhaps further add to this formulation by suggesting further, that which of the two frames of reference is actually drawn up will be situationally determined; more specifically, it could be hypothesized that in situations where purely abstract evaluations are called for, the dominant value system will provide the moral frame of reference; but in concrete social situations involving choice and action, the negotiated version – or the subordinate value-system – will provide the moral framework (1972, pp. 92–3).[2]

This version of ambivalence has most recently been advanced by Howard Newby in his research into class relationships in rural England. Torn between the contractual elements of his relationship to the farmer and the personal, particularistic loyalties inherent in that same relationship, the farm worker is often ambivalent in his moral assessment of the social and economic position of his employer. The ambivalence of the relationship itself is reflected in the worker's image of society. Newby is not surprised by his findings:

If one accepts a fairly basic sociological premise that an individual's social consciousness is to a large extent influenced by his immediate social context then there is no reason to assume, except in certain limiting cases, that the interpretations provided to and by the individual will always be cumulative or commensurate one with the other. The pattern of most individual's social relationships is such that they are provided with different, conflicting and often contradictory beliefs about the nature of society at large and their own position within it. From this no single unambiguous image of society is built up. . . . Such ambivalence is therefore not a very remarkable nor unexpected outcome, given the admixture of work and community situations which most agricultural workers experience (Newby, 1979, pp. 402–3).

Newby takes great pains to distinguish this form of ambivalence from that suggested by Philip E. Converse (1964) and Michael Mann (1978).

Mann's interpretation of working-class consciousness rests, of course, on his now widely adopted model of a mature class consciousness as comprising four elements: class identity (of oneself as working-class); class opposition (to capitalism and the capitalist class); class totality (analysing one's own situation and one's society in class terms); and, finally, a conception of an alternative society. Rarely, according to Mann, are all four elements found together. Their differing admixtures help explain variations in consciousness among working classes in the industrial West. Variations aside, however, Mann's general conclusion is that the working classes of the West neither need nor possess a coherent social consciousness: 'only those actually sharing in societal power need develop consistent societal values'. Social cohesion in liberal democracies rests, according to Mann, on a lack of consensus among members of the working class, which is sustained by 'pragmatic role acceptance' and 'manipulative socialization'. The latter, practised via schools, media, and the state, may be challenged by 'deviant' values introduced by an external radical agent. However, confronting the realities of concrete everyday life and able only intermittently to relate these to abstract principles of political philosophy, 'the attachment of the lower classes to the distant state may be expected to be far less normative and more pragmatic than their attachment to the primary familial group' (Mann, 1982. See also Blackburn and Mann, 1975 and Blackburn in this volume). It is debatable whether it is worth distinguishing this particular form of ambivalence from that proposed by Newby, since – as even Newby concedes

empirically it is not very easy or possible to distinguish between these two forms . . . since the end product, in terms of articulated views, is substantially the same – a hotch-potch of ideas and beliefs without the appearance of any underlying ideological rationale (1979, p. 404).

The thesis of working-class ambivalence, however conceptualized, has recently been endorsed by many who have focused their research interests upon female workers. Anna Pollert, for example, suggests that the women working in a Bristol tobacco factory in the early 1970s displayed contradictory self-images and an ambivalent class consciousness because of their dual identities as dependent wives, in the family and home, and workers selling their labour power, on the shop-floor. Summing up her findings she concludes:

Class society is torn by contradictions. So is class consciousness. Here we see an aspect of what Gramsci called 'common sense', which 'even in the brain of one individual is fragmentary, incoherent and inconsequential'. Working-class, working women face a double yet interconnecting set of contradictions: those of class and those of sex. Those we have so far seen . . . revealed they both accepted and rejected their inferior position, that they were at once satisfied and dissatisfied, that they lived an unresolved conflict. . . . Their concrete experience of work, their self-image and self-confidence as workers, was constantly confused and undermined by their awareness of being women and their role in the family. This was the essence of their 'commonsense' conceptions of their lives. How did this happen? (1981, pp. 87–8).

It happened, according to Pollert, because common sense is a mixture both of ideas received from ruling-class ideology and of the everyday practices of making sense of the world. For women workers, the ambivalence engendered by their simultaneous location in structures of social production and of human reproduction was simply reinforced by the patriarchal assumptions implicit in the hegemonic ideology of the ruling class (see also Purcell, 1978 and 1979; Porter 1978).

While one school of thought has resigned itself to the conclusion that working-class consciousness is apparently ambivalent, volatile, even self-contradictory, an equally influential group of observers has argued that, far from being ambiguous, working-class consciousness forms a perfectly consistent though narrowly focused whole. Quite simply, workers are instrumentalists, more or less rational maximizers of pecuniary returns to themselves. John H. Goldthorpe has probably been the most forceful proponent of this view. In an attempt to explain inflation in Britain as a consequence of distributional conflict, he has argued that, because of the progressive decay of traditional status orders, the realization of citizenship, and the emergence of a demographically and socio-politically mature working class, rank-and-file 'pushfulness' for pay increases is perfectly intelligible from the worker's point of view and is likely to increase. These secular changes are present, in a less developed form, in most advanced capitalist societies. They are most developed in Britain, which explains its pre-eminence in inflationary league tables and the leap-frogging wage demands that apparently sustain this. Rejecting the view generally held by economists that the British working class has recently developed a *new* consciousness, based on greed, acquisition, or envy, Goldthorpe proposes the alternative thesis that

what the mass of wage- and salary-earners have learned from capitalism is not acquisitiveness *per se* – which they probably never lacked – but, of far greater consequence, the practice of exploiting one's market position to the full. This includes, of course, maximizing the gains to be had from any 'strategic' advantage that may present itself; and, more importantly still, using the power of organization to improve a weak position or to reinforce and maintain a strong one (1978, pp. 200–1).

Goldthorpe's inflation-generating 'rational economic worker' is, of course,

103

the 'privatized instrumentalist' of the Affluent Worker Study. The world view of the latter was explained by Lockwood, Goldthorpe's co-author, in these terms:

The social environment of the privatised worker is conducive to the development of what may be called a 'pecuniary' model of society. The essential feature of this ideology is that class divisions are seen mainly in terms of differences in income and material possessions. . . . Basically, the pecuniary model of society is an ideological reflection of work attachments that are instrumental and of community relationships that are privatised. It is a model which is only possible when social relationships that might provide prototypical experiences for the construction of ideas of conflicting power classes, or of hierarchically independent status groups, are either absent or devoid of their significance (1975, pp. 21–2).

The authors of the Affluent Worker Study, neo-Weberians to a man and woman, were taken to task by their Marxist critics for having rediscovered (at last) Marx's and Engels's 'cash nexus'. John Westergaard, for example, was not surprised by the *fact* of workers' instrumentalism (the toleration of uninteresting work and acceptance of a working relationship with management for the sole purpose of collecting the wage packet) but by the *interpretation* that the Affluent Worker team placed upon it. This included in the first instance,

the implication that the worker's monetary orientation to his job is somehow a new phenomenon, which is the trigger for developing 'privatization' of the affluent workers' entire social outlook. For this 'monetary orientation' seems to amount to something remarkably like a recognition of the 'cash nexus', which Marx identified as the main residual binding force of capitalist society well over a hundred years ago (1970, p. 120).

If workers are tied to their work only by their wage packets then their commitment to their jobs, and to everyday co-operation with management, seems to Westergaard to be a brittle one. 'The "cash nexus" may snap just because it is *only* a cash nexus – because it is single-stranded; and if it does snap, there is nothing else to bind the worker to acceptance of the situation'. Note, however, that Westergaard accepts the fact of workers' instrumentalism (suitably relabelled, of course, as the cash nexus). He is separated from the Luton team only by the interpretation he places upon this 'orientation to work' in terms of its potential for releasing large-scale discontent or militancy, which ultimately will become socialist radicalism. Instead of deducing socio-political quiescence from instrumentalism (by postulating privatization), Westergaard paints a picture of a working class precariously balanced between attitudes of co-operation or resignation, on the one hand, and a nascent class consciousness, for when the tenuous thread of the cash nexus is broken, on the other. Working-class instrumentalism is real enough. The dispute is about its implications for the timetabling of the revolution.

Problems of the current impasse

These discussions of working-class ambivalence and instrumentalism reveal the debate about the nature of working-class consciousness to be grinding to a confused and untimely halt. The current impasse is untimely because of the increasing weight given to the ideological or cultural sphere in explanations of the stability of advanced capitalist societies. This is true of commentators of the right as well as of the left. Even those who have argued that late capitalist societies are increasingly *unstable* have tended to rest their accounts on a developing conflict between the techno-economic, organizational, or social structural and the ideological, expressive-symbolic, or cultural spheres of social existence.[3] Both analyses rest on an implicit understanding of the social consciousness of the average worker-in-the-street. However, there is some confusion about the precise nature of the social consciousness in question. Sociologists are faced with contradictory assertions. On one hand, working-class perceptions of inequality are said to be highly limited, their understanding of an opaque hierarchy of rewards very unclear, and their reference groups extremely modest (W. G. Runciman, 1966); on the other hand, distributional conflict is purportedly the direct result of workers' great awareness of social and economic injustice and of a sophisticated understanding of their own strategic strengths in pursuing specific class interests (Goldthorpe, 1978). Confronted with these views, sociologists seem to be capable of little more than an intellectual shrug of the shoulders. ('Such is the nature of working-class ambivalence.')

Of course, critics have not been slow to identify specific weaknesses in the literature discussed above. Their attempts to move the discussion of working-class consciousness forward, however, have tended simply to reiterate a limited number of related, fairly well-established criticisms of earlier studies. Those most commonly voiced are the following.

The ontological status of the dependent variable – class consciousness – remains obscure

It has been widely suggested that insufficient thought has been given to exploring the possible differences between an image of society, subculture, orientation to work, and social or class consciousness. Elementary distinctions, such as that between the cognitive and evaluative aspects of 'moments' of class consciousness, have commonly been overlooked. Social imagery or consciousness can allegedly exist at many levels and can be differentiated in respect to several distinct spheres of social life, but little attempt has been made to distinguish these (see, for example, Nichols and Armstrong, 1976; Willener, 1975; Prandy, 1979; Stewart and Blackburn, 1975).

The sources of social imagery or consciousness are not fully explored

A number of important sources have been identified, and it remains to be seen if these can be incorporated within an overall framework. For example, little thought has been given to the question of relating sources in the immediate milieu to possible influences emanating from outside the occupational community or subculture, such as that of the mass media. Similarly, the possibility that different levels of imagery or consciousness might originate in different sources is not considered (see, for example, Martin and Fryer, 1973; Moore, 1975; Westergaard, 1975; Batstone, 1975; Scase, 1974).

The relationship between social imagery and social action is unclear

The debate here is principally about the extent to which social actors may be constrained by the structural context in which they act. If the degree of constraint is considerable, as has been suggested by R. M. Blackburn and Mann (1979), among others, then the highlighting of individual and collective value-orientations gives a falsely voluntaristic gloss to accounts of working-class life. Thus adherents of the 'action frame of reference' tend to interpret an accommodative world view as implying consensus with the status quo, when it might well be the result of a pragmatic compromise with it. In this respect the possibilities of feedback between experience, imagery, and situational context have not been satisfactorily explored. An overemphasis on class imagery at the expense of class action can perhaps be attributed to the widely held belief among academic observers that it is somehow necessary for men and women to encompass society intellectually before they can attempt to change it. This premise is not confirmed by the history of class action on either a revolutionary or on a more modest scale (see Stewart and Blackburn, 1975; Cousins and Davis, 1974; Chamberlain and Moorehouse, 1974 a and b).

The nature of class action is itself a matter of contention

A number of important distinctions have yet to be explored; for example, that between class solidarity and the sociability of mere friendship. Researchers may have mistaken the localistic, parochial solidarity of traditional, homogeneous, working-class communities as the political solidarity of a universalistic, class conscious proletariat. The former may, in fact, be in large part antithetical to the latter. Traditional working-class values of collective action, mutuality, and communal solidarity may simply be the instrumental response of a group of labourers to the realities of their market situation, to be modified if the context of their use changes, rather than a commitment to communal as opposed to individualistic concerns (see Westergaard, 1973 and 1975; Whelan, 1976; Goldthorpe in this volume).

Class consciousness and social imagery have been conceptualized in an unrealistically static and ahistorical manner

This is because little attempt has been made to show how consciousness in part emerges from, and may change in the light of, the past as well as the present experiences of everyday life. This problem is often illustrated by reference to Lockwood's ambiguities concerning the status and historical location of his threefold ideal-types of traditional proletarian, deferential, and privatized instrumental images of society. His ideal-typical approach, his suggestions of prototypicality, and even his terminology (*traditional* proletarian and deferential) are said to have confounded rather than shed light upon questions of chronology and historical process (see Nichols and Armstrong, 1976; Curran and Stanworth, 1979; Davis, 1979).

Research techniques that have been employed are probably not appropriate
More appropriate techniques are needed for the complexity of the interplay between immediate milieu and national context, or the interplay between consciousness, action, and structural context, to be grasped, or for the meaning to social actors of their friendships, work, and voting habits to be uncovered (see Bulmer, 1975; Edelman, 1980; Platt, 1971; Webb, 1973).

While these and other more particularistic criticisms may be well founded, they do not, of themselves, point towards future research strategies. Few positive suggestions as to how the debate might proceed have been made, and even these have remained programmatic, possibly because their authors are themselves committed to the framework within which discussion has thus far taken place. Blackburn and Mann, for example, after interviewing workers in Peterborough in 1971, quickly reached the rather significant conclusion that their survey methodology had successfully made itself obsolete. For further research into social consciousness they suggested that

our demonstration that coherent, consistent ideologies in the conventional sense do not exist now renders inadequate our kind of attitude survey data. . . . It is now necessary to move on to other methods because of our demonstration. . . . We need to know not simply the final result of whether workers are able to synthesise ideological contradictions, but also the process by which they attempt to do this. One method would be an intensive, though structured, set of discussions with individual workers, actually challenging them about contradictory lines of thought. Another would be discussions among groups of workers in which argument is encouraged. Complementing these would be projective techniques using hypothetical situations of ideological significance. Alongside these approaches there remains a need for more methodologically conscious studies of workers' responses to actual contradictory situations, not only the occasional dramatic strike but also more mundane day to day processes of accommodation (1975, p. 156).

Significantly, neither author has attempted, in the ten years since, to implement this research strategy, and both have continued to couch their published studies of workers' consciousness in a heavily modified, less voluntaristic, more dynamic, but still clearly recognizable orientations-to-work framework. Nor has the obsolescence of their research instrument prevented them from employing it, and the Peterborough data, to reconfirm Mann's earlier diagnosis of working-class consciousness as essentially pragmatic and ambivalent.

Thorough as many of these criticisms may appear to be, they do not offer a way out of the impasse that has been reached in studies of working-class consciousness precisely because they are not thoroughgoing enough. The currently fashionable theses of working-class ambivalence and pecuniary instrumentalism rest on analyses that share at least three serious shortcomings. These shortcomings have been much underplayed or, arguably, in some cases entirely overlooked. They concern the place of individual actors in the analyses, the model of consciousness underlying the various interpretations of working-class action, and a curious, almost paradoxical combination of an

107

implicit historicism with a lack of sensitivity to historical matters and processes.

The first of these might be called 'the problem of the disappearing subject'. The shortcomings of certain variants of contemporary Marxism are well documented in this regard and, indeed, are all too obvious, not only in contributions to the boundary debate, but also in accounts of ruling-class cultural or ideological hegemony. Poulantzas effectively sets the terms of the boundary debate, as far as the question of human agency is concerned, by his ruling that social classes are to be seen as objectively defined locations in the class structure rather than as discrete collections of individuals:

> The principal aspect of an analysis of social classes is that of their places in the class struggle; it is not that of the agents that compose them. Social classes are not empirical groups of individuals, social groups, that are 'composed' by simple addition; the relations of these agents among themselves are thus not inter-personal relations. The class membership of the various agents depends on the class places that they occupy: it is moreover distinct from the class origin, the social origin, of the agents (1979, p. 17).

Human subjects are simply the bearers of class relations. They occupy the places that are marked out in the structural determination of classes by relations of production, by political and ideological domination and sub-ordination, but social classes are not reducible either to the sum total of the individuals themselves or to the sum total of the interpersonal relations between them. Discussion of class *actors* is thus eliminated in favour of descriptions of abstractly defined class *locations*.

Poulantzas's structural definition of classes at the economic, political, and ideological levels (in terms of the distinctions between productive and unproductive, supervisory and non-supervisory, and mental and manual labour), especially when combined with the flexibility of concepts of relative autonomy and overdetermination, gives him great scope for identifying 'fractions' of classes as these are 'objectively' defined in the economic, political, and ideological spheres. So much so, that – as is demonstrated clearly by Lockwood in the previous chapter of this volume – his argument often dissolves into self-contradiction in the attempt simultaneously to distinguish the various class locations in terms of these instances and to remain true to a recognizably Marxist notion of materialism or economic determinism. Be that as it may, his 'structural super-determinism' reduces social actors to the status of simple executants of strategies imposed on them by the system. Dismissing the problematic of the subject as mere 'anthro-pologism' Poulantzas, following Althusser, maintains that the 'structure of relations of production determines the places and functions occupied and adopted by the agents of production, who are never anything more than the occupants of these places, in so far as they are supports of these functions' (1978a, p. 66).

Poulantzas's critics within the boundary debate, however much they may take him to task for shortcomings elsewhere, never succeed in recovering the individual subject for analysis. Wright's redescription of the class boundaries of advanced capitalist societies is simply a different way of conceptualizing the objective locations of the several social classes that comprise a particular social formation. Wright does not group people: he circumscribes locations. Unlike Poulantzas, however, he does not fall back upon the metaphysics of relative autonomy and overdetermination in order to render the social class locations he identifies mutually exclusive. He simply concedes, instead, a variety of contradictory class locations. Note that it is the locations within class relations that contain the contradictory elements. These are no less objectively specified than Poulantzas's own structural categories. Wright nowhere considers the possible problems raised by his argument that the class structure is in part peopled by contradictory agents.[4] Nor, perhaps, is this surprising, since as Poulantzas himself points out, it would be a perfect absurdity to say that a specific individual was both a proletarian and a bourgeois or both a manager and a worker. Wright's demarcation of class boundaries is simply 'an alternative way of dealing with . . . ambiguities in the class structure' by regarding 'some positions as occupying *objectively contradictory locations within class positions*'. It is an attempt 'to clarify the structure of positions defined by social relations of production' (as these are derived from Marxist theory) 'and to link these to other positions in the social structure' (Poulantzas, 1978b, p. 119). The concrete activities of real people or of groups of people and, more importantly, how they themselves define these activities are nowhere to be found.[5]

This is true also of accounts that paint the picture of a corporate working class imprisoned within the ideological terms imposed by the hegemonic capitalist or ruling classes. However, whereas the boundary theorists have eliminated subjects in favour of abstractly defined categories referred to as 'classes', hegemony theorists have achieved the same end by concentrating their attention on the internal structures of ideologies at the expense of their alleged effects. The most obvious example is provided by research into the media. An abundance of studies have demonstrated in increasing detail the bias of news bulletins, the hidden meanings of films and television programmes, and the dominant values reinforced in magazine articles and newspaper reports. Although great pains have been taken to unpack and expose the hegemonic values implicit in all of these, there is little research into the audience reactions of those who, it is assumed, internalize the message. The studies conducted by the Glasgow Media Group are entirely typical in this respect. Arguments about hegemony postulate subjects who are absorbing the devious meanings of the hegemonic medium, but it is only the message itself that is scrutinized. We are left to assume that, by some social or psychological process, hegemonic values are unproblematically internalized by the working class and that they shape the consciousness of its individual members. For all the talk of 'mechanisms of reproduction' and 'processes of ideological subordination', detailed analysis of the actual dynamics of such reproduction is conspicuously absent. (One notable exception is Paul Willis's study of how working-class boys 'learn to labour', to which we shall return below.) Moreover, as both Goldthorpe in this volume and Stanley Cohen

(1980) have pointed out, where such an analysis is offered, it usually amounts to little more than a redescription of known facts in a new, and more impressive, language. Many of the descriptions of cultural hegemony produced under the auspices of the Centre for Contemporary Cultural Studies at the University of Birmingham, for example, employ the language of neo-Gramscian Marxism favoured by that institution simply to restate facts of working-class quiescence rather than to explain them.

More seriously, proponents of the hegemony thesis are guilty of an ecological fallacy when they transfer uncritically the hegemonic characteristics of an ideology or 'ideological apparatus' to the individuals who purportedly internalize that ideology or 'bear' it. This type of methodological error is evident in both Marxist and 'bourgeois' models of 'hegemonic ambivalence'. The interpretation of working-class consciousness offered by Mann thus rests on the unjustified assumption that the contradictions evident in the cumulative findings of a variety of studies into value commitments indicate contradictions between the values subscribed to by the individuals studied. From the obviously inconsistent preferences and beliefs of the various *samples*, drawn across two continents and over a period of twenty years, Mann draws the conclusion that 'working class *individuals* . . . exhibit less internal *consistency* in their values than middle-class people' (1982, p. 388). For example, faced with two samples of Secondary Modern school children, one of which reports 88 per cent of respondents agreeing that 'hard work (and not luck or influence) is how to get on' while the other reports only 30 per cent concurring with the proposition that 'status is achieved by effort', Mann concludes that the working-class children are ambivalent in their commitments. This is explained in terms of the contradictory values to which they are exposed by the school as an agent of manipulative socialization and by their family or peers as representatives of the 'populist deviant tradition'. Mann is here guilty of committing at least two types of ecological fallacy: one, aggregating data over social groups and over time and, two, imputing the correlations found among groups to the individuals comprising them (see Robinson, 1950). Associations computed from group means or proportions cannot, of course, be taken as valid estimates of the associations that would be derived from individual data. The ecological associations between social classes and a range of contradictory beliefs or values tell us nothing about the individual worker and his or her particular attributes. Mann's unit of analysis is the group – he has data about group attributes – but he persistently applies his conclusions both to the groups themselves and to the individuals that comprise them. Instead of theorizing about ambivalent or consistent groups, he theorizes additionally, and erroneously, about ambivalent or consistent individuals.

Mann is not alone in using this kind of ecological reasoning. Several of the contributors to the discussion stimulated by Lockwood's paper, 'Sources of variation in working-class images of society', switch levels and units of analysis in mid-exposition in precisely this manner. Roberts and his colleagues, in their account of the 'fragmentary class structure', report data about the characteristics of the several groups that comprise this structure but apply their results indiscriminately both to the groups themselves and to the individual employees or workers within them. This slippage is frequent, though unobtrusive, throughout the analysis. Close scrutiny of their text reveals that the socio-political, ideological, and cognitive dispositions of 'proletarian', 'central working-class', 'middle-class', and other groups have generated 'the proletarian worker' and 'bourgeois manual worker', in short, a series of individual employees, each of whom is apparently imbued with the precise characteristics of the group as a whole (see Roberts *et al*, 1977, ch. 3). The ecological reasoning of such studies does not necessarily invalidate their conclusions regarding working-class ambivalence. It does mean, however, that their conclusions do not follow from the data that are presented.[6] They do not do so in large part because of the absence of individual subjects as legitimate units of analysis, rather than as hypothetical constructs or statistical artifacts derived from group aggregates.

Theorists of working-class consciousness who have diagnosed instrumentalism display an equally marked tendency to lose their subjects, but for a rather different reason. If the ambivalent worker is often the simple aggregate of a variety of *divergent group* characteristics then the instrumental worker appears to be the result of a shallow arraying of data for each *individual* along a *single* dimension. That so many working-class respondents, when asked about their orientation to work, choose to answer in pecuniary and instrumental terms should not, after all, come as a surprise to sociologists. Numerous studies have confirmed: that the great majority of manual workers have almost no control over their own fate; that employers tend to treat labour as simply one more commodity in the production process, to be controlled, exploited, and disposed of when it is rendered superfluous; that most unskilled and many skilled jobs are boring, physically exhausting, and mentally debilitating; that many workers expect to be made unemployed at least once if not several times during their working lives, an expectation all too frequently realized; and that huge numbers of people, many more than ever appear on welfare state casualty lists, are engaged in a permanent struggle to maintain living standards only just this side of poverty. Yet the same workers live in the consumer-oriented, status-conscious societies of the affluent West, exhorted at every turn to acquire goods and services that are available only in exchange for money and that, as they are also constantly reminded, others around them have already secured even if they themselves have not.

Under these circumstances the thesis of working-class instrumentalism may be true, but it seems trivially so. It does little more than restate the obvious: the dictates of a modern market economy ensure that workers are interested in their pay-packets. Of course workers will, more often than not, articulate their ambitions and worries in pecuniary terms. Since money is increasingly the generalized medium of exchange in capitalist societies, people are constrained to think in monetary terms. The question is, what do these monies mean to the individuals concerned? Having discovered that workers

111

are, with good cause, concerned about the size and security of their pay-packets, some sociologists have simply declared their investigations closed, instead of pursuing them further to probe the wants, preferences, feelings, interests, or even the cynicism that lies behind this. The interview schedule for the Affluent Worker study, for example, asks a great many questions about the workers' perceptions – of their jobs, of the role of their unions, of the profitability and structure of their firms, and of the hierarchical structure of society generally – but very few were designed to elicit the workers' feelings about these topics. Nor is there much opportunity for the respondents to explain why they do or do not vote Labour, would or would not strike for better conditions, and do or do not own a refrigerator. This general failure to distinguish cognitive, practical and ethical judgements is surprising, since Goldthorpe himself has pointed to the difficulties involved in deducing value-commitments and changes in these from behaviour and changes in behaviour, which may simply be a pragmatic response to particular circumstances.[7]

Despite Goldthorpe's warnings elsewhere against the strictures of essentialism, his most recent account of working-class instrumentalism rests ultimately on the model of an unchanging instrumentally oriented worker, whose ability to pursue his or her essential interest in money is governed entirely by changes in the social structure that are unrelated to workers' demands:

I would maintain that over recent decades the generally rising rate of inflation reflects a situation in which conflict between social groups and strata has become *more intense* and also to some extent *more equally matched*, with these two tendencies interacting in a mutually reinforcing way. Less advantaged groups and strata have tended to become more free of various constraints on their actions in pursuit of what they see as their interests. . . .

Once, therefore, this analytical context is established, it is possible for rank-and-file 'pushfulness', distributional dissent, union militancy and 'irresponsibility' etc., all to be viewed in a rather different way to that of the economists . . . it no longer seems so necessary, in attempting to account for such phenomena, to invoke new cultural or ideological currents sweeping across the Western world, nor to give such prominence to rapidly rising expectations and to the psychological effects (however characterized) of the failure to realize them. It is not so much that *new* influences on wage- and salary-earners and their organizations need to be recognized, but rather the disappearance of old ones – that is, the weakening of the inhibitions formerly imposed by the status order . . . (1978, pp. 195–6 and 200–1).

Somewhere between the Affluent Worker Series and the above diagnosis of the causes of inflation, the excessive voluntarism of the worker freely accommodating his or her chosen orientation to work has given way to a model of the natural condition of capitalist humankind, in which workers are essentially rational economic actors whose ability to realize their pecuniary passions is wholly determined by changes in the structural order of the wider society. Ironically, one of the leading exponents of the action frame of reference is here guilty of a straightforward structural determinism.

Working-class instrumentalism can be and has been identified in every era of capitalist development (see, for example, Crossick, 1978, ch. 7). What money has meant to the individuals concerned, however, has varied considerably, to say the least. The 'strike-happy' line-workers at Ford's Halewood plant in the 1960s, with one eye on the clock and the other on their pay-packets, appeared to be concerned with 'money and nothing else'. But responses to questions about the nature of work and the role of management, responses that were at first sight indicative of pure instrumentalism, could readily be seen as imbued with a moral dimension when they were placed in the context of the plant and its history. Monetary demands often had a moral or political meaning for the workers at the factory. For example, the company 'ought not' to ask the men to rearrange their shifts, or change their work-practices, without offering extra payments; it was 'morally wrong' of management simply to impose decisions on shop-floor workers regardless of their feelings (Beynon 1980). Just as empirical research has shown that the meaning of a strike can vary among different respondents at the same time, or the same respondents at different times, so the meaning of a wage demand, or an instrumental attitude to work in general, can vary in the same way. Demands for increased remuneration may be based on conceptions of fairness, equality and comparability, incomparability (the justice of 'main-taining differentials'), what is customary (taken-for-granted increase in money-wages), or a wide variety of other values and aspirations. A single form or strand of a social relationship can be imbued with an enormous variety of meanings and therefore with a variable content (see Gilbert, 1981, p. 188 and Sahlins, 1974, chs. 4 and 5). Unless working-class instrumentalism is located firmly in its contexts, and unless some attempt is made to penetrate the one-dimensional and entirely predictable pecuniary responses generated by attitude surveys about social consciousness and orientations to work, the hypothesis imputing an economistic mode of consciousness to the working class remains unsubstantiated. We simply cannot say, on the basis of the Luton and similar material, whether it is Goldthorpe or Westergaard who has imputed the correct meaning to declarations of pecuniary intent.[8]

The curiously one-dimensional nature of the subjects of the instrumentalist model raises, in turn, the question of how both schools of thought have conceptualized the phenomenon of class consciousness – revolutionary or otherwise. Throughout the debate, 'consciousness' has tended to remain something strangely ethereal. While all talk has been of grounding it in the experiences and practices of everyday life, of locating its social origins firmly in the immediate or distant milieux of social and cultural life, often it has been located in this manner at the front door only to slip out again, spirit-like, at the back. Earlier contributors to the debate adopted a strict dualism with respect to social experience, which was viewed as comprising distinct subjective and objective elements, namely, people's consciousness of society and the structural sources of this. J. C. Leggett, attempting to assess the effects of ethnicity and geographical mobility (uprootedness) on working-class consciousness, measured the latter as a series of verbal responses to attitudinal questions, which he then scaled as four mental states in a linear progression from class verbalization, to scepticism, to militancy, and, finally, to egalitarianism (1965, pp. 235–47). In this way class consciousness became detached from class experience except as a spiritual reflection of it. Certain structural features relating to social-class membership (the nature of work situations, occupational communities, and the like) automatically generated an awareness of the world that, though not entirely free-floating, was permanently at a distance from other aspects of social experience and that was held in place only by a limited number of rigid and readily identifiable guy-ropes. Consciousness was something akin to a knapsack carried around on one's back – or, in this case, in one's head – and dipped into when the occasion demanded. Furthermore, this detachment of social consciousness from social action was reinforced by a related tendency to view 'images of society' or an 'awareness of the world' as something static, as unchangingly determined by the objective characteristics of which it was the reflection, a problem to which I shall return below.

While later commentators were quick to condemn this crude dualism, it is by no means clear that they themselves transcended it. Newby, for example, rejected the conventional approach to the study of deference, which took deferential ideology to be '*an attribute*' of individual actors guiding their social and political conduct. He proposes, instead, to move 'away from the study of deferential *people* to the study of deferential *relationships*: who defers to whom, under what circumstances and over what issues', in order to avoid the 'fallacious correspondence [of] deferential attitudes and deferential people'. His purpose is to ground social consciousness in everyday life and in the historical process as to avoid conceiving of consciousness as each individual's neatly packaged, discrete collection of attitudes and attributes, a 'comprehensive and monolithic ideological system which they bring to bear on the various situations which they find themselves in and which determines their actions accordingly'. 'Indeed', Newby continues, 'the evidence on the sources of variation in images of society suggests the reverse: rather than a coherent ideological system guiding the actor's relationships, deference, or other class ideologies, can be seen as emerging *from* a particular set of relationships':

As far as deference is concerned, this suggests that the concept should be considered not as an ideological attribute of individual workers but as typifying certain relationships which they enter into, and how situational factors affect these. Thus deference is best considered not merely as a particular form of behaviour, since this ignores the problem of its meaning to the actor, not as a set of attributes, since this is too over-deterministic, but as a form of social interaction. Specifically deference can best be defined as the form of social interaction which occurs in situations involving the exercise of traditional authority. . . . This seems to do less violence to an understanding of how the agricultural worker lives out his daily life than either of the other two approaches to the concept (1979, pp. 381, 385–6, 416).

However, having in this way tied social consciousness inseparably to social action, at least in so far as deference and deferential relationships are concerned, Newby subsequently detaches it again, in an attempt to relate his findings to the general debate about the nature of working-class consciousness as a whole. The contradictory strands in the social relationships between farmer and farm worker are reflected spontaneously in the ambivalent world-view of the farm worker, which has, once again, taken on the incorporeal qualities of an ideology:

. . . many agricultural workers lacked any single abstract model of society which constituted their entire social consciousness. Instead, many seemed to operate with a multiplicity of images and half-formed beliefs and opinions which did not add up to any single coherent image. . . . They did not have one image of society which provided a constant point of reference, but many, a particular model being utilized when it seemed to best explain the issue in question. . . . Although many agricultural workers do hold what appears to be a coherent and easily identifiable image of society, there are many who do not. They either hold a multiplicity of class images from which they will draw upon the one most appropriate to explain a particular social context, or they hold no overall image of society at all. . . . This fragmented form of social consciousness was the most typical of the images of society among the farm workers who were interviewed (1979, pp. 387–8, 394, 402, 405–6).

Social consciousness has, once again, become detached from social action; and, if attitude questions elicit a series of apparently contradictory responses, then clearly they originate in a knapsack, the contents of which must be hopelessly jumbled.

The legacy of dualism emerges even more forcefuly in Howard H. Davis's recent *Beyond Class Images* (1979). Here, the author adopts the theoretical framework of Alain Touraine's 'Actionalism' explicitly to transcend the dualism of opposing consciousness to structure. 'What is required', in Davis's eyes, 'is a theory of the constitution of meaning and a method to establish the underlying unity between the analysis of social situations on the one hand and the knowledge of opinions and attitudes on the other'. In Touraine's theory of action Davis finds a conception of consciousness as 'a way of defining the labour *movement*', which becomes apparent at various levels, including not only 'the participation of individuals in the process of constitution of meaning and values', but also the particular 'projects' of individual actors. In other words, and simplifying drastically the arguments of both Davis and Touraine, we may say that consciousness is inseparable from action:

. . . if the analysis of action begins with social relations, as Touraine intends, consciousness can also be interpreted as a relation: not just the recognition by an actor of his place in a social situation but a property of social action at the highest social level (the system of historical action), the consciousness of labour in seeking to recognize itself and to be recognized through its products, the 'will to freedom and the struggle against alienation, against the opaqueness of society which is forgetful of its own process of constitution'. Just as the notion of social action is an instrument of analysis and not a way of describing behaviour, 'workers' consciousness' is an analytic and not a descriptive term (Davis, 1979, pp. 40–1).

Be that as it may, it does not prevent Davis from subsequently offering an entirely conventional account of working-class consciousness, in which maintenance fitters, steelworkers, and clerical workers are described as possessing, respectively, a 'craft', 'proletarian', and 'collusive' consciousness.

115

Despite his repeated insistence that social consciousness 'can only be understood properly as part of a wider system of social action', Davis slips throughout into the customary usage. Thus, a person's consciousness becomes a distinct though discarnate entity, which, for example, gives more weight to certain topics than to others, which can be constituted from materials of the worker's own experience or from external ready-made images, and which, as each individual's dominant consciousness, is to be set against his or her action. Once again, as in the case of Newby's analysis of deference, a critical attempt to theorize the relationship between action, structure, and consciousness ends in a neo-Hegelian reification of consciousness in a manner barely distinguishable from that practised by earlier proponents of a crude structure–consciousness dualism.

The attempt to transcend this dualism by introducing the concept of action raises, of course, the whole question of the dynamic nature of social reality. What are we to make of the copious references in the literature on class consciousness to the necessity of understanding this phenomenon in the light of 'the full complexities of the historical process'? Here again, it seems to me, spectators on the sidelines of the debate must be careful to distinguish between what the participants claim to be doing and what, in reality, they succeed in doing. In much of the writing on working-class consciousness, insufficient attention has been given to individual biography and historical context and to the dynamic relationship between structure, action, and consciousness, as these have conventionally been distinguished.

The importance of taking into account the 'career trajectories' or social mobility experiences of working-class subjects in an attempt to identify the sources of their values and orientations has long been emphasized. R. F. Hamilton (1965), for example, argued that the values and behaviour of skilled manual workers were similar to those of unskilled manual workers, but wholly unlike those of white-collar workers, and that this could be explained in terms of the common 'unskilled manual' social origins of the skilled workers in question. A deviant group of middle-class-oriented skilled manual workers was found generally to have been recruited via downward mobility from white-collar backgrounds: genuine 'converts' from blue-collar to white-collar values and behaviour were a minor exception to this pattern. Job-histories, home-life and school-life experiences, position in family, personal life-cycles, and histories of geographical mobility have also been investigated with a view to determining their impact on orientations to work, images of society, and class consciousness. There has thus been a broad recognition that '"orientations to work" can most usefully be seen as likely to change as a result of new social experiences and changes in social situation' (Brown, 1976, p. 31).

In practice, however, the great majority of commentators have been reluctant to adopt a genuinely historical approach to the study of social consciousness and how it is generated and sustained. As both Goldthorpe and Lockwood demonstrate in this volume, Marxists are prevented from doing so because a genuine sensitivity to historical processes would present difficulties for the implicit historical determinism that informs their analyses. Such criticisms seem to be well founded. Wright, for instance, insists that 'many positions in the class structure have essentially a zero-probability of being mapped into certain class formations: bourgeois positions, for example, cannot be organised into working class trade unions or revolutionary socialist parties'. He adds the rider that

this does not mean, of course, that individuals who occupy bourgeois class locations cannot support trade unions or, for that matter, join revolutionary socialist parties. Engels is a classic example of a bourgeois who, as an individual, played an important role in working class organisations. But the position itself cannot be mapped into trade unions or working class parties. When Engels died, there was no reason whatsoever for the next incumbent of his bourgeois class location to be tied to the working class. When an industrial worker dies, there are systematic social forces which link the next incumbent of the same position to working class organisations. It is important throughout this discussion to remember that the analysis refers to the forging of social relations between positions, not simply between individuals. Both processes are important, but the logic of positions has an analytical priority over the analysis of individual relations within these positions (1978, p. 106).

In this remarkable paragraph Wright succeeds, in the space of a few sentences, both in legitimizing the interventionist activities of radical socialist intellectuals (his own included) and in defining away as epiphenomenal such apparently inconsequential matters as working-class conservatism and strike-breaking, intra-working-class conflict along gender or racial lines, and the proletarian nationalism displayed on the battlefields of Flanders and on the beaches of Normandy. The next step in this logic, which accords ontological priority to theory over the everyday practices of historical subjects, is, of course, to distinguish 'real' or 'objective' interests from 'immediate' interests or from merely subjective 'preferences'. The floodgates of 'false consciousness' are then opened with all the many and familiar problems associated with that concept and a teleology is established whereby all interpretations of working-class consciousness must start from the assumption that 'socialist theory . . . is a form of consciousness which is . . . active and . . . mass-based (i.e. it is not the preserve of a socialist intellectual elite)' (Downing, 1979, p. 129). The complexities of the historical process are thus eliminated in favour of the certainties that accompany the axioms of socialist historicism.

Mainstream proponents of working-class ambivalence and instrumentalism also succeed in exorcising history, but they do so by somewhat different means. While sociologists of the various neo-Weberian stances represented by Goldthorpe, Parkin, Mann, Lockwood, and Newby have rightly condemned the strictures imposed by Marxist and Marxisant historicism, they have been seriously constrained by the methodological limitations inherent in their own approach. Despite their eloquent testimonies to the historical nature of sociology elsewhere (Lockwood, 1960; Goldthorpe, 1977), they have adopted, in practice, the extreme Weberian position of distinguishing sociology from history and defining the purpose of sociology as the construction of ahistorical 'types'. Weber himself, despite his programmatic identification of discrete

117

subjects (for sociology, the empirical uniformities of typical modes of action and, for history, significant individual events), was far too astute an observer of social reality to follow his own precept. His sociologies of religion, law, domination, and legitimacy are distinguished by their pursuit of individual historical explanations, through comparative analysis, for the emergence of particular social phenomena. Irrespective of what he may have set out to do in theory, Weber's ideal-types of such concepts as the 'Protestant Ethic' and the 'Spirit of Capitalism' are historically situated, and his causal explanation of how changes in one led to changes in the other rests, in practice, on an historical analysis of a series of developments in the great world religions and economies (see Weber, 1968, p. 29; compare Marshall, 1982).

Contributors to the debate about working-class consciousness in the mainstream of sociology seem to have followed Weber's theory rather than his practice. The underlying premise of their approach is that there exist identifiable value-complexes, images of society, or types of social consciousness that can be related directly to highly visible factors in the actor's immediate social milieu. Earlier commentators, up to and including Lockwood, accorded ontological or theoretical priority to a limited number of such factors and then ignored the question of changes in these. Lockwood's own tendency to reify his ideal-typical images of society while remaining ambivalent about their precise historical locations has been commented on above. The historical and sociological realities reflected in his types subsequently, and not unreasonably, became a matter of some dispute. Sensitivity to the historical process demanded that the significant milieu be extended beyond the confines of immediate occupational, familial, and local communities to include each individual's past experiences and present expectations. The problem, then, was to analyse the complex effects on identifiable images of a proliferation of historical variables (experiences of geographical, occupational, and social mobility, patterns of socialization, family and home-life, and so forth) within the limits imposed by conventional attitude surveys or structured interview schedules and by the dualism of opposing structure to typical consciousness. The solution has been to adopt one (or a combination) of several alternative strategies in order to simplify the analysis.

Thus, those who concede that working-class consciousness can be affected by a large number of diverse influences prefer to diagnose consciousness itself as ambivalent. At a certain point in the analysis the profusion of causal factors requires the delineation of a multiplicity of types of consciousness, which commentators are either not prepared to pursue or apparently find it unconvincing to document. If people are exposed to diverse, confusing, and contradictory influences, then it is pronounced reasonable to expect them to display diverse, confused, and contradictory thoughts about these. The complexities of working-class consciousness are therefore dissolved by such as Mann and Parkin, into ambivalence, self-contradiction, and volatility (although little attempt is made to identify the reasoning or processes behind such volatility). Others, like Newby, preface a conventional and ahistorical account of the effects of a limited number of factors in the actors' immediate milieu on their social consciousness with an entirely unrelated section entitled 'The historical context'. In this way, the history of agricultural labour between 1851 and 1971 becomes the subject of one study, while the work and market situations and social consciousness of farm workers in 1971 are isolated as that of another. Somewhere between the two are lost the life histories and previous experiences of Newby's respondents, along with their present reflections on unfulfilled ambitions, their aspirations changed or reaffirmed, their expectations met or unrealized, and their projects for the future. Still others adopt Goldthorpe's strategy, and postulate a working class made up of subjects who possess constant wants and interests (originating in an unspecified source or sources). Apparent changes in workers' demands and behaviour can therefore be explained only by reference to changes in the present system of constraints holding these in check. Goldthorpe's instrumentalists, like the ambivalent workers uncovered by Newby, Mann, and Parkin, appear to be almost entirely devoid of a biography. Their essential humanity, as beings capable of rational changes in beliefs and behaviour following self-reflection or changes in the world about them, would seem to be denied. This, too, is a form of historicism, for it leaves working-class consciousness without the complexities of historical processes, detached from class practices or action and, if only by implication, unaffected by changes in these.

Conclusion

I have argued that recent studies of working-class consciousness have converged on two broad interpretations, one based on workers' instrumentalism and the other on workers' ambivalence. These theses, whether formulated explicitly or hidden within accounts of working-class incorporation or heterogeneity, lend present discussions of workers' consciousness an air of exhaustion. After all, if workers are uniformly ambivalent or unambiguously pecuniary in proclivity, what more is there to say on the matter? In view of the prominence of the concept of ideology in many of the current macro-theories of advanced capitalist society, such an impasse is untimely and confusing. Moreover, despite extensive discussion, commentators have tended to understate at least three related weaknesses that appear to be common to the analyses of the leading proponents of both theses and that cast some doubt upon their respective interpretations of their data. The next question obviously must concern the possibilities for repairing these weaknesses. How might one more profitably study working-class consciousness in a manner that neither eliminates the subjects of the analysis nor detaches them artificially from a consciousness that is reified and suspended outside the aknowledged complexities of the dynamic social reality in which we all live?

An appropriate research strategy must first address the problems arising out of the analytical priority accorded thus far to the dichotomous couplet of structure–consciousness. The principal consequence of this has been to squeeze the notion of social action out of analytical framework. This, in turn, has reinforced the idea that consciousness is a discrete component of social reality carried around inside people's heads and dipped into at pertinent moments. The underdevelopment of the concept of social action has also given the debate its ahistorical taint. There has been little sense of progress, of reflective social actors engaging social structures in ways that might change their awareness and evaluation of their social world.

The first step toward more constructive research into the nature of working-class consciousness, therefore, must be to reintroduce social action into the analysis. Research strategies that detach consciousness from action are forever fated to generate images of society that are as much an artifact of the research instrument – the particular wording of questions, their perceived level of generality, topicality, and so on – as they are a genuine attribute of the working-class subject. Consciousness is generated in and changed by social action. Consciousness is, in fact, an integral component of social action rather than a distant something that somehow causes or is caused by it. The two cannot be studied in isolation. Experience has shown that it is the relationships between attitudes and actions that are important and that these can only be studied contextually (see Schuman and Johnson, 1976).

Social actors neither automatically translate professed attitudes into actions consistent with those attitudes nor behave in a manner unambiguously indicative of consciously held values or beliefs. Between statements of cognition or evaluation and patterns of social conduct lies a complexity of conditions that make the relationship between beliefs and action indeterminate and, in each case, a matter for empirical investigation. Actors may be constrained or may perceive themselves to be constrained by such things as lack of material resources, the requirements of some normative order, or by subjection to the power of others. Moreover, these constraints are not necessarily constant and may prevent the pursuit or realization of particular value-complexes at one time but not at another. Partial attainment of desired ends may then change the subject's perception or evaluation of these ends or of the ordering of the social world (see, for example, Kornblum, 1974; Cumbler, 1979). Since there is no necessary correlation between speech and action, satisfactory explanations of either require independent evidence as to both the action and the subject's perception of it. Without regressing to the complete relativism of an ethnomethodological analysis of the indexical characteristics of all speech, it is nevertheless true that language is not self-evidently meaningful. Its meanings are always a function of its use: its intended audience, the circumstances under which it is employed, and so forth. This is true of statements of political awareness and belief no less than any other. Working-class consciousness cannot therefore be studied, in the abstract, using highly structured attitude surveys or isolated interviews. It must be investigated as a component or dimension of everyday class practices (see, for example, Cumbler, 1979; Beynon, 1980; and Willis, 1979).

A second step for investigating working-class beliefs about the nature of social hierarchy is an awareness that there is no a priori reason why class consciousness should be measured according to a datum provided by one, albeit eminent, nineteenth-century theorist of early capitalism. The theoretical frameworks of classical sociology may continue to serve the discipline well in other areas but the concept of class consciousness that can be extrapolated from Marxist and Marxisant social theory is patently no longer appropriate to the economic, political, and ideological realities of advanced capitalism in the West. Only if one assumes an elective affinity between the working class and socialism, thus engaging in the type of historical determinism rightly criticized by Goldthorpe, does it make sense to suppose that working-class consciousness must necessarily take the form of allegiance to a socialist party or programme. Class-conscious workers may, in fact, go beyond the 'economism' of wage claims to raise class issues and to press class demands for fundamental changes in the social order, but these issues and demands may not be in the particular direction of socialist alternatives. They can as easily take the form of a movement toward distributive social justice within the framework of the capitalist mode of production. What is therefore required is an analysis of political beliefs, of perceptions of hierarchy, and so on, that does more than merely scale these phenomena as a series of stages *en route* to revolutionary socialist consciousness. To study class consciousness as if it were a simple continuum from right to left, or from trades union to political-revolutionary awareness, is to exclude an enormous variety of other dimensions of class consciousness.

As a third step, we need to uncover the ways in which subjects take up particular beliefs, as well as to document the content of the beliefs themselves. Workers' responses to sociologists' questions are not all of one piece; they may perform a variety of cognitive, emotional, and social functions for the subject. They may be a complex mixture of *ex post facto* self-directed rationalizations for earlier or projected conduct, attempts to present a favourable image to an audience, spur-of-the-moment opinion slightly held, positive preferences long subscribed to, fatalistic restatements of the recognizably unavoidable, or cherished hopes and ambitions that render difficult circumstances tolerable (see, for example, Chinoy, 1955, pp. 123–34). What has been rather too simply conceptualized as a single or unitary phenomenon – an image of society, an orientation to work, a class consciousness – is, in reality, a diverse collection of subjective components of action, performing a variety of functions for the subject, and employed by him or her with varying degrees of awareness. Sociologists therefore must employ research instruments that are capable of distinguishing between, for example, unanalysed stereotypes, whimsical reflections, beliefs founded on misinformation or ignorance, cynical or authentic attempts to preserve favourable images of self, and reasoned conclusions often verified by the exigencies of everyday life.

These requirements suggest to me that research energies and resources should be channelled in the direction of intensive, longitudinal ethnography, in which different aspects of consciousness are located firmly in the context of class practices – everyday work at the factory, leisure time at home and in the club, the recent protest, the strike – and conceptualized at the outset as inherently dynamic phenomena. Such studies must be based on the realization that class consciousness, like class itself, is a relational phenomenon. It does not exist as a separate entity with a reality *sui generis* but only as consciousness *of* something: of the structures that impinge on workers' lives and the opportunities for action within these. The necessity of uncovering the diverse ways in which components of an awareness and evaluation (or consciousness) of the social order are taken up, employed, and perhaps subsequently disregarded, requires intensive observation and interviewing of respondents over an extended period of time. Qualitative techniques alone, among sociological research methods, are capable of uncovering the relationship between attitudes and actions that is class consciousness.

A variety of such techniques can and should be used: group discussion, participant observation, intensive interviewing on a series of occasions. These are complementary rather than mutually exclusive. For example, the in-depth interviews with workers in 'Eastport' conducted by Robert Lane (1962) would suggest that the ambivalence or instrumentalism revealed in more perfunctory exchanges between respondent and investigator may simply be the gloss on a more sophisticated understanding of the world, and of one's position within it. Ambivalence may turn out to be nothing less than a conscious refusal to extend personal experiences indiscriminately to situations about which one has only limited information: it may be indicative of intellectual openness and sophistication as much as lack of understanding. Probing may reveal apparently contradictory beliefs to be entirely consistent and the result of contextual thinking and applications of general principles – again, perhaps, an indication of intellectual maturity rather than confusion. Willingness to accept conflicting accounts of the world may be a purposeful act of democratic goodwill rather than a testimony to the effects of ruling-class ideological hegemony. Conversely, as Michael Burawoy discovered, workers' testimonies concerning their own exploitation, which appear to indicate a mature class consciousness, may when examined carefully, be nothing more than anger narrowly focused on a management team that has 'cheated' on the informally agreed rules for the game of 'making out' at work. Unlike working-class consciousness, may, when examined carefully, be nothing more than anger altering the institutional order of the capitalist labour process (see, for example, Burawoy, 1979, pp. 82 ff). These and similar possibilities can only be assessed and cross-checked in extended observations of everyday life, group discussions, and in the construction and reconstruction of life histories.

Is this simply to reiterate the familiar plea for a proper balance between the validity sought through intensive fieldwork techniques and the reliability guaranteed by statistically sophisticated social surveys? I think not. It is difficult to see how the shortcomings of social surveys, as a means of studying class consciousness, can be overcome simply by a more thorough piloting of survey questions or a more careful aggregation of survey data. It is not that qualitative research of the kind here advocated *complements* surveys in this field. Rather, such research provides a more suitable *alternative* to the large-scale survey, and it generates data that the latter are incapable of uncovering no matter how much care is taken in piloting the survey and in compiling the questions. Survey research cannot report on action directly observed; consciousness can only be studied contextually as a component of class practices; therefore surveys are inappropriate to the study of class consciousness.

Of course intensive ethnographic studies have their own problems. Although Paul Willis does unpack at least some of the processes by which cultural hegemony might be reproduced, there is no denying that his theory of cultural forms and social reproduction rests upon the observed activities of but four people. The most important aspects of his thesis are invariably illustrated by reference to the lives of two working-class boys, Joey and Spanksy, and their respective fathers. It is obviously an open question as to how representative his subjects are of the working class in general. In a similar study, William Kornblum became part of the blue-collar community he writes about. His own life became entangled in the lives of his subjects. Kornblum the sociologist and Kornblum the steelworker are indistinguishable in the text: the analyst metamorphosed into a partisan and became a deeply committed organizer of the very local political competitions he had set out to study. To doubts about Willis's reliability may be added reservations about Kornblum's validity. It is quite possible that the alleged working-class culture of South Chicago residents is in some part the creation of the sociologist rather than of his respondents. This may also be true of the shop-floor culture of machine operators at the Allied Corporation plant studied by Burawoy – although in this instance for the converse reason that we know absolutely nothing about the nature of the investigator's relation to his subjects. In both cases the coherence, dimensions, and meanings of blue-collar lives may be no less a child of the sociologist than working-class ambivalence is the artifact of a rigid and narrowly focused interview schedule. Still, there is no reason in principle to suppose that the possible weaknesses of these particular accounts points to insuperable difficulties for the ethnographer of working-class life. Recognized ways exist, and new ways can be found, for controlling the narrator and for determining the nature of his or her influence. It is difficult, however, to see any means by which the techniques of the social survey can be improved upon, such that they might more adequately uncover the realities of a phenomenon as complex as a class consciousness.

It has not been the purpose of this chapter to offer tidy solutions to such fundamental issues of sociology as those of validity and reliability or methodological individualism and holism. It has had the infinitely more modest objective of highlighting some of the principal problems of studying class consciousness. If I have gone some way beyond this by arguing for the revival of ethnography in studies of working-class consciousness, that is emphatically not because I believe that instrumental and ambivalent workers are entirely the fictitious creations of inappropriate research methodologies. I maintain, simply, that these conclusions do not follow unambiguously from the data currently offered, that their widespread acceptance in the sociological community helps perpetuate the practice of sociology as an historically insensitive discipline oriented more to the construction of neat and tidy theories or schemata than to understanding the complexities of everyday life, and that a more appropriate and productive research strategy for the study of class consciousness is available and ought therefore to be more widely employed. In this way we might at least begin the difficult task of reconciling theory and empirical research in this field. To call for sociological ethnography, and hence to draw the discipline (in this area at least) closer to a narrative mode and away from the numerical precision of large-scale social surveys, may be academically unfashionable or even politically unwise, given the current intellectual climate and the widespread agitation in favour of 'hard' rather than 'soft' techniques. But if these are the costs of achieving a more satisfactory answer to the questions posed by Machiavelli and Hobbes, then so be it.

Notes and references

1 It is worth noting that one of the principal difficulties in arriving at a systematic overview of the various studies of working-class consciousness is the tendency among leading authorities to change their position on key issues in the course of their analyses. The authors of the Affluent Worker Series are noted for this: see Benson, (1978); Mackenzie (1974); and Davis and Cousins (1975).

2 The idea that working-class consciousness is ambivalent because it rests on two sets of values – a manifest version of the dominant value system and latent, intermittently drawn upon, oppositional values – has been widely employed in order to explain away contradictions between responses to specific and abstract attitudinal questions posed in surveys of the lower classes and between statements of belief elicited in surveys and behaviour observed in practice. In addition to Rodman (1971), see Erikson (1976).

3 See, for example, Bell (1976); Habermas (1975); Shils (1981); Hirsch (1978); and Offe (1976). In parallel fashion, many historians have argued that one characteristic feature of early capitalist-industrial societies was a conflict between the traditionalistic culture of the pre-industrial work-habits and leisure-habits of first-generation factory labourers and the new work-discipline and division of labour imposed in the factories. See, for example, Thompson (1965) and Gutman (1973).

4 At one point he touches upon this issue but only to dismiss it as a problem of minor importance:

> We will not discuss contradictory locations that occur because an individual ·simultaneously occupies two class positions within social relations of production. For example, a craftsman who works in a factory on weekdays may operate as a self-employed petty-bourgeois artisan on weekends and evenings. While such dual class membership may be important in certain historical circumstances, it does not pose the same kind of analytical problem as positions which are themselves located in a contradictory way within class relations (Wright, 1978, pp. 74–5).

5   See Wright (1978). This chapter takes no account of Wright's more recent reconceptualization of contradictory class locations (1985) but see Rose and Marshall (1986) and Marshall *et al.* (1988) for criticisms of this new class model.

6   Although both Parkin and Newby claim to have identified ambivalent individuals, rather than conflicting views among members of a group (which amounts to group ambivalence), it does not follow that their data are necessarily more convincing than those proffered by Mann. Parkin and Newby avoid ecological reasoning, but they characterize as ambivalence the cumulative responses of individual subjects to a number of particular and general questions appropriate to a great variety of contexts. Both accounts therefore ignore the fact that questions posed in the abstract and questions relating to particular and varying contexts will, as is widely recognized, elicit divergent (and ultimately contradictory) responses. And yet, each author had earlier explicitly acknowledged this particular problem and, indeed, the general difficulty in collecting valid data on attitudinal variables via relatively short, synchronic, data-collection instruments.

7   See Goldthorpe, this volume. It is especially surprising that Goldthorpe should accept pecuniary instrumentalism to be an adequate characterization of working-class consciousness, since he argues also that 'within a growing market economy, market relations and the principle of "equal exchange" tend to enter into an ever-enlarged area of social life, as the dynamics of the "commercialisation effect" work themselves out' (Goldthorpe 1978, p. 199).

8   Goldthorpe's paper on inflation itself implies that workers may be peculiarly concerned about their wages for a variety of reasons, not the least of which is an awareness that the distributive mechanisms of market capitalism are morally unjust and do not square with the principles of citizenship that are supposed to apply in liberal-democratic societies (1978, pp. 201–4). Goldthorpe ignores the implications of this aspect of distributional conflict for his thesis of working-class instrumentalism (namely, that one can as readily interpret this in Westergaard's terms as one can in terms of 'privatized instrumental collectivism'), just as he earlier ignored the background threat of unemployment to the security of the workers in Luton when he came to interpret their 'instrumentalism'. Seventy-one per cent of the affluent workers may have stated that they felt their present jobs to be 'fairly safe' but 52 per cent of these seems spontaneously to have volunteered the corrective that '*no* job is dead safe' (Goldthorpe *et al.* 1968, p. 118; and 1970, pp. 37–8, 155).

Further reading

Nicholas Abercrombie *et al.*, *The Dominant Ideology Thesis*, London: George Allen and Unwin, 1980 and 1984

Duncan Gallie, *Social Inequality and Class Radicalism in France and Britain*, Cambridge: CUP 1983

Ewa Morawska, 'East European labourers in an American mill town, 1890–1940: the deferential-proletarian-privatized workers?', *Sociology*, **19**, no. 3 (1985), p. 364–83

Gordon Marshall *et al.*, *Social Class in Modern Britain*, London: Hutchinson, 1988

5   Neither angels in marble nor rebels in red: privatization and working-class consciousness*

R. E. Pahl and C. D. Wallace

It is becoming more widely understood that the links between the social structure and social attitudes and behaviour are much more complex than has seemed to be the case in the conventional sociological wisdom of the past twenty-five years. The neat causal chain, linking position in the class structure to a given form of social consciousness and consequent political action can no longer be uncritically accepted. In this essay we address ourselves to the notion of privatization, which has been invoked to account for the putatively distinctive working-class attitudes and behaviour that have been described in various studies and surveys in the 1980s. To say that 'the working class' are retreating from active political involvement or are voting against their apparent 'class interests' evidently begs many questions about the normative assumptions underlying these and similar statements. To go one step further and to claim that the notion of privatization may explain such seemingly problematic attitudes or behaviour simply compounds the problem, as we argue at length below. We are ready ourselves to share part of the blame for contemporary confusions when we earlier distinguished between voluntary and obligatory privatization as responses by working-class households to the prevailing conditions (Pahl and Wallace, 1985).

In much contemporary discussion of privatization it is generally not clear whether it is an umbrella concept that subsumes a number of constituent elements, such as domesticity, familism and fatalism or whether these latter terms are rival concepts, which may serve the same purpose but with greater precision. Furthermore, it is not clear whether these constituent elements or rival concepts operate in the same way to elucidate the links between structure, consciousness and action (and, we may add, inaction) or whether they, as it were, pull against each other, influencing in both a positive and a negative way the patterns and style of working-class behaviour. Even more importantly, it is not clear whether these and similar concepts, that have been invoked in the recent literature, are merely refining the definition and character of status categories or whether, indeed, the discussion about privatization involves a more fundamental attack upon the very concepts of class and status, as these have been traditionally understood in sociological

* The collaborative work on which this chapter is based was supported by grants from the Joseph Rowntree Memorial Trust. Dr Peter Taylor-Gooby provided substantial intellectual stimulation which we are glad to acknowledge.

analysis. This concern with the putative relationship between consciousness and action comes at a time when sociologists have turned from armchair theorizing to a greater involvement with empirical fieldwork: it is now easier than perhaps it was a decade ago to find empirical verification for some of the interesting and imaginative hypotheses that are being adduced. Indeed, some of the more conceptual discussion has arisen directly from the result of empirical investigations and our own contribution falls into this category. However, we readily acknowledge that early interpretations of pilot studies or preliminary computations can be false or misleading and we recognize that, as the debate moves on, many whose work we discuss below will inevitably modify and elaborate their positions. This is as it should be in a lively and developing scholarly field. We offer our present contribution in that spirit. The study of social stratification in Britain is in a particularly fluid state and it may not be possible to be more definitive until more empirical research has been reported.

Returning, then, to the enduring puzzle for political sociologists, it is certainly true that there is a pleasing intellectual coherence in the idea that class consciousness provides the crucial link in the chain between objective conditions, subjective awareness and radical action. Many have been influenced by Marx's suggestion indicating how a class-in-itself might turn into a class-for-itself, although such notions have been trenchantly demolished by Lockwood (Chapter 3, this volume). That intellectuals had become habituated to using the Marxist model as the 'crucial agency for the achievement of their own socio-political goals' was also neatly exposed by Goldthorpe (Chapter 2, this volume).

Finally, Marshall (Chapter 4, this volume) in an exemplary view of the theories of working-class instrumentalism and working-class ambivalence, concludes that research has reached a stalemate. He cites the work of Mann (1978) and Pollert (1981) to illustrate 'that working-class consciousness is apparently ambivalent, volatile, even self-contradictory'. Goldthorpe is held to be mainly responsible for the clear articulation of working-class instrumentalism, first in the Affluent Worker Studies and, later, in his work on the sociology of inflation (Goldthorpe, 1978). Marshall suggests that the way forward should depend on empirical research based on the action frame of reference. First, working-class consciousness cannot be studied in the abstract: 'it must be investigated as a component or dimension of everyday class practices'. Second, 'there is no a priori reason why class consciousness should be measured, according to a [nineteenth-century] datum'. A contemporary goal of social justice within capitalism is a valid alternative. Finally he advocates that

We need to uncover the ways in which subjects take up particular beliefs, as well as to document the content of the beliefs themselves. Workers' responses to sociologists' questions are not all of one piece; they may perform a variety of cognitive, emotional and social functions for the subject. They may be a complex mixture of *ex post facto* self-directed rationalizations for earlier or projected conduct, attempts to present a favourable image to an audience, spur-of-the moment opinion lightly held, positive preferences long subscribed to, fatalistic restatements of the recognizably unavoidable, or cherished hopes and ambitions that render difficult circumstances tolerable.

These effective exercises in demolition and constructive criticism now leave an embarrassingly clear problem to be faced by sociologists: if class, however defined, does not serve as a neat way of defining the basis for social consciousness and the source of distinctive patterns of political behaviour, what alternative concept or concepts can we put in its place? In a phrase, the conventional model of structure → consciousness → action is a highly problematic notion: it needs to be carefully unpacked and each part scrutinized carefully.

It is now almost a convention when writing about class to begin by admitting that the classical theories do not have the power that was originally attributed to them. Nevertheless, most commentators press on to make the best of the situation. It is generally agreed that class can be used in two distinctive ways: first it is a theoretical concept, historically and dynamically related to the technical, sectoral and social divisions of labour and, second, it can be used as a descriptive device, a statistical artifact, based upon the categorization of specified occupational categories. As a theoretical concept class is seen to have some intellectual power as a means of understanding the strains and contradictions generated by the social relations of production (Wright, 1985). In the second, descriptive, sense class is seen to have significant correlation with differential access to health, education and other societal resources. In this second sense class is simply a way of labelling the categories in a hierarchically structured system. It is a descriptive not a theoretical concept and is used by the Registrar General in the analysis of official demographic and medical statistics. In practice there has been an uneasy alliance between the dynamic (theoretical) and static (descriptive) aspects of class: the various descriptive devices that were devised to divide up the occupational structure were also used by those seeking to develop a theoretical model based on a dichotomized class struggle. Debate then focused on which side of a significant division specific occupational categories should fall (Parkin, 1972). It is now recognized to be a risky, if not a foolhardy, undertaking to construct theoretical classes from descriptive categories, although one of the bravest and probably the most effective attempts has been made by those working on the Nuffield social mobility study (Goldthorpe and Hope, 1974; Goldthorpe, Llewellyn and Payne, 1980).

Thus, despite major criticisms, the arbitrary classification of occupations – first formulated in 1913 for purposes quite other than sociological investigation – was used as the basis for the empirical construction of social class (Szreter, 1984). Not only was there an uncritical acceptance of descriptive devices as building blocks for a more elaborate theoretical structure but the structure itself – a dichotomously divided class society – was taken as given. For example, in the influential debate about class imagery, prompted by the now classically provocative article by Lockwood published in 1966 (Bulmer, 1975), it was argued that some of those doing certain kinds

129

of male manual jobs had a more 'accurate' awareness of their class position – whom we may refer to as the 'rebels in red' – whereas others in the same kinds of jobs 'mistakenly' thought that their social superiors were more fit to govern – the 'angels in marble' (McKenzie and Silver, 1968). A final category, the privatized workers also doing manual work, were described as being more instrumental but still demonstrated their 'real' proletarian consciousness by voting Labour. Thus, Marxist and non-Marxist scholars alike were guilty of what Goldthorpe has termed 'wishful, rather than critical thinking' (Goldthorpe, Chapter 2, this volume).

More recently, contributors have recognized the arbitrary and atheoretical nature of occupational categories and have focused upon the precise nature of the job and the social relations in which it is embedded as being a better basis for defining occupational groups. Further, they have analysed the labour process and the fragmentation and decomposition of work in the hope, first, of making better theoretical links between occupational categories and class and, second, in the hope of finding a working class that would be potentially truly radical (Braverman, 1974; Goldthorpe and Hope, 1974; Wood, 1982). Similarly, Carchedi (1975a and 1975b) and Wright (1978 and 1985) have provided their own formulations of the 'new' proletariat. The ultimate goal of these and other writers appears to be to determine, at least to their own satisfaction, who could be potentially marshalled under the red banner once the barricades are up.

As the industries that supported the 'traditional' workers collapsed, the breathless search for substitutes became almost embarrassing as 'proletarianized' white-collar workers, council tenants or low-paid women in the service sector were dragged on to the stage to play their part in the drama of history (Crompton and Jones, 1984). Yet, however elegantly their parts were written, the workers in practice stubbornly refused to play them. The attribution of a putative class consciousness – and hence implicit 'interests' – to economic origins alone implied that working-class Tory support had to be accounted for as some kind of deviant behaviour. Parkin (1967) was an honourable exception. This paradigm has lasted for some twenty years and, while it has wobbled in the 1980s with three successive victories for the Conservative Party led by Mrs Thatcher, prompting some general discussion of 'dealignment', it only needs a Labour victory in the next decade for the conventional paradigm to reassert itself.

The abstract and tortuous business of defining class need not detain us further here, since other contributors to this book demonstrate in their distinctive ways that simple-minded notions of classes as putative groups that can be collectively mobilized no longer hold. More importantly, we argue that there are other significant determinants of consciousness, apart from the occupation of the male head of household, that create people's subjective awareness of positions in the social structure. New divisions have become more salient or have been belatedly recognized. These are based on race, religion, gender and even life cycle stage and geographical context. Thus, young, black unemployed people in the inner city are likely to have a different basis for social consciousness from unemployed, white and middle-aged agricultural workers in Wiltshire or Dorset. Similarly, operatives in the new so-called sunrise industries of the 'golden arc' from Cambridge to Bristol are likely to think differently from those working in the declining smoke-stack industries of the West Midlands and the north. To be earning much the same income and to be apparently in the same relationship to the means of production is of itself not enough. The new divisions of employment and unemployment are sociologically too strong to be ignored (Parkin, 1979; Massey, 1984). As we show below, sociologists specializing in the study of social stratification no longer have a monopoly on their subject, as urban sociologists and specialists in women's studies have come to make their own distinctive contributions.

Recent debates on class affiliation and voting behaviour have, indeed, highlighted the importance of factors other than simply the occupation of the male head of household in determining voting patterns and, hence, class consciousness (Rose and McAllister, 1985; Dunleavy and Husbands, 1985; Heath, Jowell and Curtice, 1985). Commentators have identified four factors in particular – state dependency, gender, production and consumption-sector cleavages – which have helped to fracture traditional class alignment. Considering, first, state dependency, it is clear that there are an increasing number of 'non-working' class – those who are not presently in paid employment, who could hardly be expected to derive their complete present consciousness from sources of which they have either no direct experience or, if they have, it was long since past. The increasing numbers in such groups encouraged one social theorist to bid *Farewell to the Working Class* (Gorz, 1983). This non-working class is increasingly dependent upon state benefits, leading some to hypothesize that it is this experience, rather than employment, that shapes their perceptions (Dunleavy and Husbands, 1985).

Indeed, perhaps the most cogent critique of traditional approaches comes from studies of women's consciousness, either in the home or in the workplace, showing that occupational definitions and modes of analysis related to male workers are less obviously applicable to women (Pollert, 1981; Hunt, 1980; Porter, 1983; Westwood, 1984; Murgatroyd, 1984). Some now argue for a reformulation of traditional measures of social class, based upon the occupation of the male head of household, which they see as inadequate in determining the class position of the entire household (Heath and Britten, 1984; Stanworth, 1984), although this has been challenged by Goldthorpe (1983b and 1984b). Much depends on the purpose for which such a composite household class index would be used: there are indications that, for a significant minority, voting behaviour is influenced by specific combinations of men and women's occupational class (Britten and Heath, 1983; Missiakoulis, Pahl and Taylor-Gooby, 1986; Rose and McAllister, 1985). The third factor identified as being an alternative source of consciousness is that of consumption position. With the increasing emphasis on privatized provision of services and the residualization of state services (Dunleavy, 1979; Saunders, 1981; Dunleavy and Husbands, 1985) differential access to private

131

and public service provision is said to produce 'consumption-sector cleavages' that cross-cut class allegiances and affect voting behaviour. Furthermore, there is evidence that these may be more salient in the 1980s than they were hitherto. Hence, it is not so much affluent workers *tout court* who are now being singled out, but rather the affluent *home-owning* workers. Given this complexity of potential sources of consciousness, it is hardly surprising that studies of working-class imagery have demonstrated a fragmentary and confusing reality (Nichols and Armstrong, 1976; Roberts *et al.*, 1977). Similarly, there is evidence that differences between public and private employment and especially self-employment have a salient impact on political behaviour (Heath, Jowell and Curtice, 1985).

However, these recent studies were necessarily based upon large-scale survey designs and pre-coded questions. There is still need for an appreciation of both how consciousness is shaped and how it changes. These kinds of question can perhaps be best answered through detailed qualitative investigation (see Marshall, Chapter 4). It was for this reason that our own approach to social status and social consciousness was shaped by our detailed empirical investigation of a specific social context – the Isle of Sheppey in Kent (Pahl, 1984). However, we have gained much in discussion with our colleagues at the University of Essex and we share with them a certain similarity of approach. Like them we see the centrality of qualitative evidence (Rose *et al.*, 1984, p. 153) but there is scope for further refinement in their approach. They rightly acknowledge that 'we know we cannot read off class consciousness and action from social structure and we also know that the structure has real consequences for the individuals who constitute it' (Rose *et al.*, p. 156). This attempt by the Essex group to move beyond previous analyses accounts for their emphasis on the centrality of status, which they urge their colleagues to take more seriously, claiming that status

is concerned with how people are placed in what one might call the moral order of society. Status is evaluative. It has a symbolic basis, and is generally associated with life style, that is, with what different groups consume and how they consume (p. 152).

This argument was developed in the field of urban studies in the early 1970s (Dunleavy, 1979; Saunders, 1982). However, the Essex group develop the point by emphasizing people's own perceptions of where they stand in society – these being conditioned by status and consumption (or perhaps simply by style of life), which they then define as cultural privatization – in contrast to structural privatization – that

would be reflected empirically in such matters as central life interests being home centred; the recognition of a domain of control which lies within the home in contradistinction to the world outside which is unpredictable and uncontrollable, an instrumental orientation towards social relations outside the home and/or family etc. (Newby *et al.*, 1985, p. 101).

This notion of cultural privatization is perceived as a novel social process by the Essex group: 'We would argue that recent changes both in the nature of local communities and in patterns of consumption are combining to produce increasingly privatised life styles and increasingly home- or family-centred social identities based on them' (Newby *et al.*, p. 95).

This process that they identify produces, in turn, not only a new social consciousness or new 'social identities', but also, in their terms, it produces new conceptions of political interest (Newby *et al.*, p. 99). This new cultural privatization and political consciousness has encouraged the Essex group to argue that working people do not see their identities in terms of broader class structuration (in terms, that is, of conventional sociological analysis of the class structure), and hence, inevitably, they do not act collectively in defence of some assumed class interest. It is this line of reasoning that leads the Essex group to suggest that it does not necessarily follow that the only way that the working class can show that it is conscious of its class interests is to vote for a socialist party and that this must be the Labour Party. Other forms of distributional conflict can become more salient and these need not be directly reflected in the conventional left–right political debate. Simply because manual workers did not all vote Labour in 1983 does not necessarily mean the permanent collapse of class-based politics as some have suggested (Crewe, 1983).

This concern of the Essex group both with people's private lives and with their perceptions of the social order has helped to advance stratification analysis theoretically – by examining some of the intervening factors between 'structure' and 'consciousness' – and empirically through their accounts of cultural privatization. However, they would be the first to acknowledge that certain conceptual and empirical difficulties remain.

For example, they propose a dynamic model that assumes that whatever is taking place in contemporary society is in some distinctive and crucial way different from a previous set of social, economic, and political circumstances. Inevitably, there has to be some implicit base point from which change is inferred to have taken place. This often implies an assumption about some putative 'Golden Age' of collectively solidaristic working-class communities, where common deprivation and poverty was said to produce 'real' fraternal values: the working class, in such a romantic view, were poor but happy. These assumptions are implicit from Richard Hoggart's *Uses of Literacy* to the contemporary journalism of Jeremy Seabrook. As Raymond Williams has so astringently reminded us, the happy community is always a generation or so before the time of the person referring to it (Williams, 1973).

The Essex group seems to fall into this trap in a number of ways. First, they imply that the contemporary working class is, in some significant way, 'retreating' into the family in a manner distinct from their behaviour in the past. However, we have reason to suspect that in the past the working class were never anywhere else, since most of what we know from the work of oral and social historians makes us sceptical of the view that the life of the street or the pub was ever more important than the life of the home, except for a very poor and occasionally segregated minority (for example, Kerr, 1958).

Moreover, it is not clear what the working class are retreating from: we suspect that the Essex group have some unstated vision of where the working class were before they started to retreat. A further example of the implicit decline from the good old days is an assumption that the working class has some 'natural' tendency to vote Labour, so that if they deviate they are somehow guilty of unnatural practices. The 'marked decline in support for altruistic social policies' (Rose *et al.*, 1984, p. 155) is tacitly deplored. Almost without question, the Essex group seem to accept that the working class is being deviant if members engage in instrumental voting and the 'breakdown of class-based politics (or, more precisely, the working-class support for the Labour Party)' (Newby *et al.*, 1985, p. 101) is implicitly perceived as regressive.

Our second point of criticism is that the 'retreat' into the private world of the family is somehow seen as a negative process preventing involvement in wider collective activities. The assumption that familism militates against altruism is of doubtful empirical validity. It is equally plausible to argue that an appeal to familism, as an ideology defending the family, is an extremely effective means of mobilizing people at times of national crisis, such as in the last two world wars, or even the Falklands campaign. Similarly, family values were emphasized at the time of the miners' strike to mobilize workers' collective action. The whole question of familism and family values is complex and contradictory and is open to manipulation from parties of the left and right. Given such complexities and ambiguities, the notion of familism can be used on both sides in many arguments. Indeed, there is a tradition stretching back to the early nineteenth century whereby the institutions of male working-class solidarity attempted to redefine women's position in the family through their emphasis on the so-called family wage (Land, 1980; Barrett and McIntosh, 1980).

Third, the Essex group refer to privatization as a kind of historical process related to a period of lesser privatization with which the present pattern is contrasted. One of the difficulties of their style of argument is that it is very difficult to see precisely what normative framework they are working from. We would have little difficulty in understanding structural privatization of, say, housing (through the sale of local authority housing) or the sale of British Telecom, since it is quite obvious what that form of privatization involves. However, when we move to cultural privatization the indicators of change appear inevitably more blurred and difficult to measure.

Finally, their concern with familism, the retreat into the home, privatization and a falling away from solidarity can hardly be faced without considering questions of gender. Both structural and cultural privatization involve relations of gender, following sexual differentiation in both the public and the private sphere, and these matters are not pursued. Recent contributions to this field would suggest that the discussion of familism would be considerably enhanced if gender relations were taken into account. For example, Porter's work (1983) suggests that male manual workers did not necessarily bring their class consciousness home with them together with their wage-packet and that their wives often had a very different view of the class war. Couples do not always share ideologies even though they may share a bed: a conflict model can be extended to social relations inside the household as well as outside. Research results depend upon which partner is being interviewed and under what circumstances.

Without question the contributions by the Essex group, to which we have referred, certainly advance the debate in a most fruitful way. However, we need to be very sure what it is that is to be explained. If the issue is 'Why doesn't the working class behave in the way that previous theorists thought the working class ought to behave' then there is a danger of being trapped in a prison of outmoded concepts. Class structure derived from a set of positions is an abstract formulation which we would not expect to find reflected in people's minds in any precise form. However, people *do* construct more clearly articulated identities and ideas about their social position from other sources of experience in their everyday lives: one of the welcome developments in some recent empirical research is that there is now much more concern to allow people to frame their own worlds, rather than to insist that the investigators' frames are self-evidently true but require, perhaps, a little modification. Unpublished research by the Essex group illustrates very well this new sociological humility but, in turn, it creates new theoretical dilemmas. In preparatory qualitative research they did not desperately dredge people's attitudes for evidence of their class position but instead allowed them to report, without devious prompting, what they thought about their social identities and their position in society and – according to the Essex group – none mentioned class.

In our research on the Isle of Sheppey we were primarily concerned with the connection between employment and other forms of work carried out by household members in and around the home. It would not strengthen our argument to refer to our quantitative data relating to the Isle of Sheppey here, since the more recent national surveys making the same points may carry more weight (Dunleavy and Husbands, 1985; Rose and McAllister, 1985). Instead, we draw on the open-ended qualitative interviews that we each carried out, which helped us to understand how consciousness is formed and reproduced in practice. Certain kinds of occupations allow people the time, and provide them with the money, to do more work outside employment. This other work might be self-provisioning work, such as vegetable-growing or home-decorating, or it might be informal, unpaid work for others, such as doing tasks for elderly or handicapped people. From our perspective it became increasingly odd to concentrate on one form of work carried out by one member of the household, when it was clear that the household should be considered as a collective unit engaged in a variety of forms of work. We were pushed by our empirical material to a position which saw the work of all the household members as constituting, by that set of practices, a given 'household work strategy'. We must emphasize that this does not necessarily imply a kind of utopian consensus among household members. There were, of course, sharp and sometimes bitter divisions among household members. But as long as members of a household were staying together under the same roof and sharing most catering arrangements, then we considered what members actually did as the household work strategy. These strategies could be fitted more readily to stages of the life cycle – hardly surprisingly – and this alerted us to the idea that individuals' images of society were likely to be structured to a significant extent by all their experiences in the household as a social unit. Certainly, the idea that one household member's employment experience should overwhelmingly colour his or her world-view and identity, as well as others who shared the same dwelling, seemed intrinsically implausible, although we recognized that this was counter to conventional sociological wisdom.

The Sheppey study convinced us of the importance of the domestic life cycle for social identity. People experience social, political and economic change through personal biographical milestones related to the family life cycle: these provide them with co-ordinates of more general social and political concerns. Bertaux (1981), for example, has illustrated in his interviews with bakers that social consciousness, putatively deriving from employment, was distorted by the biographical experiences of the individual. Those who became self-employed had very different perceptions of employment from those who remained employees, but that does not imply that employment history is the only salient element in determining contemporary consciousness. One has to avoid the danger of imputing some permanent effect of certain employment experiences that individuals carry around within themselves like a birthmark. Our social identities are constructed in a far more complex way. Social images, we suggest, may be constructed less in terms of class and more in terms of family and personal biography. Thus, unexceptionally it is clear that people's knowledge of historical events, affecting the society in which they live, impinges on them through the prism of individual experience. The social constructs, that to the social theorists may appear as clashes between labour and capital, may impinge on an individual's social consciousness through biographical life events, very often related to the life cycle, such as a marriage brought forward or a birth postponed. Thus wars are remembered in terms of tangible reminders such as bundles of letters, a medal, photographs, the loss of a loved one and real or imagined personal experiences. Few talk about the struggle between fascism and democracy. The class war is even more remote, as Lenin and Trotsky, in their different ways, quite rightly observed. Without political organization, inspiration and education, people do not perceive themselves as part of broad social collectivities. From Gramsci to Raymond Williams the importance of the immediate world of everyday existence of households and families has been emphasized.

As an example of this we can note that certain historical events in a particular year or month – October, May or whatever – are often commemorated in squares and street names by the guardians of the collective consciousness. These different dates in different countries help to recreate the collective conscience in a Durkheimian sense – and often provide good excuses for a private party. These obligatory celebrations and days of remembrance help to create forms of social cohesion, but it is important to remember that the date or month being commemorated will have impinged on people at different ages and stages in their life cycles. The event will be filtered through idiosyncratic personal activities. Thus VE day might mean for some the long-awaited return of a fiancé, husband or father, while for others it meant a day off school or in some other way the beginning of a new phase in life. Hence, all such national events throw up a patchwork of memories, since the dynamic element is the domestic life cycle and the household work strategies related to it. Women, in particular, are more likely to construct meanings to their lives in terms of births, deaths, marriages, divorces and family disruptions or celebrations, and to relate even their occupational careers to these. (This theme is further substantially elaborated in the associated work of Evans, 1984.) Men, on the other hand, are more likely to measure their occupational identities in terms of employment experiences, but this, too, is interpreted in terms of their individual biographies rather than in broader historical terms. Thus, for example, one of the most significant things to have happened to the Isle of Sheppey was the closure of the naval dockyard in 1959, but men still, as it were, wrapped their personal biographies round that event when drawing on their experiences of employment.

Both men and women on Sheppey mentioned moves between houses and between areas as being of particular significance, and these often provide the main focus and goal for their family biography or household work strategy. They perceived the present in the context of the significant events of their past. Those events that are perceived most significantly are likely to be gender-differentiated. This was also the case with their perceptions of the future. Young adults (studied separately) tended to perceive housing, transport and other items which located them in particular consumption sectors in terms of their own individual life plan (Wallace, 1985).

In addition to life events and consumption plans, which were largely expressed in an individualistic way, people also perceived themselves in terms of collective identities. However, this did not necessarily imply an oppositional socialist consciousness. We do not deny that we found a degree of collective identity based on occupation, but this was often a form of collective action that supported Mrs Thatcher's Conservative administration. First, workers in one of the largest centres of employment in the island collectively combined to fight the workers from other steel plants who attempted to picket them. They valued their own jobs more than any putative class loyalty – an example, perhaps, of the distributional conflict to which the Essex group have drawn our attention.

Second, our attempt to seek some collective consciousness among the representatives of organized labour was unsuccessful, since we found many of the union leaders were as likely to be involved with organizing the Conservative Party as the Labour Party. Certainly, most of the firms on the island were unionized, many of them operating a closed shop, so there was some collective activity, but in no way did it seem to us that this reflected a specifically radical consciousness of a form and style traditionally associated

137

with proletarian life. Had we not been bemused by the expectations generated by the conventional wisdom in sociology, our understanding might have developed more quickly.

Initially we were very impressed by the number of working men's clubs on the island and we expected them to be filled with traditional workers. However, they were mainly social clubs, providing a friendly environment for cheap drinking in a context of convivial collectivism. Much the most successful of these was the Conservative Club. Thus, while we found that working people did organize themselves collectively, there was no obvious link with the Labour movement. The general style of organization was, apparently by general agreement, rigidly hierarchical.

Third, there were occasions when the people of the island took to the streets in relatively spontaneous collective action – the last one being a torchlight victory celebration at the end of the Falklands war. This collective action was not a reflection of some form of subordinate deference, since it was organized with both pride and confidence: it had its own internal hierarchy and while it was certainly fundamentally collective in nature, it was not radical or proletarian in the sense of the stereotypes put forward for example by Parkin (1972) or Lockwood (1966). We discovered neither the solidarity of workers intent on smashing the capitalist system (the rebels in red), nor the deferential privatized worker (the angels in marble), although there were, to be sure, individual examples of these. The kind of collectivism we did find had deep historical roots: it was claimed that the co-operative movement pre-dated Rochdale, and some of the many working men's clubs had records stretching back over one hundred years.

While it might be argued that male manual workers would be expected to base their social identities on a degree of collectivism, regardless of whether this be more conservative or oppositional in nature, we found that there was a strong element of working-class individualism among our sample. This took a number of forms. First, there was a belief in looking after yourself and an individualistic pride in survival strategies.

I've always kept something, a couple of pigeons or chickens or something, so when I got to this situation of coming out of work, I just started doing that sort of thing again. Like, I extended the garden down there, took off a bit of council land, stuck a few chickens on it . . . they call me a right old rogue, but this is how you've got to live isn't it? And then there's totting – honest fiddling I call it. It's just that I see a shilling where you wouldn't (Disabled decorator, mid-fifties).

Second, a sense of personal identity was derived from the way in which people individually threaded a path between the confusing and conflicting demands of the life cycle and family events, various forms of work and 'them' – meaning not the forces of capital as much as complaining neighbours or the ubiquitous state. One man, in response to our question about the welfare state felt particularly trapped:

They've got records. It's just like being a criminal. The only thing is you haven't got bars on the windows. That's the way I feel. There isn't bars on the windows and I'm not locked up. But they do make you feel like a criminal.

This desire to escape from impositions by alien and threatening others was at times extended into a desire to be self-employed.

Male school-leavers often expressed a commitment to self-employment as an ideal pattern of work which would give them freedom from supervision and more personal autonomy. Other social investigators have observed this yearning to be self-employed, even if it was enacted at the level of fantasy more than reality (Chinoy, 1955; Blackburn and Mann, 1979). This aspiration involves cutting links with any class identity – whether 'middle' or 'working' – and 'going it alone' as they would put it. To some extent this was also a *petit bourgeois* reaction against the very elemental constituent of working-class consciousness – mass production. Alienation was a recognizable syndrome, but the solution was not to reappropriate the means of production, but to flee into a totally different and more humanly controllable working environment. A study of school-leavers on Sheppey illustrated a preference for outdoor labouring as a reaction to factory work when they experienced it for the first time (Wallace, 1986).

Another major source of social identity was the distinction between 'rough' and 'respectable', a distinction that probably emerged early in the nineteenth century (Williams, 1956; Klein, 1965; Gray, 1976). Many of the consumption patterns of those we interviewed appeared to be ways of demonstrating a sense of 'respectability' to others in the local area:

A lot of the people round here, they are not our type of people. They run around with no tax and insurance and scruffy old houses. You've only got to drive around and see what they're like. You've only got to look at somebody's windows and curtains I always say, to see what they're like inside.

This had strong moral connotations: those who were able to demonstrate their respectability through having comfortable, affluent life-styles also thought of themselves as morally superior to the less fortunate. Thus, they were unlikely to form alliances with those whom they perceived to be the 'undeserving poor'.

An additional moral dimension of the rough/respectable distinction relates to sexual conduct and to 'matter out of place'. Cleanliness, sexual propriety and strict rules of public and private conduct all help to reinforce the apartness of certain households from others:

The lot up the road, up the rough end, they are always in and out of each others' houses borrowing their husbands and stuff like that. That's why I am glad I'm up this end. . . . You've only got to look at the outside to see they're rough. It's all scruffy and dirty with their trash and broken-down cars and that up there. It's like a slum.

In so far as people would talk of class, it was in reference to a disparaged style of life associated with poverty, large families and fecklessness. The 'lower class' was thus morally tainted as well as simply unfortunate. Thus working people tended to define themselves in relation to other status groups

139

in the vicinity rather than in relation to 'bosses' or to the middle class generally.

This distinction, which is often rather generally referred to as status divisions within the working class, could perhaps be better understood as a value system reinforcing the traditional nuclear family. A particular pattern of gender identity and sexuality is inherent in the 'respectable' life-style and, since gender identity, as expressed through sexuality, is an essential part of social identity more generally, the link between gender, respectability and social consciousness is crucial. Those who do not subscribe to the respectable life-style are perceived to be immoral and potentially sexually deviant.

Furthermore, consumption patterns serve to reinforce these status divisions in the community – particularly the purchase of housing. The purchase of consumer goods is important in the construction of social consciousness because they contribute towards distinctive life-styles. They also help to define stages in the life cycle, particularly in the transition to adulthood. Young adults argued that they would postpone getting married until they had saved up the money for a house, a proper wedding and the material goods for the matrimonial home. People need symbolic landmarks to provide meaningful punctuation as they pass through different stages of their lives: it is not helpful to disparage the acquisition of consumer goods, as for example, Seabrook (1982) does, claiming that these in some way undermine the putative collective solidarity of common deprivation, without recognizing the social meanings attached to these goods and the way in which they are transformed and incorporated into personal biographies.

In our earlier discussion of privatization we were critical of the Essex group for their implicit processual model that seemed to lack a point of departure from which to measure the changes they note. We adopt no implicit mode of change ourselves but argue that this has always been an enduring aspect of the lives of manual workers. *Familism* is concerned with a particular set of attitudes related to the early socialization of and the care and responsibility for children. It may take a variety of forms ranging from the perhaps over-protective cosseting of some skilled manual workers and the lower-middle class to the apparently less protective style variously reflected in the easy-going approach ('bringing themselves up') of the rough working class to the distanced dependence on boarding schools in the commercial sector to which sections of the middle class subcontract so much of the daily care and attention to their offspring.

Domesticity, on the other hand, is a set of values relating to the use and living arrangements within a domestic dwelling and is not linked to any particular household type, although it may differ according to stage in the life cycle. It is an essential ingredient in how the majority of people lead their lives and is, in a sense, the end-product of their efforts in the labour market. The roots of domesticity as a working-class value have been well explored by social historians. Daunton (1983) has written of a cult of domesticity based on the intensification of home-based consumption in the late nineteenth century and Elizabeth Roberts (1985) has shown how family-centred values encouraged the reproduction of respectability from generation to generation. Daunton argues that:

The working class turned away from dependence in their experience of work, towards a search for purpose in the life of the family and home, which came to be seen as a source of assertive dignity. The reality of working-class life in the late nineteenth century was one of dependence at work and of deference in the community. The working-class institutions of self-help, and the creation of a home-based culture of domesticity, may be seen as a response to this. The outcome might be a conservative retreat from wider issues, but it might also be a mechanism to assert independence and identity within a setting of subordination (Daunton, 1983, p. 266).

Daunton is at pains to point out that the working class was not simply responding to pressure from above but there was an internal working-class dynamic based on rising real wages and greater regularity of employment. Thus, those who claim to find a true, communal working-class life in local neighbourhoods may again be engaged in wishful rather than critical thinking. 'The respectable working man would argue that the streets were for those who did not have a decent home. An active street life was a sign of the slums' (Daunton, p. 272). Mrs M. E. Loane observed in 1905 that 'the vast majority of men above the age of 26 are distinctly domestic in their tastes' and she provides little support for those who imagine that the working class were somehow less materialistic or consumption oriented in the past. As she remarked in *An Englishman's Castle* (1909) 'the expensive furniture is desired . . . as incontrovertible evidence of character and position' (quoted in Daunton, 1983, p. 279). Similarly Benson (1955) has argued for the importance of work outside employment for constructing working-class identities, lending support to our view that it is not so much the working class that has changed in its fundamental beliefs and attitudes over the past century but rather the attitudes of those who have commented on them.

Domesticity, then, is not a value born of contemporary consumerism but has been an essential element in working-class life for as long as we have any historical knowledge of the context and nature of everyday life. A concern with snugness, cosiness, togetherness by the fire, family meals, reunions and collective activities are not simply defensive measures designed to offset oppression, but may be seen as positive affirmation of a sense of social identity. Indeed, it could be argued that instrumental collectivism, that may have developed at specific historical conjunctures, has not been designed to change familial domesticity but rather to defend and enhance it. The goal of workers' movements, where they have existed, has been to make the conditions of ordinary everyday existence more secure. Domesticity, indeed, is as much the goal of collective action as its cause. We therefore take issue with both the radical left (Barrett and McIntosh, 1982) and the radical right (Mount, 1982) who perceive family values to be at odds with collective action, albeit for dramatically different reasons. Our position is that the set of values surrounding domesticity are among the most salient determinants of social identity. Domesticity is a set of values relating to the use of and the living

141

arrangements within a domestic dwelling: it is not linked to any particular household type or stage in the life cycle. The majority of people lead lives that are remarkably domesticated – in the sense we are meaning. Indeed, the 'home' provides not only the chief marker of social status for those living in it and one of the main goals for which people take employment, but also provides a sense of ontological security at a more abstract level. We should emphasize that we make these remarks in a descriptive, not a normative sense. Williams (1983) has referred to 'mobile privatization' and his description is worth quoting at length:

The identity that is really offered to us is a new kind of freedom in that area of our lives that we have staked out inside these wider determinations and constraints. It is private. It involves, in its immediate definition, a good deal of evident consumption. Much of it is centred on the home itself, the dwelling-place. Much of it, in those terms, enlists many of the most productive, imaginative impulses and activities of people – moreover sanely so, as against the competing demands of orthodox politics. Because what you put in, in effort, in this way, you usually get to live with and have its value.

At the same time it is not a retreating privatization, of a deprived kind, because what it especially confers is an unexampled mobility. You may live in a shell of this kind in which you and your relatives, your lovers, your friends, your children – this small-unit entity is the only really significant social entity. It is not living in a cut-off way, not in a shell that is just stuck. It is a shell which you can take with you, which you can fly with to places that previous generations could never imagine visiting. You can move all the time in the society, choosing the places you're going to. You take the shell with you. You're given this sense that is offered as a primary identity, as your real life. And most people underwrite it as their real life, against which those big things, in whatever colour of politics they appear to come, are interpreted as mere generalities, mere abstractions, as at best rather boring interferences with this real life and at worst destructive interventions in it (p. 16).

The expansion of market capitalism has encouraged a shift of symbolic meaning from older, and often well-worn artifacts to new and more ephemeral objects in order to increase the demand for goods. In pre-industrial times, with limited material objects and artifacts in the domestic dwelling, considerable meaning was invested into, say, an old chest, a treasured garment or a set of well-cared-for tools. The fact that these were handed down from generation to generation served to bind family and domestic values in a distinctive way. It is a general part of capitalist marketing strategy to change the arrangement and patterning of objects – or designs for living, in the language of the Sunday paper supplements – so that each generation at different levels in the social structure to some extent defines itself by the way it comes to terms with this distinctive style of consumerism. This, of course, underlines the way social consciousness is created in the sphere of consumption for those with the means to participate.

While domesticity may be seen as encompassing an enduring set of values, the *form* these values take in a given context is related to the changing social and material circumstances. Domesticity may seem to some to have strong Victorian overtones, implying a rigid gender-based division of activities wherein the female was the manager of the bourgeois retreat to which the busy entrepreneur or factory owner returned at the end of the day. Such a model of the separation of spheres would imply a full-time domestic role for women in order to ensure that the domestic support system functioned efficiently. Such a stereotype from Victorian England was adopted to a considerable extent by the Labour Party in planning post-war reconstruction after the Second World War (particularly in the way it fossilized the pattern on the ground in its New Town planning). This model linking familism and domesticity was embodied in much legislation established in the post-Beveridge period of welfare state legislation, assuming a male breadwinner and dependent family. We are not limiting ourselves to that concept of domesticity in our present discussion, although there are common threads between ideals of domesticity. First, the very rapid increase of married women's activity rates has highlighted the increasingly obvious point that maintaining and running the domestic dwelling is a form of work which takes up a substantial proportion of women's time even when they are in full-time employment. Martin and Roberts (1984) show that just over a quarter of wives in their sample said that they shared the domestic housework equally with their husbands. Most women spend some two-thirds of their working life in the labour market but of course the older the age cohort the lower the proportion. However, there were important differences according to the wife's employment status: wives who worked full time were much more likely than those who did not work to say they shared the housework equally with their husbands: 44 per cent did so, while 23 per cent of wives who worked part time said they shared the housework equally. In our more detailed and precise work on this topic, reported in *Divisions of Labour* (1984) we come to broadly the same conclusion, based on a wide range of actual tasks carried out rather than on eliciting general statements. We do not, of course, suggest some over-simple model of a 'symmetrical family': rather, there is a process of negotiation based on forms of work and gender relations.

The ingredients of consciousness based on the domestic sphere are not generally based on a breadwinner and his supportive housewife but are a very complex and dynamic set of dialectics, involving not only each partner but other adult members of the household, whose employment histories weave together over the life cycle in distinctive patterns. Given that only 5 per cent of households are based on a single breadwinner supporting a wife and two dependent children and that 40 per cent of all households have two or more earners, the exact mixture of sources of consciousness from different forms of work experience in and outside the dwelling changes significantly over the life cycle (Pahl, *ibid*, pp. 132–4). In the same way that the domestic cycle generates a distinctive pattern of wealth and poverty, so too does it produce distinctive sources of consciousness. This essential dynamic element in the creation of consciousness is based upon the household as the unit of analysis and, as we have shown elsewhere, different forms of work intermesh over the life cycle. Clearly, it hardly has to be argued that the social consciousness of a social class is not entirely male determined. Distinctive gender-linked

143

variations in attitudes to employment have been documented which may be partly explained by gender-linked occupational segregation (Hakim, 1979) but Martin and Roberts also demonstrate that women have different orientations to employment at different stages in the life cycle, at different ages and, finally, whether they are full-time or part-time workers (1984, pp. 62–3). This fluctuation in degrees and sources of commitment to work by women is likely to affect to some degree how their partners perceive the world, but little research on this kind of interaction has so far been carried out (Dex, 1985). Men's attitudes and orientations to work also change over the life cycle, adding to the inadequacy of a mechanistic approach linking employment experience and social consciousness. Furthermore, the involvement of men in other forms of work in and around the home is likely to have some effect on consciousness although devising surrogate variables for precise analysis of this issue is still at an early stage (Missiakoulis, Pahl and Taylor-Gooby, 1986). New divisions of labour surely produce new forms of social consciousness: as a result of changes both in the labour market and the domestic division of labour, the Victorian or Beveridge model of domesticity applies to an increasingly small minority of the population. But this does not imply that domesticity has been undermined: it simply means that it has changed in its contemporary guise. Paradoxically, the recent increase in married women's employment has served to reinforce domesticity, since the increasing purchasing capacity of multi-earner households allows a greater focus of self-provisioning through the purchase of more domestic consumer goods and materials (Pahl and Wallace, 1985). As an interesting modification of this point the Sheppey survey showed that when the male breadwinner was unemployed he was likely to do less work in and around the home; there was less self-provisioning; there were fewer consumer durables and the domestic division of labour was more traditional (Bell and McKee, 1985; Pahl and Wallace, 1986). Clearly, for the unemployed domesticity implied a different set of values. Hence there is a kind of polarization in domestic values between multiple-earner households and those based on an unemployed breadwinner.

We have argued that the consciousness of working people is inevitably fragmented, based as it is on the changing experience of household members as they move through the domestic life cycle. Furthermore, there is an assumed interactive effect taking place inside the household, where it is presumed the experience of all forms of work colours the consciousness of each individual in a distinctive way and then each, in turn, affects the others. We are not claiming that the significance of women's increased participation in the labour market, of increasing home-ownership or of increasing self-provisioning have not been already noticed as potentially important elements in developing social consciousness. However, this consciousness may be focused specifically on gender identity or domesticity: it would be a gross mistake to assume that all sources and manifestations of social consciousness necessarily relate to class consciousness. Indeed, it is this obsession with the search for class consciousness alone that has misled or distracted many observers from coming to terms with contemporary social reality. It is our contention that these other social values are more important and may vary at different stages in the life cycle. Thus, women may at one stage of their life cycle be more concerned with their occupational identity and at another stage with their gender identity.

Turning now from social consciousness generally to political behaviour, it is evident that some of the variables which we have described above can also help to explain political behaviour. The Conservatives have been in power since 1979, with the benefit of a substantial working-class vote – in 1983 having 39 per cent of the C2 and 29 per cent of the DE vote (BBC/Gallup Survey 1983, quoted by Kellner, 1985). Therefore it would appear apposite to attempt to understand the appeal of the Conservative administration in terms of the values of domesticity.

The rise of the New Right and its political success since the late 1970s has been the source of considerable commentary and speculation (Fitzgerald, 1983; and Elliott *et al.*, Chapter 11, this volume). This new political force – often called 'dynamic conservatism' – has managed to create an increasingly divided and polarized society, while at the same time using an aggressive meritocratic egalitarianism. This apparent contradiction is achieved through an appeal to the kinds of archetypal 'respectable' values which we have been describing. It is also worth considering the vocabulary in which such appeals are based in order to understand how and why they resonate in this way. Recent statements by Mrs Thatcher illustrate the way national political statements echo the home-centred values of Sheppey.

The 1983 Conservative Party Manifesto taps a fundamental value set:

Freedom and Responsibility go together. The Conservative Party believes in encouraging people to take responsibility for their own decisions. We shall continue to return more choice to individuals and their families. That is the way to increase personal freedom. It is also the way to improve standards in the state services (Conservative Party Manifesto 1983, p. 24).

Fitzgerald has indicated the importance of this ideal of the family for Conservative welfare policies and he shows how it has been used as a metaphor for far wider society in the appeal to national unity and sensible budgeting. However, the ideal of the family is also used as a way of overcoming class conflict:

Our fifth task is ownership for all. The desire to have and to hold something of one's own is basic to the spirit of man. We are battling for a Britain freer from class conflict, where property is the right of the many and not the privilege of the few. That is the way to build one nation (Thatcher, 1985).

Thus, ontological security implicit in property-ownership to which we referred above, is invoked: the importance of the family, private ownership and privatized consumption are fused. Rather than calling upon occupationally-based allegiance, this rhetoric appeals to consumption goals and domestic values – precisely the values expressed by many of our respondents. Moreover, this appeal is extended to include self-provisioning and the work

145

of the family in the domestic dwelling. The symbolic importance of housing is an important theme:

Also basic to the hopes and ambitions of the overwhelming majority of our people is the ownership of the family home. It means more than ownership of bricks and mortar. It brings a sense of pride and independence, of having something to hand on to the next generation, of having roots. Do-it-yourself becomes a hobby with all the satisfaction that gives. And as you know, I speak from recent personal experience (Thatcher, 1984a).

For the majority of our respondents, the physical ownership of the home embodies the family itself and its status in the world. The value of home-ownership extends beyond the financial advantages it undoubtedly confers. Thus when it is claimed that the right to buy 'is the biggest single step towards a home-owning democracy ever taken' (Manifesto 1983, p. 24) many working-class constituents would obviously agree. The fact that they regard property-ownership of this kind as a new form of citizenship and a route out of the subordinate class, both as we found in our interviews and as the Essex group found in theirs, clearly makes sense in these terms. In the words of one man who built his own house, 'You get an independent feeling and there's a lot to be said for that.' However, as the Essex group point out, this serves to disenfranchise the non-property-owners from membership of the new democracy, and implicitly leads to sharper polarization (See also Hamnett, 1984).

Dynamic conservatism appeals to values of domesticity in other ways too. We have already indicated that an important source of social consciousness is the experience of the life cycle and the new politics makes reference to this too. The Conservatives claim to help to free the individual from debilitating dependency on the state, either in housing or employment, thus appealing to the kinds of anti-state values described previously; the welfare state appears as the people's enemy rather than the people's friend.

This movement towards more responsibility for the individual and a family-based philosophy involves a change in values:

I came to office with one deliberate intent: to change Britain from a dependent to a self-reliant society. From a give-it-to-me to a do-it-yourself nation. A get up and go instead of a sit-back-and-wait Britain (Thatcher, 1984b).

This has clear parallels in the individualistic, self-reliant ethic which we observed among our respondents and emerged also from the qualitative and quantitative results reported by the Essex group.

These are some of the ways in which conservatism has managed to tap essential values in the British electorate. These values – of domesticity, self-reliance and the like – are not in themselves conservative; they can equally be harnessed to more socialist goals, and indeed have been in the past, as Humphries (1980) illustrates. Rather, particular constellations of inherited values derived from a variety of different sources of consciousness become politically salient at particular times.

146

Conclusions

It would not be necessary for us to emphasize the multifaceted sources of social consciousness were it not for the strong grip of traditional class analysis on the political sociology of the last forty years. As Pahl argued in *Divisions of Labour*, the period of dichotomized and seemingly class-linked politics in the 1950s and 1960s, based on full employment, can be seen as atypical and has, perhaps, blinded us to longer-term tendencies. With hindsight, the Labour voters of the post-war years should, perhaps, be seen less as class warriors and more as pragmatic opportunists, selecting the best available strategy to get better health, housing, education and so on. Labour Party policies may have presented the most effective means of achieving given ends in the post-war period. There is no need to invoke any long-term commitment to a radical ideology on the part of its supporters. Even those who have recognized working-class Conservatives in the past have seen them as deviants from their 'true' position of developing the collective interests of the working class.

Our perspective, based on seven years research in one locality, encourages us to emphasize the complex mosaic of social experience out of which people construct their social identities. That people's primary concern is with their homes, their families and the individual life events of themselves and others accords with the particularism of the individualistic English. Whether this particularism has roots extending deep into pre-industrial times as Macfarlane has suggested, or whether, following Hobsbawm, the crucial factor was that Britain led the world as the first industrial nation, initially free from international competition, does not have to be finally decided. Either way the English may be seen to be more individualistic than most of their fellow Europeans. Indeed, the way the English use the national past in the contemporary world may be peculiarly characteristic (P. Wright, 1985).

Radicals of the left have typically scorned aspirations towards respectability by working people, since these are often perceived to undermine collective action for collectivist goals. Radical socialists in Britain do not express their goals in terms of *petit bourgeois* respectability, even if that is what most workers seem to want. The stereotype of traditional workers as tattooed beer-drinking machos with clenched fists raised high is out of phase with the reality of the world of the men and women who shop in the British Home Stores, Habitat or Marks and Spencer. Such people would resist the stereotype of either angels in marble or rebels in red: their goals and aspirations may be closer to their '*petit bourgeois*' counterparts in Denmark or the Netherlands than their 'radical' labour leaders imagine. This position, popularized by Eric Hobsbawm and others in recent polemical writing, is countered by those who stress the vulnerability of routine workers in the restructuring of contemporary capitalism. However, we see no reason why a pragmatic approach and more distributional conflict need be alternative ways of responding to current circumstances. We certainly do not intend to suggest by anything that we have written that working people are not, indeed, highly vulnerable. The

147

possibility that subsidiaries of multinational corporations based on the Isle of Sheppey might close and move to Portugal or elsewhere served as a real or imagined threat to all members of the work-force we studied. The point we want to emphasize is that few workers believed that by voting Labour they could add the slightest amount of security to their vulnerable position. Rationally and realistically they considered that more security could be obtained from owning their own dwelling – and more craft skill could be exercised by decorating and maintaining it once it was theirs. Bending nature to one's will and exercising craft skills, as Karl Marx or William Morris would have wished, may be more successfully and agreeably accomplished in the sphere of self-provisioning than through employment or even self-employment. As most routine workers are implicit supporters of the process of capitalist accumulation through their collective interest in their pension funds, it is debatable whether workers who support or who oppose capitalism show the most false-consciousness. In the face of such absurdity it is surely time to escape from such false dichotomies.

In this chapter we have mounted an implicit attack on neo-Marxist class-based theories of political action on two fronts. First we have emphasized the importance of *all* forms of work and have suggested that perceptions of these are mediated within the household. Second, we have joined with others, particularly the Essex group, in emphasizing the importance of social status, recognizing that this dimension of stratification gets its life and being in the sphere of consumption. However, it is important not to reify these distinctions. By focusing on all forms of production we are undermining the distinctions between production and consumption, as these are conventionally understood by economists, and in our attempt to unify the spheres of work and social evaluation we are trying to be more conscious of the way people actually express themselves and perceive the world, rather than forcing them into pre-coded categories. Typically, those adopting a more Weberian approach have been at pains to make sharp analytical distinction between the class and status dimension of social stratification. Certainly it is right to match the divisions of production with the divisions of consumption; but we are uneasy about the very distinction between production and consumption and future theorizing is likely to be based on the conflation of these two spheres. With the promise of a new wave of empirical sociological studies, reporting from specific localities what men and women say and do in response to their specific forms of consciousness and social identities, we may be in a better position in the 1990s to forge a new link in the chain between material and existential circumstances and social consciousness. However, it is very unlikely that those who follow us will wish to deny the fundamental importance of economic interests. The rather simple-minded notion that class explains everything cannot be replaced with the equally simple-minded notion that class – as the distillation of economic interests – explains nothing. The fact that the analysis of class is crumbling with the collapse of our traditional industrial base and the dispersal of the population from the tightly-packed Victorian cities is to allow our sociology to be controlled by the geography of the global restructuring of manufacturing industry. Economic interests may become more opaque but they do not disappear. Perhaps the real problem, as Durkheim noticed nearly a century ago, is that there has been an elision between class struggle, socialism and matters of the stomach. In his essay on *Socialism and Saint Simon* Durkheim rightly perceived that *laissez-faire* economists also say they want to ameliorate the conditions of working people. They just want to go about it in a different way. Hence the current crisis in class analysis may, if we follow Durkheim, be less a crisis of theory and more a crisis of morality. Workers in the late 1980s have no clear conception of the unity of purpose linking their individual efforts with the collective productive effort of society. As Raymond Williams, freed from the burden of sociological theory, put it:

It would be alright if we all really cared for each other or had a sense of common responsibility. But that kind of positive position, announced on its own, is comparatively weak when confronted with the real pressures in what is still the majority situation, in which, with whatever fear and under whatever pressure, this private and mobile kind of life may still be available to you; even if an increasing number of your neighbours drop off the list and simply become unemployment statistics. In other words, I think that socialists have now to recognise that the central problem of the coming period is to create an authentic rather than an inherited sense of what a society is and should be. Not a society which is crudely counterposed to conditions of individual security, freedom and achievement, for these are not going to be given up except under force (1983, p. 17).

If what is needed is a new sense of moral purpose then it may be that political parties have outlived their usefulness as agents of social change. Durkheim's insistence on the need for society to be integrated by the moral norms of individual obligation and corporate solidarity requires the mass of ordinary working people to be neither rebels in red nor angels in marble but, perhaps, angels in red. Privatization, in the sense used by Williams, or domesticity in the sense used by us here, are not going to go away in the interests of a nineteenth-century theorist's model of class struggle. The force for change will come through the difficulty of maintaining social cohesion. Sociologists should not be disturbed if the divisions do not follow traditional lines. Rather, we should recognize that material interests and moral concerns are the central sociological forces determining the system of stratification we are seeking to understand. It remains to be seen how these forces face up to each other in the decade ahead.

Further reading

M. J. Daunton, *House and Home in the Victorian City*, London: Arnold, 1983

J. Klein, *Samples for English Cultures*, London: RKP, 1965

R. E. Pahl, *Divisions of Labour*, Oxford: Blackwell, 1984

R. E. Pahl, and C. D. Wallace, 'Household work strategies in economic recession', in N. Redclift and E. Mingione (eds), *Beyond Employment*, Oxford: Blackwell, 1985

R. Williams, *Towards 2000*, Harmondsworth: Penguin, 1985

Part Two

Empirical Research

6 After redundancy: economic experience and political outlook among former steel employees in Sheffield

John Westergaard, Iain Noble and Alan Walker

We have three aims for this chapter. One is to tell the story of what happened to nearly 400 people who lost their jobs with a Sheffield steel firm in the late 1970s, and whom we interviewed about three years after they had been made redundant – at least the story, in outline, of how they fared in the labour market and in their everyday life circumstances over the three years. Second, we shall try to explore their socio-political orientations – their views on politics, industrial relations and a range of related matters on which we asked them to comment – and to assess the effects of their economic experience over the three years on their outlook in these terms. Third, we want to draw out some implications of our findings, as we see them, for the understanding of present and prospective class relations.

Our conclusions under this last heading will be fairly straightforward in one respect. The impact of redundancy on individual welfare was, for very many of our respondents, harsh in ways that underline familiar economic inequalities of class. Our results re-expose, in the stark light of recession, the vulnerability of people whose livelihood at its best depends on ordinary wage-earning jobs, manual or nonmanual; and the particular vulnerability of those among them who are short of recognized skills, who are past the working prime of life, or who are women. They throw into sharp relief the important part played in the determination of class situation by inequalities of access to employment; and the pressures on people with poor access to give up – to substitute withdrawal from the labour market for formally acknowledged unemployment.

But when we turn from the brute facts of economic life and welfare division retold in this story to the matter of how, politically and ideologically, people react to their varying experience of these facts, the conclusions are a good deal less straightforward. Our informants generally were not galvanized into leftward-directed radicalism by their experience of recession, not even when they drew the shortest straws in the process. By a number of signs, on the contrary, there was a drift among them away from traditional labour movement support, similar to that which seems to have been going on nationally in recent years. Yet if there is such a drift it is not, from our evidence, one that can be readily summed up as a drift to the right or towards eclipse of class-based political conflict. There are too many uncertainties, ambiguities and ostensible paradoxes to the orientations involved for that.

153

The study and its setting

The firm which had employed the men and women whose experiences after redundancy we followed up was a privately-owned company in Sheffield's main steel-manufacturing district. Established in the latter half of the nineteenth century, it was below the threshold for nationalization in 1967, and remained under control of the founding family until take-over, in 1978, by a large multinational corporation. Even then it retained much of its local reputation – which many of our respondents confirmed – for conscientious paternalism in everyday management and for quiet labour relations. But the market was ominously contracting and competition increasing. In 1979 the board decided to close its Forging Division and to combine this with a general reduction of its payroll, mainly in the division but with some scope also for other employees to take redundancy under the scheme negotiated with the union conveners. Just over 600 – out of altogether some 3700 – were made redundant, all but thirty-seven of them on a formally voluntary basis which entitled them, over and above statutory redundancy pay, to a tax-free sum in lieu of notice and a further sum calculated by reference to length of service and age.

A further 400 left the company by negotiated transfer to another private steel firm (which acquired the Forging Division's order book) and to a large local plant of British Steel. Many of these people are said since to have lost their new jobs, on poorer terms than had they opted out altogether in 1979; and further redundancies followed at the firm itself, until it finally closed in 1983. But we did not have the opportunity to follow up these many other victims of economic decline; our account is of the first cohort to be made redundant.

We were able to interview most of them because – after an initial approach from the firm, followed by board hesitations eventually resolved to the effect only of some delay – management and union conveners agreed, 'without strings', to allow us use of a list of those made redundant. This contained their names, addresses at the time, and some individual details from which in due course we could check the representativeness of those whom we succeeded in tracing and interviewing some three years later: a total of 378 – over 70 per cent of the people effectively available from the list, and a good cross-section of all those who had lost their jobs in 1979.[1]

The research opportunity offered us here was welcome. There is no general sampling frame available from which one can readily identify people made redundant at a given time, in order to follow up their experiences thereafter. Moreover, the group on our list, though from only one firm, was both relatively large and usefully mixed in composition. About two in every three came from manual jobs with the firm, roughly equal numbers from skilled and from non-skilled work; the remaining third or so had been in nonmanual work – about 15 per cent in clerical and similarly routine jobs, about 20 per cent in work of higher grades, supervisory, managerial or technical. True, there were relatively few women – some 13 per cent, almost all made redundant from routine-level office jobs. And, as could be anticipated from the nature of the firm and the redundancy situation, the composition of the group was skewed towards middle age and above, and towards long service with the company. Over half our respondents were 55 years old or more when we interviewed them, only one in eight below 30; nearly half had served with the one employer for twenty years or more, only 15 per cent for under five years. But the impact of recession on the middle-aged and older has attracted less attention than it warrants. Our results can go some way to remedying that; and they relate to people sufficiently varied in their socio-economic circumstances to allow fruitful comparisons of post-redundancy experience and reactions among them.

The study is, of course, only local. But we saw advantage – over and above the practicalities of access – to Sheffield as its site. That city offers rather special opportunities for assessment, in particular, of some of the socio-political repercussions of economic decline. It can be seen as a 'test case' in this respect for two reasons. First, the transition from relative affluence to depression has been both recent and abrupt in Sheffield. Large-scale steel production, associated manufacture and engineering have been central to the local economy for well over a hundred years. Growth and relative prosperity from that base were interrupted only briefly, though acutely, even in the 1930s. But from the latter half of the 1970s the base – not least its core in production of 'special steels' – has been crumbling; and, formerly somewhat below the national average, registered unemployment in Sheffield has risen to equal or even slightly exceeding it – to 5 per cent in 1979 (when our respondents lost their jobs), to 14 per cent in 1982 (when we interviewed most of them) and to 15 per cent in May 1985.

Second, the city is a stronghold of the organized labour movement. Even in 1983, after depletion of the Labour vote in the general elections both of that year and 1979, five of the six Sheffield parliamentary constituencies remained in the party's hands – as before, and like the eight other constituencies in South Yorkshire. Control over local government has for long been firmly with Labour; and the style and ambitions of the leadership at that level have recently boosted the tongue-in-cheek reputation of the city as the metropolitan centre of a 'Socialist Republic of South Yorkshire'. But the degree of match between organized politics and grassroots opinion remains a question for exploration; radicalization of the former cannot be simply read off from the conjunction of heightened militancy on the public stage with deepening recession.

Economic experience after redundancy

Announcement of the plant closure did not come as a bolt from the blue. Looking back, about half the manual workers in our group said that they had expected it. So did two in three of the office workers and supervisors who, even when in routine jobs, may have been better placed to pick up reliable

155

hearsay. But, irrespective of work level, most remembered having been 'upset'; and anxieties proved well founded. All the people we interviewed had regular full-time work until the moment of redundancy, mostly over a long period with the same employer. Three years later, only four in every ten had paid work; and for a few of these – mainly women – even that was only part time.

Table 6.1 *Employment at interview by age*

Employment status at interview	Age at interview			All informants
	Under 40 %	40–59 %	60 and over %	
In paid work	69	62	13	41
Unemployed	18	27	15	20
Retired –				
early	–	–	43	17
normal	–	–	12	6
Other	13	11	17	16
Total: %	100	100	100	100
(no.)	(81)	(113)	(152)	(346)
Percentage economically active	87	89	28	61
Percentage unemployed among economically active	20	30	53	31

Notes:

1 The table is confined to informants for whom a full record is available
2 Unemployed = registered *and* looking for work
3 Retired, normal = retired at (or after) normal retiring age
4 Other = Out of labour market for reasons other than retirement
5 Economically active = those in paid work and the unemployed.

Of course the outcome varied with age (Table 6.1). The number of people without paid work included many of 60 years and over who had now taken retirement. But even these had done so usually before normal retirement age, often only reluctantly and not infrequently after hard personal experience of inability to find new work. We shall discuss later the combination of pressures which so frequently led older people in our group to choose premature retirement in preference to employment market insecurity. Differences of age, however, were relatively unimportant in the outcome for people under 60. Among these, young and middle-aged more or less alike, about one in every three was still without work – unemployed or out of the labour force – three years after redundancy. We say 'still', because those who did not find a new place in the job market early on were unlikely to do so later; and their chances depended very much on the level of their work before redundancy and the qualifications – or lack of them – commonly recognized to be associated with it.

Table 6.2 *Informants under 60 at interview – summary of employment status at different times by occupational level*

Occupational level before redundancy	Percentage in paid work at time			Percentage unemployed among economically active at time		
	A	B	C	A	B	C
Non-skilled manual	28	53	42	70	43	51
Skilled manual	61	80	86	37	17	13
Routine non-manual	43	60	40	46	22	37
Higher non-manual	66	83	83	29	13	8
All informants under 60	49	69	64	47	25	26

Notes
1 The table is confined to informants u..der 60 years old at the time of interview for whom a full record, including details of work level before redundancy, is available: a total of 185, of whom 169 were 'economically active' (in work or registered as unemployed and looking for work) at times A and B and 161 at time C.
2 A = immediately after redundancy; B = six months after redundancy; C = at interview approximately three years after redundancy.

Just under half the people under 60 walked into a new job more or less straight after redundancy. Over the next six months more found work, and a little over two in every three were then employed. Thereafter, very few hitherto jobless made their way into paid work; some who had previously managed it lost their new jobs or withdrew from the labour market; and the net effect was a downward slippage of the numbers in paid work to rather less than two-thirds at the three-year point of time when we interviewed (Table 6.2, left-hand side).

That is the picture overall. It takes much sharper social shape when we look at variations in experience according to 'class' – the level of work before redundancy. Skilled manual workers and those who came from supervisory or managerial work – more or less alike – *both* had far greater ease than others in finding alternative employment straight away, *and* maintained or improved their still higher six-month point employment figures over the following two-and-a-half years. By extreme contrast, manual workers without recognized skills started off on a poor footing – with little more than a quarter in new jobs. Over the next and crucial six months another quarter or so managed to find work; but as further time passed, employment in their case slipped back. When we interviewed, 'non-employment' (whether registered unemployment or retreat from the job market) was three to four times as high among the non-skilled under 60 (58 per cent) as among the skilled (14 per cent) and the higher-grade nonmanual people (17 per cent).

'Non-employment' – the reciprocal of the 'paid work' rates shown in the left-hand side of Table 6.2 – is in fact a notion that makes good sense of the post-redundancy experience of many respondents. Even for those as yet without the option of early retirement, either personal exposure to fruitless job-hunting or a general sense of the scarcity of jobs is liable to discourage continued participation in 'economic' activity – on grounds of ill-health not serious enough to have that effect before redundancy; or because domestic commitments now loom larger as a realistic priority; or for no other stated reason than despair of finding work. It is not surprising that of the non-skilled under 60 still without a job three years after redundancy, one in four had by then opted out of the labour market on just these counts – by contrast with hardly any of the much fewer skilled workers who were still workless. For throughout the three years it was the non-skilled who, if they remained 'economically active', had the least chance of finding – and holding on to – work. Even so, most neither wanted nor could afford to give up entirely, but kept a foot in the labour market despite the odds against success. These features of the story are summed up by the conventional measure of unemployment, the rate of joblessness among people still engaged in the market for work (Table 6.2, right-hand side). At each stage, this rate was consistently highest for the non-skilled – indeed desperately high, at over 40 per cent even at the six-month 'employment peak' and at some 50 per cent for a full three years after redundancy. It was consistently lowest – at the time of interview six times lower – for former supervisors and managers of the firm: they had comparatively little trouble in finding new work and, if they pulled out as a few did, it was by choice rather than *force majeur*.

The experience of the 'routine nonmanual' group is coloured by the fact that, uniquely in the sample, it comprised mainly women. More in this group found new jobs early on after redundancy than of the non-skilled men; but after three years just as many (60 per cent) were without paid work. Over half of these had left the labour market – usually, as they said, to become full-time housewives. But while some would no doubt have done so anyway, even in better circumstances, it is clear from their accounts that the scarcity of jobs often tipped the scales in their decisions between the employment market and domestic commitments. Among those who remained 'economically active', in fact, the rate of unemployment three years after redundancy was (at 37 per cent) almost as high as it had been right at the outset and now much closer to the rate among the non-skilled than to those for the skilled and for their former nonmanual superiors. For such women – once 'semi-skilled' workers of the office world – retreat from an insecure labour market into unpaid work at home offered an alternative to formally acknowledged unemployment with the advantage of some conventional dignity. If this was an 'option', however, it was one heavily conditioned by the pressures of the economic climate.

For older people, early retirement could offer a similarly dignified alternative to hardship in the labour market. Well over half the people 60 years old and over when we interviewed had then retired, the great majority of these before reaching official pension age (Table 6.1). Quite often the decision to retire was a positive one, taken with a sense of relief and of pride in having 'done my bit and earned a rest'. Commonly, moreover, retirement carried some financial advantage over the likely alternative of unemployment. A recent change in social security provisions had given a benefit-incentive to unemployed men aged 60–64 to declare themselves retired before reaching pension age; and many who retired could also then begin to draw on private pension arrangements, including their former firm's scheme.

For all this, however, the choice was often difficult. Not only had some three in every four of those who, sooner or later, opted for early retirement had no thought of doing so before redundancy came on to the agenda, but about half said they would have preferred to continue working, and about a quarter went through a spell of unemployment before opting out. Choices again were conditioned by pressures; and the often delicate balance sheets which the older people drew up in their minds to weight continuation in the labour market against withdrawal from it differed substantially according to 'class situation'.[2]

Among the older respondents, manual workers were by all signs more anxious than former members of the nonmanual staff – routine as well as higher grade – to keep the door to employment at least a little open: less inclined throughout the three years to pull out of the labour market; slower to do so when they took this step; and less likely then to choose definitive retirement in preference to regarding themselves as out of circulation for the time being, on grounds especially of ill-health. This was so particularly in the case of skilled men – among whom, for example, fewer than a third had fully retired even after three years, compared with about half the non-skilled men of the same 60 and over age group and nearly three in every four of those – men and women – who had been made redundant from nonmanual work of different levels.

That the skilled were still more reluctant than the non-skilled to give up all idea of paid work could have been because they thought their chances of success – like those of their younger counterparts – to be better. In fact, however, in this age group unemployment among the 'economically active' was not only very high in general (over 75 per cent immediately on redundancy, over 50 per cent three years later after many had pulled out); but it also varied rather little, and in no consistent way, with previous occupational level. It was simply hard for the older people, as older people, to get new work when they tried. But a decision to opt out altogether could be no less hard – and often was so, for the manual workers especially.

For women, concentrated previously in clerical work, retirement at 60 was at least conventional even though financially problematic. And the former supervisors and managers, though drawn only from the low-to-middle ranks of the firm's management hierarchy, could usually retire on relatively comfortable terms. Not so the manual workers, among whom the skilled could expect to find the premiums which they had once enjoyed over the non-skilled in the employment market reduced or eliminated in retirement.

True, the skilled took more money away with them in redundancy pay than the non-skilled – in this age group with the largest handshakes, an average of some £7000 for the former, under £4500 for the latter and less than £3000 for the routine clerical group. But these were all quite modest sums – more usable, and in fact used and run down, for everyday expenditure to supplement otherwise reduced resources than for investment to yield a lasting boost to retirement income – by contrast with the supervisory and managerial group's average, some £16,000. And for those who had retired by the time of interview in 1982/83, the gap in regular incomes (respondent and spouse together) between this 'top' group and the rest was indeed marked. With relatively generous occupational pension payments and other private income to add as much again to public benefits – the latter fairly similar for all – the one-time supervisors and managers averaged after tax about £105 a week in retirement: not a very grand sum even then, but a good deal more solid than the averages of some £60–70 for those who had retired from essentially wage-earning work, manual or routine nonmanual, skilled or non-skilled. When many people of these kinds were reluctant to commit themselves to premature retirement, it was not without good reason.

Suggestions have recently become prominent that, under the impact of 'de-industrialization' and wider economic change linked to technological innovation, a new line of social division will increasingly separate many skilled wage-earners who, together with professionals and technicians, have resources of recognized specialism and collective organization sufficient to protect their places in the employment market by tactics of 'closure', from a mass medley of others – the non-skilled, women, members of ethnic minorities – who, lacking these resources, will find regular work progressively harder to get and ill-paid, their links with the world of organized employment more and more tenuous, their dependence on a publicly funded 'social wage' correspondingly more crucial. The 'working class', in scenarios of this kind, is at imminent risk of dissolution into two quite distinct groups.[3]

A good deal of the evidence we have summarized so far could be seen to support such prognoses. Once they had been made redundant, the non-skilled manual workers and the women who came from routine office work certainly proved to have a far looser hold on the labour market than skilled blue-collar workers and former supervisory and managerial staff. In terms of access to re-employment of some kind, the dividing line was – from our data just as from other data on unemployment – much as Bauman or Gorz would anticipate: a line *within* the 'working-class' (however defined in detail), rather than around it.

There were signs of this too in some other respects relevant to the thesis of 'infra-class polarization'. Even when unemployed, for example, over half the skilled retained membership of a trade union, but hardly any of the non-skilled or the routine nonmanual group did. If severance of union ties is a symptom of individual isolation in recession so, more generally, is loss of income when it entails reduced expenditure and less recreational activity – as it did especially, again, for the non-skilled. They reported themselves as worse off over the three years – whether through loss of work or through lower earnings – still more often than others (nearly four in every five of them, compared with two in every three of the skilled and little more than half of either nonmanual group). When they did so, moreover, they also almost invariably said that they had had to cut down spending in consequence. Among others who reported loss of income, by contrast, quite a number had not had to reduce spending – at least not to a degree which they felt worth mentioning. This was so for four out of ten among skilled men and routine nonmanual women alike; and for nearly three in four former supervisors and managers – for whom savings or a fair margin of previous earnings over outgoings evidently cushioned such loss of income as they had to cope with.

Even so the pattern here involved not a sharp line of division separating the experience of the skilled manual and higher nonmanual groups alike from that of the others, but a gradient. And this was the case also in a number of other respects where, in particular, skill in former manual work provided only limited – or even no – distinctive protection against economic vicissitude following redundancy. Unless 'old', the skilled certainly had comparatively very good chances of re-employment in some form: even if their skills were not directly transferable, they probably had a fair 'know how' about openings in the local labour market and bore a hallmark as 'good workers'. But that was no guarantee of re-employment in *skilled* work. In fact, one in three of those among them who had a job three years later was now in a non-skilled job (and hardly any, as might be expected, in higher grade work than the work they had lost).

'Down-grading' on this scale was indeed a common trend for those who found and kept employment after redundancy: a drift into unskilled labour from the ranks of the formerly non-skilled (whose work at the firm had been generally 'semi-skilled'); into manual work from among women once in routine office work; into a range of blue-collar and lower-grade white-collar work even in the case of former supervisors and managers. The latter, however, while not immune from downgrading, retained on average a distinct advantage in income over all others still at work: jointly between respondent and spouse a mean of some £135 a week after tax in 1982/83, compared with around £115 for the formerly skilled, £100 for the non-skilled and rather less for the routine nonmanual group.

At quite a risk of downgrading when they found re-employment the skilled, moreover, could expect circumstances little different from the non-skilled and the women previously in routine clerical work when, by force or choice, they did not. They had to cope with much the same low income if unemployed – though, age for age, with rather more redundancy pay to help out until this was exhausted. And, as we said earlier, they had much the same income as former non-skilled and routine-grade office colleagues if they retired – again at a low level, though with a small benefit-and-pensions bonus over income in unemployment. On these material scores, and in much of the way in which respondents themselves assessed their changed circumstances, experiences of unemployment and of withdrawal from the labour market were similar for most of those who had been ordinary wage-earners, the skilled more or less on a par with the non-skilled: financially hard, commonly seen as difficult, associated both with mental stress and a degree of social isolation in unemployment especially.

Only the former supervisors and managers, as a group, stood out from this pattern. Their redundancy pay was generally well above that of others – by a factor of two or more relative to the skilled, except in the youngest group – and of 'investable' proportions (even though virtually never used for a new start in small independent business, as the current government might have liked). If they retired or pulled out of 'economic activity' in other ways, they did so usually on at least moderately comfortable incomes; with some past accumulation of resources to cushion loss of direct earnings; and in a welcoming rather than a grudging or anxious mood. They shared with skilled manual workers distinctly good chances of re-employment in some form after redundancy, unless they were 'old'. But they carried more resources with them to cope with downgrading in work, and above all with life out of paid work. These were not high executives, members of well-established professions, let alone tycoons: those levels of the class structure are well outside the range of this survey. Even so, their defences against redundancy and its aftermath were a good deal stronger than those of skilled blue-collar people. Once the latter slipped, either within the labour market or right out of it, they shared stringent circumstances in common with others whose livelihood had centred on ordinary wage-earning work, manual or nonmanual. Industrial skill does not, on this evidence, give durable security or set a new line of social cleavage below itself. The well-known line between wage-centred and even rather low-level salary-centred life still seems prominent.

Political orientations

There is, as our results emphasize, no very sharp distinction to be drawn between unemployment and withdrawal from the labour market as consequences of curtailment of paid work opportunities. And, as personal experiences, both are liable to be coupled with mental stress – but unemployment almost invariably so, and most acutely. By a standard measure of psychological tension (Bradburn's scale of 'negative affect'), for example, average levels of personal stress over the previous few weeks before interview were twice as high, in our group, for respondents who had by then pulled out of 'economic activity' as for those in paid work – with no such heightened anxiety in the case only of former supervisors and managers, whose decision to opt out had often been relatively free. But it was three times as high among people who had stayed on in the labour market yet were still without a job. They had not only the lowest incomes, the sharpest experience of cuts in expenditure and recreational activity, a common despair of getting the jobs for which they were still at least nominally looking. But also, because they usually shared with most others the conventional assumptions of a 'work ethic' (more accurately a 'paid employment ethic'), they often suffered from self-doubt. Neither they nor others in fact generally subscribed to the view that unemployment is the fault of the unemployed themselves. Yet they still half-suspected such stigma in the eyes of the world, and tended to turn anxieties about loss of respect from others into qualifications of their self-respect.

This is a familiar finding about the personal impact of unemployment, at least on people who – like our respondents – have been long in the world of work before being forced to its margins. It may also give some help to explaining why in the 1980s, as at earlier times, deep recession has not on the whole mobilized its prime victims for political radicalism on the left. Indeed on the first face of our evidence, any shift in ideological outlook among this group in Sheffield resembled simultaneous trends in the country more widely in pointing rightwards.

Take the most obvious index, political party support – though this is also, as we shall argue, a rather crude and uncertain index. Four in every five respondents overall described themselves as having usually supported one or other political party before 1979 – the year of the first Thatcher-led Conservative election victory and, as it happened, of the redundancies. And of these party stalwarts, some six in every seven had supported Labour – the manual workers among them almost *en bloc*, irrespective of skill level; substantial majorities even of the people in the two grades of nonmanual work before redundancy. But in 1979 and over the next few years support for Labour ebbed away among these hitherto dependable adherents of the party (see Table 6.3).

One in every three of those many on whom Labour had normally been able to count earlier 'defected' from the party either in 1979 or – if respondents stuck to the intentions they expressed in interviews which happened to be conducted over a period shortly followed by the next general election – in 1983. Defection of this sort was on a fairly small scale in 1979, concentrated mainly among nonmanual respondents and favouring Conservatives over Liberals in a ratio of two to one; hardly any of these people saw themselves as returning to Labour the next time round. The main fall-out from Labour, if we can rely on stated intentions, was to come in 1983 – then more into a limbo of electoral abstention or uncertainty than into positive support for other parties; and among the latter into support for the new Liberal–SDP Alliance more than for the Conservatives. But though 'defection' yielded fewer gains for Labour's opponents than it involved losses for Labour – and the latter also attracted, or could hope to attract, a little more new support than its opponents from the minority who had been uncommitted to any party before 1979 – the drift away of former adherents left Labour in 1983 with definite

163

Table 6.3 *Defection from Labour among previous Labour supporters – by employment status at interview and by pre-redundancy occupation.*

	Employment status				Occupational level				All respondents
	Emp.	Unemp.	Ret.	Other	OM	SM	RNM	HNM	
% of all in category who usually supported one party before 1979	83	74	84	76	80	89	69	71	80
% of these 'usual supporters' who supported Labour before 1979	83	92	80	95	93	94	78	66	86
% of latter who 'defected' from Labour 1979–83	38	30	31	30	24	37	46	42	34

Notes:

Employment status at interview – Emp. = in paid work; Unemp. = registered unemployed and looking for work; Ret. = retired, whether 'early' or 'normal'; Other = otherwise withdrawn from labour market.

Occupational level before redundancy – OM = non-skilled manual; SM = skilled manual; RNM = routine, nonmanual; HNM = supervisory, technical, managerial staff.

'Defected' from Labour – are among those 'usual Labour supporters' before 1979 who either did not vote Labour in 1979 or expressed an intention at the interview 1982–83 not to vote Labour at the next election.

support from little more than half our respondents overall, compared with well over two-thirds before the 'electoral break' which brought the first Thatcher-led government to office.

Yet these were all people who had experienced recession at first hand at least in the form of redundancy. True, support for Labour waned rather less among those with the hardest experience after redundancy – the 'non-employed' of all kinds – than among those who still had paid work three years later (Table 6.3, bottom row). But the differences on this score were small; and on closer inspection they prove to reflect not so much the varying direct impact of experience after redundancy as the 'class' differences which helped to make for those variations in experience. Non-skilled manual workers were, as we have shown, hardest hit by redundancy and its aftermath; but, more or less irrespective of this, they stayed more loyal to Labour anyway. 'Only' a quarter of *their* pre-1979 Labour stalwarts withdrew support for the party, compared with over a third of their skilled counterparts and more than 40 per cent of those whose work before redundancy had been nonmanual. For all else that they entailed, variations in immediate labour market experience over the three years were thus little connected with shifts of electoral inclination. What mattered politically far more, it appears, were larger and longer-standing differences of socio-economic situation – between skilled and non-skilled manual, the former now more prone than the latter to question their previous party commitments; between manual and nonmanual, the latter even in this Sheffield group less attached to Labour from the outset.

The drift away from Labour went hand in hand with scepticism towards some of the policies and approaches commonly associated with the party or the movement. The term 'scepticism' is justified because the current of opinion among respondents – on a wide range of questions concerning industrial relations, causes and remedies for unemployment, justice and injustice in current social arrangements – showed a complexity that resists ready classification into conventional categories of 'left' and 'right'. Commitments remained strong, for example, to generally formulated notions of trade unionism and working-class co-operation as defences against employers' self-interest, and to perceptions of wealth and power in British society as unfairly concentrated. But some more specific actions or measures which might seem consonant with orientations of that sort – union militancy, public ownership of major industry or workers' control as measures for economic regeneration – evoked divided views or majority dissent. And in terms of opinion it was disagreement over these matters which, among pre-1979 Labour supporters, distinguished those who withdrew their support from those who maintained it.

The way in which basic orientations sympathetic to the labour movement – especially among manual workers – were mixed with doubts or distrust in respect of militant action is illustrated in Table 6.4. This sets out only a limited number of the issues on which we asked for comment, concerning matters mainly of industrial relations though also of British social structure at large; but the patterns of response are similar to those which emerge from

Table 6.4 *Expression of 'leftward inclined' views in response to selected propositions.*

	Percentage assenting or dissenting among		
	All	Manual	Nonmanual
1 Working class people have got to stand together and stick up for one another: % Yes	83	90	69
2 If it weren't for the unions bosses could do what they wanted with their workers and most of them would: % Yes	68	79	48
3 Given half a chance most managements will try and put one over on their work-force: % Yes	44	50	34
4 Most major conflicts in industry are caused by agitators or extremists: % No	30	28	30
5 Trade unions don't have enough power – it's time they started to take a tougher line against employers and the government: % Yes	19	25	6
6 If my union called on me to strike I'd do so even if I disagreed with the decision: % Yes	62	72	45
7 Unions should not be allowed to stop people working when they want to: % No (i.e. disagreeing with statement)	36	42	24
8 A union member should be prepared to strike in support of other people even if they don't work in the same place: % Yes	37	45	24
9 If you go on strike it should only be about matters that affect you directly in your own workplace: % No	22	24	21
10 . . . If your union (had) asked you to strike for a day to support the health workers' claim, would you (have) do(ne) so? % Yes	56	67	37
11 In Britain today wealth is concentrated in the hands of too few people: % Yes	85	91	75
12 People from wealthy families who have been to public schools have too much influence and power in Britain: % Yes	75	81	65
13 The poor have only themselves to blame for their problems: % No	72	72	72
14 In Britain today anyone with brains and initiative can get to the top regardless of who their father was: % No	35	36	33

Note: The classification manual/nonmanual is according to the last job before redundancy.

analysis of the whole range of propositions – including suggested policies to tackle unemployment – which we put to informants. These were mostly provocative propositions, couched in words of conventional wisdom whether 'left' or 'right'; each individually therefore liable to trigger responses off-the-cuff, of a pre-packaged and maybe superficial kind, variable in thrust according to the particular wording and context of the originating question. But these familiar methodological problems of opinion polling recede when one looks, not at responses to this and that provocative statement one by one, but for any pattern that may connect them. And there is a pattern to be seen.

There is first, as we have said, a tension between endorsement of abstractly formulated values of unionism and worker unity *vis-à-vis* employers who are seen to be out for themselves (statements 1 and 2, more ambiguously 6 and more marginally 3) and widespread reluctance or opposition to engagement in strike action in other than limited forms (statements 4, 5, 7, 8 and 9). The former – sentiments of employee solidarity as against management – co-exist with almost universal acceptance of a stock view that 'industry is like a football team' with workers and managers on the same side: an ostensible paradox which we are not the first to find. The latter – suspicion of militancy and lack of support in particular for 'secondary', 'sympathetic' or 'politically directed' industrial action – may seem hard to square with the notions of common working-class interest expressed in the first-listed responses or loosely implied in criticisms of the concentration of wealth and influence in British society (statements 11 and 12). But there is no necessary contradiction. Industrial militancy in effect over the preceding years had often been 'particularistic' – conducted by this or that union, trade or section for itself, with little but rhetorical reference to larger interests of class and of a kind, arguably, to foster commitments to unionism which in practice exclude 'other people's unions' from sympathy. Even so, moreover, a specific question about one current dispute which seemed to put wider issues of social justice on the agenda of public debate (statement 10) in fact attracted majority support for at least a token of sympathy.

A second feature of the pattern concerns 'class' differences in response. We have used a simple occupational distinction in Table 4 between manual and nonmanual because, generally, it was by this familiar social fissure that opinions were divided. Though the skilled among manual workers had more often withdrawn their votes from Labour than the non-skilled, the 'opinion profiles' of the two groups on the issues we put to them were in many respects closely similar – and, as illustrated in the table, often sharply different from those of the nonmanual informants, whether routine or higher grade. Almost throughout, 'blue-collar' men, irrespective of skill, showed by far the stronger sympathies for ideas of labour movement inspiration; and, though small numbers hamper detailed analysis, 'white-blouse' women tended to side in contrary opinion with their former male superiors. Even so, there are strands of opinion worth noting as a sign, in this small sample at least, of scepticism *across* class lines concerning some aspects of current conventional conservative wisdom: majority rejection of the view that the poor are responsible for their own problems, for example (proposition 13); and sizeable though minority dissent from the notion that careers are now equally open to all talent (proposition 14).

By the generally 'class-split' character of the pattern hangs also a third feature. The socio-political orientations of the manual workers in our group seem to have been more uncertain – more characterized by ostensible paradox, more liable to be affected by specific question-wording and context – than those of nonmanual respondents. On the whole, as can be seen from the table, the tension between generalized sentiments of common working-class interest and misgivings about militant practice is greater for the former than the latter. (Contrast, for example, statements 1 and 2 with 4 and 9.) Moreover, when two or three questions were directed to the same general issue but in different form, the difference in wording or contextual reference made for a greater shift in expressed opinion among 'blue-collar' than among 'white-blouse/white-collar' informants. (Compare the 'milder' and 'sharper' formulations of the proposition that employers are self-interested in statements 2 and 3 respectively; and the various statements concerning 'secondary' or 'sympathetic' strike action, 8 to 10.)

When question-wording and context have a large impact on the pattern of answers it is a fair assumption – supported by survey methodological research – that opinions are uncertain and liable to change. It is significant – though neither surprising nor an entirely new finding – that they should be so among manual workers especially, over issues on which people of the 'traditional working class' in recent years have been caught up in intense cross-pressures from their established collective organizations on the one hand, newer influences from a changing economic scene and from the mass media on the other.

Conclusions

It is more than just convenient to draw a line between class as a matter of rooted inequalities of economic situation and class as a matter of socio-political consciousness and action in collective recognition of the conflicting interests implied by such inequalities. That distinction – in shorthand between class-in-itself and class-for-itself – also makes sound socio-historical sense. Certainly no ready reckoner has been found with which to translate the former into the latter. And if ready reckoning would have predicted a popular swing to the left in response to the sharpening of inequalities associated with recession – especially when recession followed a long period of economic growth and self-assertion on the part of organized labour – both recent national political trends and our limited local findings confirm the futility of such ready reckoning.

Indeed on this score the very limitations of our study help to make the point stronger. For in Sheffield, more than in many other places, both the local culture of organized politics and the abruptness of the recent transition to slump might have been thought conducive to militancy and left-wing defiance in the adverse economic and political climate of the early 1980s. And that has been the case, to a degree, in the conduct of local government; but not, correspondingly, at the grassroots to judge either by electoral trends in the city or by our findings. Moreover, if our findings could be thought suspect because our respondents came from a firm with a reputation for 'paternalist' industrial relations, neither their usual support for Labour till 1979 nor detailed internal analysis of the data suggests that unusually 'deferential' attitudes among informants played much part in the drift away from the party or common qualms about militancy and some other features of conventional left-wing policy.

It is not, on reflection, surprising that the people worst affected by redundancy – those unemployed over long periods of time – disappointed simplistic ready reckoning by failing to be galvanized into new or renewed radical activism. As others have found before us, for people geared to paid work as a source of both livelihood and self-respect, unemployment is an individually isolating experience. The announcement of redundancy itself, from the accounts we obtained, divided the work-force as much as it united them; and such unity as there might have been – insufficient as in fact it was for even token collective resistance in a firm known to be in decline – was quickly dissipated as people left to find their own individual ways in a tightening labour market. Those who then came to face severe adversity – no job at all, a short-term job here and there and then none, reluctant withdrawal to early retirement or domestic commitments, no such face-saving option as an alternative to 'stamped' unemployment, exhaustion of redundancy pay – reached their individual crisis points at different times; in any case in little or no contact with former workmates; and isolated still more by lack of money and by self-doubt. 'Privatization in recession' can be more potent, and more corrosive in its effect on political activism, than any 'privatization in affluence'.

But if this helps to explain the absence of a positive shift to the left, it does not do much to explain the drift in what appears to be the opposite direction. Four points about that seem to stand out from our results. First, although the drift away from Labour may in the event have been smaller at actual polling date in 1983 than suggested by respondents' vote intentions before that, the local culture and situation clearly did not 'immunize' these Sheffield people from larger trends at work in Britain as a whole. Second, differences in immediate economic experience following redundancy – even over three years – can account only in a very small way for the differences in electoral inclinations and socio-political outlook which emerge from the analysis. In particular – and despite differential 'defections' from Labour involving skilled more than non-skilled manual workers – skilled and non-skilled more or less alike retained general sympathies and perceptions consonant with the labour movement's traditions, to a degree which set them off quite clearly from the low-to-middle grade nonmanual people among our respondents.

This evident persistence of an old line of political division suggests a

169

significant continuing influence on popular ideology of lifetime or at least long-enduring – as distinct from short-term however dramatic – socio-economic experience. And seen in this context, two questions arise from the fact that even so – here as nationally – skilled manual workers have been more ready than the non-skilled to take their votes away from their traditional party. One question is why. The answer to that may need to take account of new differences in long-term 'class situation' between skilled and non-skilled, perhaps especially in respect of effective access to important private-market consumer goods such as owner-occupied housing. Another question is whether, in future, the skilled are more likely to realign their general social values and perceptions to fit their voting inclinations of recent years; or to shift back again into a voting pattern more in line with the basic labour movement sympathies which, by our evidence, they continue to hold. Neither question can be answered from our data.

A range of recent electoral research has found signs of increased volatility of voting behaviour; a decreasing influence on individual voting – or abstention from voting – of longstanding class commitments; an increasing influence of hard-nosed *ad hoc* appraisals of party performance and practical promise, within the limits set to such utilitarian judgements by the capacity of media and politicians to shape the electoral agenda. The third point of note from our results on this front is that they are consistent with such findings – or at least not inconsistent with them. When a good many of our respondents failed to give Labour their wonted support in 1979 and/or 1983, it was from their own accounts often because the party seemed associated with an industrial militancy which had come to be regarded as self-seeking and counterproductive, and with policies some of which – though laudable in their goals of economic regeneration and equity – seemed to lack sufficient practical credibility either in themselves or at the hands of a Labour Party then very visibly divided within itself.

But if this was a 'drift *from* the left' it was not – and here is the fourth point to be noted – correspondingly a 'drift *to* the right'. It is essential to reiterate this feature of the pattern and the complexities of opinion which go with it. The manual workers among our respondents, in particular, remained strong in their views of employers as concerned mainly with their own interests; of working-class unity and unionism as essential in defence against that; of wealth and influence as unfairly skewed, though individual opportunity much less so. And while opinions were – in liberal eyes disturbingly – divided on the notion that further immigration control might ease unemployment, our respondents had not otherwise come to subscribe to loudspoken right-wing views of the time. They had not commonly embraced the ideas, for example, that the remedy for poverty and unemployment lies with their victims or in holding down wages, or that married women should be discouraged from paid work to give more of it to others.

So overall – and especially among blue-collar workers – there were tensions here between pragmatic political judgements and more general socio-ideological orientations. In the uncertainties of opinion which went with these

170

tensions, there seemed to be considerable leeway for change in the future; but in which direction the data cannot say.[4]

The results of the study are more clear-cut in respect of class-in-itself. Yet there are limits here too – which arise less from the local character of the project than from the very fact that its focus was experience *after* redundancy. So, because the risk of redundancy is itself highly skewed, the 'sample' too is highly skewed – skewed no doubt in its selection of people from the firm (though we cannot say how much, because the management felt prevented by their own crisis from offering detailed information about the decisions which led to redundancy and the processes of selection and self-selection involved); skewed still more because it leaves entirely out of sight those levels of the class structure where the risk of redundancy is insignificant or has no meaning.

But if supervisory staff and skilled workers may have been a good deal less likely than others to be made redundant at all in 1979, the post-redundancy labour market experience of those among them who were certainly gave sharp evidence of their better economic life-chances. We have noted in particular the much better access to 'replacement jobs' of skilled than of either non-skilled manual or routine nonmanual workers because, while disparities of class situation between 'staff' and 'wage-earners' are well known, disparities *among* wage-earners between the better and the less protected raise significant questions about possible new or widening fissures in the lower ranges of the class structure.

Generalizations from our findings on this score are hazardous. Skilled workers from the declining steel industry in Sheffield are not necessarily representative of that category of organized and privileged employees whom some commentators see as able to close themselves off from current and prospective processes of labour market marginalization – processes which, they project, are liable to produce a new and numerous ill-protected substratum under, rather than of, the old working class. At first sight, however, our evidence could be read in support of this scenario. Yet at the same time it includes reminders of some of the doubts that beset the thesis.

Union strength established in boom conditions does not carry over into recession to block redundancy. Once-recognized skills – and what else goes with them – can give potent help after redundancy in the search for alternative employment; but as quite a number of the skilled people, especially the older men, in our group found, they give no guarantee of continued status, earnings and security as skilled. Once out of regular paid work, moreover – as unemployed, as sick, as retired – the formerly skilled face much the same conditions of life as the formerly non-skilled. These are conditions, if not of penury then often of hardship and usually of stringently tightened belts and uncertainty for the future, which they share in common, as people whose lives have centred on jobs. By contrast people whose working lives have been geared rather to careers – management and associated staff employees, even at quite modest levels – generally carry a bonus of security and comfort with them into life beyond work. That division of economic class is, for the present at least, still plain.

171

Notes and references

1 We are grateful to the Social Science Research Council (now Economic and Social Research Council), which funded the study. The interviews, using a mainly structured schedule, took an average of over two hours. Deaths, serious illness, errors on the list and other reasons reduced the number available for interview to about 530, of whom some 100 proved untraceable after a move and just over 50 refused. Those interviewed were well representative of the 600 odd made redundant in respect of age, length of service, gender and occupational level – about which the original list gave details – except that young and middle-aged informants with less than five years service were somewhat underrepresented, though to negligible effect on the overall results.

2 We have discussed the post-redundancy experience of our older respondents in some detail in an earlier paper, 'From secure employment to labour market insecurity', in B. Roberts, R. Finnegan and D. Gallie (eds), *New Approaches to Economic Life* (1985).

3 Among forecasts to broadly these effects, though accompanied by different readings of the political implications, are Z. Bauman, *Memories of Class* (1982) and A. Gorz, *Farewell to the Working Class* (1982). The notion of 'closure' has been elaborated especially by F. Parkin, e.g. in his *Marxism and Class Theory* (1979).

4 Among recent work on shifts in electoral behaviour and the complex cross-currents of popular socio-political orientations the following are especially relevant: P. Dunleavy and C. T. Husbands, *British Democracy at the Crossroads* (1985); B. Sarlvik and I. Crewe, *Decade of Dealignment* (1983); P. Taylor-Gooby, *Public Opinion, Ideology and State Welfare* (1985); A. Heath *et al.*, *How Britain Votes* (1985).

Further reading

On unemployment in the 1980s:

B. Crick (ed), *Unemployment*, Methuen, 1981
A. Sinfield, *What Unemployment Means*, Martin Robertson, 1981
B. Showler and A. Sinfield (eds), *The Workless State*, Martin Robertson, 1981

On contemporary patterns and changes of economic life more generally:

P. Abrams and R. Brown (eds), *UK Society – Work: Urbanism and Inequality*, Weidenfeld and Nicolson, 1984
E. Gamarnikow *et al.* (eds), *Gender, Class and Work*, Heinemann Educational Books, 1983
R. E. Pahl, *Divisions of Labour*, Blackwell, 1984
B. Roberts *et al.* (eds), *New Approaches to Economic Life – economic restructuring: unemployment and the social division of labour*, Manchester University Press, 1985

On the theses of polarization within the working class and occupational closure:

Z. Bauman, *Memories of Class – the pre-history and after-life of class*, Routledge and Kegan Paul, 1982

A. Gorz, *Farewell to the Working Class – an essay on post-industrial socialism*, Pluto Press, 1982

F. Parkin, *Marxism and Class Theory: a Bourgeois Critique*, Tavistock, 1979

On voting behaviour and socio-political attitudes:

M. Bulmer, (ed), *Working Class Images of Society*, Routledge and Kegan Paul, 1975

P. Dunleavy and C. T. Husbands, *British Democracy at the Crossroads – voting and party competition in the 1980s*, Allen and Unwin, 1985

A. Heath *et al.*, *How Britain Votes*, Pergamon, 1985

R. Jowell, and S. Witherspoon (eds), *British Social Attitudes: the 1985 Report* Gower and SCPR, 1985

B. Sarlvik and I. Crewe, *Decade of Dealignment*, Cambridge University Press, 1983

P. Taylor-Gooby, *Public Opinion, Ideology and State Welfare*, Routledge and Kegan Paul, 1985

7 Conceptualizing the place of redundant steelworkers in the class structure

C. C. Harris and R. M. Lee

This paper arises from the attempt to understand the labour market experience of a sample of steelworkers made redundant from the British Steel Corporation's Abbey Works at Port Talbot.[1] Out of a complement of 12,476 workers in March 1979, a total of 5807 workers was made redundant under the corporation's 'slimline' plan which was put into effect in May 1980. The steelworkers were made redundant at a time when the market for labour was falling very sharply and was already extremely loose. This differentiates the present study markedly from earlier redundancy studies whose subjects were operating in much tighter markets (see, for example, Kahn, 1964; Wedderburn, 1965; and MacKay et al., 1980).

The behaviour of redundant workers has to be understood not only in terms of their previous employment and labour market histories, but in terms of the redundancy process itself, which the investigator is rarely there to observe. By 'redundancy process' we do not refer simply to the process of selection of workers for redundancy but to the whole sequence of events leading up to the workers' actual discharge. While the actual mechanisms of selection remain obscure, the events leading up to the redundancies are clear at least in outline and what Wood has termed 'the social production of redundancy' (Wood and Cohen, 1978) therefore merits some discussion. So, however, does the social institution of redundancy itself.

The background to the redundancies in BSC

Employment at the Abbey works reached its peak in 1969 when it employed just under 18,000 workers. The work-force has been steadily reduced since then by natural wastage; indeed, an annual manpower review and allocation of *job* reductions between plants and departments had become a well-established feature of BSC management policy long before the 1979 crisis which resulted in the redundancies. Since 1974–5 BSC had been operating at a loss and its sales of steel were falling. While these were important factors in the programme of cuts and closures the precipitating factor was unquestionably the policy of the 1979–83 Conservative administration which in BSC's own words 'deliberately created intense pressures upon all BSC's operations' (BSC, 1981) by imposing what Morgan (1983, p. 182) has described as 'the most stringent cash limits ever imposed on a nationalised industry in Britain'. These required a reduction of BSC's capacity from 21.5 m. tonnes to 15 m.

174

tonnes and a reduction of 53,000 in the work-force (over a third) in a mere eight months (Morgan, 1983).[2]

In spite of the size of the reduction in the labour force and the speed of its implementation, the redundancies were selective and also involved a change in the character of the labour process. First, the redundant were predominantly older, longer-service workers, a substantial proportion of whom appear to have been in ill health prior to redundancy: those 'exposed' by the redundancies were those less advantaged in the labour market in terms of the negotiability of their skills, their personal characteristics and their labour market experience. This had two consequences: it resulted first in a large proportion of the redundants (36 per cent) withdrawing from the labour force, i.e. moving out of the market[3] and it resulted in a substantial proportion (30 per cent) of the remainder remaining unemployed for the two years following the redundancies.

Second, the redundancies did not result simply from a decision to make less steel but from a decision to make steel in a new way. This change in the labour process itself also had a significant effect both on who was made redundant and on the labour market experience of the redundants who remained in the market. To understand both these effects more has to be said about the redundancy process at Port Talbot.

The generation of redundancies at Port Talbot

The effect on demand

The redundancy agreement between management and unions, required under the terms of the 1978 Employment Protection Act, specified that some work previously performed by BSC's permanent work-force would be put out to contractors. In other words, some of BSC's peripheral workers were, in future, not to be BSC workers at all but employed by contractors. The redundancies were not *simply* a result of a cutback in production but of the excision of certain functions which were to be outsourced. Morgan has noted that

despite BSC's abysmal market prospectus . . . since 1979 BSC has extracted a miraculous improvement in productivity, particularly at Port Talbot and Llanwern where hours per tonne [were] reduced from 10 to 5.7 and 4.6 respectively . . . such productivity advances have been won from *two sources*: from the assault on working practices and from mass redundancy (Morgan 1983, p. 184, emphasis added).

While we concur with Morgan that both mass redundancy and changes in working practices (also specified in the Redundancy Agreement) are largely responsible for the improvement in productivity, we insist that it has also resulted from the increased use of contractors. This increased use can be and probably was legitimated at the time, in terms of the lower level of production leading to the creation of dead time in some departments, especially those concerned with maintenance. However there is evidence that the use of contract labour at Port Talbot continued to expand after the redundancies and it is at least uncertain that the volume of contract labour now employed is warranted simply on the grounds of lower production levels (Fevre, 1984). It is certainly the case that some redundant workers were asked to report to contractors immediately after their redundancy took effect, thus indicating that some of the functions excised were vital to the plant's operation at the time of their excision.

The result has been that the redundancy event has had a marked effect on the demand side of the market. The replacement of some of the jobs lost by other jobs with contractors, fulfilling short-term contracts, has increased the proportion of employments which are fixed term. This change in the type of employment indirectly generated by steelmaking in Port Talbot has interacted with the character of the flow on to the labour market, on whose disadvantaged labour market position we have already commented.

The effect on supply

Under European Coal and Steel Community (ECSC) provisions redundant steel-workers are entitled to have their pay in subsequent employments made up to 90 per cent of their pre-redundancy pay for one and a half years. Originally designed to ease their transition from steel to a permanent job in another industrial sector, this provision now makes ex-steelworkers highly attractive employees who can be paid low wages in situations where wages are easily negotiable. Contracting, characterized as it is by sub- and sub-sub-contracting, is such a sector of employment. Hence the 1980 redundancies created a supply of suitable cheap labour for contractors to the steel industry and these contractors were thereby enabled to tender very competitively for contracts to carry out functions whose excision had brought their labour on to the market in the first place (Fevre, 1984).

The relatively disadvantaged labour market position of the redundant is to be explained by the way in which the redundancies were implemented. Management, in consultation with the unions, determined which departments should be closed and the number and distribution of *job* losses in the remaining departments. At the same time the offer of redundancy with substantial redundancy payments and other benefits was made to *workers*. Naturally there was a mismatch between *workers who applied for redundancy* and *the jobs which were scheduled to disappear*, and this was accommodated by transferring workers whose jobs were to be cut to similar jobs whose occupants had applied for redundancy (a procedure called 'cross-matching'). While this mismatch may appear to have been a problem for management it was, it can be argued, an opportunity in so far as management was able to control information flows about potential vacancies to workers whose jobs were due to go, thus enabling them to retain valued workers at the expense of others. At the same time, since redundancy payments are related to lengths of service, it is likely that the more voluntary redundancies were positively related to the age, length of service, and ill health of workers. A union official described the 1980s redundancies as, in the main, 'soft' redundancies (that is, they involved workers who volunteered or were relatively easily persuaded to accept redundancy) as opposed to any further and feared redundancies which would be 'hard'.

Nevertheless there *were* 'hard' redundancies in 1980. The task of deciding which men – of those who didn't want to go but had to – were to be made redundant was left to the fifteen unions in the plant. Though they were somewhat coy about the selection procedures used, 'last in, first out' would seem to have been at least one of the criteria. The net result of the interaction of these processes was to create a population of redundants, a large proportion of whom went out of the market leaving a remainder whose labour market position was relatively poor. The exception to this statement is the workers, not cross-matched, from departments which had been abolished. It was these workers who were needed immediately by the contractors who were to perform the functions which had been excised.

The wider significance of the Port Talbot redundancies

Most of the redundants had little experience of the external labour market because they had been existing in a large internal market. Labour reductions had previously been possible without redundancies because of the possibility of transferring workers from one part of the plant to another.

Now a large internal labour market is a rational response to labour shortage. Labour is retained during temporary recession (resulting in overmanning) against the occurrence of certain labour shortage in the coming boom. Internal labour markets are associated with *labour hoarding*. The opposite of this situation is constituted by a product market in which demand is falling and uncertain, and a labour market in which there is a substantial unutilized supply. In these circumstances, especially in the case of steel,[4] it makes good economic sense to reverse the labour hoarding/internal labour market policies of more prosperous times and replace them by the attempt to create what has been called 'the flexible firm' (Atkinson, 1984). This concept involves separating a firm's activities into core and peripheral functions, core functions being defined as those necessary for the maintenance of productive capacity. These are discharged by a permanent labour force whose tenure is guaranteed, while all other labour is bought in as required.

The effect of a shift from internal labour market/labour hoarding firm to the flexible firm is of course both a consequence and a determinant of the character of the labour market: a consequence, because a loose labour market makes hoarding unnecessary; a determinant, because a market whose demand side is made up of flexible firms will be characterized by flows on and off the market as labourers are hired and discharged according to varying production levels in response to varying product market demand.

The effect of the shift to the flexible firm is vastly to expand what has been termed the 'secondary sector' of the labour market. First, by abolishing a large proportion of the jobs constituting the internal labour market, it forces labourers on to the open market. Second, it does not replace the jobs lost by relatively permanent jobs of the same kind, but rather produces an irregular demand for short-term labour as *a persistent feature* of labour demand. We wish to argue, however, that the terminology of primary and secondary sectors of the *market* cannot be accepted on the grounds of the existence of differences among employments alone. We are only entitled to infer from differentiation of employments to the existence of market sectors if it is the case that *there is a corresponding division on the supply side such that there exist categories of workers, identifiable in terms of their different positions in the social structure*, the members of which share similar chances of obtaining secondary types of employment, which chances are greater than those of workers in other social locations. The emergence of the flexible firm makes the conventional use of 'sector' or 'segmented' terminology doubly problematic, however, since the primary/secondary distinction may be applied to employments within the same firm. The emergence of such firms does, however, signal, not a growth of the secondary 'sector', but a growth of secondary *employment*.

There is, however, a difficulty which stands in the way of capital's shift to the flexible firm and its associated transformation of the labour market: the employment protection legislation. The present legislation (the 1978 Employment Protection (Consolidation) Act) incorporates a number of earlier provisions, the first of which was the 1965 Redundancy Payments Act. If the first post-war Labour government had made the right to work a reality for the labouring classes as collectivities, so the second post-war Labour administration created individual rights in employments and redundancy payments as compensation for the loss of those rights. This may be viewed as another stage in the *incorporation of the working class* in which the *possession* of employment ensured by the successful pursuit by successive administrations of full-employment policies was transformed into a legal right (as understood in bourgeois, i.e., individualist societies) to possession, i.e., jobs became a form of private *property*. It was the Labourite version of the attempt to create a 'property-owning democracy'. Naturally such an attempt to incorporate the working class involves an alteration of the consciousness of workers and moderates the sharpness of 'class struggle' (see Callender, 1985). It only becomes *merely* an attempt to shed labour and obtain worker compliance when the substantive positive right to full employment is withdrawn both ideologically and practically, as is at present the case. This does not mean, however, that at the personal level the operation of the legislation has not *always* provided cooling-out mechanisms (Goffman, 1952, pp. 451–63; Lee, 1985) which facilitate the transition of individuals to a new and unsought status.

Workers certainly tended to regard redundancy payments as a right but not as a right deriving from the loss of property, but as a recognition of years of *service*. In the words of Sewel's study of redundancy in mining:

Entitlement to redundancy pay . . . was seen as being earned by virtue of the large proportion of the worker's life that had been given to mining. . . . It was length of service, together with a belief that his present plight was the consequence of misguided policies,[5] that formed the basis of the miner's belief in his automatic right to redundancy pay (Sewel, 1975, p. 38).

That the relations between capital and labourers should be conceived more as a status relation than as a market relation is scarcely surprising when the labourers in question are redundants from the coal and steel industries, whose experience of the external market is brief and remote and whose experience of the internal market (which involves the filling of positions on the basis of knowledge of workers' personal attributes, affected by communication flows along a network of relationships), is extended and immediate. This suggests that the shift to the flexible firm, and the consequent increased incidence of frequent and extensive periods on the market, is likely to effect a change in the way in which those affected experience their relation to the means of production. Where such a transition occurs, employer–employee relations (for those not on the permanent work-force) are more likely, *ceteris paribus*, to be experienced as 'class' relations than as 'status' relations because of workers' *greater experience of the market*. This does not, however, mean that they are more likely to experience any sense of belonging to a collectivity of labour sellers than before. On the contrary, competition between individuals in the market is more likely to increase their individualism at the same time as it tends to increase the class characterization of their position in both the social and technical divisions of labour.

The fate of the redundant in the market

As steelworkers our respondents constituted a highly privileged sector of the local labour force by virtue of their employment in the primary sector, as the local name for the works, 'Treasure Island', implied. They are privileged also in redundancy – by abnormally large redundancy payments, make-up pay, opportunities for retraining – while some enjoyed a higher probability of obtaining employment with contractors than other workers in a market where jobs are scarce.[6] This is not to say, however, that ex-steelworkers are, in absolute terms rather than relative terms, in a highly favourable position. The size of redundancy payments appeared to the public and to the men themselves as astronomical, since they amounted in the majority of cases to 'many thousands of pounds'.[7] This ignores the fact that the annual wages of steelworkers amount to 'many thousands of pounds',[8] and hence the payments only provide a substantial cushion if it is the case that redundancy does not lead to long-term or very long-term unemployment and if capital is disregarded in the estimation of entitlement to social security payments after eligibility for unemployment benefit is exhausted, i.e., after twelve months. Neither of these assumptions holds good. Fifty-five per cent of the total sample had never worked during the two years following redundancy, and those obtaining employment immediately, or after a spell of retraining or unemployment, constituted only 16 per cent. Moreover, not only are redundancy payments taken into account by the DHSS, but also social security payments are conditional on proof by the claimant that exhausted redundancy payments have been 'properly' spent (Leaver, 1985).

The redundancies took effect in 1980, before the depths of the recession had been plumbed and before its severity was realized. The assumptions of most redundant workers at the point of redundancy who intended to remain in the market were not dissimilar to those underpinning the redundancy legislation and the ECSC provisions: that the function of the payments and other benefits was to tide them over until they resumed regular employment when the market picked up. Having had no recent market experience, they were unaware of how loose the market already was and how difficult obtaining permanent employment would be. Hence redundancy payments were used to supplement unemployment benefit and/or spent on the renewal of domestic capital.[9] The absence of any DHSS disregard provided no incentive to eke out the payments over a long period of unemployment, even where such an eventuality was expected. As a result a considerable proportion of the long-term unemployed among the redundant were in severe financial difficulties two years after employment (Leaver, 1985).

However, the most significant characteristic of the members of the sample who remained in the market is not their relatively privileged position in the labour market, and in relation to the market for wage goods compared with other workers; nor their relatively disadvantaged position compared with those not made redundant and the population investigated by earlier studies in much tighter markets. Rather it is the *diversity* of labour market experience of the steelworkers. The labour market histories over the two-year period between the redundancies and the last wave of interviews in autumn 1982, show a range of between one and eight statuses. Excluding those not in the market, the mean number of statuses was 2.7 and 42 per cent had three or more statuses. Their experience has been diverse therefore in two senses: first, a large proportion of the histories are diverse (i.e. contain a large number of different statuses); and second, there is a wide range of variation in the pattern of statuses and number of statuses as between redundants. That is to say that not only have the redundancies created a category of labour sellers which is in some sense distinct from the rest of the work-force currently on the market, but this category is itself highly diverse. Hence the task of conceptualizing the place of redundant steelworkers in the class structure does not simply involve conceptualizing their position as a category: it requires conceptualizing a diversity of positions within that category in relation to one another.

The distinctiveness of the category derives not only from the special benefits redundant steelworkers received when coming on to the market, but also from their remoteness from, or lack of previous open-market experience and their experience of a large internal market.

The diversity of the labour market experience of the redundant is illustrated by our attempt to categorize their labour market histories, the results of which are set out in Table 7.1. Table 7.2 shows, for those who

Table 7.1 *Types of redundancy history: mid 1980 to end of 1982*

	History type	Description	% of all		
	Withdrawn only	*Withdrew* (W/D) and no other status	20.5		Out of market: 38.5%
	Withdrawn no employment	*Last status W/D* some previous unemployment or retraining	15.4		
	Withdrawn, employment experience	Mixed history; some employment; *last status W/D*	2.6		
A	Unemployed only	*Unemp.* and no other status	13.8		In market: 61.2%
	Unemployed plus	No employment. All *unemp.* plus retraining & W/D; *last status Unemployed*	4.7	19.8	
	Employment to unemployment	Employed/self-employed at first; *last status Unemployed*	1.3		
B	Self-employed	All *self-employed* or employed and then self-employed	2.9	4.5	
	Returned to self-employment	Unemployed, W/D, Retraining, then *self-employed*	1.6		
C	Employed only	All statuses *employed*	8.2	16.2	
	Returned to employment	Unemployed/Retraining, then *employed*	8.0		
D	Chequered pure	Mixture of *employed and unemployed*; no other status types	10.5	20.7	
	Chequered plus	As above but with some other types as well	10.2		
			100.0		

Table 7.2 *Labour market experience types for those who remained in-markets*

	%
A Unemployed only Unemployed plus, incl. Emp. to Unemp.	32.4
B Self-employed only Self-employed plus	7.2
C Employed only Employed plus	26.4
D Chequered pure Chequered plus	34.0
	100.0

remained in the market, the distribution between the four major 'labour market experience' types which we distinguished.

In view of the character of the redundant population, the high withdrawal rate (38.5 per cent) is not surprising. In view of the looseness of the market, the high proportion (32 per cent) of those remaining in the market who failed to secure employment over a long period is also not unexpected. What is significant about Table 7.2, however, is the large proportion of those remaining in the market who had type 'D' or 'chequered' labour market histories. We have coined the term 'chequered' to describe those histories which are not merely diverse in the sense of having a large number of statuses, but which are made up solely or predominantly of the status types 'employed' and 'unemployed'. The creation of this category constitutes the chief structural effect of the BSC redundancies. Its coming into existence both demands explanation and poses the question of how the transition from BSC employee to chequered worker is to be conceptualized.

There can be little doubt that the size of this category is the result of the shift by BSC (and indeed other employers) in the direction of the 'flexible firm' by means of the increased use of contractors. The size of the chequered category, however, cannot be explained simply by reference to changes in the labour process and employment policy, nor by reference to the existence of ECSC make-up pay, or by any combination of these factors. Other factors must be operating to ensure that some redundant workers but not others are regularly supplied with fixed-term jobs with contracting firms thus producing a distinct labour market category whose members have a distinct position among the redundant and whose working life is characterized by frequent spells *on* on the market: who regularly sell their labour power to an employer and therefore inflate the numbers of redundants with type 'D' labour market histories.

We wish to claim that the coming into being of this category of worker requires explanation in terms of differences in social location and identity among those made redundant and that the recognition of the importance of these aspects of social reality have important consequences for the way in which we *understand* labour markets, and conceptualize the class structure and the processes of hierarchical differentiation which go on within it.

The notion of a *local* labour market involves reference to a population defined in terms of its inhabitancy of a distinct geographical location within whose boundaries labour is bought and sold. It has a structure when specified in economic terms which is constituted by the relation between the supply and demand for different types of labour power in that area. In these terms workers with different types of labour have different chances of obtaining different types of employment, that is, occupy different positions within the market. We shall term this sense of market position 'market position$_1$'.

A local labour market may also be conceived, however, as being structured in the sense that it is composed of a plurality of categories of people – buyers and sellers of different types of labour power – who have distinct identities defined by their membership of social categories (other than buyers and sellers of labour power), some of which may have their own customary moralities to which a definite social meaning is attached. At the same time the members of the population are related to one another through a network of social relationships which connect buyers and sellers with one another. Unless all points of the network are interconnected, location within this field of social relationships will differentially determine the access of buyers to different types of labour and of sellers to different types of employment opportunity. Social identity, category membership and network location are different aspects of what we shall term 'the social location of market members', that is to say of their position in a local market conceived as a social structure. This we shall term 'market position$_2$'.

We wish to argue that market position$_2$ is an important determinant of market position$_1$. Our theoretical reasons for this claim concern the distinctive nature of labour power as a commodity. What the employer gets in the labour contract is labour power, i.e. a capacity or potentiality. What the employer requires is actual labour. The employer is therefore faced with the problem of actualizing the labour power thus acquired. The employer is therefore interested, at the point of contract, in predicting the probability of the labour power of the applicant being actualized. This will depend on the 'character' of the person in whom it is embodied. It will be predicted on the basis of first, that person's identity as socially constructed, and second, on that person's reputation as a worker transmitted to the putative employer by third parties. The chances of the applicant being hired will be greater, the higher the probability that can be assigned to his labour power being actualized. That probably will be higher the more appropriate his identity, while assessment of reputation will depend on buyers and sellers already being related through third parties, i.e. being members of the same network.

Labour market position$_2$ will only have an important effect on labour market position$_1$ where the employer has an effective choice between actual or putative applicants. This choice will be greater the looser the market. Hence the importance of labour market position$_2$ in determining the fate of workers on the market will increase in time of recession and unemployment and be negligible in times of labour shortage.

This model of the process of labour contract has important implications in two main respects. It entails that unemployment, in the sense of unsuccessful job search, will be experienced by the unsuccessful as personal rejection. It entails also that greater experience of the market, i.e. more frequent attempts to sell one's labour, will not be of interaction in which persons are reduced to their economic functions: it will not be experienced therefore as class *interaction*. Yet, paradoxically, it will sharpen workers' sense of their class position, i.e. their position in society as sellers of their labour power, and of their powerlessness in the market, i.e. *vis-à-vis* labour buyers.

The importance of social location

There are a number of empirical grounds for attaching considerable importance to social location (market position$_2$) as a determinant of labour market experience. The first concerns a quantitative characteristic of the market, the ratio of number of unemployed (labour sellers) to vacancies (the demand for labour). The survey data show a substantial reliance on informal means of labour marketing (the use of friends and acquaintances as information sources) in both job search and job acquisition (see Lee, 1983a; 1983b). We interpret this finding in terms of the advantage, to both seller and buyer, in the use of informal methods. The buyer will be inundated with applications if formal means are used,[10] while sellers soon discover that few jobs are advertised and those that are have usually been filled by the time they apply, while direct application to firms ('giss a job') is time-consuming, expensive, exhausting and frustrating. While it is likely that most people use all methods of job search, the significant proportion (a third in each case) of jobs last applied for or obtained by informal means, attests to the utility of the informal in a loose labour market (Lee, 1983a).

Second, the greater the part of labour demand in a given market which is composed of demand for contract labour, the greater will be the reliance on informal means, since the administrative costs of continually recruiting numbers of workers which are large relative to the administration of a contracting firm are prohibitive. Outsourcing functions necessary to a plant's operations, but which are not continuously performed, by the use of contractors increases the number of short-term contracts and increases the burden of recruitment. The solution is the increased use of sub- and sub-sub-contracting, and the smaller the subcontract the more it is the case that 'firms' supplying such contracts are individuals who recruit acquaintances to assist them.

Third, workers in some types of contracting firm may be employed as lump labour which avoids tax and insurance contributions or may be using the (often low) wages obtained to supplement (illegally) social security benefits. In such circumstances acquaintance and mutual trust are necessary prerequisites of the labour contract.

Fourth, contractors (and subcontractors) often need to be able to recruit quickly – hence knowledge of which of a field of eligibles is on the market and therefore available is vital.

Last, knowledge and experience of the steel industry are desirable attributes in workers for firms holding some types of contract with BSC.

We do not include as a reason for the importance of the informal the particularism of Welsh culture; but there are certain empirical conditions which have to be fulfilled if such a system of labour recruitment is to operate and which are, we believe, fulfilled by the west industrial South Wales labour market, and by the Port Talbot sub-market in particular. These are past geographical stability of population and the existence of a relatively highly interconnected social network. The fulfilment of these conditions does not however entail that every resident in the local labour market (LLM) area is a long-term resident with an extensive ego-centred social network. (Indeed, in some circumstances, as Lee (1983b) has argued elsewhere, such bounded networks of strong ties may drastically limit employment opportunities.) Nor does it entail that those with such networks will have networks of a kind which connect them with opportunities for contract work, or indeed any work. Nor does it follow that interconnectedness in itself improves ego's labour market position, since networks are composed of links of different kinds and may be characterized by what Lee has termed 'preferential channelling', i.e. the transmission of valued information to some network members and not others.

It is no part of the argument of this paper that previous labour market experience, work experience, type and level of skill, are not important determinants of sellers' labour market chances. However categories of workers who are positively privileged on these dimensions cannot actualize the higher theoretical probability of employment unless they can get into a situation in which these favourable attributes are recognized by someone with employment in his or her gift.

Nor is it part of the argument of this chapter that the only way such attributes can be recognized is through the employment of informal means, though it has been argued that in certain types of labour market (so defined in economic language) and under certain social conditions (defined in sociological language), informal means will be prominent and even crucial to certain categories of worker.

The labour market in which the redundant workers were seeking employment was both loose in economic terms and exhibited high degrees of interconnectedness in certain sub-areas. Under these conditions it is reasonable to expect that informal methods of 'application' and recruitment involved both social identity recognition and cognisance of reputation. If so we would expect to find differences between successful and unsuccessful applicants according to whether or not they had been recommended to their prospective employers by third parties (reputation), high levels of job bestowal (employers' use of both reputation and network), differences between redundant workers with different network types and differences according to social identity.

In fact, Lee has shown job acquisition to be characterized by high rates of bestowal and, where applicants had heard of the job applied for through a third party, for jobs to be more often obtained when that party had 'put in a good word' for the applicant with the employer (Lee, 1983a; b). In one of the publications arising out of her field study of the domestic organization and local networks of a random sub-sample of the main sample of redundants, Morris distinguishes three social-activity types which stand as surrogates of the network types of her respondents, which she terms the 'collective', the 'dispersed' and the 'individualistic'. Very crudely, individualistic respondents' social contacts do not know each other, are geographically separated and ego's interaction is dyadic in private settings. Collectivistic respondents' contacts all know each other, are geographically concentrated in the same locality and are seen by ego together as a group in a public setting. Some dispersed respondents' contacts know each other, are relatively geographically concentrated and ego's interaction is dyadic in a mixture of public and private settings.

Morris argues that the labour market experience (LME) of these categories differs, the individualistic being more likely to *end up* in relatively secure employments, but only after a considerable period on the market involving a long period out of work. The collectivistic in contrast are more likely to have 'chequered' labour market histories (LMHs) associated with work for contractors. Now obviously these differences are *related* to pre-redundancy skill levels and LMHs: in particular Morris suggests that the dispersed category who were most prone to long-term unemployment had fewer skills and more chequered pre-redundancy LMHs, but social-activity type does differentiate the LME and labour market position$_1$ of more favourably situated workers (Morris, 1984).

Indicators of Morris's social-activity types were included in the third wave survey schedule and analysis of LMHs in terms of this variable reveals that the individualistic workers have distinctive behaviour patterns as well as distinctive network types. They are more likely to have retrained, to have retrained early rather than reluctantly after a period of unemployment, and to have made use of formal means of job application, particularly direct application to employers. In other words, the individualistic behave in a way which more closely approximates to sellers' behaviours as specified by models of economically rational labour market behaviour: they respond to a loose market by increasing their human capital and, because the market is falling, do so quickly before it falls further; they have a wide range of information sources and make applications for the sorts of jobs they want at places where they are likely to be available. As a result more end up in relatively stable jobs, stable because they haven't the social relationships which connect them with contracting work and stable because those are the sort of firms and positions they apply to or for in the first place. This pattern of behaviour has all the marks of customary morality or mode of life which we associate with the respectable working/lower middle 'social classes' in T. H. Marshall's sense (Marshall, 1934), and of which the individualistic activity pattern is an outcome.

There is evidence therefore from different data sources which suggests that reputation, network type and identity, that is to say the different aspects of social location, are important demarcators of the population of labour sellers by virtue of which they may be thought of as occupying different positions in 'the market' conceived as a social structure, and that workers' market position in this sense (market position$_2$) affects their market position$_1$: their chances of obtaining different types of employment.

When we turn specifically to consider the category of workers with chequered labour market histories we find that they are younger, less skilled, and have had more previous experience of unemployment and their redundancies were 'harder' than the sample as a whole. In these respects they are more like those with 'unemployed' labour market histories. They have by far the highest proportion of those who volunteered the information that they had worked for BSC contractors since being made redundant, and the 'pure' chequered (see Table 7.1) have an even higher proportion (50 per cent) with 'contracting' experience. The field data strongly suggest that what also distinguishes the chequered from the unemployed is their network type. Unfortunately it is difficult to devise instruments to replicate *intensive* field data in *extensive* survey research and the crude instruments used in the survey failed to show major differences between the labour market history categories in respect of network type; nor do any clear differences emerge between chequered and other workers on a range of attitudinal variables which do however demonstrate the distinctive character of the small 'self-employed' LMH category.

It seems likely, however, that the chequered LMH category comprises two distinct sub-categories: those upon whom contract work is regularly bestowed by contractors using information originally obtained from BSC about 'suitable' labour, and those who have collective, i.e. interconnected, networks which both link workers with employers offering fixed-term work and among whose members a reputation as a '"tidy" lad' is maintained and known by employers who are members of that network.

Conceptualizing the class position of the chequered

The problem posed by our material is that of conceptualizing the way in which the class position of the workers with chequered labour market careers has changed as a result of their redundancy. Harris has argued elsewhere (Harris, 1984a) that class theory has neglected the market dimension of the Marxian notion of class in 'class' societies: production classes are internally differentiated according to their access to markets for the commodities they produce and the relations of class members to one another and to members of other classes *in the market* must, in such societies, be species of class relations. Classes in 'class' societies are necessarily theoretically constituted as such by *both* production *and* exchange positions/relations: in Marx's words: 'anarchy in the social division of labour and despotism in the manufacturing division of labour mutually condition one another' (Marx, *Capital* I, ch. 14).

187

Since what distinguishes the members of the different LMH categories is their position in and experience of the market, it is the market aspect of class relations which must be addressed, but here it is not, in Marx's phrase, 'the play of chance and caprice in the market' produced by the competition of *different capitals* that concerns us: the preceding section is concerned with attempting to understand what *appears* to be the play of chance and caprice in the *labour* market so long as its members are defined *solely*, as Marx and some modern economists would have us do, as bearers of economic functions.

This paper has argued that in the years after the redundancy event those made redundant can be seen to have occupied different positions in the market: they have actualized different probabilities of obtaining different types of employment when placed in competition with one another for a scarce number of jobs. It has therefore denied that the outcome is the result merely of chance and caprice, and claimed that it is rather a manifestation of a previously existing market structure. If, however, a set of relations between different sets of sellers of a commodity have been exhibited then what has been made manifest is a set of class relations. The process which the study reports is the emergence of different relations to the means of production within the category 'wage labourer' which market processes have made visible precisely because, since wage labourers share in common the necessity of selling their labour power in a labour market, those relations are always mediated by the market.

The emergence of the chequered category among the redundant has to be understood, however, not as the manifestation of a latent probability but as a new phenomenon produced by the 'mutual conditioning' of the labour process and the labour market. Some of the redundant have, that is to say, come to occupy a new class position. The nature of this new position can only partly be comprehended in Marxian terms. Clearly the chequered workers have not, like the self-employed, exchanged 'the despotism of the manufacturing division of labour' for the 'play of chance and caprice of the market': rather they occupy an interstitial position in which they are continually forced on to the market in order to obtain the opportunity to participate in the labour process. They cannot, however, like the unemployed, be thought of as part of the reserve army of labour since their employment and unemployment is not related to the expansion and contraction of economic activity.

To take this comparison further, however, requires that we abandon Marxist categories. Like the unemployed, the 'chequered' have lost their secure *status* (i.e. a set of rights) in an employing organization, but unlike the employed they have no opportunity to acquire those rights by virtue of their subsequent employment. But this change in class position is perfectly intelligible in Marxian terms once we recognize, as many of the workers themselves do, the historical significance of what has occurred. The redundancy event involved the extinction of a certain form of property, an employment, which guaranteed workers access to the means of production. Those in secure employments, those with employed LMHs, have re-established their property rights and access: the unemployed have lost both. The chequered have regained (albeit intermittent) access, but have not regained their rights.

The reason that Marxist terminology is not readily available to conceptualize this category is that the relation to the means of production of workers with chequered LMHs is that of the whole proletariat in Marx's day which was that of 'a class in civil society which is not of civil society' (Marx in O'Malley, 1970, pp. 141–2) but most of which has since been slowly incorporated into civil society by the legal recognition of workers' rights. The change in class location experienced by redundant workers with chequered LMHs is that involved in a movement out of this incorporated class, protected by law from experiencing the full rigours of a free labour market, and back into the proletariat proper, as Marx originally understood it, whose members' survival depended on their ability to sell their labour power in the labour market.

This return to the proletariat 'proper' might be thought, since it involves the abolition of property, to be the beginning of the creation of a politically radical proletariat, of 'the formation of a class with radical chains . . . a class that is the dissolution of all classes . . . a sphere of society claiming no particular right . . .' (Marx in O'Malley, 1970) in contrast to the reformist Labourism of the traditional working class or the privatized instrumentalism of the 'affluent worker'. Yet as Ollman (1971, p. 209) has pointed out, 'competition [not in the neoclassical economic sense, but as Marx defined it: "avarice and war among the avaricious"] may be viewed as the activity which produces class'. Ollman does not refer here merely to competition between parties to the social division of labour, however, for he continues:

Among the proletariat competition first rears its head at the factory gate where some are allowed in and others not . . . it is such competition, at all levels, with its accompanying attitudes which makes organising the proletariat such a difficult task (1971, p. 250).

The chequered category should be seen, then, as the result of competition between members of the working class, as a class fraction characterized by competition between its own members which, together with their geographical dispersion and distribution among the labour force, militates against any possibility of the development of class consciousness, let alone organization.

To follow Ollman in his frank recognition of the obstacles to the development of working-class consciousness and action in 'class', i.e. capitalist, societies, to which markets, and especially labour markets, are central, is not to accept his interpretation of Marx's views on the character of the relation, at the phenomenal level, between members of the same class. 'Here too', says Ollman, 'people react to one another as one of a kind rather than as real living individuals'. All the evidence of our study argues against this. Indeed, Harris has argued elsewhere (Harris, 1984a, p. 14) following Rose (1981, p. 216) that this sort of conclusion owes more to Marx's

189

inadequate theorization of subjectivity than to any necessary characteristic of social relationships in capitalist society.

It is clearly no part of our argument here that Marxian categories cannot and should not be deployed in the effort to conceptualize the change in the class position of 'chequered' workers, but we do wish to argue that however successfully that task is accomplished, the character of social relationships cannot be read off from that description: Marxian categories are not adequate for understanding the response of 'real, living individuals' to one another. To understand this one needs to think of a local labour market as the historical product of past economic processes around which have developed cultural (i.e. intergenerationally transmissible) ways of thinking, feeling and acting. It is not so much *men* who cannot *make history* according to their own will, but *tendencies in the system of economic relations* which cannot *express themselves* fully in social relations because they have to do so under cultural and historical conditions which those tendencies themselves did not originate.

To understand the salience of network, identity and reputation in the structuring of the flow of job opportunities and to render intelligible the effect that redundancy and subsequent labour market experience has on the relationships, beliefs and actions of redundant workers, it is necessary to think of the local labour market as a social entity made up of 'social classes' in Marshall's (1934) sense: i.e. a set of groups each of whose identity depends on its members sharing a customary morality and way of life which is the culturally encoded response of subjects to past economic conditions and transformations. Social classes, for Marshall, are not functionally differentiated (like classes) and 'their objectivity consists not in the criteria that distinguish [them] (like both classes and status groups – CH) but in the social relations [they] produce' (Marshall, 1934, p. 94; and see also Harris, 1984b).

Networks of relationships are the origin, and their structuration the expression, of the existence of identity groups according to whose normative standards reputation may be judged. In the labour market behaviour of the redundant we are witnessing the attempt to maintain social identity by the employment of means which are themselves constitutive of it – a situation which, logically, exactly parallels that of class reproduction.

Marshall's essay on 'social class' does not attribute the constitution of identity to social group membership alone, thus precluding any but indirect determination of identity by the effect of the experience of material life. He writes,

Property, however small gives security and insurance against misfortune and liberty for new adventure, thus cultivating a sense of proprietorship in a civilisation, of independence of status, which makes governments appear as servants, not as masters, and institutions as the means to freedom not to servitude (Marshall, 1934, pp. 112–13).

It has been the argument of this last section that redundant workers have lost their only property, however small that may have been, while their redundancy pay, it has been shown, was for the majority insufficient insurance against misfortune. Like the self-employed, the chequered workers have experienced the play of chance and caprice of the market as a routine feature of working life but, unlike them, they also experience 'the despotism of the manufacturing division of labour' where the pay earned is insufficient to provide security against misfortune and renders them periodically dependent for benefits upon state institutions. It cannot be that these changes will not affect both their social and political attitudes and behaviour, but it will do so as a result of the interpretation, by chequered workers, of their experience in terms of the customary morality of their 'social class'. It is as absurd to suppose that, as a result of their changed class location, the sense of identity and belonging that social-class membership provides will be dissolved, leaving an aggregate of nakedly competing individuals, as it is to suppose that these workers will develop truly proletarian forms of consciousness and action.

Notes and references

1 This paper arises out of research funded by ESRC Grant GOO 230023. Both the financial support of the Council and the understanding and academic support of the appropriate committees during a period of considerable difficulty on both sides are gratefully acknowledged. For a general account of the research see Harris *et al.* (1985). The authors are, respectively, Grant-holder and Senior Research Officer. Though we take full responsibility for any inadequacies this paper may contain, it could not have been written without the field research insights and ideas of our two colleagues, Dr L. D. Morris and Dr R. Fevre. It was Dr Morris's field data that first drew our attention to the chequeredness of labour market histories, while Dr Fevre's subsequent work on the settlement and labour market of Port Talbot has clarified our thinking about the relation between labour market experience and changes in the labour process, amplified our knowledge of the redundancy process, and contributed enormously to our understanding and knowledge of 'contracting' on which his separate study is now focusing. The authors wish to acknowledge the assistance of Philip Brown in resolving the classificatory and computing problems which made possible the final labour market history classification on which Table 7.1 is based.

2 Announced in December 1979, BSC's labour-shedding plans were in fact delayed by the 1980 steel strike. Workers at Port Talbot were made redundant during a period from mid May to the end of September 1980.

3 This is the proportion describing themselves as 'sick' or 'retired' or otherwise unavailable for work.

4 The need for flexibility in employment was particularly important in the case of the steel industry for two reasons. The technical nature of the steelmaking process requires large plants in continuous production and the process is capital-intensive with a high proportion of capital tied up in

plant. Second, BSC's investment programme in the 1970s was based on the assumption that optimization of plant size

would automatically command lower operating costs so as to offset high fixed costs and interest charges. The effect of a high proportion of fixed costs was to increase BSC's break-even point . . . so that in 1975 BSC had to operate at 85% of its capacity before it could even begin to earn profits (Morgan, 1983; see also Bryer, Brignall and Maunders, 1982, *passim*).

5 It is the burden of Bryer *et al.*'s work (1982) that in steel the redundancies (though precipitated politically) were in fact the result of misguided policies. A similar belief was involved in the 1984 Coal Dispute. It may be suggested that what is at issue in contemporary industrial relations is less the right of management to manage than the ability of management to manage.

6 The unemployment/vacancies ratio in Port Talbot stood at 12.5:1 in February 1980, reached 52:1 in November 1980, and in May 1982 stood at 37:1 (Fevre, 1985, Table B6.1, p. 51).

7 Around two-fifths of the sample had received a redundancy payment of £5000 or more (Lee, 1983c).

8 In 1980 wages of operatives in iron and steel establishments employing 750 employees and over averaged £6412 pa – Census of Production 1980, Business Monitor PA 221, Table 4. Eighty-two per cent were satisfied or very satisfied with their pay when at BSC.

9 Forty-eight per cent spent some of their redundancy money on major items of domestic capital. For 54 per cent savings was the item to which the *largest amount* of redundancy money was applied, but purchases of large domestic items (23 per cent) was the next most important use.

10 According to the *South Wales Evening Post*, Fords of Swansea (foolishly) advertised a storeman's job and were inundated with applications.

Further reading

R. Kreckel, 'Unequal opportunity structure and labour market segmentation', *Sociology*, **14**, 1980

D. I. Mackay, *et al.* 'Redundancy and displacement', *Department of Employment Research Paper No. 16*, 1980

T. Manwaring, 'The extended internal labour market', *Cambridge Journal of Econ.* **8**, 1984

S. Wood and I. Dey, *Redundancy*, Gower, 1983

8 Political quiescence among the unemployed in modern Britain

Gordon Marshall, David Rose, Howard Newby, Carolyn Vogler

I

During the 1970s large-scale unemployment once more became a fact of economic life in the United Kingdom. Somewhere between 3 million and 5 million persons are now jobless – the precise figure depends upon the definition that is applied. Most of these are registered unemployed. They are men and women available for work which, tragically, is not available for them. It is not necessary to debate the precise parameters of this phenomenon here, since it is sufficient for our purposes to note that unemployment is now seen universally to have reached unacceptable proportions. The majority of politicians, industrialists, trades unionists and ordinary citizens alike are agreed that too many people have been involuntarily out of work for too long.

The 1970s and 1980s also witnessed the emergence of increasingly well-organized pressure groups of the disadvantaged on to the British political scene. Many among the hitherto unorganized and unpoliticized found platforms from which to make their voices heard and, not infrequently, they gained a measure of success in securing some of their most important objectives. Women, homosexuals, racial minorities and the handicapped, among others, have all become highly visible in this way during the past fifteen or so years. Legal and welfare systems reflect the changes that have occurred. To some extent this may even be true of public opinion itself. But herein lies a puzzle. Given the parallel emergence of mass unemployment on the one hand, and politicization of many previously unorganized groups among the disprivileged on the other, one cannot help but be struck by the quiescence of the unemployed themselves. There is no effective national union of the jobless, no network of support groups, and no self-help telephone switchboard. Others may campaign on behalf of the unemployed but they themselves are largely silent.

The extensive literature on unemployment offers a number of putative solutions to this puzzle. Most straightforwardly it could be argued that the unemployed are not really suffering undue economic hardship, either because they enjoy the protection of welfare state payments, or are enthusiastic participants in an informal economy that generates much hidden income. Some would maintain that 'the unemployed' are, in any case, not a category but rather a flow of population. They are not an identifiable social or

193

economic group since, for most people, unemployment is temporary and short-term. Again the suggestion is that 'the unemployed' do not need to be politically active. Others view the personal consequences of unemployment less favourably but argue that unemployment is unevenly distributed, being concentrated in particular occupations, areas and social groups, so that those suffering a common financial hardship are nevertheless effectively isolated from each other. To physical isolation could be added psychological, social, and political isolation. Unemployment is said to induce pessimism, loss of self-respect, fatalism, perhaps even clinical depression in the individual. He or she loses contact with workmates, lacks financial resources to socialize outside the home, so becomes compunctious and introversive as a result. Finally, since the unemployed are disproportionately working-class, black, and either very young or nearing retirement, they may be said to lack the resources and skills necessary to gain access to the political process. In other words, mass unemployment has not induced social disorder and political activism among the unemployed because they do not *want* representation, do not *need* representation, or are *incapable* of organizing to secure it (see, for example, Henry, 1982; Ditton and Brown, 1981; Daniel, 1981; and Sinfield, 1981).

We cannot attempt to test all of these propositions here. There are, in any case, good grounds for suspecting that either separately or together they provide an adequate solution to our puzzle. Recent research confirms that the safety-net of welfare provision nevertheless leaves many of the unemployed in households not far removed from poverty. Some are unambigiously impoverished. Most of those in receipt of welfare payments would prefer to be in work. Formal employment remains the goal since the unemployed have neither the financial nor social resources that facilitate informal economic exchanges. Similarly, evidence about subemployment or the discontinuously employed shows that it is a minority of the labour force which flows through unemployment over the months and years, so that the same individuals and groups are repeatedly (if not strictly continuously) disprivileged. Nor is it clear why the experiences of powerlessness and isolation should prevent the unemployed from organizing in pursuit of collective ends while other similarly placed groups have overcome these same obstacles to political activism (see, for example, Norris, 1978; Townsend, 1979; Pahl, 1984; Hakim, 1984; and Jahoda 1982).

How, then, is the puzzle to be resolved? By far the most rigorous attempt to explain quiescence among the unemployed has been made by the American political scientists Kay Lehman Schlozman and Sidney Verba. In the mid 1970s they set out to determine why it was that the increasing numbers of jobless workers in the United States did not experience a process of political mobilization akin to that undergone by other disprivileged groups. In principle, they suggest, this process of mobilization can be seen as a series of hypothetical steps leading from deprivation to political activity (Table 8.1). The specific application of the model to the unemployed would yield the predicted result only if a number of conditions were met. There must be an

Table 8.1 *The process of political mobilization*

	(1)	(2)	(3)	(4)	(5)
General Model	Objective condition	Subjective strain	Politicization of the strain a Perception of governmental relevance b Group consciousness	Policy preferences and programme	Level and direction of political activity
Specific Application	Unemployment and/or low socioeconomic status	Sense of economic dissatisfaction and deprivation	a Perception that government is responsible b Class consciousness and/or 'jobless' consciousness	Preferences for economic policies designed to ease problem	Protest; organized group activity; issue voting; electoral activity

From Schlozman and Verba, 1979: p. 13

195

objective situation that creates strain for the individual – in this case unemployment. He or she must then perceive that situation as stressful. Unemployment must be accompanied by feelings of dissatisfaction. Next, Schlozman and Verba identify two perceptions that are crucial in linking subjectively stressful problems to collective political responses; namely, that government action is somehow relevant to the problem, and that the problem itself is experienced by others. In the case of the unemployed, they must come to define their economic circumstances as a consequence of social forces rather than personal weakness, and see that this requires a solution based on state intervention rather than wholly individual efforts. The jobless must recognize that they cannot simply get on their bikes. Moreover, the problem of joblessness needs to be seen to be an injustice shared, one that crosscuts cleavages of class, ethnicity, sex, or location. Again this will mitigate against attempts to solve the problem through purely personal initiatives. Individualistic strategies – investing all of one's energies in looking for a job – will give way to collective pressure on the state to raise unemployment benefits or stimulate the economy. As a prior step to pursuing these demands an agreed programme of policy preferences must be reached. Not only would the unemployed express common dissatisfaction with their lot: they would also share, as a group, similar preferences for policies designed to meet their needs. Finally, there is the step of mobilization itself which in America at least can take several forms. Individuals might engage in protest activities or electoral politics, acting through formal bureaucracies or self-help groups, and resort to more or less militant tactics once organized.

As Schlozman and Verba were aware at the outset, the unemployed are not exemplars of the process of political mobilization, since they quite obviously do not move from the condition of objective strain, through the steps of subjective strain, group consciousness, shared perceptions and preferences, to that of joint political activity. On the contrary, the American survey data suggest a plausible explanation of why it is that nothing happens when, as the authors put it, the injury of joblessness is added to the insult of the ongoing disadvantage associated with low socio-economic status, race, sex or youth. These data show, first of all, that unemployment hurts. When compared with those who are in work, the unemployed are much less satisfied with their income, and with life in general. Objective economic disadvantage produces strain. Crucially, however, there is no evidence of systematic forward links from the strain associated with economic condition (step 2) to support for particular components of political and social ideology (step 3). Interviews both with workers and the unemployed alike showed little evidence of class consciousness. What was evident, instead, was a widespread belief in the American Dream of individual opportunities for success. Indeed the two findings are closely connected: confidence in the American Dream is associated with low class consciousness. But this is true across all occupations and economic circumstances. The unemployed were no more cynical about the American Dream, and no more 'class conscious', than were their job-holding peers.

For this reason the survey findings about who the unemployed hold responsible for their condition, and their preferences for policies to change it, are somewhat contrary. On the one hand, unemployed interviewees did not blame themselves for their joblessness, and most agreed that the government had a responsibility both to create more jobs and to improve benefits for those without work. On the other hand, they also believed that it was the duty of individuals to find new jobs, take care of themselves, and manage their financial affairs more astutely. The effect of this ambivalence on preferences for specific economic policies is to render the unemployed largely indistinguishable from their working counterparts, except in the matter of policies directly concerned with government intervention to provide jobs or benefits for the poor, of which the unemployed are of course generally more supportive. Nor was any relationship found between social class and policy preferences. (Though the authors do cite evidence from the 1930s which tends to suggest that there was a much closer affiliation between social class, unemployment, and class consciousness in earlier periods of American history.) They therefore conclude that

Quite consistently we have found the long-term economic deprivation associated with social class to have weak effects; the impact of the short-term deprivation concomitant to joblessness is far more severe, but is contained. It is associated with real personal unhappiness and with preferences for certain policies designed to ameliorate the situation, but not with general disenchantment with American life, wholesale changes in social ideology, or adoption of radical policy positions (Schlozman and Verba, 1979, p. 349).

Not surprisingly, therefore, Schlozman and Verba find no evidence to suggest that the unemployed are mobilized to higher levels of political activity than might be expected from a group with their general social characteristics. The jobless are selectively recruited from social groups that are not ordinarily politically active, so in fact participate less than those actually in work, but even allowing for this still show no signs of organizing in order to pursue the specific interests of those involuntarily without employment. With the single exception of withdrawal from union activity, the political behaviour of the unemployed can be seen to be a function of their long-term characteristics (political partisanship in the American case), rather than a consequence of joblessness itself. Thus, the authors conclude, their data tell a consistent story:

The effects of unemployment are severe but narrowly focused, manifest in ways that are proximate to the joblessness itself. Many of the connections we had originally expected between unemployment and political beliefs and conduct simply were not made. However, we did find islands of coherence: material condition was related to personal dissatisfaction but not much else; aspects of social ideology were related to one another, but neither backward to material conditions nor forward to political attitudes; political attitudes were related to political behaviour as manifested in the

197

voting choice, but they were linked strongly neither to general social ideology nor to material conditions (Schlozman and Verba, 1979, p. 351).

In short, at the centre of this elegant account sits an ideological block to political mobilization among the unemployed that is familiar to us from the writings of Werner Sombart about the American working class as a whole at the turn of the century, namely the American Dream of individual advancement and opportunity (compare Sombart, 1976). It is this, ultimately, that undermines class consciousness and so explains the failure of the unemployed to rise up in their own defence.

II

Schlozman's and Verba's argument is not without weaknesses – even in its application to the United States. Some of the indicators used are ambiguous or simplistic. Rather crucially these include the measurements for 'dissatisfaction', 'class', and 'class consciousness'. Similarly, the interpretation of key findings is perhaps suspect, as for example when the authors take as evidence of a principled commitment to the American Dream, the widespread belief among American workers in hard work as a means of getting ahead. It could equally well be argued that this belief is simply a pragmatic assessment of prevailing circumstances among those who realize that they are at the bottom of the heap produced by an unjust system.

It is not necessary to pursue these issues here. More obviously, we might question the relevance of the substantive conclusions from the American survey, as these can be applied to the circumstances of the United Kingdom. There is an established tradition of research which shows that British society is – and always has been – more explicitly conscious of class than has North America. So, for example, British proletarians are much more inclined towards trades unionism than their American counterparts. Class-voting patterns are more pronounced in this country, as are class identities, and class-based interpretations of social injustice (see, for example, Giddens, 1973). Moreover, the 'American Dream' scarcely offers sufficient explanation for political quiescence among the unemployed in these islands, if not by definition alone then because social ideologies and public rhetoric in Britain have been structured historically by class-based interpretations of the world rather than a vision of wholly individualistic achievement. Not only the ideologies but also the social institutions of the country (for example the system of public schooling) support this world-view (see, for example, Westergaard and Resler, 1976).

On the face of it, therefore, the explanation offered by Schlozman and Verba is of questionable relevance to the British situation. At a minimum their central thesis about the American Dream and its relationship to class consciousness and political activity requires systematic scrutiny against data for this country. Can the conclusions for the United States be transferred across the Atlantic? If not then why not? These are the questions addressed in this chapter.

Our data are taken from a project on the impact of economic recession on class processes in contemporary Britain. As the first stage of this research the authors organized a national sample survey of people between the ages of 16 and 64 (excluding those in full-time education) during the period March to June 1984. A total of 1770 interviews were completed in two polling districts in each of 100 representative parliamentary constituencies by a specialist survey agency working under the close supervision of the research team. Among the major categories of data gathered in the survey were those concerning relationships at work, standard of living, class biography, and the impact of economic recession on households, together with a range of attitudinal questions including the usual party political identification items.[1]

Though not collected with the analysis of Schlozman and Verba specifically in mind these data shed some light on the problem with which they were concerned. Because our study was of class processes in general, rather than the phenomenon of unemployment in particular, it contains rather fewer jobless individuals than would be ideal in a comparative exercise of the sort being undertaken. Still, we do have detailed information on 142 unemployed men and women, and this can be compared with the data for 1248 respondents in formal employment. (In our sample, 380 persons were 'economically inactive' through illness, early retirement, or because they were keeping house.)[2] Those unemployed were 93 males and 49 females, of whom all but 12 were white, and proportionately rather more were aged between 16 and 25.[3] Our results are therefore suggestive rather than conclusive, given the restricted samples upon which they are based, but they do point towards clear difficulties in applying the Schlozman and Verba thesis to the British case.

III

The extent of objective deprivation among the unemployed in our sample is consistent with what is known generally about the economic hardship experienced by those made jobless. Unemployed respondents were concentrated in low-income households: 24 per cent were in households having a gross annual income under £2800; 65 per cent had less than £5000; a mere 35 per cent enjoyed household incomes above that sum. The corresponding figures for respondents in work were 2 per cent, 11 per cent, and 89 per cent respectively. Most of those unemployed were heavily dependent on state benefits. Whereas 39 per cent of employed respondents were in households receiving no state pensions or benefits of any kind, only 7 per cent of unemployed respondents placed their households in this category, with 19 per cent claiming three or more benefits (as compared to 3 per cent of households of employed respondents). Among households having employed respondents, 65 per cent received less than 5 per cent of the gross household income in the form of welfare payments, with most of the remainder having a relatively low dependence on such sources (20 per cent or less of total income in the form of benefits). By comparison, 81 per cent of unemployed interviewees were in households where more than 5 per cent of gross income came in the form of state benefits, and proportionately more of these were heavily dependent on this income: 35 per cent of unemployed households were wholly dependent on state benefits; another 14 per cent received more than 90 per cent of household income in this way; while 16 per cent reported 50–80 per cent of total income taking the form of such payments. Among unemployed households as a whole, 57 per cent were in receipt of supplementary benefits, 49 per cent had unemployment benefits, and 15 per cent claimed housing benefits. The corresponding figures for households where the interviewee was employed were 7 per cent in the case of all three forms of benefit.

How is this state of affairs experienced by the unemployed themselves? Are they more likely to express dissatisfaction than those with jobs? Posing this question in the United States, Schlozman and Verba inquired about satisfaction with income, family life, and 'accomplishments' in general. Our own measures are somewhat different but the thrust of our analysis addresses the same question. Does unemployment hurt?

Respondents in the British survey were asked to review their standard of living over the previous five years. Among those employed there were significant class differences in answers to this question, with almost 50 per cent of Goldthorpe class I interviewees (higher professionals, administrators and managers) reporting an improvement during this period, as compared to 26 per cent of those in Goldthorpe class VII (semi-skilled and unskilled manual workers). However, unemployed respondents felt worse off even than the latter group, with a mere 12 per cent judging their standard of living to have improved, while 37 per cent thought it had stayed the same and 51 per cent reported falling living standards.[4]

The unemployed were also unlikely to judge the distribution of income and wealth in Britain to be a fair one. Again there are significant social-class differences here. The percentage of respondents agreeing with the assessment that the distribution was fair ranged from 44 per cent of the self-employed, and 32 per cent of the 'service class' (classes I and II), to 28, 25, 25 and 23 per cent respectively among routine white-collar employees, supervisors, skilled and unskilled manual workers (classes III, V, VI and VII). Unemployed respondents were characteristic of the (relatively more disaffected) manual workers as a whole: barely 25 per cent endorsed the distributional order as being just. Similarly, when faced with a description of Britain in the past as having had a political and economic system largely controlled by a dominant class, and a lower class with no control over political and economic affairs, well over 60 per cent of the service class thought that things had now changed, as did 59 per cent of the self-employed, 58 per cent of routine white-collar employees, 46 per cent of supervisors, and 43 per cent of skilled manual workers. However, only 37 per cent of unskilled manual workers saw any change, as did a mere 36 per cent of those unemployed. In other words more than 64 per cent of the latter were prepared to endorse our class-polarized picture as an accurate description of Britain in the 1980s.

In general terms then, although the questions posed in the British survey

Table 8.2 *Self-reported standard of living over previous five years, by Goldthorpe class and unemployment*

		Goldthorpe class/unemployment							
		I	II	III	IV	V	VI	VII	Unemployed
Standard of living	Improving	49.2 (60)	44.6 (103)	30.4 (77)	29.6 (34)	33.6 (36)	29.4 (48)	25.9 (80)	12.0 (17)
	Falling behind	13.9 (17)	18.6 (43)	20.6 (52)	23.5 (27)	25.2 (27)	28.2 (46)	27.2 (84)	50.7 (72)
	Staying same	36.9 (45)	36.8 (85)	49.0 (124)	47.0 (54)	41.1 (44)	42.3 (69)	46.9 (145)	37.3 (53)
		100 (122)	100 (231)	100 (253)	100 (115)	100 (107)	100 (163)	100 (309)	100 (142)

Note Figures in brackets are raw numbers

were somewhat different from those asked of North American respondents, we would argue that the unemployed in Britain are, like their counterparts in the United States, both relatively deprived and relatively dissatisfied. One caveat that should perhaps be added here (since the point bears also on our subsequent findings about everyday perceptions of Britain as being those of a specifically class-based society) is that our respondents generally were not much inclined to see an underlying distributional justice in the social order. As will be clear from the figures reported above, even among those actually in work, 71 per cent judged the distribution of wealth in this country to be unfair and 48 per cent could perceive no changes in the economic or political inequalities associated with social class. It is at this point, however, that our findings diverge from those reported by Schlozman and Verba. Hardship and dissatisfaction among unemployed Americans are not translated into common policy preferences (and thence into political mobilization), so the argument goes, because of the American commitment to an ideology of individual opportunity and responsibility which undercuts collective identities associated with class. In Britain we find precisely the opposite. It is the government that is held to be generally responsible for economic matters and so for creating work. Moreover, 'class consciousness' is more pronounced here than in America, and there is no evidence of it being offset by specifically meritocratic ideologies or world-views.

Taking the data on class first, we see (Table 8.3) that the unemployed are no less likely than those in work to claim that they normally think of themselves as belonging to a particular social class, to think that there are *important* issues causing conflicts between classes, and that social class is an inevitable feature of modern society. The unemployed are, as one would expect, more likely to describe themselves as belonging to the working class. These figures are far in excess of those obtained for comparable class self-identification items in the United States – among both working and unemployed respondents alike.

In fact social class seems to be the pre-eminent source for collective identities in Britain, being far more influential in this regard than status, gender, or (significantly) the condition of worklessness itself. A mere 21 per cent of employed respondents in our sample (N = 254) claimed that there was some other major group that they identified with. Nineteen per cent of those unemployed (N = 27) also made this claim. Among the former, the largest categories (50-plus individuals in each case) were those who identified themselves as business or professional people, or with some particular religious grouping. Twenty-eight of the employed claimed an ethnic or racial identity. Other identities, nominated by around a dozen or so employees in each case, were associated with gender, a particular age group, political party, pressure group, club or society. Half of those without work claimed an unemployed identity in particular: the remainder gave very scattered responses in terms of religion, gender, and those additional categories already mentioned. About 63 per cent both of employed and unemployed respondents identifying with these other groups stated that they thought of themselves

202

Table 8.3 *Class identity, by Goldthorpe class and unemployment*

	Goldthorpe class/unemployment							
	I	II	III	IV	V	VI	VII	Unemployed
Whether class membership claimed								
Yes	54.5 (67)	57.0 (134)	61.7 (158)	54.9 (62)	71.0 (76)	64.8 (107)	57.5 (180)	62.9 (88)
No	45.5 (56)	43.0 (101)	38.3 (98)	45.1 (51)	29.0 (31)	35.2 (58)	42.5 (133)	37.1 (52)
	100 (123)	100 (235)	100 (256)	100 (113)	100 (107)	100 (165)	100 (313)	100 (140)
Important issues causing class conflict?								
Yes	64.7 (75)	66.2 (149)	54.8 (126)	66.0 (68)	56.0 (56)	57.4 (85)	57.6 (151)	57.3 (71)
No	35.3 (41)	33.8 (76)	45.2 (104)	34.0 (35)	44.0 (44)	42.6 (63)	42.4 (111)	42.7 (53)
	100 (116)	100 (225)	100 (230)	100 (103)	100 (100)	100 (148)	100 (262)	100 (124)
Is social class inevitable?								
Yes	74.6 (91)	70.1 (164)	79.8 (198)	81.8 (90)	84.9 (90)	80.1 (125)	72.9 (213)	76.7 (102)
No	25.4 (31)	29.9 (70)	20.2 (50)	18.2 (20)	15.1 (16)	19.9 (31)	27.1 (79)	23.3 (31)
	100 (122)	100 (234)	100 (248)	100 (110)	100 (106)	100 (156)	100 (292)	100 (133)

	Self-assigned class						
	Upper	Upper Middle	Middle	Lower Middle	Upper Working	Working	Lower Working
Employment status							
Employed	0.1 (1)	3.3 (38)	27.2 (314)	14.1 (163)	12.9 (149)	39.5 (455)	2.9 (33) 100 (1153)
Unemployed	0.8 (1)	0.8 (1)	16.0 (20)	8.0 (10)	8.8 (11)	56.0 (70)	9.6 (12) 100 (125)

normally in these terms rather than as members of a social class. Only forty-nine employed respondents (and five of those unemployed) claimed that they routinely saw themselves neither in class terms nor as members of (one or more) alternative social groups.

Schlozman and Verba asked not only about class identities but also about social conflicts more generally. We have already seen the majority of our respondents claim that there are important conflicts between social classes. Asked to describe these conflicts, some three-quarters of the employed and unemployed alike referred to distributional conflicts about income and wealth more generally, with fewer than 7 per cent and 9 per cent respectively making any reference to class conflicts as implying wider political issues – far less some sort of struggle for control over the productive means in society. (There were no significant social class differences in the patterning of responses here.) Only three of those without jobs saw unemployment itself as an issue causing specifically class conflicts. We also inquired about conflicts in industry in particular, first by inviting interviewees to agree or disagree with the statement that 'the main conflicts in Britain today are between those who run industry and those who work for them', then asking for clarification of the nature of the conflicts involved among those who perceived them in these terms. Identical proportions – 70 per cent in each case – both of those formally employed and those without jobs agreed with this statement. Among those who disagreed, 82 per cent of the employed and 71 per cent of the unemployed subsequently agreed that there were *some* important issues causing conflict between the controllers and workers in industry. It is difficult to generalize about the precise nature of the issues that were identified as generating this conflict (see Table 8.4) except to say that pay generally was seen to be the most popularly contested area. Union militancy was viewed by about one-fifth of respondents as likely to cause conflict, as was the 'unreasonable' or 'unsympathetic' manner of management, though surprisingly few (even among the unemployed) nominated redundancies or job security as such an issue. Needless to say, few perceived industrial conflict originating in disputes about 'power in the workplace', and fewer still referred to the machinations of the capitalist system of production. Our respondents may have been generally conscious of class: incipient revolutionaries they clearly were not.

Though largely indistinguishable from employed respondents in their perceptions of industrial conflict and its parameters, the jobless in our sample were noticeably less inclined to concede that those who run industry and those who work for them nevertheless share certain interests in common, industrial conflict notwithstanding. Sixty-six per cent of those in employment nominated some such shared interest as compared with 48 per cent of the unemployed. The latter were rather more inclined than the former to see this commonality in terms of preserving jobs, but otherwise gave a broadly similar account of the interests involved, as can be seen from Table 8.5. In fact, as will be evident from the categories to which these replies were coded, many of the codes (such as those referring to the 'survival of the industry' or

Table 8.4 *Perceptions of industrial conflict, by employment status (percents and totals based on respondents)*

Conflict based on	Employed	Unemployed
1 Distribution of profits – workers not getting a fair share	4.7 (47)	2.1 (2)
2 Employers overpaid; employers' perks; employers greedy	7.3 (72)	4.2 (4)
3 Excessive wage demands by unions or workers; greed of unions or workers	12.5 (124)	15.8 (15)
4 Pay or money, when not further specified	19.5 (193)	26.3 (25)
5 The capitalist system itself	0.2 (2)	0.0 (0)
6 Hours of work, including short-time working	4.9 (49)	4.2 (4)
7 Numbers employed; redundancies; job security	6.7 (66)	8.4 (8)
8 Who has say in controlling work; management ignoring or dictating to workers	4.4 (44)	5.3 (5)
9 Power in the workplace (unequal distribution between management and workers)	1.9 (19)	3.2 (3)
10 Working conditions when not elsewhere specified (including health and safety)	7.9 (78)	5.3 (5)
11 Trades union militancy; strikes caused by unions	18.3 (182)	21.1 (20)
12 Workers' or union fear of new technology or change	2.5 (25)	1.1 (1)
13 Employers' attitudes to workers – unsympathetic and unreasonable management	14.7 (146)	16.8 (16)
14 Workers' attitudes to employers – laziness, lack of effort, expecting something for nothing	5.2 (52)	2.1 (2)
15 Employers' and employees' attitudes to each other – lack of communication and understanding	22.9 (227)	11.6 (11)
16 Weak management which gives in to unions too easily	0.5 (5)	0.0 (0)
17 Bad management – lack of expertise, failure to invest, 'old school tie'	6.4 (63)	2.1 (2)
18 Other	11.4 (113)	8.4 (8)

'expanding the company') indicate answers that also carry the clear implication of maintaining jobs or creating employment. Very few of our respondents, whatever their employment status, identified either with the firm and its products or with some greater national interest that was served by employers and employees alike.

These figures tend to reinforce our finding that class is more salient as a social source of identity in Britain than in the United States. The most popular perceptions among those both in and out of employment are that

205

distributional conflict is widespread throughout society; such conflicts are structured broadly by the phenomena of social class; and that these conflicts tend to outnumber whatever interests the principal protagonists might share – at least in so far as the different parties to production are concerned. Not surprisingly, therefore, against this background of pronounced class awareness we find little or no evidence of popular adherence to an ideology of individual achievement that might serve as some sort of functional equivalent to the 'American Dream' which, Schlozman and Verba argue, has an important influence on the cognitions and evaluations of workers in America.

It is clear, for example, that the majority of those both in and out of employment perceive class to be an ascribed rather than achieved characteristic. Asked how people come to belong to the class that they do, most respondents will nominate birth, family or inheritance as a determining factor, irrespective of their own present class position or employment status (see Table 8.6). Only about one quarter of those in each class location believe that hard work in any way contributes to one's class placement. Those in the service class are somewhat more likely to mention education and personal qualities than are those in the working class. The unemployed are noticeably less convinced that the distribution of people to classes is a function either of hard work or education and rather more likely (as one would expect) to emphasize the importance of occupation, and more generally of having employment itself. Those respondents who thought that class was (wholly or in part) a matter of ascription rather than achievement were then asked whether they approved or disapproved of people belonging to a particular class because of birth. Twenty-five per cent of employed respondents said they approved of this, 31 per cent disapproved, with the remaining 44 per cent neither approving nor disapproving. (Again there were no significant social class differences in the pattern of the responses.) The corresponding percentages among those unemployed were 25, 34, and 41. Asked further as to whether they thought it was easy or hard for a person to go from one social class to another, 78 per cent of these respondents declared that class mobility was hard ($N = 861$), as did 87 per cent of those unemployed who were also asked the question ($N = 78$).[5]

IV

Schlozman and Verba argue that the subjectively stressful problem of unemployment is not linked to a common political response in America because two perceptions are absent. The unemployed lack a collective identity and they fail to define their circumstances as resulting from impersonal social forces rather than personal failure. In large measure, both outcomes can be traced to the lack of class consciousness among American workers generally, and a corresponding endorsement of the meritocratic principles embodied in the American Dream of personal success. Thus far we have seen that, in Britain, the first of these putative conditions for political mobilization is actually fulfilled, British workers are as a whole 'class

206

Table 8.5 *Perceptions of shared interests of employers and employees, by employment status (percents and totals based on respondents)*

Shared interest in	Employed	Unemployed
1 General prosperity, pay, money	24.6 (190)	23.7 (14)
2 Survival of the company or enterprise	19.5 (151)	10.2 (6)
3 Profitability of the company or enterprise	22.3 (172)	22.0 (13)
4 Expansion or improvement of the company	8.7 (67)	10.2 (6)
5 Greater productivity	10.6 (82)	15.3 (9)
6 Safeguarding jobs	13.8 (107)	22.0 (13)
7 Company policy (all have interests in how company has run)	6.5 (50)	3.4 (2)
8 Effect of government policy on company or enterprise	0.6 (5)	0.0 (0)
9 Pride in company or enterprise, in its services or products	5.0 (39)	1.7 (1)
10 Good of the country; working for national interest	2.2 (17)	3.4 (2)
11 Other	6.6 (51)	8.5 (5)

conscious' to such an extent, and in such a manner, that social class is by far the most widely perceived, and most salient, source of collective identities. This is true of employees and of the unemployed alike. Indeed, if anything, the latter are more inclined towards class-based interpretations of the society than are the former. Is this collectivism then reflected in perceptions of unemployment itself? The model suggests that a personal trouble (unemployment) is more likely to become a basis for joint political action when it is seen as a public issue: as a shared, rather than a private condition, requiring government action and not simply personal effort for its solution. Moreover, Schlozman and Verba argue, collective political action becomes more likely if such a perception of state responsibility is translated into an agreed programme of appropriate government action. Neither condition is unambiguously met in the United States. So how does Britain compare in these respects?

Our data suggest that the unemployed in this country come much closer to sharing in the perceptions that, according to the model of political mobilization, are highly conducive to joint political activity. Unemployment is popularly seen to be a social rather than a personal problem. In our survey we introduced this topic by asking respondents whether or not they thought 'unemployment will ever fall below one million, the level it was in 1975'. Nineteen per cent of the unemployed thought it would, as did 13 per cent of those with work. The fact that well over 80 per cent of respondents in both categories could see no such reversal is itself rather significant. It suggests that

207

Table 8.6 Perceptions of factors determining class membership, by Goldthorpe class and unemployment (percents and totals based on respondents)

Factors determining class	Goldthorpe class/unemployment							
	I	II	III	IV	V	VI	VII	Unemployed
1 Birth; inheritance; family of origin	86.6 (103)	81.8 (189)	76.6 (85)	78.7 (85)	73.1 (76)	72.2 (109)	72.8 (214)	66.4 (85)
2 Innate ability	0.8 (1)	4.8 (11)	3.2 (8)	2.8 (3)	2.9 (3)	2.0 (3)	2.0 (6)	3.1 (4)
3 Hard work, ambition	27.7 (33)	24.9 (69)	25.4 (63)	22.2 (24)	27.9 (29)	20.5 (31)	23.5 (69)	11.7 (15)
4 Work; job; occupation	11.8 (14)	18.2 (42)	19.8 (49)	7.4 (8)	14.4 (15)	19.9 (30)	13.9 (41)	19.5 (25)
5 Education	31.9 (38)	29.9 (69)	21.8 (54)	27.8 (30)	21.2 (22)	18.5 (28)	20.4 (60)	11.7 (15)
6 Income; standard of living	9.2 (11)	15.2 (35)	13.3 (33)	15.7 (17)	17.3 (18)	16.6 (25)	18.7 (55)	17.2 (22)
7 Possessions (e.g. home ownership)	3.4 (4)	3.9 (9)	4.0 (10)	3.7 (4)	1.0 (1)	4.0 (6)	2.7 (8)	2.3 (3)
8 Status; associates	6.7 (8)	3.9 (9)	6.0 (15)	1.9 (2)	1.9 (2)	3.3 (5)	3.4 (10)	2.3 (3)
9 Personal qualities e.g. laziness, smartness)	5.0 (6)	4.3 (10)	2.4 (6)	0.9 (1)	2.9 (3)	1.3 (2)	1.4 (4)	2.3 (3)
10 Marriage	1.7 (2)	2.0 (5)	1.2 (3)	0.0 (0)	0.0 (0)	0.0 (0)	0.3 (1)	0.0 (0)
11 Luck	5.9 (7)	2.6 (6)	2.8 (7)	4.6 (5)	1.0 (1)	2.6 (4)	2.0 (6)	0.8 (1)
12 Other	5.0 (6)	3.0 (7)	2.8 (7)	0.9 (1)	1.9 (2)	4.0 (6)	1.7 (5)	3.1 (4)

most people are resigned to this situation irrespective of whether they approve of it or not. More interesting for our immediate concerns, however, are the responses to supplementary questions asking people to justify their initial judgment (see Table 8.7). Unemployment was seen by the vast majority of respondents as a problem to be solved (or as one unlikely to be solved) because of structural and political rather than personal factors. Thus, for example, optimists saw decline stemming from a change of government, from the policies of the present government, or from an upturn in the British or world economy. Pessimists blamed new technology, the decline in manufacturing, and demographic trends. In both cases the numbers alluding to private solutions or personal failures – a decline of the work ethic, spread of fatalistic attitudes, or problems in controlling inflation (with the implication that employees make excessive pay demands) – are relatively small.

This conclusion is reinforced by our findings about perceptions of Britain's economic problems more generally. Table 8.8 shows the main reasons for

Table 8.7 *Perceptions of unemployment, by employment status (percents and totals based on respondents)*

	Employed	Unemployed
a Reasons why unemployment will *fall below 1 million*		
1 Election of a different government	15.8 (22)	35.0 (7)
2 British economy will improve and business will pick up	35.8 (54)	30.0 (6)
3 World economy will improve and business will pick up	16.5 (23)	20.0 (4)
4 Lower wage increases will mean more jobs created	6.5 (9)	5.0 (1)
5 Present government policies will do it	13.7 (19)	10.0 (2)
6 Retirement age will be reduced; early retirements encouraged	6.5 (9)	0.0 (0)
7 Demographic or population changes (e.g. in birth rate)	7.9 (11)	10.0 (2)
8 New technology will create jobs	2.2 (3)	0.0 (0)
9 Optimism (e.g. 'it will all come right in the end')	15.8 (22)	0.0 (0)
10 Improved job training, vocational education	0.7 (1)	0.0 (0)
11 Individual solutions (e.g. self-employment; people 'getting on their bikes')	1.4 (2)	0.0 (0)
12 Government action to create jobs (where not covered by code 1)	1.4 (2)	0.0 (0)
13 Other	2.9 (4)	5.0 (1)

cont.

209

Table 8.7 *cont.*

	Employed	Unemployed
b *Reasons why unemployment will* not *fall below 1 million*		
1 World recession	10.2 (102)	8.7 (9)
2 New technology will eliminate jobs or require fewer workers	50.6 (505)	39.4 (41)
3 Decline in manufacturing or 'basic' industries	30.0 (300)	25.0 (26)
4 Population growth; too many school leavers	16.3 (163)	26.9 (28)
5 Cuts in government spending; present government's policies generally	12.9 (129)	12.5 (13)
6 Need to keep inflation down	2.2 (22)	1.0 (1)
7 Decline of work ethic or desire to work; welfare state fosters laziness	13.6 (136)	11.5 (12)
8 Britain's economic problems unsolveable or gone too far by now	8.7 (87)	12.5 (13)
9 Unemployment necessary for healthy economy; 1 million not too high	0.9 (9)	1.0 (1)
10 Wages are too low to attract people away from dole	0.6 (6)	1.0 (1)
11 More women are working nowadays, which creates job shortages	0.8 (8)	0.0 (0)
12 Immigration creates job shortages	1.5 (15)	1.0 (1)
13 Attitudes of hopelessness, despondency or fatalism	6.0 (60)	11.5 (12)
14 Other	3.7 (37)	1.0 (1)

Britain's economic problems in recent years as seen through the eyes of our respondents. The present Conservative administration came in for considerable criticism – especially from the unemployed themselves. Other commonly cited factors included the world economic recession, new technology, foreign imports, trades union militancy, and general criticisms of the political system as such. Note again, however, the relatively few responses that alluded to personal rather than systemic causes. Neither personal greed nor group characteristics which reveal themselves in individual behaviour (such as apathy, lack of effort, or unwillingness to work) feature at all prominently. As with the topic of unemployment, this question was followed up by asking respondents whether or not anything could be done to solve their nominated problem, and if so what (or if not why not). Seventy-seven per cent of those employed and 74 per cent of the unemployed said something could be done and nominated the solutions indicated in Table 8.9. Note again how many responses refer to government action and proportionately how few allude to individual efforts. Both 'changing individual attitudes' and 'improving

Table 8.8 *Reasons given for Britain's economic problems, by employment status (percents and totals based on respondents)*

	Employed	Unemployed
1 Membership of EEC; Common Market policies	7.0 (79)	10.1 (12)
2 Welfare state is a burden, or reduces work ethic	3.3 (37)	0.0 (0)
3 Policies of present government	20.2 (230)	39.5 (47)
4 Political system itself flawed (party bickering etc.)	16.9 (192)	21.0 (25)
5 Other political reasons, not elsewhere specified	3.1 (35)	0.8 (1)
6 General world recession	23.3 (265)	14.3 (17)
7 International relationship (e.g. multinationals)	1.8 (21)	0.0 (0)
8 Uncompetitive or declining industry	3.4 (39)	4.2 (5)
9 Lack of investment in industry	7.3 (83)	5.0 (6)
10 Inefficient or bad management	4.6 (52)	5.0 (6)
11 Trades unions too powerful	11.7 (133)	9.2 (11)
12 Upper classes, bosses or employers too greedy	0.7 (8)	0.0 (0)
13 Workers or unionists too greedy	4.9 (56)	4.2 (5)
14 Everyone is too greedy	6.9 (78)	1.7 (2)
15 Pay is too high (when not further specified)	2.3 (26)	1.7 (2)
16 Poor industrial relations	1.7 (19)	0.8 (1)
17 New technology or automation	9.2 (105)	5.9 (7)
18 Unemployment (NES)	3.3 (37)	4.2 (5)
19 Inflation (NES)	1.0 (11)	0.8 (1)
20 Lack of exports	3.2 (36)	3.4 (4)
21 Too many cheaper foreign imports available	7.7 (87)	10.1 (12)
22 Too much foreign aid distributed	2.0 (23)	2.5 (3)
23 Other economic reasons	14.2 (161)	7.6 (9)
24 National characteristics (apathy, lack of effort etc.)	10.0 (114)	2.5 (3)
25 Demographic factors (e.g. ageing population)	3.0 (34)	5.9 (7)
26 General fatalistic responses	0.3 (3)	0.8 (1)
27 Other	3.3 (38)	3.4 (4)

education and training' imply private solutions to public problems. Other responses call for government intervention and, in some cases, suggest clear government responsibility. This pattern is repeated among those who could see nothing being done to change things for the better: the 'because people can't change' responses form only a small proportion of the total answers given.

Table 8.9 *Solubility of Britain's economic problems, by employment status (percents and totals based on respondents)*

	Employed		Unemployed	
a Proposed solutions				
1 Increased government or public spending in new industries	2.4	(18)	1.4	(1)
2 Increased government or public spending in existing industries	1.6	(12)	0.0	(0)
3 Increased government or public spending generally	7.1	(53)	2.9	(2)
4 Greater investment in new industries	3.7	(28)	5.8	(4)
5 Great investment in existing industries	1.5	(11)	0.0	(0)
6 Greater investment in industry generally	5.2	(39)	7.2	(5)
7 Reduced government or public spending	8.7	(65)	0.0	(0)
8 Changes in directions of or priorities for government spending	9.0	(67)	2.9	(2)
9 Reduce costs for industry (e.g. reduced taxes)	1.6	(12)	1.4	(1)
10 Greater national self-sufficiency (e.g. protectionism)	12.3	(92)	15.9	(11)
11 Government action to reduce trade union power	7.4	(55)	2.9	(2)
12 More government involvement in industrial relations	0.8	(6)	0.0	(0)
13 Repatriation of foreigners; halt immigration	2.3	(17)	1.4	(1)
14 Improvements in education and training for work	5.2	(39)	4.3	(3)
15 Change attitudes of individuals (e.g. improve work ethic)	21.4	(160)	11.6	(8)
16 Reduce retirement age	4.0	(30)	0.0	(0)
17 Change present government; elect other government	13.3	(99)	33.3	(23)
18 Present government policies will do it	4.0	(30)	8.7	(6)
19 Increase economic, political, and social consensus	9.8	(73)	8.7	(6)
20 Other	3.5	(26)	7.2	(5)
b Reasons why no solution available				
1 Present government will not change its policies	6.6	(14)	13.0	(3)
2 No government or political party has the answer	11.8	(25)	13.0	(3)
3 Civil service rule the country	0.5	(1)	0.0	(0)
4 Change is impossible; problems too great	13.3	(28)	4.3	(1)
5 Too late to make any change; things gone too far	16.6	(35)	13.0	(3)
6 Attempts to change are counterproductive and create new problems	1.4	(3)	13.0	(3)

212

	Employed	Unemployed
7 People can't change; human nature	17.1 (36)	4.3 (1)
8 Problems are cyclical; things will come right in their own time	16.6 (35)	13.0 (3)
9 Lack of settled policies; lack of continuity in policies	5.2 (11)	13.0 (3)
10 Lack of co-operation between parties	2.4 (5)	4.3 (1)
11 Key groups are too powerful and hostile to change	2.8 (6)	0.0 (0)
12 UK powerless to solve problems; international solutions required	8.5 (18)	4.3 (1)
13 People are not given economic incentives to change	6.2 (13)	4.3 (1)
14 Other	1.9 (4)	0.0 (0)

V

It would seem, therefore, that there are significant differences between the United States and Britain when we reach step 3 of the formal model before us. The argument introduced for America by Schlozman and Verba is that the unemployed do not engage in joint political action because of the conjoint effects of low class consciousness and a high commitment to individual achievement and effort. There is no political programme for government intervention commonly subscribed to because joblessness, and the strain associated with it, do not have an impact on overall views of the American social and economic order: American workers generally are neither class conscious nor cynical about personal opportunities for success. The political preferences of unemployed Americans are therefore largely indistinguishable from those of their working counterparts. By comparison, British workers – employed and unemployed alike – arguably share a common class consciousness, and tend to be rather cynical about the tenets that underpin the American Dream of personal success. Unemployment seems to have no direct impact on these perceptions. Is it therefore also true that it leaves general policy preferences and political participation similarly unaffected?

The short answer to this question would be yes. The British and American data are again similar when we consider steps 4 and 5 of the formal model. We have already seen that, in terms of their perceptions of Britain's economic problems, the unemployed are not noticeably different from the wider population of those in work. The evidence from Table 8.10 confirms this earlier impression. As far as more general economic and social policy preferences are concerned, there is no evidence from our findings to suggest that unemployment intervenes in shaping these, except where specific programmes having a direct impact upon the unemployed themselves are involved. This, of course, was precisely the pattern reported for America by

Table 8.10 *Economic and social policy preferences, by Goldthorpe class and unemployment*

	Goldthorpe class/unemployment							
	I	II	III	IV	V	VI	VII	Unemployed
Leave it to market forces to revive the economy								
Agree	37.3 (44)	37.0 (81)	40.7 (92)	55.6 (60)	45.5 (46)	36.7 (55)	41.0 (116)	45.2 (56)
Disagree	62.7 (74)	63.0 (138)	59.3 (134)	44.4 (48)	54.5 (55)	63.3 (95)	59.0 (167)	54.8 (68)
	100 (118)	100 (219)	100 (226)	100 (108)	100 (101)	100 (150)	100 (283)	100 (124)
Incomes policies which increase the wages of the low paid more than the high paid								
Agree	56.2 (68)	63.3 (143)	75.9 (189)	69.0 (78)	80.2 (85)	81.5 (132)	82.9 (257)	83.1 (113)
Disagree	43.8 (53)	36.7 (83)	24.1 (60)	31.0 (35)	19.8 (21)	18.5 (30)	17.1 (53)	16.9 (23)
	100 (121)	100 (226)	100 (249)	100 (113)	100 (106)	100 (162)	100 (310)	100 (136)
Increasing income tax in order to increase welfare benefits								
Agree	23.8 (29)	25.8 (59)	26.6 (66)	18.6 (21)	32.4 (34)	34.0 (55)	28.2 (87)	35.5 (49)
Disagree	76.2 (93)	74.2 (170)	73.4 (182)	81.4 (92)	67.6 (71)	66.0 (107)	71.8 (222)	64.5 (89)
	100 (122)	100 (229)	100 (248)	100 (113)	100 (105)	100 (162)	100 (309)	100 (138)

cont.

Import controls to protect Britain from competition from abroad

Agree	56.3 (67)	58.6 (133)	80.2 (199)	71.4 (80)	73.1 (76)	85.4 (135)	79.5 (240)	75.5 (105)
Disagree	43.7 (52)	41.4 (94)	19.8 (49)	28.6 (32)	26.9 (28)	14.6 (23)	20.5 (62)	24.5 (34)
	100 (119)	100 (227)	100 (248)	100 (112)	100 (104)	100 (158)	100 (302)	100 (139)

Increased taxes on the profits of successful companies in order to maintain jobs in declining industries

Agree	24.4 (30)	34.1 (78)	55.2 (138)	36.6 (41)	46.6 (48)	65.0 (104)	62.5 (190)	63.0 (85)
Disagree	75.6 (93)	65.9 (151)	44.8 (112)	63.4 (71)	53.4 (55)	35.0 (56)	37.5 (114)	37.0 (50)
	100 (123)	100 (229)	100 (250)	100 (112)	110 (103)	100 (160)	100 (304)	100 (135)

Increased government spending to revive the economy

Agree	62.2 (74)	61.2 (137)	65.3 (164)	53.6 (60)	69.8 (74)	80.3 (122)	72.5 (219)	72.9 (97)
Disagree	37.8 (45)	38.8 (87)	34.7 (87)	46.4 (52)	30.2 (32)	19.7 (30)	27.5 (83)	27.1 (36)
	100 (119)	100 (224)	100 (251)	100 (112)	100 (106)	100 (152)	100 (302)	100 (133)

Table 8.10 cont.

	Goldthorpe class/unemployment							
	I	II	III	IV	V	VI	VII	Unemployed
Policies which make multinational companies reinvest in Britain all the profits they make here								
Agree	65.0 (78)	76.3 (171)	83.0 (205)	83.0 (93)	73.3 (77)	88.0 (139)	86.0 (259)	86.1 (118)
Disagree	35.0 (42)	23.7 (53)	17.0 (42)	17.0 (19)	26.7 (28)	12.0 (19)	14.0 (42)	13.9 (19)
	100 (120)	100 (224)	100 (247)	100 (112)	100 (105)	100 (158)	100 (301)	100 (137)
Special help for ethnic minorities over jobs and housing								
Agree	34.7 (42)	41.7 (95)	45.6 (114)	42.5 (48)	39.4 (41)	51.6 (82)	51.5 (157)	66.4 (89)
Disagree	65.3 (79)	58.3 (133)	54.4 (136)	57.5 (65)	60.6 (63)	48.4 (77)	48.5 (148)	33.6 (45)
	100 (121)	100 (228)	100 (250)	100 (113)	100 (104)	100 (159)	100 (305)	100 (134)
Special help to give women equal opportunities outside the home								
Agree	55.0 (66)	70.6 (163)	74.5 (187)	57.7 (64)	82.9 (87)	77.9 (127)	79.0 (245)	82.1 (115)
Disagree	45.0 (54)	29.4 (68)	25.5 (64)	42.3 (47)	17.1 (18)	22.1 (36)	21.0 (65)	17.9 (25)
	100 (120)	100 (231)	100 (251)	100 (111)	100 (105)	100 (163)	100 (310)	100 (140)

Respondent himself/herself would be prepared to pay higher taxes to create jobs for unemployed

Yes	60.3 (73)	54.5 (127)	52.4 (132)	40.7 (46)	64.2 (68)	59.1 (97)	59.3 (185)	72.1 (98)
No	39.7 (48)	45.5 (106)	47.6 (120)	59.3 (67)	35.8 (38)	40.9 (67)	40.7 (127)	27.9 (38)
	100 (121)	100 (233)	100 (252)	100 (113)	100 (106)	100 (164)	100 (312)	100 (136)

Respondent himself/herself would be prepared to pay higher taxes so that spending on welfare state could be increased

Yes	45.0 (54)	48.3 (112)	42.2 (106)	30.1 (34)	54.2 (58)	46.6 (76)	46.9 (144)	59.3 (80)
No	55.0 (66)	51.7 (120)	57.8 (145)	69.9 (79)	45.8 (49)	53.4 (87)	53.1 (163)	40.7 (55)
	100 (120)	100 (232)	100 (251)	100 (113)	100 (107)	100 (163)	100 (307)	100 (135)

Schlozman and Verba. We see, for example, that the unemployed are somewhat more likely to support incomes policies and higher taxes for higher welfare benefits, and significantly more likely to support taxes on profits or higher taxes generally in order to create jobs. (The extent of support among the jobless for ethnic minorities and for women suggests also an empathy and sympathy for other relatively disprivileged groups among the population – remembering here that disproportionately few among our sample of the unemployed were themselves either female or racially non-white.)

Nor are the unemployed exceptional in their political make-up. A majority vote Labour – but this is to be expected given the social characteristics of those who are selectively recruited into the ranks of the jobless. Their voting intentions are similar to those of manual workers generally (Table 8.11). Political allegiance is determined prior to the event of unemployment, and largely unaffected by it, as can be confirmed by examining patterns of vote switching among our respondents. Only 30 per cent of the unemployed (compared with 45 per cent of those in work) had *ever* voted for another party at a general election (N = 446 and 34 respectively). Moreover, unemployment itself would seem to have no direct impact on voting choice, since the overall patterns of vote switching among those in and out of work are very similar. Nor are the unemployed noticeably more cynical about, or disillusioned with, party politics as a whole than are those in work. Forty-three per cent of the latter and 42 per cent of the unemployed thought that it did not make a great deal of difference which party ran the country, and for broadly similar reasons (see Table 8.12). In other words, it would seem to be the case that the electoral politics of the unemployed in Britain are, like those of jobless Americans, not that distinctive. The severe economic strain occasioned by job loss has no obvious relationship to voting behaviour or more general political beliefs.

Finally, we arrive back at the observation from which we started: namely, that in Britain, as in the United States, there is no evidence of concerted political action by the unemployed themselves. Disproportionately high numbers of the unemployed in our sample reported that they (or their immediate family) had been affected by changes in government spending patterns across a range of public services (see Table 8.13). (In a follow-up question, to determine which change in spending had the greatest impact, 33 per cent of unemployed respondents nominated changes in supplementary benefit payments and 29 per cent that on unemployment benefits. Employed respondents, by comparison, were most affected by changes in spending on the NHS and on education, at 28 per cent and 23 per cent respectively.) The crucial point, as far as our present interest is concerned, is that 85 per cent of the unemployed (and 89 per cent of those in work) disapproved of the change they had experienced. Presumably, in other words, the great majority of employed and unemployed respondents alike had experienced *cuts* in government spending of which they were not in favour. Needless to say few had attempted to do anything about this: 13 per cent of employed interviewees (N = 165), and 11 per cent of the unemployed (N = 15), had

Table 8.11 Vote, by Goldthorpe class and unemployment

Voting intention

				Goldthorpe class/unemployment				
	I	II	III	IV	V	VI	VII	Unemployed
Voting Intention Conservative	52.8 (56)	46.6 (97)	41.0 (86)	55.0 (56)	38.0 (38)	19.1 (27)	25.1 (67)	21.6 (27)
Labour	17.0 (18)	23.6 (49)	26.7 (56)	13.7 (14)	35.0 (35)	61.7 (87)	50.6 (135)	54.4 (68)
Alliance	22.6 (24)	23.1 (48)	20.0 (42)	19.6 (20)	21.0 (21)	12.1 (17)	16.5 (44)	12.0 (15)
Would not vote	7.5 (8)	6.7 (14)	12.4 (26)	11.8 (12)	6.0 (6)	7.1 (10)	7.9 (21)	12.0 (15)
	100 (106)	100 (208)	100 (210)	100 (102)	100 (100)	100 (141)	100 (267)	100 (125)

Patterns of Vote Switching (Previous vote to voting intention), by employment status

			Employed	Unemployed
Conservative	→	Labour	7.2 (32)	6.5 (2)
Conservative	→	Alliance	17.2 (77)	19.4 (6)
Labour	→	Conservative	21.0 (94)	32.3 (10)
Labour	→	Alliance	25.1 (112)	16.1 (5)
Alliance	→	Conservative	17.4 (78)	3.2 (1)
Alliance	→	Labour	12.1 (54)	22.6 (7)

Table 8.12 *Reasons why it makes little difference which party runs the country, by employment status (percents and totals based on respondents)*

	Employed	Unemployed
1 No party has all the answers	21.6 (111)	5.4 (3)
2 All politicians look after themselves	12.3 (63)	8.9 (5)
3 One party is as bad as another	30.2 (155)	37.5 (21)
4 When in power all parties are the same	34.3 (176)	44.6 (25)
5 No party can do anything to solve the problems of the UK	14.4 (74)	10.7 (6)
6 One party just undoes what the other has done	6.2 (32)	0.0 (0)
7 The Civil Service run the country	1.9 (10)	3.6 (2)
8 Parties don't keep their promises	4.9 (25)	5.4 (3)
9 Other reasons	6.8 (35)	1.8 (1)

Table 8.13 *Reported impact of changes in government spending patterns, by employment status*

Changes in government spending on:		Employed	Unemployed
National Health Service	Affected	30.6 (377)	31.2 (43)
	Unaffected	69.4 (857)	68.8 (95)
Education	Affected	24.0 (297)	19.4 (27)
	Unaffected	76.0 (938)	80.6 (112)
Law and Order	Affected	7.6 (93)	12.1 (17)
	Unaffected	92.4 (1133)	87.9 (123)
Public Transport	Affected	24.1 (297)	39.0 (55)
	Unaffected	75.9 (936)	61.0 (86)
Council Housing	Affected	15.4 (190)	33.6 (46)
	Unaffected	84.6 (1042)	66.4 (91)
Unemployment Benefit	Affected	13.0 (160)	52.9 (73)
	Unaffected	87.0 (1074)	47.1 (65)
Supplementary Benefit	Affected	10.2 (126)	45.3 (63)
	Unaffected	89.8 (1105)	54.7 (76)

taken the (sometimes minimal) actions indicated in Table 8.14. Most had done nothing, not because they failed to experience 'dissatisfaction', nor (as we have seen) because they viewed the social order as a just meritocracy, but rather for the somewhat fatalistic – or realistic – reasons summarized in Table 8.15. Most commonly, it was argued that individuals can do nothing in this regard, since the authorities alone could implement remedial action; or that nothing could be done; or that, were the individual to take action, no one would take notice in any case.

Our data therefore confirm that the unemployed, far from being politically active as a result of hardships experienced in the context of joblessness, participate less actively in the political process than do their employed counterparts. Proportionately more would not vote at a general election (see Table 8.11 above). Few of those in our sample were likely to be involved in

Table 8.14 *Actions taken against changes in government spending, by employment status (percents and totals based on respondents)*

	Employed	Unemployed
1 Taken part in protest	9.7 (16)	13.3 (2)
2 Written to MP or Councillor	15.8 (26)	20.0 (3)
3 Written to newspaper	3.6 (6)	6.7 (1)
4 Signed a petition	18.2 (30)	6.7 (1)
5 Attended public meeting or other similar meeting	15.2 (25)	13.3 (2)
6 Joined campaign or organization	10.9 (18)	6.7 (1)
7 Been on march/demonstrated	6.1 (10)	13.3 (2)
8 Changed my vote	7.3 (12)	6.7 (1)
9 Changed to private service (e.g. BUPA, private school)	12.1 (20)	0.0 (0)
10 Complained to or contacted local council	7.9 (13)	6.7 (1)
11 Complained to or contacted a government department	9.7 (16)	46.7 (7)
12 Complained to or contacted another authority	13.9 (23)	6.7 (1)
13 Provided things privately	6.7 (11)	0.0 (0)
14 Other	2.4 (4)	13.3 (2)

Table 8.15 *Reasons why no actions taken against changes in government spending, by employment status (percents and totals based on respondents)*

	Employed	Unemployed
1 Can't be bothered; apathy	14.4 (65)	7.1 (5)
2 Individuals can't do anything – only authorities can	20.0 (90)	25.7 (18)
3 Ordinary people can't change policy	19.3 (87)	27.1 (19)
4 No point; no one would take any notice	12.9 (58)	21.4 (15)
5 Nothing that can be done about it	26.7 (120)	17.1 (12)
6 Don't know what could do	14.2 (64)	15.7 (11)
7 Change has not affected me badly enough	5.6 (25)	4.3 (3)
8 Other	2.9 (13)	1.4 (1)

Table 8.16 *Political activism, by employment status (percents and totals based on respondents)*

Percent involved in:	Employed	Unemployed
1 Political party activities	11.6 (29)	20.0 (3)
2 Residents, tenants and ratepayers' associations	13.1 (33)	40.0 (6)
3 PTA, school governors, educational pressure groups	35.5 (89)	13.3 (2)
4 Environmental, conservationist and civic amenity groups	16.7 (42)	26.7 (4)
5 Other local pressure groups	3.2 (8)	13.3 (2)
6 National pressure groups concerned with political issues (e.g. CND, Amnesty)	7.6 (19)	20.0 (3)
7 Trade union activities	25.5 (64)	0.0 (0)
8 Business groups or associations concerned with business interests	23.1 (58)	20.0 (3)
9 Membership of public bodies (elected or appointed)	5.6 (14)	0.0 (0)

pressure group activities of the kind reported in Table 8.16. This pattern of responses represents but 20 per cent of employed respondents – and a mere 11 per cent of those without jobs. The implication is clear: unemployment induces political quiescence rather than political mobilization.

VI

What conclusions can therefore be drawn about the political quiescence of the unemployed in Britain from our data? We have observed that, as was found to be the case in the United States, joblessness is accompanied by economic hardship that is experienced as such. It creates relative dissatisfaction among those who are its victims. Injury is added to insult (steps 1 and 2 of the model). Yet, as is also true for America, deprivation and strain do not induce among the unemployed a distinct and common set of preferences for policies designed to ease their lot. In both cases the unemployed show a preference for policies designed to ameliorate their immediate situation, but there is no general disaffiliation from the world-views of the employed majority, no obvious wholesale change in ideology to accompany the loss of occupation. Nor do the unemployed engage in systematic political activity as a protest against their situation (steps 4 and 5 of the model). In all these respects our data simply replicate the American findings. Rather significantly, however, British workers as a whole (including the unemployed among them) tend to share in a collective identity based on social class which is associated with a relatively low level of conviction that meritocratic principles operate to reward individual effort. This situation is the obverse of that suggested for the

United States by Schlozman and Verba at step 3 of the model of political mobilization. British workers do not lack a class identity and do not subscribe to a British version of the American Dream.

Of course our data are much less extensive than those considered for America. The British sample survey was not designed with this particular problem in mind. Our respondents are representative of the population as a whole – but those in the sample who are jobless are not representative of the unemployed *per se*. Nor do our questions entirely correspond to those in the original study. Our analysis is crude and could not hope, within the confines of a short chapter, to match the sophistication of the much lengthier American monograph. Nevertheless, the fact that we observe the same outcome as Schlozman and Verba, yet cannot replicate their crucial findings about social identities and the ideology of achievement, suggests either that Britain is very different from the United States in this respect, or that the explanation offered for America is somehow mistaken.

At this point we really do exhaust our data and perforce must simply offer the *speculation* that Schlozman and Verba may perhaps have sought their explanation for the political quiescence of the unemployed in the wrong quarter. As was suggested above, their argument stands in a long tradition of sociological research into a non-event ('Why don't the working class rebel?'), a tradition that places particular emphasis on the content and effects of working-class 'consciousness', which is seen to operate as some sort of 'intellectual block', preventing those located in a certain structural position from translating relative deprivation and discontent into collective action. There are good grounds for suggesting that this form of argument is unsatisfactory. Above all else it offers too mechanical a view of the relationship between the artificially differentiated components of 'structure', 'consciousness', and 'action'. It is a crude *Manifesto* Marxism in liberal guise.

There is no need to pursue such criticism here. One of us has already explored the problems of this tradition of writing about the working class at some length (see the chapter by Marshall in this volume). Rather, we would simply suggest that a more satisfactory explanation for political quiescence would place less emphasis on the ideological elements of any particular situation, and rather more on what might be termed the pressing realities of everyday existence. An altogether different way of looking at the data from the British study is to start with the remembrance that most of those without jobs will have considerable personal experience of relative disadvantage. Most of the unemployed consider the social and economic order to be distributionally unjust and do indeed disapprove of this. But, as we have also seen, they are at the same time aware that they live in a society structured by class inequalities, and that the existing political system is largely insensitive to the consequences that flow from this, so that not much has changed over the years. There is a resignation or cynicism – some might call it realism – evident in the responses of our interviewees which suggests that the explanation offered by Schlozman and Verba is altogether overly-voluntaristic. It is not that the unemployed share with their working counterparts a positive preference for individualistic solutions to their problems. We suspect, instead, that their experience of trades union indifference, state welfare bureaucracy, and political ineptitude on both sides of the party divide has provided the painful lesson that they must expect to fend for themselves. Faced with indifference from the top, and lacking the material resources to organize collectively from the grass roots, political quiescence and the purely private attempts to improve matters (through the individual job search) are a 'preference' born of necessity rather than choice.[6]

In short, and to put the matter into the terms of Parsonsian social theory, Schlozman and Verba accord too much importance to the normative regulation of action and altogether too little to its conditions. In order to demonstrate this convincingly we would require data rather more extensive and detailed than are available to us from our sample survey in Britain. Nevertheless, we would claim in this chapter to have cast justifiable doubts upon the particular thesis at issue, and so indirectly at least to have expressed our considerable misgivings about the tradition of sociological theory within which it is set.

Notes and references

1 The project is financed by the Economic and Social Research Council whose assistance is gratefully acknowledged. Additional technical information about the survey is available from the authors on request. It is linked to an international project on class structure and class consciousness initiated by Erik Olin Wright in the United States. Many of the results from the British survey will be directly comparable with those obtained for North America, the Scandinavian countries, Australasia, Japan and West Germany. The British survey was fielded by Social and Community Planning Research (London).

2 We are aware of the definitional problems associated with the concept of unemployment. (See, for example, the discussion in Marshall 1984.) The logic of Schlozman's and Verba's thesis is that one should contrast workers in formal employment with those who are objectively most deprived in this respect. We have therefore imposed a strict definition of unemployment such that 142 is the number of respondents in our sample who are formally unemployed, registered as such, and immediately available for work. The residual category of those economically inactive includes some who, elsewhere, one might wish to consider among the 'unemployed' themselves: women keeping house who are not registered at a Job Centre or Employment Office but say that they would take work if it was offered or was available; youths on a Community Programme or Youth Traing Scheme; the sick and disabled; and unemployed but unregistered males.

3 The detailed age distribution was as follows: 49 aged between 16 and 25 years; 29 aged between 26 and 35; 16 between 36 and 45; 27 between 46 and 55; and 21 between 56 and 65 years.

4   The Goldthorpe class schema derives from a neo-Weberian conception of
    class as contrasting market and work situations. It attempts to combine

> occupational categories whose members would appear . . . to be typically
> comparable, on the one hand, in terms of their sources and levels of income, their
> degree of economic security and chances of economic advancement; and, on the
> other, in their location within systems of authority and control governing the
> process of production in which they are engaged, and hence in their degree of
> autonomy in performing their work-tasks and roles (Goldthorpe, 1980, p. 39).

On this basis its author distinguishes seven principal classes: I – Higher
grade professionals, administrators and officials; managers in large
industrial establishments; large proprietors; II – Lower-grade professionals,
administrators and officials; higher-grade technicians; managers in small
business and industrial establishments; supervisors of nonmanual
employees; III – Routine nonmanual employees in administration and
commerce; personal service workers; IV – small proprietors, artisans etc.,
with and without employees; farmers and smallholders; self-employed
fishermen; V – Lower-grade technicians; supervisors of manual workers;
IV – Skilled manual workers; VII – Semi-skilled and unskilled manual
workers. Classes I and II are collectively referred to as the 'service class',
classes III–V as 'intermediate classes', while classes VI and VII together
constitute the 'working class'.

5   Because of an unfortunate filtering error in the interview schedule only
    those respondents who answered the initial question by reference to
    ascriptive processes were asked for supplementary information.
6   A more elaborate version of a somewhat similar argument, applied much
    more generally to capitalist societies as a whole, can be found in
    Abercrombie *et al.* (1980).

Further reading

G. Marshall, *et al.*, *Social Class in Modern Britain*, London: Hutchinson,
  1988
K. Schlozman and S. Verba, *Injury to Insult*, Cambridge, Mass.: Harvard
  University Press, 1979

9 Ideologies of work[1]

R. M. Blackburn

I feel like ashamed. I go round the back streets, and I don't want to meet people. They say 'Aren't you in a job yet?' and I feel ashamed. I don't like going out any more (Unemployed railwayman: Wedderburn, 1965).

I go terrible sometimes just thinking about coming to work in the mornings. It's not hard work but it seems to wear you out. When you don't talk its terrible – its a real drag – you could scream. Someone went like that last week. You've just got to control yourself (Woman packing foods: Beynon and Blackburn, 1972).

Introduction

Work can be perceived in quite different ways. Thus it may be seen as hateful by many with jobs while it is greatly sought after by those without. Clearly such views reflect distinct circumstances but they are not necessarily expressed by very different people. At some stage a worker may well hate his or her job and at another be unemployed; each person's understanding of work draws on the whole range of past and expected future experience. In recent years many jobs have become less attractive and harder to get, but neither the unpleasantness nor the unemployment is a new phenomenon. Both must be seen in the context of social processes embracing a longer time period. Ideologies of work are an important element of these processes; they provide forms of understanding and evaluation which help to sustain and reproduce the existing socio-economic structure, a structure in which there are great inequalities in the rewards derived from work. It is, therefore, pertinent to consider the nature of these ideologies and their basis in social experience.

Ideologies have both cognitive and evaluative aspects; they express people's understandings about existing social arrangements and their feelings about how they should be. They may also be considered at two levels: the general and the individual. General ideologies have wide currency within a population and provide familiar points of reference; they are belief systems about society which, through their application in the practical conduct of daily life, sustain social arrangements and the explanation of these arrangements. Individual ideologies are the corresponding beliefs and values of separate persons, that normally approximate to the general ideology (which otherwise would lose its general currency), but do not necessarily do so.

It will be argued that the cognitive aspect of ideologies, particularly work ideologies, is fundamental. In stable circumstances social arrangements have an external and 'given' appearance; like physical arrangements they are perceived as part of a natural reality which just is the way it is. An ideology provides a particular account of this state of affairs. It has, therefore, an explicit factual quality which inhibits evaluation by making it inappropriate.

Significant evaluations arise, therefore, only in relation to problematic elements in the factual account. At the general level this means socially problematic issues and at the individual level it indicates a disjunction between ideological accounts and the people's views of their own experience. This applies only to evaluations with practical relevance for possible behaviour. In the abstract – detached from the practicalities of experience – it is always possible to imagine things could be different and judge them accordingly. It is, however, the evaluations involved in the practical conduct of life which matter in ideologies. A crucial element in the analysis is the argument that such evaluation occurs only when, and in so far as, personal experience leads to the belief that different social arrangements are possible (Stewart and Blackburn, 1975). This provides a basis for value judgements at the level of individual ideology and so for divergence from the general ideology.

Because of the 'matter of fact' character of cognitive understanding when arrangements are not seen as problematic, there is a tendency to be aware of ideology in relation to problems, and so to emphasize the evaluative content. But it is, of course, just when an interpretation is unquestioned that it is most secure, and so has greatest conservative force. On the other hand, when evaluation does occur, individual deviations from the general ideology may provide a potential impetus for social change.

A further point of the argument is that ideologies of work, at least in western industrial societies, are markedly individualistic. This is entirely in keeping with the 'given' quality attributed to the socio-economic structure, implying that processes can only be explained by individual actions. This puts emphasis on individual choice and value judgements.

Within this individualistic understanding the existing arrangements tend to be imbued with a positive moral quality. The context of individual action is felt to be not quite so safe and secure as the cognitive account implies. This may be seen in the notion that it is wrong to interfere with nature, which can only have meaning when the 'natural' status of nature is sufficiently uncertain to be threatened. The evaluative aspects of general ideologies are of this form, protecting the cognitive interpretation.

The following discussion will look at ideologies of work, first at the general level and then in terms of individual understandings and evaluation, though the interrelation of the two will be evident throughout. The argument is then tested through an empirical investigation of a critical element of it. Finally some practical implications are considered.

Duties and rights

A basic paradox in ideologies of work is that work is held to be both a duty and a right. The duty is concerned with an individual having, or more precisely doing a job. Although sometimes associated with the 'protestant ethic', its basis and reference are strictly economic. It may be regarded as an 'employers'' ideology in the sense that it supports their need for labour, but it may also be seen as supporting the interests of society in general. The ideology is widely shared. Thus those without work are often condemned as 'work-shy' and 'shirkers' and certainly the very existence of such terms reflects the ideology, while even the unemployed are apt to blame themselves.[2] In a 'market' economy, such as Britain, the duty puts an onus on the individual workers to find work while the circumstances for doing so are not in their control. Thus it is an ideology serving the interests of capitalism while transferring responsibility to the workers, so that they receive the blame for failures of the system.

The duty implies work is not desirable for the individual. If it were enjoyable it would surely, like sex, be associated with sin rather than duty. Of course a duty may sometimes be pleasant but the concept implies sacrifice. If work were a natural need, as is sometimes suggested, then, as with eating, there would be no need for exhortation. Activity of some sort may well be a human need but not in this socially defined form.

An understanding of work as socially necessary is the basis of the ideology. This understanding is deeply entrenched; even mass unemployment has little effect, and may in fact be seen as providing confirmation since it is associated with economic recession and the unemployed represent a problem for the society. Thus the social need for work and, at a general level, its presence, are stable. The evaluative element of duty arises from the understanding of work as both unpleasant and as costing the individual effort and uncertainty in finding employment. This entails a fear not merely of people not working but of the system not functioning.

At the same time work is claimed as a right, and this claim implies that work is desirable. This may be regarded more particularly as a 'workers'' ideology, which is not entirely shared by employers, whose concern to increase productivity and reduce costs may well lead to laying off labour. This is not, in fact, a denial of the right to work but only of the employer's responsibility to provide it. However, working is a normal part of life for the relevant section of the population, and so is understood as a natural and necessary condition of life. Hence, at a superficial level there is general acceptance of work as a right. But once again significant evaluation depends on the problematic aspect of the 'natural' condition, the uncertainty of employment. Whereas the duty reflects uncertainties from the perspective of the society, and especially the owners and employers, the right more directly entails the individual worker's perceptions and interests. Those for whom the right is most important are those who are least secure. Primarily this means manual workers, and especially those without qualifications. These are also the people who tend to have the worst jobs in other respects. Work may be a highly rewarding experience for the professional with an interesting and worthwhile job, but this is hardly the case for many manual workers, such as the man packing and loading fertilizer in green bags, quoted by Nichols and Beynon (1977).

You come in here sometimes and you think 'I'd do anything to get out of this. God, what am I doing this for?' But next day you're back. I think all of us are mad. Even when you're at home you see those f****** green bags. Just lie back and shut your eyes and all you see is green (p. 16).

Paradoxically, then, the people with the most concern over a right to work are those for whom work is least attractive.[3] At one level the explanation of this paradox seems obvious and conventional. It is simply an aspect of social stratification. Those at the bottom of the stratification hierarchy are worst off in all respects, including security, and everyone needs the money a job provides in order to live.[4]

However, this is an explanation in terms of the same ideology in that it draws on the same general understanding of socio-economic processes. Thus the stratification structure is taken for granted, being part of the general understanding of the way things are. Recognition of this point then leads to new questions such as 'Why do the most deprived put up with the existing social arrangements and work within them?' 'Why do workers demand the right to work – to be exploited – rather than radical changes in the structure of inequality?' The form of these questions brings out the individualistic nature of the ideology; an ideology where understanding is in terms of individual experience and action within a given structure, as for example in notions of social mobility, educational achievement or job choice in the labour market. Located in this sort of understanding, the questions imply a centrality of choice and values, as though the workers choose or at least approve of their deprivation.

Thus, while the supposed explanation in terms of stratification may be an illusion, it nevertheless illuminates and confirms the general ideology. Within this ideological framework a need for the 'right' to be accorded is felt most pressingly among those for whom the potential jobs are the least attractive – where workers' understandings are predominantly in terms of a need to fit into the unequal structure, and so are in a form that helps to reproduce it.

A general ideology of work

It has been argued that there is a general ideology of work which permeates the understandings of people in all circumstances. In this, the existing social-economic structure is taken for granted, as part of the natural order, while interpretations of processes and relationships are individualistic. Economic activity is an essential feature of society and hence work is given a central importance. The notions of right and duty indicate different perspectives on the general evaluative beliefs associated with the form of understanding. Thus the ideology supports, cognitively and evaluatively, the maintenance and reproduction of the existing structure. A basic feature of the argument is that work is positively evaluated while inequalities in rewards are largely unquestioned. This may be illustrated with the data presented in Table 9.1.

In a recent survey[5] covering a wide range of occupations, respondents were asked 'Do you think it is desirable that someone can inherit enough wealth to be able to live off investment income without having to work?' and 'Is it desirable that someone can make enough money to be able to live off investment income without having to work?'. The table sets out the proportions who said 'No, it is not desirable'. There are no significant differences between the replies of the men and women.

Table 9.1 *Average disapproving of (a) inheriting and (b) making enough to live off the interest*

	Disapprove Inheriting %	Disapprove Making %	N
Men	53.2	14.0	215
Women	47.3	14.4	165
All	50.5	14.2	380

Inheritance is a normal part of the functioning of our society and tends to be accepted as right and proper. Thus only half the respondents saw anything wrong in the huge inequalities that are entailed in some people inheriting enough to live off the interest. On the other hand, this is a large proportion compared with the mere 14 per cent who expressed disapproval of 'making' a similar amount of wealth. Yet the degree of inequality between the level of income necessary to amass such wealth and the levels with which the respondents are familiar is hardly negligible. Indeed several of the respondents were so aware of this as to question the legality of making so much money, but given it was legal they accepted the inequality. Clearly the high level of inequality is seen as less significant than the method of wealth acquisition.

Inheritance does not have the same centrality in people's lives as work; notions of duty and right are less relevant and it is not difficult to imagine changes. Nevertheless, it seems unlikely that it is inheritance as such which is criticized, and clearly it cannot be the inequality *per se*, but rather it is the combination of the two. In contrast, high earnings represent individual achievement in an unequal environment and so can be accepted, and sometimes admired. Even successful gambling on the football pools – with 30 per cent disapproving on a similar question – seems more acceptable than passive inheritance.

At this level of generality the ideology of work entails an individualistic understanding of society, because individuals are seen as acting in a given structure of inequality where work is of fundamental importance. However, while significant in itself, its relation to individual experience remains problematic. It does not take account of variations in individual ideologies, where details of inequalities are questioned while their existence is not, or more radically and exceptionally, where their actual existence is challenged. Nor has it taken us much closer to grasping why inequalities tend to be understood in a neutral way which does not interfere with the processes of their reproduction.

Ideology, identity and experience

It is necessary to locate ideologies in the context of experience; to look beyond this general pattern of understanding and evaluation to the forms of understanding deriving from workers' positions in the social structure. We need to consider social identity, and to explain the circumstances which lead to understandings of social arrangements that inhibit or encourage radical appraisal.

Social identity may be taken to refer to the interpretative image of a man or woman which both derive from and are expressed in the person's pattern of social relations in everyday life. Roughly it is the way people see themselves and are seen by others in a shared social environment. It entails perceptions, interpretations and evaluations of actual and potential experience of social arrangements which are held not only by the persons in question but are also shared by others with whom they interact. There must be a sufficient common understanding of the circumstances of their interaction for social relations to proceed. Thus identity entails a practical understanding of social experience which is both constrained by social location and is adequate for participation in, and so the reproduction of, existing social arrangements. At one and the same time, therefore, it gives a basis of ideological understanding and defines an individual as a social person.

Because of the centrality of work in the lives[6] of virtually all men and very many women of working age, it is an important source of social identity. Holding a job is not simply important for economic reasons but also as a major element of social identity, though clearly these are not separate. Unemployment undermines such identity, while a lot of women feel an identity deriving from family domestic work is inadequate. The dole, social security or spouse's earnings may provide income but not a satisfactory identity. Thus, for example, unemployed workers still define themselves by their last job. Work is a basic part of life, and holding a job is more directly and personally problematic than the inequalities of the context in which it exists. The general ideology relates to this, as may be seen from the discussion of duty and rights. The first point to note, then, is that the right to work is a right to a significant social identity.

However, this does not, in itself, explain the general adherence to an ideological view that maintains the inequalities. For this we must take account of the constraints of experience deriving from social location. The relevance of such constraints derives from the argument that significant critical evaluation depends on experience which leads to a belief that social arrangements could be different.

231

What is understood as 'given' and 'natural' may be attributed a positive moral quality, but is no more relevant for moral judgement than, say, the force of gravity. In principle it is always possible to overcome social or physical constraints (though it seems easier to launch men into space than solve basic social problems). Control of physical nature is part of our ordinary experience; for example mastery over gravity may suggest space travel but is also to be found in the more familiar air travel and even in cycling. Similarly the social environment is external to each individual with a certain 'given' quality but is constantly being modified by everyday activities as well as by major political programmes. For many, the dominant experience may be one of constraint but there is room for a belief in the possibility of change. An understanding that things could be different may entail a sense of competence to exercise control, individually or collectively, or a belief that others could act effectively. The difference is, in fact, less a matter of who exercises control than of whether the outcome is seen as desirable. 'Others' may prevent desirable or effect undesirable change, whereas competence implies achieving a desired result; and where the outcome is desired, it is possible to share in a sense of collective achievement. For example, if it is believed that the government is failing to take practicable steps to reduce unemployment, the power is seen to reside in an alien body, whereas successful action would be a demonstration of collective competence. Individual control may often be more a matter of coping with the immediate environment than a question of changing it, but control of personal experience is likely to encourage a perception that social processes are alterable and thus open to critical judgement, and potentially to action.

Those with most concern with the right to work are, as Prandy (1979) has argued, not only those with the most to gain from more equitable rewards but also those whose experience is most likely to inhibit a sense of personal competence. He suggests a curvilinear relation such that, for different reasons, the most deprived and most advantaged are the least radical. The advantaged are more likely to have a belief in the possibilities of change, generating concern to preserve the existing order and hence support for the values of the general ideology (which should not be seen as *constructing* ideology in their interests). From the disadvantaged we might expect radical criticism and rejection of the general ideology, but the constrained nature of their experience means that they are the least likely to make the relevant evaluations.

The final, and crucial, step in our argument is that those at the bottom of the stratification hierarchy not only have the least attractive jobs but also the most constrained experience. They therefore have less sense of competence leading to a belief in the possibility that things could be different and, consequently, have less basis to make critical evaluations of social arrangements which operate to their disadvantage. The general ideology of work expresses their understanding of the way things are and, in its evaluative beliefs, of how they have to be. Compliance is essentially cognitive and in this sense alienated.

However, we must not regard the workers as a homogeneous mass or take too static a view of their ideological understandings. Circumstances vary over time and between individuals at any one time. Social changes may generate beliefs in the possibility that the situation could be different, leading to more critical and radical interpretations of social arrangements. Even in relatively stable conditions, variations in individual experience will lead to corresponding ideological variations, though we would expect radical evaluation to be comparatively rare.

An empirical exploration

If our argument is correct, it should account for differences within the relatively homogeneous grouping of those we have described as having most concern over a right to work. Accordingly, the following analysis was undertaken to test this, using the sample of unqualified male manual workers in the Peterborough labour market reported in Blackburn and Mann (1979).[7] While some were in jobs conventionally described as skilled, none had formal apprenticeship qualifications for the jobs they were doing. The level of skill required was low, below the capacities of the workers, who shared a common market position in the sense that almost all could, given the opportunity, do virtually all the jobs. Regrettably the sample is all male but there is no reason to believe a female sample would give different results here.

It is difficult to measure directly the understanding that things could or could not be changed, and the measures used are far from perfect. Since this understanding needs to be practical, it has to relate to a real problem where either a deterioration is threatened or an improvement seems possible. The former involves difficulties in identifying relevant situations and it is the latter which is used here. However, this has the limitation that meaningful questions on whether improvement is or is not possible are dependent on a prior view that something is wrong.

The main instrument used derives from a question asking, 'Do you feel that your work is a worthwhile, valuable part of your life, or is it just something you do to earn a living?' Those who answered affirmatively were then asked to indicate in what way it was worthwhile and valuable. The remainder were asked two further questions, 'Do you dislike this, or have you grown used to it?' and 'Could anything be done to make it more worthwhile and valuable?' The few who answered 'Don't know' on this last question have been combined with those answering 'No' on the grounds that they had no positive conception of the possibility. A similar set of questions were also asked about enjoyment, starting with, 'Do you enjoy the time spent at work, or don't you get much pleasure out of it?'. Table 9.2 relates the answers to these sets of questions (with affirmative answers subdivided, see below). Because relatively few said their work was not enjoyable, these questions were less useful; and thus, the analysis is presented for the 'worthwhile' questions unless indicated, but both sets give similar results.

Clearly, the questions 'Could anything be done. . .?' tap an understanding

233

Table 9.2 'Worthwhile' by 'enjoy' (showing reasons for affirmative (contented) responses, whether discontented think improvement is not (negative) or is (positive) possible, and whether they say they have grown used to or dislike their situation

| Worthwhile: and if not whether improvement is possible | Enjoy (contented): reasons | | | Not enjoy: is improvement possible? | | | | Row Total |
| | | | | No. (negative) | | Yes (positive) | | |
Number / Row % / Col %	Job	Workmates	Illegitimate	Grown used to	Dislike	Grown used to	Dislike	
Worthwhile (contented):								
Legitimate reason	151	59	17	7	0	14	0	248
	60.9	23.8	6.9	2.8	0.0	5.6	0.0	26.9
	42.9	23.7	17.0	6.7	0.0	20.3	0.0	
Illegitimate reason	58	59	12	7	0	7	4	74
	39.5	40.1	8.2	4.8	0.0	4.8	2.7	15.9
	16.5	23.7	12.0	6.7	0.0	10.1	14.3	

Not worthwhile

								Row Total
No: Grown used to (negative)	87 27.9 24.7	75 24.0 30.1	61 19.6 61.0	65 20.8 61.9	1 0.3 5.3	21 .7 30.4	2 0.6 7.1	312 33.8
No: Dislike (negative)	3 9.1 0.9	8 24.2 3.2	2 6.1 2.0	4 12.1 3.8	10 30.3 52.6	1 3.0 1.4	5 15.2 17.9	33 3.6
Yes: Grown used to (positive)	51 32.9 14.5	42 27.1 16.9	6 3.9 6.0	21 13.5 20.0	5 3.2 26.3	22 14.2 31.9	8 5.2 28.6	155 16.8
Yes: Dislike (positive)	2 7.4 0.6	6 22.2 2.4	2 7.4 2.0	1 3.7 1.0	3 11.1 15.8	4 14.8 5.8	9 33.3 32.1	27 2.9
Column Total	352 38.2	249 27.0	100 10.8	105 11.4	19 2.1	69 7.5	28 3.0	922 100.0

235

that things could or could not be different, and will provide the core of the following analysis. An affirmative answer to these questions indicates a positively critical understanding. On the other hand, the view that nothing could be done about an undesirable situation suggests a fair degree of hopelessness. For ease of presentation these responses (and the men giving them) are called 'positive' and 'negative' respectively. The remainder – those who say their work is worthwhile/enjoyable – will be referred to as 'contented' but the term should not be taken too literally.[8] For convenience the sets of questions are entitled 'worthwhile' and 'enjoy'.

Before proceeding with the data analysis, it will be useful to consider the meanings of, and relations between the types of response. Following Marx, it would be correct to argue that all these workers are alienated. Their common experience is such as to lead to an alienated form of understanding, which is expressed in the general ideology of work and inhibits pursuit of their interests through an attack on inequalities. However, there are also differences of experience and understanding.

Those who are not 'contented' may be regarded as alienated in the sense that they recognize their undesirable situation but are powerless to change it; they must go on working. It might then be argued that those giving positive responses are simply more frustrated since they perceive that others have the power to make improvements. There is, however, one form of individual control, through changing jobs. When asked if they were thinking of changing, not surprisingly most said they were not and this was more marked among the contented, while the negative group were the most likely to say they did not know and the positively discontented were most likely to have done something about it (gamma = 0.41).[9] Of course a job change may only be stepping out of the frying pan, but the positive group were more hopeful than the negative one, indicating bigger improvements in the levels of the future jobs that they would like and that they expected to get (gamma = 0.31, 0.33). Furthermore, when asked if they would move for an improvement in pay, with a set of increasing offers, the negative group seemed inclined to settle for a smaller amount. This evidence suggests that those who see the possibility of improvements do have a greater sense of individual personal competence. It remains to be seen whether the changes they have in mind are purely individual adjustments or involve a wider critical consciousness. However, it appears that alienation is relatively low among this group and comparatively high in the negative group.

Looked at from a different standpoint, to some extent the very act of not approving their work, and especially the expression of dislike, may be taken as indicative of radical consciousness. It is well known from innumerable job satisfaction studies that most workers say they are satisfied – 86 per cent in this sample – but this does not mean they find their jobs attractive. Rather it means that they find their expectations, which are realistically low, are reasonably met (Stewart and Blackburn, 1975). Thus, the expression of satisfaction is in part a reflection of alienation, in that they have come to terms with their deprivation, whereas to actually express dissatisfaction may entail an element of radical appraisal. A similar argument may be applied to the present questions. In both cases a substantial proportion answered affirmatively – 75 per cent for enjoyment and 43 per cent for worthwhile – and the answers are well related to 'satisfaction'.

We cannot just ignore the meaning of the questions, for those who do find something genuinely worthwhile or enjoyable in their work are only alienated in the more general sense which applies to all the workers. It may, nevertheless, be the case that some affirmative answers conceal a more substantial degree of alienation, and to examine this, contented responses were further divided to distinguish illegitimate reasons in relation to the form of the questions – essentially extrinsic, instrumental reasons like earning a living. While these answers do not directly express a consciousness of constraint, their extrinsic and limited character may reflect one. For enjoyment, legitimate reasons are also divided into those created through relations with fellow workers and those deriving from the job and conditions supplied and controlled by the employer. The relationships of these response patterns for the two questions are shown in Table 9.2. There are clear differences suggesting that the affirmative answers are not homogeneous in meaning. On the one hand, enjoyment of the job itself is most closely associated with legitimate 'worthwhile' responses; on the other, illegitimate responses on enjoyment are associated with the negative response on the 'worthwhile' questions – over 60 per cent apparently alienated on this criterion, as are more than 25 per cent of the others who reported enjoyment. By comparison only 5 per cent of illegitimate and 3 per cent of legitimate worthwhile responses are combined with the negative answers on enjoyment, though the illegitimate are strongly associated with enjoyment from work-mates' company.

Unfortunately it was not possible to ask the respondents who gave these different forms of contented answers whether anything could be done to remedy their situation, since they indicated no problem. For further analysis we must take the content answers at face value while bearing in mind their diversity, although this seems less serious for the 'worthwhile' question.

Turning to the distinction between the 'grown used to' and the 'dislike' responses, it seems reasonable to suppose that the former indicates an accommodation to the undesirable situation and in this sense a degree of alienation. This is supported by the relationship with negative answers on the possibility of change (enjoy: gamma = 0.39, worthwhile: gamma = 0.24). It suggests divisions within the positive and negative groupings, such that the extremes range from 'grown used to and no improvement is possible' to 'dislike and improvement is possible'. In fact, this pattern tends to be found in relation with other variables, at least for the 'enjoy' responses. However, for 'worthwhile' it is doubtful if the distinction between 'grown used to' and 'dislike' proved very meaningful for many respondents. The relationship with the question on improvement is lower, and anyway nearly 90 per cent answered that they had grown used to it. Since the focus of interest is on the positive/negative division, with very little loss of information and an appreciable gain in the ease of handling the data, the other division is dropped from further analysis using the 'worthwhile' question (giving another reason for preferring this question). The proportion expressing dislike varies from 15 per cent in the positive grouping to 10 per cent in the negative one, and so the problem of a spurious effect is negligible.

Overall there is a clear relation between the two variables with strong association particularly in positive responses. Taking the contented answers at face value (without division), the measures are encouragingly related, with little difference when 'worthwhile' is reduced to three categories (gamma = 0.50 and 0.49 respectively). In view of the various considerations in the foregoing discussion, it would be foolish to expect too clear cut results in the following analysis, but we shall see that there is nevertheless a clear overall pattern.

Dissatisfaction and radical attitudes

A common-sense interpretation would see those who felt they could do nothing about an undesirable situation as being in the most hopeless, and therefore the worst situation, which would lead to greater dissatisfaction and radical attitudes. Against this our argument suggests that those who see possibilities of improvement will be most likely to express dissatisfaction and so on, with the more alienated occupying a middle position. This is indeed what we find. In fact this tendency has already been noted in the relation between dislike and positive responses in Table 9.2. The pattern in relation to job satisfaction may be clearly seen in Table 9.3.

Table 9.3 *'Worthwhile' by job satisfaction*

Number Row % Col %	Dissatisfied	Satisfied Slightly	Fairly	Very	Row total
Worthwhile	22	143	136	87	338
	5.7	36.9	35.1	22.4	42.7
	18.6	38.0	47.4	68.5	
Not Worthwhile					
negative	42	149	110	37	338
	12.4	44.1	32.5	10.9	37.2
	35.6	39.6	38.3	29.1	
positive	.54	84	41	3	182
	29.7	46.2	22.5	1.6	20.0
	45.8	22.3	14.3	2.4	
Column Total	118	376	287	127	908
	13.0	41.4	31.6	14.0	100.0

It shows that the positive are the most likely to express dissatisfaction, while the negative express mild satisfaction and those who see their jobs as worthwhile include most of those who say they are very satisfied (gamma = −0.41). As we might expect, answers on enjoyment of the job are even more closely related to job satisfaction (gamma = −0.64), but the difference is due to the comparison between respondents saying they do or do not enjoy their work rather than between positive and negative responses among those who do not.

Table 9.4 gives coefficients of association (gammas) for a set of variables, showing that similar patterns emerged, in keeping with the general argument. The first column gives values for the whole sample with 'worthwhile' ordered as in Table 9.3, and the second includes only the workers saying their jobs were not worthwhile. As we would expect the latter values tend to be lower, but not greatly and sometimes not at all, showing the importance of the division between the positive and negative groupings.

Table 9.4 *Association between attitude measures and responses to the 'worthwhile' question (Ordered positive, negative, contented for the whole sample, and positive, negative for those saying their jobs are not worthwhile)*

	Coefficient of association: gamma	
	All	Not worthwhile
Satisfaction with job	0.41	0.42
Satisfaction with life in general	0.28	0.27
Would choose same type of job again	0.25	0.20
Reluctance to go to work*	0.35	0.18
Economism*	0.22	0.14
Generalized demands	0.37	0.38
Radical/conservative attitude	0.32	0.30
Age*	0.34	0.23
N (approx)	920	525

Positive coefficients indicate a relationship in the expected direction. Thus the three items marked * are reverse scored.

The enjoyment question would give coefficients about 50 per cent higher for the whole sample and probably a little lower in the second column (the measurements are not strictly comparable). Although there are reasons to place less reliance on this measure the results are at least consistent with those of Table 9.4.

On satisfaction with life, the pattern is the same as for job satisfaction. Similarly those who said they would choose the same kind of job if they could start their working life again tend to see their jobs as worthwhile, while the 'Don't knows' came disproportionately from the negative group; and although the majority would not make the same choice, this was most marked among the more hopeful critics. Most workers, and especially the 'contented' group, said they rarely or never felt reluctant to go to work but over half the

239

positive and a substantial proportion of the negative group felt so more often.

There is a general tendency for the negative group to express no orientation to work of any sort, which is in evidence with respect to economism. At the same time we would expect those who do not find their work worthwhile or enjoyable to be more concerned with extrinsic rewards. However, the position is further complicated since such concern may indicate greater alienation; and indeed, among the twenty-three scored at the highest level, seventeen (74 per cent) were from the negative group, against the overall trend. With these conflicting influences on the negative group, the net effect is a contrast between the contented and positive, with the latter tending to have their orientation quite strongly and more than any other (as also do workers with more radical attitudes).

The next two items come closer to direct measures of radical ideology. Generalized demands is the mean score of a set of nine items (measured on scales from 0 to 24) concerned with criticisms of employment in general. For example, two of the items contributing most of the relationship are 'To get a decent wage you have to ruin your social life by working much too long on overtime and shifts' (gamma = 0.29/0.31) and 'Nowadays managements treat people like me just as numbers and never as human beings' (gamma = 0.33/0.40). Then there is an attempt to measure a left–right 'ideology' in relation to work. Again there were nine items, in this case combined through factor analysis (see Bulmer 1975). Examples are 'The worker should always be loyal to his firm even if this means putting himself out a bit' (gamma = 0.28/0.27) and 'Most conflicts between managements and workers are caused by agitators and extremists' (gamma = 0.24/0.40). The composite measures effectively differentiate the contented and positive on the 'worthwhile' variable, especially at the extremes (gamma = 0.58 and 0.50). However, the negative group are fairly evenly distributed around a slightly left of centre position.

The final variable, age, is obviously not an attitude but is included because of its well-known relationships with relevant attitudes (unlike the other variables of the table which, apart from obvious pairings, show little interrelationship). As one would expect there is a strong tendency for young workers – especially those in their twenties – to give positive responses while the older men give contented replies.

It seems clear that, as predicted, those who see the possibility of improvements in their unsatisfactory situation are the most critical and radical. Those that I have described as negative are discontented, but they express no strong views; they emerge as mildly satisfied, slightly left wing, with no clear orientation to work. They are more alienated.

Constraints of experience: non-work life

It still remains to establish the determinants of such alienation, testing the argument that it derives from constrained experience. Again the results are quite consistent. Looking first at non-work factors we see that the negative group tend to be the least socially integrated.

Table 9.5 sets out the measures of association for a set of indicators. In marked contrast to the earlier analysis, the negative group now occupies the extreme position, which is as predicted. Thus, the comparison in the first column is between the negative group and the rest. Again the second column is based on the negative/positive division to make clear this critical distinction. The values here tend to be lower because the contented have higher values than the positive group on most items, although the differentiation between them (the extremes of Table 9.4) is often not very clear.

Table 9.5 *Non-work factors related to 'negative' responses (For whole sample and for those saying their jobs are not worthwhile)*

	Coefficient of association: gamma	
	Negative/rest	Negative/positive
Immigrant/born in UK	0.52	0.47
Number of churches and clubs belonged to	0.20	0.23
Church or club officer	0.45	0.31 n.s.
Exchange visits with relatives	0.38	0.29
Go out with or meet up with relatives	0.22	0.11
Go out with immediate family	0.33	0.19
Go out to a pub	0.18	0.25
Go out alone*	0.21	0.09 n.s.
Widowed/divorced/separated*	0.15 n.s.	0.49 n.s.
Health problems*	0.18	0.21
Status of friends	0.30	0.20
Own status	0.37	0.28
N (approx)	920	525

n.s. = not significant at the 5 per cent level (i.e. p. > 0.05)

Positive coefficients indicate the relationship is in the expected direction. Thus the three items marked * are reverse scored.

Most striking, if not surprising, is the alienation of immigrants, although it is worth noting that few were recent arrivals. There were three main groupings: Asian, Eastern European and Italian. The last two, and some of the Asians had been in Britain a good many years, while it was the Italians who showed greatest tendency to negative perceptions.

The next seven items also reflect social integration in various ways. In identifying a group who go out on their own, it seems reasonable to require that they do so quite often, so the alternative group were those who replied 'rarely or never'. For the other four social activity items the critical division was between those who do and those who do not go out or receive visits. There were variations in degree of activity along the lines we would expect but in all cases it was slight compared to the basic division. Very few (5 per cent) held even one position in a club or church so that, in spite of a clear relationship, the negative–positive figure is not significant. Similarly the small number (4 per cent) who are widowers or divorced or separated show non-significant tendencies in the expected way, but as they are rarely radical, in the sense of giving positive responses, a significant relation does emerge (with gamma = 0.21) when 'worthwhile' is ordered from negative through contented to positive. All these factors and, in a different way health problems, involve limitations in the person's experience.

It is central to the argument that the constraints of social experience are inversely related to stratification position. It is important, therefore, that the two measures of status give relations as expected. Based on occupations, they are largely intuitive attempts to differentiate occupations on conventional criteria, mainly notions of skill. Those with nonmanual friends tend to see their jobs as worthwhile while the positive discontented tend to have higher level manual friends. Given the importance of friendships to life-styles this is as we would predict (compare Prandy, 1979). Such a pattern is not possible for the occupational status of the respondents themselves, since they are drawn from a restricted range of manual work. Nevertheless, using precise definitions of their occupations, it was possible to differentiate levels so that, in spite of the narrowness of the range, there is a clearly discernable tendency for the lowest levels to be those who see no possibility of improvement.

Work experience

While the stratification positions we identified under 'status' relate to experience in the wider society outside work, the use of occupation introduces an overlap with work experience. The areas of work and non-work should be regarded as parts of an integrated whole, but in relation to our specific concern with ideologies of work it is perhaps the experience of employment that is crucial to the argument.

Table 9.6 *Background work factors by negative responses (For whole sample and for those saying their jobs are not worthwhile)*

| | Coefficient of association: gamma | |
	negative/rest	*negative/positive*
Selectivity with regard to firms	0.21	0.19
Jobs in agriculture	−0.15	−0.29
Upward job changes	0.20	0.17
Downward job changes	0.11	0.23
Changes of job level (up or down)	0.28	0.22

Positive coefficients relate negative responses to low values on the variables.

Table 9.6 shows the relation to some background work variables. The first is really an attitude variable, measuring the readiness to reject hypothetical jobs with different employers. It is included here as an indicator of a work history encouraging confidence to be choosy. The others relate directly to work history. Agricultural employment is commonly associated with different attitudes and it is not surprising to find it associated with negative responses.

242

It is interesting that workers with experience of job changes both upwards and downward tend not to be in the negative group, although the latter are more likely to express positive discontent. It appears that the experience of different levels undermines the 'given-ness' of their circumstances. On the whole it seems work histories are too homogeneous to produce much differentiation and such things as experience of self-employment or nonmanual work are too rare to have significant effects, though the trends are as expected.

Table 9.7 *Extent to which mental abilities used in doing the job by 'negative' responses*

Number Row % Col %	Used of mental abilities						Row Total
	Low					High	
Negative	81	52	99	60	35	19	346
	23.4	15.0	28.6	17.3	10.1	5.5	
	55.9	50.5	43.4	35.1	28.9	12.1	37.4
Others	64	51	129	111	86	138	579
	11.1	8.8	22.3	19.2	14.9	23.8	
	44.1	49.5	56.6	64.9	71.1	87.9	62.6
Column	145	103	228	171	121	157	925
Total	15.7	11.1	24.6	18.5	13.1	17.0	100.0

More important is current work experience. Here the finding is that the negative response is associated with low rewards at work. Table 9.7 illustrates this for the opportunity to use mental abilities. In the original study this emerged as the most important factor differentiating jobs and it is again important here. There is a clear association between the absence of opportunity to use the mind and the response that no improvement is possible. It may be noted that differentiation is greater at the higher end of the scale. To appreciate this it must be understood that the job rewards were at a very low level so the more marked difference means that those who did have some chance to think in their jobs were less likely to have 'negative' perceptions. The same sort of pattern applies to other job rewards, sometimes more noticeably.

Table 9.8 gives coefficients of association for a set of job characteristics including the one just considered.[10] For this purpose the scales of job rewards have been dichotomized into high and low. As before, the first column gives the gammas comparing the negative group with the rest of the sample and the second gives them for the relations with a negative/positive split, i.e. including only those who see the job as not worthwhile. Better rewards are desirable, so we would expect those in the higher categories to see their jobs as worthwhile and those at lower levels of reward to be critical. In fact, the

Table 9.8 *Association between job characteristics and 'negative' responses (For whole sample and for those saying their jobs are not worthwhile)*

	Coefficient of association: gamma	
	Negative/the rest	*Negative/positive*
Mental abilities required	.47	.27
Skill (including manual dexterity)	.43	.32
Object variety	.45	.31
Responsibility	.44	.24
Autonomy	.45	.17
Physical effort	.05 n.s.	.29
Working conditions	.29	.04 n.s.
Status in the firm	.33	.26
General interest	.49	.30
Hours of work (long)	.12	.21

Coefficients measure association between negative responses and low values on the variables, except for hours.

n.s. = not significant at 5 per cent level (i.e. $p > 0.05$).

various rewards are positively related so that high rewards on one aspect tend to mean a better job in general, thus strengthening the point. It will be seen that the relationships are lower in the second column, as we would expect, but the general pattern is clear. It is the negative group who have the worst jobs.

'General interest' is a composite of the first three variables plus work cycle length and is included as a summary measure. The two problematic aspects are physical effort and working conditions. Indeed the latter is essentially just an indication that the contented tend to be working in better conditions, but at least those in bad conditions are no more likely to be positively critical. Low physical effort is primarily inactive machine minding which is associated with negative rather than positive responses but also with contented responses. In fact the negative responses tend to be found at both extremes, while it is mainly a comfortable pace which is associated with contented responses and a high strength content that accompanies positive responses.

Overall, the data presented clearly support the general argument. The contented tended to be in better jobs and were generally less critical or radical in outlook. Given the low levels of job rewards, this looks like contentment with relative advantage in a highly restricted context, suggesting a substantial degree of cognitive acceptance of a 'given' situation. However, it is the division within the discontented that is critical for the present analysis. Those whose ideological understanding did not allow for improvements in their situation were those with the most constrained experience. Their jobs were generally worse, particularly in an absence of opportunity to exercise mental and manual skills, and socially, they tended to be isolated and disadvantaged. In keeping with an alienated understanding of circumstances as given and unchangeable, their attitudes were largely neutral, showing no critical evaluation. This contrasts with the circumstances and attitudes of the workers who believed that something could be done to improve their situation. Within the range of unrewarding work that we have been considering, those whose understanding included practical possibilities for change had less constrained experience and are the ones who were most critical and most radical.

Implications for present circumstances

Finally let us consider briefly the implications of this argument for the present economic situation and possible developments. Quite obviously this is a time when unions are weak and control rests more firmly with the employers. This is likely to have heightened the experience of constraint for workers, and hence, their understanding that this is the natural way of things. But of course there are a great many people who are out of work, particularly among the unqualified.

Insecurity is always a problem, as was seen in relation to the concern over the right to work. Therefore, the experience of unemployment does not entail a disjunction with former understandings. Rather, it tends to reinforce these, and the fact that many others are out of work can only add further support. Not only is it part of the 'natural' order, but for the individual it involves a particular loss of control, with the loss of the social identity required by the duty to work. For the young who have never worked, the experience is rather different but for many the step from school to the dole must appear as the natural progression. At the other end of the age scale, in so far as early retirement is experienced differently from redundancy it is still hardly likely to be a radicalizing experience. All this points not to any organized radical action based on a critical ideology, but a growing alienation.

However, it is a mistake to take too static a view. Changes occur, and these are liable to make people conscious of other possibilities and so more positively critical. In the first place unemployment is not a constant state for all who lose their jobs: there is continual movement in and out of work, and as Schlozman and Verba (1979) observe, those who have recently found jobs tend to be more radical. Among the sample analysed here, all of whom were in work, there was a tendency for the men with extensive experience of unemployment to have a more constrained understanding but for those with fairly limited unemployment in more recent (post-war) years to have a positive, critical understanding.

If unemployment continues to grow, the prospects of support for a radical movement of protest seem remote. To be sure, suffering will increase but so will the alienated understanding which inhibits action, and in so far as individuals do gain a sense of competence, it is likely to emerge in action which is individualistic, 'deviant' and unorganized.[11] On the other hand, the promised economic recovery may come, and open the way to a fresh ideological understanding where current deprivations are not inevitable and beyond remedy. 'Discontent' is already widespread; economic recovery could add a 'positive' belief in the possibility of improvements. Whether or not

245

unemployment falls (though some decline may be necessary to influence understandings), the perception of an improving economy may well start a growth of radical protest. This may not be very dramatic, in view of the inequalities and constraints on experience that will remain, and the initial result may be erratic, unorganized protest. Yet, the marginal effect that is possible may prove quite significant in its impetus for social change.

In general, the deprivations of work and unemployment serve as a form of social control – though not necessarily a deliberate one – through their influence on alienated understanding. None the less, it is a potentially unstable control. Compliance does not mean acceptance, and changing circumstances – particularly recognizable improvements – may open the way to more radical ideologies. In extreme cases the outcome is revolution, but in Britain this remains unlikely.

Notes and references

1 This paper is based on research conducted jointly with Michael Mann, Sandy Stewart and Ken Prandy. My thanks go also to Frank Heller and Jonathan Turner for valuable comments on an earlier draft. I am also indebted to the ESRC for their support of the projects, and to NIAS for a perfect environment for writing.

2 Thus subsidy of the poor is criticized as discouraging the duty to work. Subsidy of the affluent is defined as in the national interest, on the grounds that it stimulates the economy, maintains employment and so on (Turner and Starnes, 1976).

3 The claim of the right to work by 'middle-class', qualified women is a significant exception, in that they are concerned with access to more attractive jobs. Their situation is problematic for different reasons, though we may note that even if the work itself is rewarding the total strain from domestic and job commitments is likely to be greater than for male colleagues. In any case, for most women, as for men, the right to work is more commonly an issue where work is unpleasant.

4 In fact this conventional explanation may not seem quite so obvious when we consider women but, if anything, this adds support to the argument that follows.

5 Part of a project financed by ESRC and carried out with Ken Prandy and Sandy Stewart.

6 This does not imply centrality in preferences. The common confusion on this point reflects the general ideology: the structure of employment is taken for granted so that 'centrality' is just a matter of individual preferences. However, if work is not liked it does not follow that it is unimportant.

7 Details of the sample and of findings relevant to the following discussion may be found in Blackburn and Mann (1979).

8 The term is strictly relative, referring to the nature of the responses, and is not meant to imply a general feeling.

9 The measure of association used throughout is gamma, and unless otherwise stated all relations are significant at the level $p < 0.05$ (and in most cases $p < 0.001$). There is no entirely satisfactory measure of association which is comparable between tables. However gamma has the advantage of not being affected by marginal distributions, so that it can always occupy the range 0 to 1, which is appropriate here. The disadvantage is that it is affected by tables size. Therefore, when it seemed appropriate, variables have been dichotomized to increase comparability, but too much attention should not be paid to the actual magnitude of the gammas. It is the general patterns that matter.

10 Occupations were systematically observed and scored on a range of features, most of which were then grouped by factor analysis.

11 Rioting is one possible form, though this has to draw in people who at other times would be unlikely to consider action.

Further reading

R. M. Blackburn and M. Mann, *The Working Class in the Labour Market*, Macmillan, 1979

T. Nichols, and H. Beynon, *Living with Capitalism*, Routledge and Kegan Paul, 1977

K. L. Schlozman and S. Verba, *Injury to Insult*, Cambridge, Mass.: Harvard University Press, 1979

10 Tackling subordination during economic decline: a pattern of business proprietorship among women

Richard Scase and Robert Goffee

The major focus of attention in studies of the British class structure has been the working class. If, in the 1960s, social research tended to concentrate upon the effects of 'affluence' for the attitudes and life-styles of industrial manual workers, in the late 1970s and 1980s, studies have been more concerned with the consequences of economic recession. As other chapters in this volume illustrate, a major emphasis of many studies has been the experience of redundancy among different sectors of the working class, and the extent to which contracted work opportunities are affecting attitudes and behaviour. But one of the implications of this research orientation has been that the effects of economic recession upon *middle-class* life-styles have been neglected. There have been few studies of how the lack of corporate growth, the impact of technological change and the restructuring of large-scale organizations are destroying opportunities for managers to enjoy reasonably stable and predictable career paths (Handy, 1984). Equally, there have been hardly any investigations of the manner in which the stagnating economic conditions of the 1980s are affecting the *petit bourgeoisie*; that is, of those who use small-scale assets for trading purposes.[1] Studies have shown that small-scale business proprietorship is often seen as a reward by employees who, with their savings and limited borrowings, try to 'buy' themselves independence from the employment relationship. It is, according to many observers, a 'dream' for many members of the working class (Bechhofer and Elliott, 1968; Chinoy, 1955; Mackenzie, 1973; Scase and Goffee, 1980). But what is the significance of *petit bourgeois* ownership under conditions of economic recession? Does it still offer this traditional appeal or has the meaning and significance of small-scale business proprietorship changed? Could it be that in the absence of suitable job opportunities, increasing numbers of people are being forced to adopt strategies of 'self-help' and to start their own businesses, particularly those for whom there is an absence of other feasible paths of action?[2]

It is within this context that small-scale business ownership among women is of significance. But, so far, it has hardly been studied. Although the position of women in the economy has been the subject of much theoretical discussion, their *actual* or *empirical* working experiences have not been much investigated (Evans, ed., 1982; Oakley, 1982). Further, a research emphasis upon women as working-class *employees* (Herzog, 1980; Pollert, 1981,

248

Wajcman, 1983) has led to a neglect of those who are *employers* and who, as proprietors of small-scale enterprises, may be regarded as members of the *petit bourgeoisie*. But what is the role of small business proprietorship among women and how may its significance and meaning be understood within the economic recession of the 1980s? Does business proprietorship enable women, like men, to obtain a degree of personal autonomy (Scase and Goffee, 1980) or are there other gender-related factors that are also salient? Does it, for instance, enable them to overcome gender-related experiences of subordination which many encounter in their domestic and work spheres? As a corrective to those investigations which have been preoccupied with the attitudes and behaviour of working-class male employees, we wish to discuss these issues in the present chapter.

With high levels of unemployment in many 'female' sectors of the economy (Sinfield, 1981; West, 1982), business start-up is becoming an important means of income for those who would otherwise be economically marginalized. In other words, because of the absence of opportunities for paid full-time employment, many women have no option but to start their own businesses as a source of earnings (Goffee and Scase, 1983). Indeed, even those who are gainfully employed are becoming attracted to entrepreneurship because of their experience of subordination in the 'secondary' sectors of the labour market.[3] As a result of very limited promotion opportunities, low pay and their concentration in low-skilled occupations, a considerable proportion of women have little job satisfaction (Wainwright, 1978; Webb, 1982). Even the small minority of those who are located in the 'primary' labour market, in the more financially and psychologically rewarding managerial and professional occupations, are likely to encounter gender-related prejudices that can heighten their levels of stress and restrict their career prospects (Hennig and Jardim, 1979; Silverstone and Ward, eds. 1980; Cooper and Davidson, 1982). Accordingly, many are attracted to business proprietorship as a means of acquiring earnings *and* for overcoming their various experiences of subordination. It is in these terms that the motives for business start-up among many women have to be understood. What, then, are the characteristics of these enterprises?

A very large proportion start with very low levels of trading, using the proprietor's own skills with the required finance obtained from personal savings and very limited bank overdraft facilities (Scase and Goffee, 1980). Such a pattern of small business start-up has been encouraged by the growth of the 'informal' economy which, during the present economic recession, has promoted a context within which many women and men can, on a very limited scale, 'test' the market for their products and services (Handy, 1984; Pahl, 1984). In Britain, there has been a tendency for the 'informal' and the 'cash' production of goods and services to substitute those produced within the formal, 'market' economy (Gershuny, 1978). Thus, as the level of unemployment among women has increased, many have sought ways of acquiring a means of living through these 'informal' and 'cash' patterns of trading. This, in turn, has provided a springboard for legitimate business

249

start-up and the acquisition of talents necessary for proprietorship. In these ways, then, an increasing number of women have started their own businesses, even though they remain a very small minority of all women. Furthermore, a large number of such self-employed women are only *formally* economically 'independent' since, in a real sense, they are often little more than low-paid and easily expendable 'out' or 'home' workers providing subcontracting services for larger corporations (Cragg and Dawson, 1981; Allen, 1983). Even so, more women are starting their own *independent* enterprises during the 1980s economic recession than in the past.

On the face of it, the overwhelming concentration of women in the secondary sector of the labour market as well as their general position of subordination at work, are not conducive to their acquisition of technical and financial skills which are necessary for starting businesses. It is not surprising, therefore, that although the number of women business owners is increasing, there are still very few of them. In Britain, as in most western economies, it is difficult to determine exact numbers, since there are no comprehensive data; only the United States government has recently attempted to collect quantitative data on women proprietors. There are, however, in Britain, official statistics on women classified as 'employers', 'self-employed' and those 'working on their own account'. Unfortunately, there are major problems in interpreting these figures since it is almost impossible to distinguish between those who may be genuinely regarded as independent business proprietors and those who, classified as 'self-employed', are, in all but the legal sense, the employees and outworkers of others (Leighton, 1983). Bearing this in mind, however, it is possible to obtain a general, albeit rudimentary, pattern. Thus, it would appear that women who are classified as either 'employers' or 'self-employed' constitute no more than 4 per cent of the total female labour force. Even so, their numbers have increased from around 300,000 in the 1950s to over 400,000 in the 1980s (Royal Commission on Income Distribution and Wealth, 1979, Table 2.11; Office of Population and Censuses, 1981). They still, however, only make up 20 per cent of all those people officially classified as 'self-employed' or 'employers' (Eurostat, 1981, Table 18.1, 29). The occupational distribution of these female proprietors reflects the broader gender-based segmentation of the labour market. According to the Royal Commission on Income Distribution and Wealth (1979), over three-quarters of all women employers and self-employed are in the categories of 'sales' (40 per cent), 'services, sports and recreation' (26 per cent), and 'professional and technical' (11 per cent).

Included within these broad categories are women who own businesses providing secretarial services; proprietors of retail outlets (including, for example, fashion shops, hairdressers, beauticians, and dry cleaners): owners of boarding houses, hotels and restaurants and cafés, and women running contract catering and cleaning businesses. The proprietors of enterprises offering technical and professional expertise in areas such as advertising, market research, public relations, accounting, financial and insurance services are also included, as well as the owners of publishing and literary agencies. In absolute numbers, there were, in 1975, 37,000 self-employed women engaged in the provision of 'professional and technical services' in Britain, 30,000 self-employed female hairdressers and 53,000 self-employed women running hotels, snack bars and cafés (Royal Commission on Income Distribution and Wealth, 1979, Table 2.14). Outside these activities – all of which are normally regarded as falling within the service sector – there are very few women proprietors of manufacturing enterprises, although a strong tradition of craft production is maintained by self-employed women who are engaged in, for example, leather work, pottery, engraving, clothes production and interior household furnishing.

In general, the greater majority of female proprietors in Britain are engaged in lesser-skilled activities, while only a minority is to be found in the provision of the more highly-skilled and prestigious professional and technical services. This, of course, is to be expected in view of the broader experiences of women in the labour market, the economy and society in general. There are, however, two further features of female-owned businesses. First, they tend to be of recent origin and of a small scale with few or no employees. Second, they are more likely than men to be founder-owners because of the tendency for businesses to be passed on by fathers to sons rather than to daughters. In the United States, the evidence suggests that the majority of women-owned enterprises are run by founders rather than inheritors. Further, the more recent origin of most women-owned businesses is a function of their concentration within the service sector which has rapidly grown during the post-war era (Goffee and Scase, 1985). With the exception of a very small number of well-known proprietors who run large businesses, almost all women business owners are in charge of very small concerns.

But how can business start-up be seen as a means for women to improve their position in a period of economic recession? It can be argued that individual forms of proprietorship are likely to have little or no impact upon the position of women in general; that only more broadly based collective action can bring about fundamental changes in their structural location and overcome economic marginalization (Oakley, 1982). But although the labour movement in Britain has been, and is, committed to improving the economic position of women, its achievements as yet have been far from impressive (Hunt, 1982). Even though women in Britain who belong to trade unions tend, like men, to have better pay and working conditions than others, 'women's issues' remain marginal within the labour movement and subordinate to the overriding needs of male trade unionists (Mackie and Patullo, 1977). Further, trade unions have been unable to recruit in those occupations where women predominate as employees and where there are no traditions of collective organization. Thus, because a high proportion of them are employed in 'secondary sector' smaller firms and concentrated in lower-paid, part-time occupations, they remain largely outside the influence of organized labour. As far as unemployed women are concerned, they, of course, have no vehicle for trade union representation.

How, then, can women overcome their own personal experiences of

251

economic marginalization within an economy with declining job opportunities? It is here that business start-up is pertinent since this, together with the pursuit of occupational careers, offers two ways whereby they can *individually* confront economic subordination. But, given the concentration of women in lower-paid, secondary sector occupations, the opportunities available for personal success through career mobility within employing organizations are very limited (Heath, 1981). Of course, a small number of women *do* enter managerial and professional jobs and occupy senior executive positions within large-scale corporations (Marshall J., 1984). Such women, however, are more prone to stress than men, a characteristic which, it is claimed, is derived from their lack of role models, feelings of personal isolation, experiences of gender-based discrimination and for married women, tensions associated with combining work and domestic roles (Kanter, 1977). The repercussions, when combined with other management-related sources of tension, can be severe and lead to a high 'incidence' of sleeplessness, smoking and alcohol consumption (Cooper and Davidson, 1982). If, then, the opportunities available for women to pursue managerial and professional careers are very limited, the very few who do succeed seem to experience considerable personal costs – if only because of retaining a 'latent' subordinate identity while occupying corporate positions of power and authority.

The entrepreneurial route, then, offers an alternative for those who wish to escape their conditions of economic marginalization and subordination. Historically, this has been the tradition in capitalist economies, where members of various ethnic and religious minorities have started their own businesses as means for achieving economic well-being (Stanworth and Curran, 1973). Business proprietorship, in other words, offers economic opportunities for those who, because of prejudice, low educational qualifications, language difficulties, and other reasons, are unable to gain entry into various occupations or who are altogether excluded from the labour market. Similarly, women may be regarded as a minority group and, thus, business start-up offers them a means whereby *individually* they can confront their experiences of not only economic but also social and psychological subordination. Indeed, for a number of reasons, female proprietorship possesses a radical potential which is often overlooked. First, setting up a small business does not necessarily constitute a personal commitment to the capitalist principles of accumulation; on the contrary, it can represent an explicit rejection of the exploitative nature of the capitalist work process and labour market (Scase and Goffee, 1981). In this sense, then, business proprietorship may be seen as a radical – albeit short-term and psychological – response to subordination. Second, even though some women business-owners are committed to the ideals of private property ownership and profit, their roles as proprietors and as entrepreneurs can query traditionally defined assumptions about gender-based divisions in society. Thus, women who both own and manage business enterprises – especially those in exclusively male-dominated sectors of the economy – can serve to undermine conventional and stereotypical notions of 'a woman's place'. Female proprietors such as these, therefore, have a *symbolic* importance which can and does explicitly challenge popular conceptions of the legitimate position of women in society. Finally, proprietorship can enable some women to enjoy a degree of material independence from men and, in many circumstances, the opportunity to control the products of their own labour. Thus, as members of a *petit bourgeoisie*, they are able to achieve a degree of personal autonomy and escape from some of the experiences associated with both class-based economic marginalization and gender-related subordination.

Obviously, not *all* women who engage in business start-up wish to challenge conventional assumptions about the position of women in society, nor are they all committed to radical ideals (Goffee and Scase, 1985). But some are, as our interviews, conducted with fifty-four female proprietors between 1981 and 1983, suggest.[4] A selection of business-owners were contacted in a non-random fashion, using personal recommendations, business directories and media publicity. Subsequently, interviews were conducted with those who were running businesses in, for example, various retail sectors, catering, cleaning, accommodation (guest houses), secretarial and clerical services, professional services (advertising, market research, public relations), and craftwork (dressmaking, pottery, engraving). Most of the businesses which they owned were fairly small with less then twenty employees and most had been founded within the previous twenty years. However, a small number running relatively large businesses were also included so that the final selection ranged from home-based, self-employed proprietors to owner–managers of international enterprises. All of them had founded or co-founded their businesses and were directly involved in day-to-day manage-ment. Almost three-quarters were in their thirties or forties. Twenty-eight were married or living with an intimate partner. In all, thirty of the respondents had children.

These interviews – perhaps not surprisingly – show there is no *single* experience of enterpreneurship among women (Goffee and Scase, 1985). While, for some, it is a reaffirmation of the traditional principles governing personal material gain, for others, it provides a vehicle for overcoming personal experiences of economic, social and psychological subordination, and for yet others, it is linked with more radical and collectivist aims.[5] It is these *radical* proprietors that are strikingly different from the others in that business trading is perceived by them as a means for obtaining material support in ways that are compatible with the goals and accepted practices of a more broadly-defined women's movement. Consequently, their businesses are not geared primarily to profit-making but, instead, any economic surplus which is generated is regarded as a resource which can be used to further the interests of other women. The intention, then, is to create a social and economic environment within which alternative life-styles can be pursued while, at the same time, providing services needed by other women. If successful, they 'create space' which is largely free from men's influence both in and beyond the sphere of paid work. Thus, unlike other female proprietors, they do not see themselves – nor wish to be seen by others – as 'entrepreneurs'; indeed, they are determined to reject the motives, life-styles and attitudes typically associated with conventional business-owners (Kets de Vries, 1977). As one of the women we interviewed stated:

Mrs Thatcher's idea of economic independence and small business is based very much on capitalism. On the fact that you tread all over everybody else in the process. I don't think the women's movement can actually set up things like this business without having a strong sense of sisterhood – call it support, call it what you like. The only way we can do something like this is to have that sense of support, to support each other, bringing the whole mass of women up with us. Anything that we do that enables women to become more independent – for example, to be able to go out on their own because we provide a taxi service – that is what *we're* talking about. We're not talking about lining our own pockets which is what Margaret Thatcher wants people to do (Aged 34, single, two partners).

For such women, then, business start-up is neither geared to self-advancement nor to profit-making for its own sake; on the contrary, it is directed to collective feminist goals. Thus, the overriding objective of business-ownership is seen as the provision of various goods and services for women which are not currently provided by, for example, the national state, local authorities and private enterprises. Indeed, the inadequacy of existing services is regarded as a reflection of the patriarchal organization and values of contemporary capitalist society. As two of the women explained, the existence of these unsatisfied needs is seen as an important reason for business start-up.

Essentially, this is a co-operative but the basic fundamental difference is that we're creating this business as a centre whereby we train women. They can get involved, get put on a skills and service register and train up other women. Then we try and find them employment. We hope that women will phone in for services so that we actually keep the whole flow within the women's circle. It's the 'women help women' rationale, as opposed to setting up a business and breaking into an already established male market. . . . It's non-profit-making. . . . It's got mutually subsidising facilities. One area subsidises another, like the crèche which we don't want to change (Aged 35, single, ten partners).

We actually want the shop somewhere which is very accessible to women. We want to provide a range of literature and books that women want to read who aren't necessarily very strong feminists in any particular way. It means that a lot of the books we stock don't really have a political message of any kind but we consider them to be very well written by women who have a connection with the history of women's autonomy and women's expression. We do actually have a very strict stocking policy and we don't stock books which have nothing to do with the women's liberation movement. So, for example, if Mrs Thatcher were to write her diaries we wouldn't stock it. We would get it for any women who wanted it, of course. We didn't stock Mrs Wilson's diaries, and we haven't stocked Shirley Conran's *Superwoman*, to name a few that might ring a bell. And there are other popular sellers that we haven't been very keen on (Aged 29, single, six partners).

Support and service for other women, therefore, takes overriding priority; profits which may accrue are usually 'ploughed back' and are regarded as the means by which further feminist ends can be achieved. Indeed, many see their businesses as experiments in women's self-help which can be imitated by others in an effort to overcome their subordination. In other words, there are few 'trade secrets'; on the contrary, business skills are regarded as resources to be shared so that more women-owned enterprises can be established. As one of them said:

We're accountable to the women's movement. You can say that we've given the women's movement, or anybody who wants to try, an absolutely convincing model that it can be done. . . . Publishing, books, writing, ideas, the lot. If you look at the map of England to work out what is happening in relation to women, you need never see a flat plain any more because there's a very strong model of how it can be done, which is incredibly valuable. . . . It's de-ghettoising. Nobody can say that it's a woman's enterprise and therefore it's going to be small (Aged 32, single, eight partners).

If a major objective is to cater for the unmet needs of women, a further goal is to 'carve out' areas of feminist activity which are removed from male influences. Indeed, some proprietors deliberately run their enterprises in a way which minimizes their direct contact with men. This is achieved through explicitly providing goods and services for women only – for example, taxi services, printing facilities, training resources, and so on – and by giving priority in their purchases to various female suppliers. In these cases, women-owned businesses are encouraged and an alternative 'feminist reality' is created within patriarchal capitalism. This, then, provides a context within which it is often considered possible to foster self-confidence among women, to increase feminist activities and advance feminist aspirations more generally. One woman expressed these views as follows:

We don't see ourselves as providing a service for men – we are providing a service for women. This is one of the areas where our own personal politics comes out. We all feel very strongly that we do not want to put our energies into men at all. This comes out strongly in the way that we feel about men in the shop. We don't want them here. . . . We want to save all our energies to help women. . . . All of us have found that in working with men we simply don't have the space to express our feminist politics. . . . We're an all-women collective because we are working primarily for feminism. I've never come across any man who was prepared to do that, or, indeed, could do that. So, it's simply not operative to have men working here. Women have a deeper understanding of emotions and are prepared to put more energy and commitment into understanding each other's emotions. Therefore, we have a very different way of relating to each other personally . . . there's a spirit of generosity and of kindness and a lack of competition which you simply would not get anywhere else – even if it was a left-wing mixed alternative organisation. . . . Certainly, when men are working together, they work on the spirit and basis of competition which is an anathema to what we are doing here. We see ourselves as an expression of the women's liberation movement and competition is one of those things which oppresses women (Aged 29, single, six partners).

However, there are often contentions or tensions in these enterprises. Some women fear that feminist goals may be undermined by becoming too 'profit or money orientated' and they feel uneasy about generating profits through trading with other women and by having other women as employees. Therefore, they often experience a contradiction between the need to trade at a profit – or at least be financially self-sufficient – and their commitment to the egalitarian, non-exploitative goals of sisterhood. How do they cope with this? There seem to be two ways. First, they use any profits for the provision of additional services for women; and second, they take a similar rate of pay as any employees they may have. In these ways, then, the goals of business-ownership and sisterhood are, to some extent, balanced. However, considerable tensions persist, as the following account illustrates:

There's a real kind of ethos about not making money out of the women's movement. Broadly speaking, I agree with that. If you're a political movement, the idea is to aim for radical change and not to make a living out of it. . . . I've never restricted myself entirely to feminist staff . . . we offer our services to other co-ops, voluntary organisations, trade unions. It's still within the broad sphere of what we're concerned with. It's not the terrible compromise. . . . I'm more interested in making the entire radical movement anti-sexist. I don't think I've sold the women's movement out. It's fairly obvious I'm not making a fortune. . . . In fact, I do reject being totally poverty striken. . . . One of the reasons I felt quite funny about setting up business was that I thought quite a few people would be judgemental of me – and quite a few were – I must be one of the few people on the left of the women's movement who has actually run two businesses in her life. But the last thing in the world I see myself as is a businesswoman. . . . The left generally has a very irrational attitude to money (Aged 32, single, two partners).

Furthermore, because of a firm commitment to sisterhood, they often express a strong attachment to the ideals of co-operative work within small, non-hierarchical organizations. Indeed, the development of such groups is often seen as a primary objective (Gould, 1979). High priority, therefore, is given to equally distributing work tasks, rotating jobs and sharing skills in order that the traditional divisions between 'managerial', 'clerical' and 'productive' activities are avoided. The characteristic emphasis upon flexible working relationships, personal expression and continual consultation about business operations and objectives is extensively illustrated in the following remarks:

A basic thing when people come here is that they can do the job. . . . [But] another criterion is that people should get on with the group. We have a three-month trial period for people coming in. They have to be compatible as we are actually very close as people. . . . We have a meeting every day. We have lunch around that table every day so that in a certain sense one can bring oneself to work as opposed to bringing a façade to work. So you need to know that the people working together have certain levels of compatibility. I'm afraid I can't define them, they're feelings. . . . [In other businesses] there'll be secretaries and bookkeepers and various servicing people – servicing the business. We don't have any of that superstructure. We don't have levels here at all – other than levels of expertise and length of time in the business – which are kind of natural. We don't have juniors. . . . We usually get a majority decision. . . . Usually it's resolved through discussion – we rarely go to a vote. . . . We are individuals with needs and difficulties and problems. We have a very sympathetic attitude to mothers. We have a concept that we do things for mothers – it depends on the people here – what their needs are. As the need comes up, people will speak about it and then something will be decided. There's no fixed rule (Aged 38, single, nine employees).

This commitment to sisterhood, then, provides a set of principles for determining the organization of work and, often, the form of business-ownership. But it is also the basis for two major dilemmas. First, the emphasis upon co-operation can limit business growth. This is because skills can be more easily shared within small tightly-knit working groups than within larger enterprises where impersonality can undermine the ideals of sisterhood. Second, the need for continual consultation and personal expression can conflict with the necessity, within the context of a capitalist market economy, to make swift decisions on the basis of specialized expertise (Wajcman, 1983). These tensions between the administration of growing businesses and the ideals of feminism are well illustrated in the comments of two women:

We actually want to break into the commercial markets. It's very important for our credibility that we don't have that begging-bowl mentality. We want to be hard-headed businesswomen without the profiteering motive at the expense of other people's work. . . . Although we're committed to collectivism, actually to be collective in every minor detail is an impossible way to run a business. So, collectivism, in its purest form, has to go to the wall. So, there is an element of cynicism that could swell up. I don't see that as a problem as long as we make sure that people's positions aren't abused by retaining the trust and the sisterhood. Also, that we never exploit labour power and that we have specific areas of responsibility which we trust each other to actually fulfil. The hard-headedness and ruthlessness comes in if women don't live up to what's expected of them. Because it's not just one woman they're pulling down, it's the whole gender. . . . We should need to eject people who didn't come up to scratch and not have nervous breakdowns about it. I just hope that that's not going to be a problem (Aged 35, single, ten partners).

The decisions are so interrelated. If the magazine became much bigger, for example, it raises the question of how many people in a collective really can work effectively together. We would have to discover for ourselves what the optimum was. . . . One of the problems here is that the work is so monumental and neverending that maybe there is one area we neglect [already] . . . I feel we don't talk enough about our inner feelings in a collective situation (Aged 39, single, fifteen employees).

In their attempts to avoid the more impersonal and economically calculative features of modern work organizations, these proprietors often give priority to the cultivation of close personal relationships. There is a strong expectation that participants will totally commit themselves to the collective enterprise which thus encompasses all facets of their personal life-styles. Their businesses, then, are not simply alternative economic organizations, but also vehicles for the expression of feelings and emotions normally found within family and other intimate relationships. This fusion of work and non-work life is often expressed in a physical dimension; within their businesses, for example, there can be discussion areas, crèche facilities, rest rooms, recreation spaces and other amenities normally associated with the

257

conventional household. Such enterprises are, then, a 'way of life'. As two of them explained:

Jill and Ann have a common interest in the Women Against Nuclear Power Group. Ann and I know each other well personally and Elaine and Jill knew each other very well. Susan and Lynn have a friendship of some years' standing. . . . We don't go out and do things together because, in fact, we see so much of each other here. . . . We have had a situation where two women in the collective were lovers for some time and that seemed quite all right (Aged 29, single, six partners).

Actually, I must admit, that through the business I've made a lot of new friends because of the women I've helped, and women that have come to work in the office. A hell of a lot of really nice people. . . . In terms of women working for themselves generally, I think the amount of support and good feeling that is created is incredible. It gives women much more strength because it gives them the feeling of being in control of their own situation and that is absolutely vital (Aged 34, single, two partners).

Despite their efforts, however, many of these owners we interviewed feel strongly that the economic and social circumstances of women in general in the 1980s are deteriorating. Recession and government policies are said to be increasing unemployment, reducing career prospects and forcing women back into the domestic sphere to perform their traditional roles. If there have been any improvements in the position of women during the post-war era, these are now seen to be seriously threatened. Two expressed these pessimistic views in the following ways:

Until the whole system changes, women are going to be in the same position or a worsening situation. Women are in a worsening position now, there is no doubt about that whatsoever. When there's unemployment, women are the first to be unemployed, and women's wages go down. Nursery schools are closing, as are crèches . . . the whole position of women is getting worse. . . . As long as this system lasts, it will continue to get worse. I don't think this is a bend in the recession – I think this recession is the end of the system, or the beginning of the end . . . I see structural change as inevitable (Aged 48, separated, nine employees).

At the moment, the gains that women have made are either at a slight standstill or even moving backwards. It's not just Thatcher's government. It's a time of economic recession and it's also a time of ideological reaction. . . . It's just a question of one step forward and two steps back. I would see feminism as getting stronger and stronger but not necessarily the women's movement (Aged 39, single, fifteen employees).

What should be done? For most, the major task for the women's movement is to restructure society since only in this way can gender relations be fundamentally altered. Socialism – with the production of goods and services for need rather than profit – is seen by most to offer the long-term solution.[6] Present-day capitalism, by contrast, with its inherent dependence upon exploitation and competition, is regarded as incapable of bringing about the real liberation of women. Within the short term, therefore, many argue the need for 'positive action' so that, for example, women who want to start their own businesses should be given special state-funded assistance. As one of them stated:

It will be really good to have women business owners helped specifically. Given that there's money around, precious little of it gets into the hands of women – that's my feeling. There's also very specific pressures on women's businesses. There are a lot of people who would like women's businesses not to succeed because we are challenging the status quo, which is that everything should be run by men. . . . If we make a small mistake, very much is made of it, whereas if the mistake is by Joe Schmoe Ltd, then nobody would even notice it. We have to be *extremely* successful to be as successful (Aged 34, single, five employees).

Clearly, then, the views expressed by these business-owners suggest little commitment to profit-making, business growth, and the pursuit of personal careers for their own sake. Instead, the major motive for these enterprises is the provision of different need-related services as defined by the priorities of a wider women's movement. In other words, they regard their business activities as part and parcel of a collective struggle which offers services to other women in ways that are compatible with feminist ideology. They recognize the need for an ultimate and fundamental restructuring of society but, in the meantime, their businesses provide them with an escape from economic marginalization and give them the material support for the creation of life-styles and personal identities removed from the constraints of domestic subordination and patriarchal relationships. If they are successful as proprietors – that is, according to conventional measures of profitability – they obtain the material bases for the collective pursuit of feminist ideals. In this respect, their business ventures offer a means for heightening the general level of feminist consciousness and for pursuing the economic and social rights of women in general. Thus, there can be little doubt that this form of business proprietorship enables women to challenge explicitly and forcefully conventional gender relationships while at the same to obtain a means of material support. Their often co-owned and collectively organized enterprises provide spheres of autonomy which free them from male domination. However, even the ability of women to confront their economic marginalization and their personal experiences of subordination through creating business ventures can be severely constrained by the need to trade in a capitalist-organized economy. For example, they often have to make swift business decisions which can undermine their commitment to collective consultation. Further, any growth of their ventures can lead to hierarchy and impersonality which may challenge cherished ideals of egalitarianism and personal self-expression. Finally, trading success and the accumulation of profits can lead to dilemmas over the distribution of rewards and conflicts about the allocation of resources for new projects. These proprietors, therefore, whether or not they are co-owners, are constantly confronted with dilemmas stemming from ideals of sisterhood and the need to generate self-financing profits.

Despite these tensions, the political potential of their ventures should not be underestimated (Gorz, 1982). The failure of the trade union movement in Britain to represent women's interests at work and its inability to combat class and gender-based subordination in conditions of economic recession, is likely to encourage the formation of small-scale, self-help groups and individuals geared to trading for the purposes of material support.[7] Further, the persistent strength of the women's movement and the numerical growth of highly educated and technically-qualified women should provide the ideological and material conditions for the future expansion of these radical forms of business-ownership. Sometimes these will take the legal form of sole proprietorships, while, often, they will be organized and financed on the basis of co-owned co-operatives and partnerships. The latter encourage the pooling of resources and enable organizational forms to emerge that are more readily compatible with the collective ideals of sisterhood (Wajcman, 1983).

Clearly, the development of businesses by women in the 1980s and 1990s will be shaped by a variety of economic, social and political forces. But it does seem certain that the decline in employment opportunities in large-scale organizations and the general growth of unemployment will lead to more business start-ups among both men and women (Handy, 1984). Both ends of the political spectrum in Britain now support this trend, although for totally contrasting ideological reasons. Thus, despite the persistence of large numbers of 'conventional' businesswomen who are committed to the ideals of personal gain, proprietorship is likely to expand among those who are more radical in their objectives. In our view, both are concerned to overcome their experiences of subordination and economic marginalization. But the means differ; whereas the former emphasize individual self-help, the latter stress the need for collective and solidaristic action. So, too, do they differ in their ends; while the former ultimately sustain the institutions of patriarchal capitalism, radical proprietors seek to replace these with an alternative socio-political order within which all women will be able to enjoy a greater degree of economic, social and psychological self-determination. Until then, the appeal of business proprietorship is likely to persist among many women if only because it offers, to a variable and limited extent, a measure of economic support and a degree of personal autonomy which many would otherwise be unable to enjoy. Accordingly, the numbers of such ventures are likely to increase as more women experience the day-to-day effects of unemployment and economic marginalization and, in the absence of alternative strategies, are *forced* to start their own businesses.

Notes and references

1 This, of course, is an extremely inadequate and crude definition of the *petit bourgeoisie*. Its precise nature has been the subject of considerable debate among writers. For a reasonably comprehensive review of definitions, stemming from various theoretical perspectives, see Scase and Goffee (1982).

2 Certainly, the Conservative government has introduced a number of policies to encourage the unemployed to start their own businesses. This, of course, is linked to a political philosophy that emphasizes self-reliance

and 'liberal-market' solutions to the economic recession. For a discussion of the ideological influences of the 'new right', see Elliott *et al.* in this volume.

3 Many writers draw a distinction between 'primary' and 'secondary' sectors within a 'dual' labour market (Doeringer and Piore, 1971; Gordon, 1972). According to Barron and Norris (1976), for example, primary sector jobs offer higher wages, personal autonomy and responsibility, good employment conditions, security and prospects of career advancement while secondary sector occupations are characterized by low pay, poor working conditions, limited career prospects, little autonomy and responsibility, and virtually no job security.

4 The interviews were conducted by Maxine Pollock, Mina Bowater and ourselves. The research was funded by the Economic and Social Research Council and by a small grant from the Nuffield Foundation. The interviews were tape-recorded and later transcribed. The quotations that are cited in this chapter are taken from these.

5 Indeed, on the basis of our interviews, we suggest that the experience of business proprietorship among women is, among other things, highly influenced by two sets of factors. First, their attachment to entrepreneurial ideals such as profit-making and 'self-help' and, second, the extent to which they accept conventionally-defined male–female relationships. This leads to the following classification, consisting of business proprietors who may be described as *conventional*, *innovative*, *domestic* and *radical*.

		Attachment to Conventional Gender Roles	
		High	Low
Attachment to Entrepreneurial Ideals	High	Conventional (1)	Innovative (2)
	Low	Domestic (3)	Radical (4)

Radical proprietors have a low attachment to both entrepreneurial ideals and to conventional gender roles. For a detailed discussion of this classification, see Goffee and Scase (1985).

6 The form of socialism envisaged by the women we interviewed fundamentally transforms patriarchal capitalism; in this sense, it is normally regarded as distinct from the varieties of socialism currently found in East European countries.

7 This point is strongly emphasized by some radical writers who argue that a path ahead for socialism in western Europe is through the development of co-owned self-help groups. This is because the large-scale automation of productive processes and the concomitant decline in paid employment is reducing the possibilities for broadly-based collective action of the traditional trade union kind. See, for example, Gorz (1982).

Further reading

R. Goffee and R. Scase, *Women in Charge*, London: Allen and Unwin, 1985

A. Oakley, *Subject Women*, London: Fontana, 1982

R. Scase and R. Goffee, *The Real World of the Small Business Owner*, London: Croom Helm, 1980

R. Scase and R. Goffee, *The Entrepreneurial Middle Class*, London: Croom Helm, 1982

J. Wajcman, *Women in Control*, Milton Keynes: Open University Books, 1983

J. West, (ed.), *Work, Women and the Labour Market*, London: Routledge and Kegan Paul, 1982

11 Anxieties and ambitions: the *petit bourgeoisie* and the New Right in Britain

Brian Elliott, David McCrone and Frank Bechhofer

Introduction

1988 sees the thirteenth anniversary of Margaret Thatcher's election to the leadership of the Tory Party, the thirteenth anniversary of that moment when the diverse forces of the New Right captured the vehicle that alone could give them the chance of real political power. They had ousted the so-called Right Progressives and in Margaret Thatcher and Sir Keith Joseph found champions of those causes, popularizers of those ideologies and advocates of those policies that promised a real break with the post-war consensus. Historically, the Thatcher years are important. The years of campaigning and of government have enabled the New Right to change the conditions of life for millions of people in the UK, and not just their material conditions (important though these are, of course, as the unemployed or the poor or the black will tell you) but also the political and moral precepts by which people live.

The political success of the New Right owes much to the remarkable growth or revitalization of associations, policy and research institutes and leagues that occurred in the mid to late 1970s. We can depict the Thatcher years as a period when business – large and small – sought new and more direct modes of representation through which to exert influence, to press the diverse interests of capital and to penetrate the institutions of the state and civil society. The role of large enterprises, of corporate capital was, of course, extremely important in this process. In response to the economic and political crises of the late 1970s, corporate business in Britain began to play a much more open, much more obvious political part. And this was unusual, for as Colin Leys (1985) observes, British capital has had weak political and bureaucratic representation for over one hundred and fifty years.

By the late 1970s and early 1980s new leaders emerged in the Institute of Directors and in the Confederation of British Industry – leaders like Walter Goldsmith and John Methven – whose bold, public pronouncements aligned big business more and more closely with the monetarist policy in the Thatcherite project. Funds from big business flowed into the coffers of Aims for Industry, the Economic League, the Institute of Economic Affairs and the Centre for Policy Studies, as Michael Useem's study shows (1983; 1984). These helped swell criticism of the Wilson–Callaghan governments, and to broadcast ideas and policies sharply different from the Keynesian and corporatist strategies used by Labour and Conservative administrations for much of the post-war period.

There was, though, another kind of mobilization taking place at the same time. Small business in Britain had traditionally shown even less capacity for collective action than its corporate counterpart and the self-employed had never constituted any kind of political force. Quite suddenly that changed. In the space of a few months in 1974 and 1975 a whole series of new organizations appeared and began to conduct highly publicized campaigns. Our long-standing interest in the *petit bourgeoisie* gave us a particular curiosity about these associations and we began to monitor their development. We found ourselves exploring their complex connections with big business, with the Tory Party, with the major right-wing league (the National Association for Freedom) and other elements of the New Right. From interviews with the office-holders in the associations, from material in the house journals and from a number of other sources including our own surveys of *petit bourgeois* groups we began to piece together an understanding of the anxieties and ambitions that fuelled these agitations. We gained too some appreciation of the ways in which these associations and the interests and values they articulated contributed to the rise and the continued political success of the New Right (see Elliott *et al.*, 1982).

Mobilization

When we began our study of what we called 'bourgeois movements' in 1976 we did not, of course, foresee the remarkable changes that were about to occur in British politics. What we did observe was an unprecedented growth of organizations among a sector of the population long held to be 'unorganizable' – the small business and self-employed elements. The failure of the traditional entrepreneurial and self-employed members of the so-called middle class in Britain to establish any durable, broadly-based associations or to formulate any coherent political ideology was generally attributed to the fragmentary character of this stratum. Its members had diverse material interests, inchoate political views and frequently worked in situations that isolated them one from another and put them in competition with each other. Moreover, they were imbued (and they often told us this themselves) with 'individualism', with an independent spirit that made them deeply suspicious of any attempts to forge collective organizations. The historical evidence and the data from relatively recent surveys seemed to lend credence to this view (see Bechhofer and Elliott, 1976).

But in 1974–5 that changed. The context was one of crisis: of economic crisis in the form of the dramatic oil-price rise, of three-day weeks, power cuts and industrial disruption; of political crisis as the Heath government fell (toppled, according to the right-wing press, by the miners) and the Labour Party was returned with a precarious majority. It was a context too in which attempts at broader mobilizations of 'the middle class' were being made. The Middle Class Association was set up by MP John Gorst; groups of armed, apprehensive patriots under the command of ex-military men were being drilled into defensive platoons against an anticipated wave of strikes; and, heralded by the shooting of its chief architect, Ross McWhirter, the National Association for Freedom was launched to defend liberty and property.

This was the heady atmosphere in which the new associations for small business-owners and the self-employed started life. Over a period of a few months a series of new organizations appeared – the National Federation of the Self-Employed (NFSE), the Association of Self-Employed People (ASP), the National Association of the Self-Employed (NASE) and the Independent Business Persons Association (IBPA). The largest of these, NFSE, recruited 40,000 members in the first ten months and from the shopkeepers, small builders, garage proprietors, hoteliers, owners of small manufacturing establishments and self-employed professionals who joined, it gathered subscriptions amounting to something like half a million pounds (Elliott *et al*. 1982; McHugh, 1979). Somewhat later the Forum of Private Business (FPB) was formed and together with older organizations like the Association of Independent Business (AIB) and the Union of Independent Companies (UIC) these gave voice to the grievances of non-corporate business in Britain. The emergence of the new associations was triggered by government proposals to raise the National Insurance levy on small business people, but underlying the outburst of indignation lay more profound disquiets.

The mobilization of these elements of the *petit bourgeoisie* reflected above all their dissatisfaction with existing means of representation. At a point where many of the smaller entrepreneurs and self-employed people felt that their livelihoods and way of life were seriously threatened by the economic crisis, the traditional bodies – Chambers of Commerce, the Small Firms Committee of the CBI and the Tory Party itself – seemed to them to be impotent or neglectful of their interests. The corporatist styles of government practised by Wilson and after 1972 by Heath, appeared to have given big business an organized privileged access to the processes of decision-making while *their* concerns, their plight, their contribution to the economy and society went unrecognized. Through their rhetoric and through the action that they organized, the leaders of the new associations gave expression to the mood of bitterness and resentment among the small business stratum. Thus, we found NFSE, ASP and other associations engaging in their early years in various forms of protest action – in a demonstration outside the Customs and Excise Office (responsible for collecting the hated Value Added Tax), in a campaign to withhold taxes and in a variety of legal battles against 'unfair' impositions. We observed too how they lobbied and courted politicians of all parties, seeking support for legislative changes that would ease their burdens and even encourage new recruits to independent business and self-employment. Through the late 1970s and into the new decade their efforts in this respect became more sophisticated as they learned the craft of influencing elected representatives and bureaucrats. They began to employ researchers and parliamentary liaison officers, forged contacts with and drew upon the expertise of policy institutes like the IEA to produce their own reports and position papers.

This unaccustomed mobilization of the *petit bourgeoisie* drew them, inevitably, into the major political struggles of the late 1970s, into tense relationships with neo-conservative organizations, with the Tory Party itself and with the diverse strands of ideology articulated by the New Right. Their success in gathering members, their claim to speak on behalf of thousands, encouraged the Tory Party under Margaret Thatcher to set up its own organization – the Small Business Bureau – to give voice to their discontent and (in a scarcely veiled way) to incorporate them and harness their energies in the 1979 bid for power. The National Association for Freedom cast itself as the champion of small business, assisting individual employees in efforts to break strikes – most notably in the Grunwick dispute – campaigning against the closed-shop and the Employment Protection Act and all those measures of the Wilson–Callaghan governments which allowed organized labour to usurp (as they saw it) the legitimate power of property-owners over their capital and their workers. NAFF also sought to provide a measure of ideological tutorship, attaching the interests of small business to the mix of libertarian and neo-liberal economic philosophy which it espoused. It attempted too the actual incorporation of small business and self-employed associations. After some flirtation with the idea, NFSE resisted this, but the Association of Self-Employed People actually did bring its members directly under NAFF's umbrella.

To the Tory leadership in the late 1970s, struggling for power and trying to establish a new 'radical' conservatism, the recently organized small business stratum represented an important resource. They saw it as a constituency – neglected under Heath – which had to be courted and attached once more to its 'natural' political vehicle. They saw it as the chief repository of those bourgeois values that they were so anxious to restore, its members as the sturdy heroes of the 'market economy' who would fight the New Corruption of 'social-democratic welfarism–corporatism' as their forebears had fought the Old Corruption of patronage, protection and monopoly more than one hundred and fifty years earlier (Leys, 1985). In reality, the ideological commitments of the *petit bourgeoisie* and of the leaders of the new associations were more diverse. In the mid 1970s there were still a good many who believed not in overthrowing but in extending corporatist principles. Conferences were held to debate the possibility of establishing small business and the self-employed as a third force to sit alongside big business and organized labour as they determined with government the management of the economy. At the other extreme the 'market anarchism' and robust libertarian views of the leader of ASP went far beyond the ambitions of Thatcherite Tories for the 'social market economy'. In between, though, there were many who found in the strands of economic liberalism and social conservatism presented by the ideologies of the New Right (see Levitas, 1986), values and beliefs that were close to their own, and expressions of class interest that addressed precisely those discontents that had stirred them to action.

The new bourgeois movements were not, then, simply incorporated by The Freedom Association (as NAFF became), the major political league or by the

Conservative Party, nor did they faithfully echo the views of those who led the associations of corporate business. But they did contribute to the swell of New Right criticism and provided important vehicles for the dissemination of various elements of New Right ideology.

The *petit bourgeoisie* in a changing class structure

Beneath much of the disquiet expressed by the small business groups was (and is) an appreciation of major, long run changes in class structure. The crises of the mid 1970s served to sharpen awareness of the declining size and importance – economically, socially and politically – of the small business and self-employed groups. Interviews with officers of the various associations and with hundreds of small proprietors in earlier projects gave ample evidence of the fact that *petit bourgeois* individuals and families felt that their place in society, their position of some substance, prestige and authority, was no longer secure (see Elliott and McCrone, 1982). Sometimes this was linked to perceptions of national decline – and in the conditions of the mid 1970s awareness of this was common; but what gave the comments their edge of bitterness and anger was the sense that the traditional entrepreneurial 'middle class' had fared badly relative to other classes. Moreover, though broad national or even international economic processes might have much to do with this, governments had a good deal to answer for. They had, throughout the post-war years, failed to defend the small entrepreneurs and the self-employed, failed to appreciate the importance of this bedrock stratum in a capitalist economy and through this neglect accelerated our national decline. Much of the propagandizing and political journalism in the 1970s sought to establish this political responsibility (for example, see Hutber, 1976).

The smaller elements of the bourgeoisie argued that their position had been undermined by the general policies and specific impositions of successive governments. They had been overtaxed and hedged about with excessive regulation. They had suffered, too, at the hands of big business which had frequently squeezed them out of markets. But again governments were implicated for, particularly in their corporatist phases, they had positively encouraged mergers, take-overs and policies that drove modest enterprises to the wall. At the same time increasing levels of state interventions, locally as well as nationally, had the effect of increasing the numbers and the power of diverse public servants. To many small business people it seemed as though the state was deliberately fostering the growth of a bureaucratic 'new' middle class. Worst of all, the Labour government in the 1974–9 period appeared to many small capitalists and to self-employed persons to be in thrall to the unions – extending the closed shop, passing the Employment Protection Act, restricting entry to the ranks of the self-employed (particularly in the construction industry), toying with the possibility of worker directors and legislating to improve opportunities and wages for women. This was a form of 'class rule', of class politics, and as such it could be contested only by the politicization and mobilization of those class elements that felt their interests to be threatened. That was the kind of analysis that underlay the *petit bourgeois* agitations of the mid 1970s.

The common-sense apprehensiveness of change was, of course, not without foundation. While corporate capitalism expanded and the ranks of the bureaucratized intelligentsia grew, Britain's class of traditional, small and medium sized employers shrivelled. The statistics are plain. By the beginning of the 1970s the proportion of employers and proprietors in the occupied population amounted to a mere 2.6 per cent, little more than half its 1951 figure. The Bolton Report (1971) pointed out that compared with other industrial countries, we had by far the lowest proportion of manufacturing workers employed in small firms, and recent Eurostats provide corroborative evidence of the relative weakness of the 'employers, self-employed and family workers' in the UK economy at that point (Eurostat, 1984 and Bechhofer and Elliott, 1985).

As the old, entrepreneurial 'middle class' declined, so the new, bureaucratized, professionalized middle class grew. Between 1951 and 1971 there was an increase of more than 200 per cent in the number of 'higher professionals' and increases only slightly less dramatic among 'lower professionals and technicians' and 'managers and administrators' (see Bechhofer *et al.*, 1978). Degrees, certificates and technical qualifications rather than capital were the passports of the rising class. Of course, its expansion had been evident for many years but there is no doubt that the decade from the mid 1960s to the mid 1970s saw particularly rapid development as education, health and local government services were greatly extended. By the mid 1970s, it seemed to many in the small business class that there was a stark contrast between their fortunes and those of this new middle class. Those with a little capital staked in their own businesses feared loss of income, loss of control, ultimately loss of their livelihoods, as inflation soared. The professional and technical employees appeared to the old entrepreneurial middle class to have built for themselves positions of entrenched privilege – regular salaries, ladders of promotion, even inflation-indexed pensions in some cases. While small business owners feared that capital transfer legislation would prevent them from handing on their businesses to their sons and daughters, members of the 'new' class seemed to be using their comfortable positions as bases from which to launch their offspring on successful career trajectories. The Oxford study of social mobility showed that indeed, the 'service class' as the authors termed it was one from which rates of *downward* mobility had decreased (Goldthorpe *et al.*, 1980). The trend in the post-war years was for the service class both to grow and to become more stable. When Sir Keith Joseph talked about this class as a new 'establishment' dominating the principal institutions of British society – civil service, local government, schools and colleges and the media – many of the *petit bourgeoisie* shared his view. In the small business associations no less than in The Freedom Association antipathy towards the bureaucratized middle class, to what was sometimes termed an 'intelligentsia', was profound.

Reducing the size and the power of this class was part of the New Right agenda which many entrepreneurs heartily endorsed.

But the new middle class was not the only object of bourgeois hostility. The election, in 1974, of a Labour government with a very slim majority, raised fears about the 'old enemy' – organized labour. In the mid 1970s, though, this was not a working class of traditional, manual workers. Rather it was a more diverse work-force which included many white-collar employees, but one which was becoming more comprehensively unionized. Through the late 1960s and the 1970s trade union recruitment flourished and many thousands of clerical and even administrative employees were, through their unions, drawn close to the TUC and to the Labour Party (see Stewart *et al.*, 1983). What triggered the bitter attacks by the business associations, the research institutes and the New Right ideologues was the prospect of a Labour government being unduly (illegitimately, so it seemed to them) influenced by the unions. And it was not just influence over central government that was pointed to. For many of the smaller businessmen, local politics was an important arena of struggle, not least because the use of direct labour – invariably *unionized* direct labour – reduced the contracts available to them. Moreover, along with increasing unionization in the 1970s went a more radical, more ideological socialism. There emerged in the Parliamentary Labour Party and in the constituency associations and local government administrations a new generation of labour activists, many of them arguing for a democratic socialism that owed a little more to Marx and rather less to the Fabians (see Gyford, 1983 and 1984). In these circumstances it was easy for the representatives of the New Right to condemn Labour for its 'Marxism'. Though the business associations were generally careful not to align themselves too closely with the fierce anti-unionism or the passionate anti-communism to be found on the pages of *The Free Nation* (The Freedom Association journal) there is no doubt that many of their officers and members sympathized with 'radical conservatives' who attacked organized labour in these terms.

Our interviews suggest though some even deeper and more diffuse sources of hostility to the working class among the *petit bourgeoisie*. What rankled most was the change in the actual *relations* of class that had occurred during the period of the long boom and the emergence of welfare capitalism. By the mid 1970s it was plain that small employers could no longer count on the acquiescence of their workers in the day-to-day routines involving long-established patterns of superiority and inferiority, or in the assumptions about property's rights and privileges. Workers no longer showed 'proper' respect, no longer deferred in any general way to *petit bourgeois* claims to status. Whatever else it had done, the post-war boom had equipped ordinary, propertyless men and women with a new conception of their rights, with a taste for the products of consumer capitalism and from time to time, with an awareness of their collective power.

Small wonder then that the old entrepreneurial middle class saw itself by the mid to late 1970s as embattled, fighting both organized labour and the bureaucratized middle class. For them there were two fronts in the class war.

Material interests

Anger, resentment and fear – the central motifs in the *petit bourgeois* agitation of the mid 1970s – were occasioned not just by broad shifts registered in changes in the occupational structure. They were called out by threats to real material interests, for in those years inflation made even substantial enterprise vulnerable. In 1974 the rate was 16.0 per cent; in 1975, 24.2 per cent; in 1976, 16.5 per cent; and in 1977, 15.9 per cent. Inflation at these levels could swallow the profits of a business very easily and raised the costs of borrowing to extraordinary heights. It was perceived by businessmen large and small as profoundly damaging. Indeed, those with small amounts of property – retired people with money in the bank, people living on fixed incomes – all had reason to view inflation with grave disquiet.

In these circumstances the analyses offered by writers like Hayek and Friedman had considerable appeal. Andrew Gamble observes that it was Hayek who

knitted together the monetarist explanation of inflation with a much broader sociological and political account of why it was that governments constantly infringed the principles of market order. Between them Friedman and Hayek ensured that the debate over monetarism would not stay at the level of macroeconomic models but would re-ignite the debate on the principles of political economy which had seemingly been settled by the triumph of social democracy and the rise of interventionist governments (1986, p. 38).

In the late 1970s the Institute for Economic Affairs and the Freedom Association strove vigorously to disseminate monetarist ideas and found considerable support from some of the small business associations. The most 'ideological' of these – the Association of Self-Employed People – organized an 'Open Door' TV programme with a video-taped address by Friedman, and among many association leaders we encountered support for Friedmanite policies to restore 'sound money'.

Inflation threatened not only immediate economic interests. Sustained over a few years it tended to affect the actual distribution of earnings. The general relationship had been known for many years: periods of high and rising inflation led to some convergence of income; periods when inflation declined produced a widening of earnings disparities (Noble, 1985). The mid 1970s gave proof of this. The overall pattern of earnings did show some reduction of differentials – managers, for instance, did particularly badly and though hard evidence about the earnings of *petit bourgeois* individuals is hard to tease out of the official statistics, there are good reasons to suppose that many small entrepreneurs fared badly too. To many people – but particularly the owners of modest businesses – there was something deeply offensive about the state of affairs in which debtors benefited at the expense of creditors. New Right commitments to change this and to restore earlier and (in the view of many small business and self-employed people) justifiable inequalities were well-received. Sir Keith Joseph's promise to create a *less* egalitarian society appealed to many in business.

The economic conditions of Britain in the 1970s also had other effects on the owners of productive property. Overall assessments of profit levels are always subject to some doubt but the best estimates suggest that company profits (pre-tax inflation-corrected rates of return on UK industrial and commercial capital) fell from around 8 per cent in the early 1970s to barely 3 per cent by 1980 (Useem, 1983).

The fortunes of capital, large and small, could not be restored unless profit levels were somehow raised. Again, the New Right analysis addressed this issue and promised that a radical programme of tax cuts would be implemented allowing the corporations and the individual 'creators of wealth' to retain more of their earnings. There would also be deliberate promotion of the private sector and a great many unnecessary forms of state regulation would be swept away, liberating the entrepreneurial spirits that alone could reverse our national decline. Such was the rhetoric. And again, this had obvious appeal in the ranks of small business, and their associations gave space in the house journals to the broadcasting of the 'new economic realism' as they perceived it.

As the campaign to promote a new economic philosophy gained momentum in the approach to the 1979 election it became plain that the effort to sweep away restrictions and restore a competitive market economy was intended to produce rather more than economic effects. The Centre for Policy Studies, the research institute set up by Sir Keith Joseph and Margaret Thatcher, expressed this clearly: 'The market economy . . . by dispersing economic power throughout society . . . establishes a countervailing force against the concentration of political power, thereby promoting democracy, personal liberty and wider choice of both goods and jobs. . .' (1979).

To those who ran family businesses or worked on their own account this rhetoric seemed to offer a comprehensive justification for rebuilding an economic order in which they and their activities could flourish.

Cultural concern

The years of the long boom produced changes not only in occupational and class structures, and in relative economic fortunes, they also saw – particularly in the decade of the 1960s – profound changes in values, mores and laws. Many of the social controls that had survived since the Victorian era were relaxed as gambling was licensed, literary and dramatic censorship was largely removed and male homosexuality ceased to be a criminal offence (at least for consenting adults). Abortion became legal and the reform of divorce and matrimonial property laws swept away some of the anachronistic and evidently patriarchal arrangements governing conjugal relationships (compare Marwick, 1982). Informing all these changes was a desire for 'liberation' and

271

the ability to live with fewer of those external constraints that appeared to many people, but especially to the young, to be out of date, shaped by religious precepts they no longer acknowledged, and imposed by state agents and agencies that themselves seemed often dubious about their value.

The 'liberating' motif can be found too in the debates and the legislation relating to a particularly crucial area of institutional reform: to education. Grammar schools, with their traditional emphasis on high scholastic standards for an elite, were attacked because they inhibited the potential of those not allowed to attend them. 'Comprehensive' reorganization was called for in the Labour government's famous Circular 10/65. Education at every level from preschool to university was under scrutiny, and expansion in the levels of provision was accompanied by changes in teaching style and curriculum content. New colleges and universities were set up, and new programmes of technical and social science study appeared alongside the traditional subjects. Reformed and vastly expanded, the education system, it was hoped, would provide positive freedom for individual citizens and the impetus for a radical modernizing of Britain's economy and society.

The 1960s was thus a decade of rapidly rising expectations and, not surprisingly, in insidious and occasionally very public and dramatic ways, this was accompanied by challenges to those in authority whether in the home, church, school or college. A variegated youth culture developed, and provided in music and dress modes a personal expression signalling diverse kinds of 'opposition' (compare Martin, 1981). The events of May 1968 in Paris, however, became the most potent symbol of the efforts to contest established relationships and practices. For many young people they continued to shine as a beacon of hope, of possibility: for many of their elders, for those in authority, they were no less powerful as a symbol of threat.

These changes in the cultural fabric had implications for all major institutions and for many of the ordered and taken-for-granted practices of everyday life. Not only was divorce easier and sex outside marriage more acceptable, but by the early 1970s feminists, along with a number of well-known psychiatrists, were busily attacking 'the middle class myth of love and marriage' and the hurtful, confining and even destructive relationships of the modern nuclear family. For them the changes of the 1960s opened the way for new gender relationships and for alternatives to the bourgeois family (see, for example, Greer, 1970 and Mitchell, 1971).

As the New Right developed, mobilized opinion and gained influence in a Conservative Party in power there emerged alongside the specifically libertarian and neo-liberal strands a distinctive thread of social conservatism. Roger Scruton (1984) and others contributing to the *Salisbury Review*, as well as a number of prominent cabinet members, began to articulate criticism of the 'permissive' reforms of the 1960s and early 1970s. In their view, these cultural developments spelled trouble. The neo-conservatives were quick to connect the rising divorce rate and increasing numbers of single-parent families with the growth of juvenile crime and disorder. The 'breakdown' of the family seemed to be at the root of many problems. Not only was its alleged decline responsible for the loss of informal social control but it no longer provided the source of capital formation through savings nor did it exercise its traditional responsibilities in providing for its members in illness, unemployment and old age. It seemed to the ideologues of the New Right that the family as the central institution for the reproduction of society and of private property needed to be defended.

From our earliest interviews with small business people, conducted in 1969–70, through others in the mid 1970s, to the discussions with leaders of NFSE, ASP and other associations in the early 1980s, we encountered unease among our respondents about many of these cultural changes. A sense of cultural estrangement was evident. And that was scarcely surprising. After all, a good many small enterprises were run as *family* businesses. Not only was the family a source of labour and of capital but very often in the life projects of the *petit bourgeois* the enterprise was seen as something run *for* the family. There were no sharp divisions between 'work' and 'family life'; property and kinship were intimately bound together. Moreover, small business and self-employed people derived opportunities – even a measure of status and power – from local political systems and local institutions such as grammar and selective schools, the very structures that were subject to 'reform'. Reform, often, meant for them displacement (see also Scase and Goffee, 1980 and 1982).

The result was certain sympathy for aspects of the emerging social conservatism and particularly for those arguments that identified the 'new' middle class as the agents of unwelcome change. In their criticisms of a left–liberal intelligentsia, which, it was said, had established their ideas as the dominant ones, Tory politicians, members of the Social Affairs Unit and the editors of *The Free Nation* articulated views with which many of the *petit bourgeoisie* could identify. New Right attacks on the role of bureaucrats and more generally on public employment echoed the sentiments of many who gained their livelihood by 'independent' means. As Andrew Gamble has pointed out, the years of Thatcher government have seen astonishing attacks on public servants. Apart from the police and the armed forces, almost all other public employees and state institutions have been castigated for being 'inefficient, overstaffed and indifferent to enterprise and commercial success' (Gamble, 1985, p. 2). In the lexicon of the New Right, public is sinister: private is right. That strikes a chord with those who see themselves as oppressed by state regulation.

Over the last ten years members of the New Right have argued that they need to learn from the success of the left–liberal elements, from those certificated, qualified members of the new class who had supposedly penetrated all the principal institutions of British society. The task is to 'turn the tide on every front in civil society and moral life as much as in economic habits and expectations' (Hall, 1984). This means re-establishing specifically bourgeois values and morality. Stedman Jones (1983) observed: '. . . Mrs Thatcher's own real preoccupation is, ultimately, not so much economic

273

recovery itself as the restitution of a desired pattern of belief and behaviour, from which, it is assumed, "genuine" economic recovery will in due course, follow'. Those patterns of belief and behaviour are the ones by which the great majority of small entrepreneurs and their families live. Lacking, as most of them do, extensive education, many from this class are alienated from the attitudes and aspirations of the liberal intelligentsia and take comfort from the new conservatism that inveighs against the social changes of earlier decades.

The reconstruction of bourgeois society?

The remarkable mobilization of small and independent business in the mid to late 1970s is best seen as an effort not simply to win a few specific fiscal advantages but as an attempt to persuade governments that what was needed for the economic and moral health of the nation was the re-creation of a class and the re-establishment of the values by which its members lived. Among some of the big business associations, the neo-liberal research institutes, the political leagues and the Thatcherite elements in the Tory Party they found champions, advocates and allies. It was not, of course, the case that the interests of the *petit bourgeoisie* were invariably coincident with those of these groups, but rather that small business had a degree of political and symbolic importance that made it worth their while to support it. In the run up to the 1979 election, promises were made to attend to the grievances of the minor entrepreneurs, to re-create the conditions for their survival and even their growth. After nine years of Conservative rule we can try to see to what extent the pledges have been redeemed.

There is no doubt that, once in power, the Conservative government acted in ways that would affect the class position of small businesses, producing, through no fewer than eighty pieces of legislation, a host of schemes to provide loans, subsidies and advice. It sought to act as midwife to what Norman Macrae (1976), deputy editor of *The Economist*, had termed the new 'entrepreneurial revolution' by encouraging large enterprises, public as well as private, to devolve many of their operations to independent, usually smaller companies, thereby creating new opportunities for non-corporate businesses.

The government acted too, in ways designed to reduce the size and the influence of the 'new' class, most obviously through its efforts to slim down the civil service and other public bodies. Since 1979 the central civil service has declined by 10 per cent, the numbers of school and university teachers have been reduced and local government has shed some 4 per cent of its employees. Those working for public corporations declined by nearly 22 per cent between 1978 and 1984, many, of course, being transferred to the private sector as a consequence of the privatization of British Aerospace, Cable and Wireless, the National Freight Corporation, British Gas, British Telecom and other concerns (see Richardson, 1985).

The power of organized labour, feared by business large and small, and so often the subject of strident complaint in the 1970s, has been directly addressed through trade union legislation, through the careful game plan and the shouldering of massive costs that produced the defeat of the miners' strike, and through the licensing of vengeful industrial relations practices. The efforts of Michael Edwardes at British Leyland, of Ian MacGregor first at British Steel and then at the National Coal Board, and most recently of Rupert Murdock in the newspaper industry, illustrate the determination to subordinate labour. Together state and assertive management have done much to weaken labour's resistance to policies aimed at turning Britain into a 'market' society. In 1979 union membership peaked out at 13.3 million. Since then it has declined steadily, falling by 17 per cent in the Thatcher years (Department of Employment, 1985). Much of the decline reflects the collapse of the manufacturing sectors of the British economy and the inexorable growth of unemployment, but it is encouraged too by constant rhetorical attacks of government and right-wing groups on the labour movement. Labour, it is said, is largely responsible for our economic decline, labour stands now in the way of progress and the restructuring of our economy, labour is untrustworthy, harbouring 'enemies within'. In some circumstances, as at GCHQ, organized labour must be banned.

But the efforts to defend or to ensure the reproduction and growth of the bourgeoisie in general and small business in particular have not been conspicuously successful. The official statistics do show that the decline of the small business sector in Britain has stopped. There has even been some proportional growth. Employers, self-employed and family workers (to take the classification of the Statistical Office of the EEC) have increased from 6.6 per cent of the non-agricultural employed population in 1979 to 8.0 per cent in 1982, and among the industrial work-force the increase is more substantial – from 5.4 per cent to 7.3 per cent over these years (Eurostat, 1984). Data on intergenerational mobility show that there has been an increase in the tendency for those from manual backgrounds to be upwardly mobile into forms of self-employment over the last decade (Goldthorpe and Payne, 1986). People have sought and have been encouraged by governments to create 'own-account' forms of work. But a modest increase in self-employment under the present conditions is hardly to be taken as evidence of a major 'entrepreneurial revolution'. When hundreds of thousands lose their regular jobs every year, when some of them have lump sum redundancy payments, a growth in self-employment is precisely what we would expect. It is as much an indicator of economic decline as of any economic regeneration (see Harris and Lee, Chapter 7).

Nor are the statistics showing a reduction in forms of public service employment without their difficulties. They do not add up to convincing evidence of any substantial overall decline in the size of the public sector (in areas like the health service there has been an expansion in numbers), still less do they show a reduction in the ranks of the bureaucratized intelligentsia so often reviled by the New Right and by small business people. We know of no adequate disaggregated data but we can be confident that most of the actual job losses have occurred in the manual and semi-skilled echelons of the public service structures. The long-run secular trend showing growth in the 'service class' continues.

As for the attack on organized labour – even there we need to qualify the right-wing claims to success. In so far as one of the objectives was to detach unions from the Labour Party, to erode their specifically political influence, we have to notice that all the union ballots on whether or not to maintain the political levy have shown that workers are determined to maintain their link with Labour. Tory legislation aimed at weakening the unions may, in the long term, prove to have encouraged a series of reforms making these collective bodies more democratic and more powerful.

The material interests of business large and small have, since Thatcher came to power, been addressed in a variety of ways. Inflation, which was the pre-eminent concern, has been greatly reduced from its double-digit levels in the 1970s to 5 per cent or less in the mid 1980s. Profit levels have certainly increased for many of Britain's large companies. Whether they have also increased among small and medium sized companies, though, is hard to assess. The assumption, common since the publication of the Bolton (1971) and the Wilson (1980) reports, that profit levels in small firms were, on average, greater than those in large firms is challenged by some recent research in which it is argued that in the late 1970s and early 1980s, they were in fact lower and were declining (see Burns, 1985).

Fiscal reforms undoubtedly contributed to the growth of company profits just as they led to major changes in the distribution of income and wealth. The annual reports of the Inland Revenue provide data on income changes and from these we can see the changes that have taken place. Reports from the Institute of Fiscal Studies show that for top earners like the directors of sizeable companies, the 1979 cuts in higher tax rates provided a substantial boost in real incomes and in the years since then, pay increases and tax allowance changes have produced for them improvements in earnings of around 35 per cent. Senior managers have gained by around 22 per cent under the Tories, middle managers by 10 per cent, but at the bottom of the distribution a council manual worker has actually lost 1 per cent in earnings while a jobless man with a family is now more than 14 per cent worse off since the election of a Conservative government. Britain has indeed become a more unequal society.

The leaders of small business associations have welcomed the control of inflation and the specific measures to assist small enterprises. They take some pride in the fact that their parliamentary officers and researchers have given them credibility in Westminster and Whitehall. They applaud when 97,908 new firms are registered in a single year, as they were in 1984 (Department of Employment, 1985), but they know that these are qualified 'successes'. The principal beneficiaries of the Thatcher years have not really been the independent entrepreneurs. Alongside figures for the creation of new (mostly small) companies we need to put the information that bankruptcies have also been running at an all time high. The flow into and out of small business has greatly increased but the overall size has grown only moderately. In its rhetoric the Thatcher government makes much of its desire to create a more competitive form of capitalism, but in practice it has presided, like its predecessors, over a growth in corporate power. The sales of public assets – Associated British Ports, British Aerospace, British Telecom and large quantities of public land and property – would all, it was said, contribute to the spread of ownership and to an economy rich in opportunities for small businesses. In fact most of the assets found their way into the hands of large institutions and corporations. State monopolies were turned into private monopolies and some of the richest rewards from these 'privatization' processes went to those who organized them. City firms made £128m from the sale of British Telecom alone (Thomas, 1986). Managers and directors of large businesses, brokers and merchant bankers – these are the people who have gained most in the Thatcher years. The small entrepreneurs have done little more than pick up a few crumbs that have fallen from the table.

In its determination to turn the tide on the nation's moral life the New Right has certainly addressed many of the sources of disquiet that we encountered among our respondents. As articulated by Margaret Thatcher and representatives for the right-wing groups the new conservatism was a complex creed in which there was a coupling of '. . . the anti-Labourist, anti-statist, anti-equality, anti-welfare spirit with the revitalising gospel of the free market'. What emerged by the time the Conservatives took office was a new combination of 'national patriotism, religion of the free market, competitive individualism in economic matters, authoritarian state in social and political affairs' (Hall, 1984). It was a social philosophy whose appeal stretched beyond the boundaries of any one class or stratum, but there can be little doubt that many of its elements found particular support among Britain's small business people.

The commitment to reinstate bourgeois values of hard work, thrift, acceptance of authority, personal ambition and an enthusiasm for capitalism – a commitment which flowed naturally from this philosophy – was understandably welcome. To engineer such a shift meant, of course, the manipulation of the chief agencies of socialization: first the family, then the education system. Both of these were perceived by many we spoke to as 'undermined' by the liberal reforms of the 1960s, so attempts to 'restore' them were approved.

Shifting responsibility for the provision of care and financial support away from state agencies and back to the family was consistent with the beliefs, and often with the practices, of the *petit-bourgeoisie*. Tory rhetoric about the need to make the family once more the prime source of authority and control, fiscal reforms that allowed the easier transfer of property within families, thereby providing incentives to accumulate and participate in profit-making activities – these too seemed to address heartfelt concerns. The Conservative ambition to restore the family to something like its nineteenth-century, middle-class form was echoed in the desire of some crusading groups and individuals to restrict abortion, fight pornography, censor sexual material on TV and restore patterns of conjugal, social and sexual relations to forms that were common before the liberalizing moves of the 1960s (see also Shapiro, 1985; David, 1986; and Price, 1985). How far these things enjoyed the backing of small business and self-employed people is unclear but our guess would be that what is sometimes referred to as a new 'puritanism' certainly has some roots in this sector of the population.

Education, long the object of neo-conservative complaint, has emerged in the 1980s as an institution of particular concern to the New Right (see, for example, Cox and Dyson, 1969; Boyson, 1975; Griggs, 1972; and Wright, 1977). Much responsibility for the country's ills has been laid at the teachers' door. A lack of respect for authority, the unpreparedness of youngsters for employment and a devaluing of the entrepreneurial spirit are all deficiencies for which, it is claimed, the schools must take the blame. Colleges and universities too have been roundly condemned for their alleged inefficiency and their supposed indifference to the commercial and practical application of knowledge. These strictures also fit, and to some degree reflect, the prejudices of many who make a living from minor businesses.

The cultural crusade to restore bourgeois values and to supplant those that underlay the 'welfare consensus' of the post-war years has, of course, been a broad one, reaching well beyond the items discussed here. It is a crusade made in the name of 'freedom', but one that has acquired ever greater levels of coercion for its accomplishment. It is proving extremely difficult to create in Britain in the 1980s the kind of moral framework in which competitive capitalism can thrive. And that is hardly surprising, for the bourgeois values, or the Victorian values (as Mrs Thatcher prefers to call them), developed under specific historical conditions which cannot be recaptured. Culture and structure are intimately related. To be sure, a Conservative government can try to dismantle much of the institutional framework of the welfare state as it was constructed in the post-war years (though even that has met substantial resistance) but it cannot reverse the long-run secular trends that have transformed the economic, occupational and class structures throughout the industrial, capitalist world. The moment when, in the early phases of industrialism in Britain, small property-owners had considerable economic and cultural significance is passed. The New Right may have promised those mobilized small business people of the 1970s that their anxieties and ambitions would be addressed, but what they have delivered, and what they can deliver, falls far short of the reconstruction of a bourgeois society.

Further reading

B. Elliott, et al. 'Bourgeois social movements: repertoires and responses', Sociological Review, **30**, no. 1, 1982.

R. King and M. Nugent (eds), Respectable Rebels: Middle Class Campaigns in Britain in the 1970s, London: Hodder and Stoughton, 1979.

R. Levitas, The Ideology of the New Right, Cambridge: Polity Press, 1986.

Bibliography

Abercrombie, N. *et al.* (1980), *The Dominant Ideology Thesis*, London: George Allen and Unwin

Abrams, P. and R. Brown (eds) (1984), *UK Society – Work, Urbanism and Inequality*, London: Weidenfeld and Nicolson

Allen, S. (1983), 'Production and reproduction: the lives of women homeworkers', *Sociological Review*, **31**, no. 4: pp. 649–65

Allen, V. (1978), 'The differentiation of the working class', in Alan Hunt (ed.), *Class and Class Structure*, London: Lawrence and Wishart

Alt, J. (1979), *The Politics of Economic Decline*, Cambridge: Cambridge University Press

Althusser, L. (1971), 'Ideology and ideological state apparatuses', in Louis Althusser, *Lenin and Philosophy and Other Essays*, London: New Left Books

Anderson, P. (1964), 'Origins of the present crisis', *New Left Review*, no. 23, pp. 26–53

Anderson, P. (1965), 'Problems of socialist strategy', in Perry Anderson *et al.*, *Towards Socialism*, London: Fontana

Anderson, P. (1966), 'Socialism and pseudo-empiricism', *New Left Review*, no. 35, pp. 2–42

Anderson, P. (1968), 'Components of the national culture', *New Left Review*, no. 50, pp. 3–57

Anderson, P. (1976–7), 'The antinomies of Antonio Gramsci', *New Left Review*, no. 100, pp. 5–78

Argyris, C. (1957), *Personality and Organization: the Conflict between System and the Individual*, New York: Harper and Row

Atkinson, J. (1984), 'Flexible firm takes shape', unpublished paper, *Institute of Manpower Studies*

Avineri, S. (1968), *The Social and Political Thought of Karl Marx*, Cambridge: Cambridge University Press

Badham, R. (1984), 'The sociology of industrial and post-industrial societies', *Current Sociology*, **32**, no. 1, pp. 1–141

Baran, P. A. and P. M. Sweezy (1966), *Monopoly Capital*, New York: Monthly Review Press

Barker, D. and S. Allen (1976), *Independence and Exploitation in Work and Marriage*, London: Longman

Barrett, M. and M. McIntosh (1980), 'The family wage: some problems for socialists and feminists', *Capital and Class*, **11**, pp. 51–72

Barron, K. and G. Norris (1976), 'Sexual divisions and the dual labour market', in D. Barker and S. Allen, (eds), *Independence and Exploitation in Work and Marriage*, London: Longman

Barry, B. (1970), *Socialists, Economists, and Democracy*, London: Routledge and Kegan Paul

Batstone, E. (1975), 'Deference and the ethos of small town capitalism', in Martin Bulmer, (ed.), *Working Class Images of Society*, London: Routledge and Kegan Paul

Bauman, Z. (1982), *Memories of Class – the pre-history and after-life of class*, London: Routledge and Kegan Paul

Bechhofer, F. and B. Elliott (1968), 'An approach to a study of small shopkeepers in the class structure', *European Journal of Sociology*, **9**, no. 2, pp. 180–202

Bechhofer, F. and B. Elliott (1976), 'Persistence and change: the *petit bourgeoisie* in industrial society', *European Journal of Sociology*, **17**, no. 1, pp. 74–99

Bechhofer, F. and B. Elliott (1985), 'The petit bourgeoisie in late capitalism', in R. H. Turner and A. J. Reiss Jr. (eds), *Annual Review of Sociology, 1985*, Palo Alto: Annual Reviews Inc.

Bechhofer, F., B. Elliott and D. McCrone (1978), 'Structure, consciousness and action: a sociological profile of the British middle class', *British Journal of Sociology*, **XXIX**, no. 4, pp. 410–56

Bell, C. and L. McKee (1986), 'His unemployment: her problem', in S. Allen *et al.*, *The Experience of Unemployment*, London: Macmillan

Bell, D. (1960), 'America as mass society', in D. Bell, *The End of Ideology*, Glencoe: Free Press

Bell, D. (1976), *The Cultural Contradictions of Capitalism*, London: Heinemann

Bell, D. (1978), 'The future that never was', *Public Interest*, no. 51, pp. 35–73

Bendix, R. (1964), *Nation-Building and Citizenship*, New York: Wiley

Benson, J. (ed.) (1985), *The Working Class in England 1875–1914*, London: Croom Helm

Benson, L. (1978), *Proletarians and Parties*, London: Tavistock

Bertaux, D. (ed.) (1981), *Biography and Society: the Life History Approach to the Social Sciences*, Beverley Hills: Sage

Beynon, H. (1980), *Working for Ford*, Wakefield: EP Publishing

Beynon, H. and R. M. Blackburn (1972), *Perceptions of Work*, Cambridge: Cambridge University Press

Blackburn, R. (1977), 'Marxism: theory of proletarian revolution', in R. Blackburn (ed.), *Revolution and Class Struggle: A Reader in Marxist Politics*, London: Fontana

Blackburn, R. M. and M. Mann (1975), 'Ideology in the non-skilled working class', in M. Bulmer (ed.), *Working Class Images of Society*, London: Routledge and Kegan Paul

Blackburn, R. M. and M. Mann (1979), *The Working Class in the Labour Market*, London: Macmillan

Bober, M. M. (1948), *Karl Marx's Interpretation of History*, New York: Norton

Bolton Report, The (1971), *Report of the Committee of Enquiry on Small Firms*, Cmnd. 4811, London: HMSO

Boyson, R. (1975), *The Crisis in Education*, London: Woburn Press

Braverman, H. (1974), *Labor and Monopoly Capital*, New York: Monthly Review Press

British Steel Corporation (1981), *Annual Report and Accounts*

Britten, N.and A. Heath (1983), 'Women and social class', in E. Gamarnikow *et al.* (eds), *Gender, Class and Work*, London: Heinemann

Browder, E. (1959), *Marx and America: A Study of the Doctrine of Impoverishment*, London: Victor Gollanz

Brown, R. (1976), 'Women as employees: some comments on research in industrial sociology', in D. L. Barker and S. Allen, (eds), *Dependence and Exploitation in Work and Marriage*, London: Longman

Bryer, R. A., T. J. Brignall and A. R. Maunders (1982), *Accounting for British Steel*, Aldershot: Gower

Bulmer, M. (1975), *Working Class Images of Society*, London: Routledge and Kegan Paul

Bulmer, M. (1975), 'Some problems of research into class imagery', in M. Bulmer (ed.), *Working Class Images of Society*, London: Routledge and Kegan Paul

Burawoy, M. (1979), *Manufacturing Consent*, Chicago: University of Chicago Press

Burns, P. (1985), 'Financial characteristics of small companies in the UK', *mimeo*, Cranfield School of Management

Callender, C. (1985), 'Gender inequality and social policy: women and the redundancy payments scheme', *Journal of Social Policy*, **14**, no. 2, pp. 189–214

Carchedi, G. (1975a), 'On the economic identification of the new middle class', *Economy and Society*, **4**, no. 1, pp. 1–86

Carchedi, G. (1975b), 'The reproduction of social classes at the level of production relations', *Economy and Society*, **4**, no. 4, pp. 361–417

Carchedi, G. (1977), *On the Economic Identification of Classes*, London: Routledge and Kegan Paul

Central Statistical Office (1985), *Inland Revenue Statistics, 1985*, London: HMSO

Central Statistical Office (1986), *Social Trends 16*, London: HMSO

Centre for Policy Studies (1979), *Why Britain Needs a Social Market Economy*, London: Centre for Policy Studies

Chamberlain, C. W. and H. F. Moorehouse (1974a), 'Lower class attitudes to property: aspects of the counter-ideology', *Sociology*, **8**, pp. 387–405

Chamberlain, C. W. and H. F. Moorehouse (1974b), 'Lower class attitudes towards the British political system', *Sociological Review*, no. 22, pp. 503–25

Chinoy, E. (1955), *Automobile Workers and the American Dream*, Garden City, NY: Doubleday

Cockburn, A. (1969), 'Introduction', in A. Cockburn and R. Blackburn, *Student Power*, London: Penguin Books

Cohen, S. (1980), *Folk Devils and Moral Panics*, Oxford: Martin Robertson

Conservative Party (1983), *Election Manifesto*, London: Conservative Party Central Office

Converse, P. E. (1964), 'The nature of belief systems in mass publics', in David E. Apter (ed.), *Ideology and Discontent*, Glencoe Ill.: Free Press

Cooper, C. and M. Davidson (1982), *High Pressure: The Working Lives of Women Managers*, London: Fontana

Cousins, J. M. and R. L. Davis (1974), '"Working class incorporation": a historical approach with reference to the mining communities of SE Northumberland 1840–1890', in F. Parkin (ed.), *The Social Analysis of Class Structure*, London: Tavistock

Cox, C. B. and A. E. Dyson (1969), *Fight for Education: A Black Paper*, London: Critical Quarterly Society

Cragg, A. and T. Dawson (1981), *Qualitative Research Among Homeworkers*, Research Paper no. 21, London: Department of Employment

Crewe, I. (1983a), 'The disturbing truth behind Labour's rout', *Guardian*, 13 June 1983

Crewe, I. (1983b), 'How Labour was trounced all round', *Guardian*, 14 June 1983

Crick, B. (ed.) (1981), *Unemployment*, London: Methuen

Crompton, R. and J. Gubbay (1977), *Economy and Class Structure*, London: Macmillan

Crompton, R. and G. Jones (1984), *White Collar Proletariat: Deskilling and Gender in the Clerical Labour Process*, London: Macmillan

Crosland, A. (1956), *Future of Socialism*, London: Cape

Crosland, A. (1959), 'What does the worker want?', *Encounter*, **XII**, no. 2, pp. 10–17

Crosland, A. (1960a), 'The future of the left', *Encounter*, **XIV**, no. 3, pp. 3–12

Crosland, A. (1960b), 'On the left again', *Encounter*, **XV**, no. 4, pp. 3–12

Crosland, A. (1960c), *Can Labour Win?*, Fabian Tract 324, London: Fabian Society

Crosland, A. (1961), 'New moods, old problems', *Encounter*, **XVI**, no. 2, pp. 3–6

Crosland, A. (1962), 'The mass media', *Encounter*, **XIX**, no. 5, pp. 3–14

Crossick, G. (1976), 'The labour aristocracy and its values', *Victorian Studies*, **19**, pp. 301–328

Crossick, G. (1978), *An Artisan Elite in Victorian Society*, London: Croom Helm

Cumbler, J. T. (1979), *Working-Class Community in Industrial America:*

Work, Leisure, and Struggle in Two Industrial Cities, 1880–1930, Westport, Conn.: Greenwood Press

Curran, J. and J. Stanworth (1979), 'Self-selection and the small firm worker: a critique and an alternative view', *Sociology*, **13**, no. 3, pp. 427–44

Currie, R. (1979), *Industrial Politics*, Oxford: Clarendon Press

Cutler, A., B. Hindess, P. Hirst and A. Hussain (1977), *Marx's Capital and Capitalism Today*, London: Routledge and Kegan Paul

Dahrendorf, R. (1959), *Class and Class Conflict in an Industrial Society*, London: Routledge and Kegan Paul

Daniel, W. (1981), 'Why is high unemployment somehow acceptable?', *New Society*, **55**, pp. 495–7

Daunton, M. J. (1983), *House and Home in the Victorian City*, London: Edward Arnold

David, M. (1986), 'Moral and maternal: the family in the right', in R. Levitas, *The Ideology of the New Right*, London: Polity Press

Davis, H. H. (1979), *Beyond Class Images*, London: Croom Helm

Davis, R. L. and J. Cousins (1975), 'The "new working class" and the old', in M. Bulmer (ed.), *Working-Class Images of Society*, London: Routledge and Kegan Paul

De Man, H. (1928), *The Psychology of Socialism*, London: George Allen and Unwin

Dennis, N., F. Henriques and C. Slaughter (1956), *Coal is Our Life*, London: Eyre and Spottiswood

Department of Employment (1985), *Employment Gazette*, **93**, no. 9, London: Department of Employment

Ditton, J. and R. Brown (1981), 'Why don't they revolt? "Invisible income" as a neglected dimension of Runciman's relative deprivation thesis', *British Journal of Sociology*, **32**, pp. 521–30

Doeringer, P. and M. Piore (1971), *Internal Labour Markets and Manpower Analysis*, Lexington, Mass.: D.C. Heath

Downing, J. (1977), 'Grave diggers' difficulties: ideology and the class struggle in advanced capitalism', in Richard Scase (ed.), *Industrial Society: Class Cleavage and Control*, London: George Allen and Unwin

Dunkerley, D. and G. Salaman (eds) (1979), *The International Yearbook of Organisation Studies*, London: Routledge and Kegan Paul

Dunleavy, P. (1979), 'The urban bases of political alignment', *British Journal of Political Science*, **9**, pp. 409–43

Dunleavy, P. and C. T. Husbands (1985), *British Democracy at the Crossroads*, London: Allen and Unwin

Durkheim, E. (1952), *Suicide*, London: Routledge

Durkheim, E. (1957), *Professional Ethics and Civic Morals*, London: Routledge and Kegan Paul

Eagleton, T. (1978), *Criticism and Ideology*, London: Verso

Edelman, M. (1980), *The Symbolic Uses of Politics*, Urbana, Ill.: University of Illinois Press

Elliott, B., F. Bechhofer, D. McCrone and S. Black (1982), 'Bourgeois social movements in Britain: repertoires and responses', *The Sociological Review*, **30**, no. 1, pp. 71–96

Elliott, B. and D. McCrone (1982), 'The social world of petty property', in P. Hollowell, *Property and Social Relations*, London: Heinemann

Elster, J. (1978), *Logic and Society: Contradictions and Possible Worlds*, Chichester: Wiley

Erikson, K. T. (1976), *Everything in its Path*, New York: Simon and Schuster

Eurostat (1981), *Economic and Social Position of Women in the Community*, Luxembourg: European Economic Community

Eurostat (1984), *Employment and Unemployment 1970–1982*, Luxembourg: Statistical Office, European Communities

Evans, F. (1984), *Women's Unemployment – A Domestic Occupation? A Reconsideration of Women's Employment, Unemployment and Domesticity*, Ph.D. thesis, University of Kent

Evans, M. (ed.) (1982), *The Woman Question*, London: Fontana

Femia, J. (1975), 'Hegemony and consciousness in the thought of Antonio Gramsci', *Political Studies*, **23**, pp. 29–48

Fevre, R. (1984), 'Contract Work in the Recession', paper presented to BSA Annual Conference, Bradford. Forthcoming in S. Wood, *The Changing Experience of Work*, London: Macmillan

Fevre, R. (1985), 'Employment and unemployment in Port Talbot: a reference paper', *School of Social Studies Occasional Papers Series*, no. 6, University College, Swansea

Fitzgerald, T. (1983), 'The New Right and the family', in M. Loney, M. Boswell and J. Clarke, *Social Policy and Social Welfare*, Milton Keynes: Open University Press

Fromm, E. (1962), *Beyond the Chains of Illusion*, New York: Trident Press

Gallie, D. (1978), *In Search of the New Working Class: Automation and Social Integration within the Capitalist Enterprise*, Cambridge: Cambridge University Press

Gamarnikow, E. *et al.* (eds) (1983), *Gender, Class and Work*, London: Heinemann Educational Books

Gamble, A. (1985), 'Smashing the state', *Marxism Today*, **29**, no. 6, pp. 21–6

Gamble, A. (1986), 'The political economy of freedom', in R. Levitas, *The Ideology of the New Right*, London: Polity Press

Gellner, E. (1978), 'Nationalism, or the new confessions of a justified Edinburgh sinner', *Political Quarterly*, **49**, pp. 103–11

Gershuny, J. (1978), *After Industrial Society*, London: Macmillan

Giddens, A. (1973), *The Class Structure of the Advanced Societies*, London: Hutchinson

Giddens, A. (1982), *Sociology: A Brief but Critical Introduction*, London: Macmillan

Gilbert, M. (1981), 'A sociological model of inflation', *Sociology*, **15**, no. 2, pp. 185–209

Glyn, A. and B. Sutcliffe (1972), *British Capitalism, Workers and the Profits Squeeze*, Harmondsworth: Penguin Books

Goffee, R. and R. Scase (1983), 'Business ownership and women's subordination: a preliminary study of female proprietors', *Sociological Review*, **31**, no. 4, pp. 625–48

Goffman, I. (1952), 'On cooling the mark out', *Psychiatry*, **15**, no. 4, pp. 451–63

Goldthorpe, J. H. (1964), 'Social stratification in industrial society', in Paul Halmos (ed.), *The Development of Industrial Society, The Sociological Review*, Monograph no. 8, pp. 97–122

Goldthorpe, J. H. *et al.* (1968a), *The Affluent Worker: Industrial Attitudes and Behaviour*, Cambridge: Cambridge University Press

Goldthorpe, J. H. *et al.*, (1986b), *The Affluent Worker: Political Attitudes and Behaviour*, Cambridge: Cambridge University Press

Goldthorpe, J. H. *et al.*, (1969), *The Affluent Worker in the Class Structure*, Cambridge: Cambridge University Press

Goldthorpe, J. H. (1971), 'Theories of industrial society: reflections on the recrudescence of historicism and the future of futurology', *European Journal of Sociology*, **12**, no. 2, pp. 263–88

Goldthorpe, J. H. (1972), 'Class, status and party in modern Britain', *European Journal of Sociology*, **13**, no. 2, pp. 342–72

Goldthorpe, J. H. (1977), 'The relevance of history to sociology', in Martin Bulmer (ed.), *Sociological Research Methods*, London: Macmillan

Goldthorpe, J. H. (1978), 'The current inflation: towards a sociological account', in F. Hirsch and J. H. Goldthorpe (eds), *The Political Economy of Inflation*, London: Martin Robertson

Goldthorpe, J. H. (1980), *Social Mobility and Class Structure in Modern Britain*, Oxford: Clarendon Press

Goldthorpe, J. H. (1982), 'On the service class, its formation and future', in A. Giddens and G. Mackenzie (eds), *Social Class and the Division of Labour*, Cambridge: Cambridge University Press, pp. 162–85

Goldthorpe, J. H. (1983a), 'Social mobility and class formation: on the renewal of a tradition in sociological inquiry', *Working Paper of the CASMIN Project*, no. 1, Mannheim

Goldthorpe, J. H. (1983b), 'Women and class analysis: in defence of the conventional view', *Sociology*, **17**, no. 4, pp. 465–88

Goldthorpe, J. H. (1984a), 'The end of convergence: corporatist and dualist tendencies in modern western societies', in J. H. Goldthorpe (ed.), *Order and Conflict in Contemporary Capitalism*, Oxford: Clarendon Press, pp. 315–45

Goldthorpe, J. H. (1984b), 'Women and class analysis: a reply to the replies', *Sociology*, **18**, no. 4, pp. 491–9

Goldthorpe, J. H. (1986), 'Employment, class and mobility: a critique of liberal and Marxist theories of long-term change', Nuffield College, Oxford; *mimeo*

285

Goldthorpe, J. H. and K. Hope (1974), *The Social Grading of Occupations: A New Approach and Scale*, Oxford: Oxford University Press

Goldthorpe, J. H. and D. Lockwood (1963), 'Affluence and the British class structure', *Sociological Review*, **11**, no. 2, pp. 133–63

Goldthorpe, J. H. and C. Payne (1986), 'Trends in intergenerational class mobility in England and Wales, 1972–1983', *Sociology*, **20**, no. 1, p. 1–24

Gordon, D. (1972), *Theories of Poverty and Underemployment*, Lexington, Mass.: DC Heath

Gorz, A. (1982), *Farewell to the Working Class*, London: Pluto Press

Gould, M. (1979), 'When women create an organisation: the ideological imperatives of feminism', in D. Dunkerley and G. Salaman (eds), *The International Yearbook of Organisation Studies*, London: Routledge and Kegan Paul

Gramsci, A. (1980), 'State and civil society', in A. Gramsci, *Selections from the Prison Notebooks*, New York: International Publishers

Gray, R. Q. (1973), 'Styles of life, the "labour aristocracy" and class relations in later nineteenth-century Edinburgh', *International Review of Social History*, **18**, pp. 445–52

Gray, R. Q. (1976), *The Labour Aristocracy in Victorian Edinburgh*, Oxford: Clarendon Press

Greer, G. (1970), *The Female Eunuch*, London: MacGibbon and Kee

Griggs, C. (1972), 'The Conservative approach to education', in D. Rubinstein, *Education and Equality*, Harmondsworth: Penguin

Gutman, H. G. (1973), 'Work, culture and society in industrializing America 1815–1919', *American Historical Review*, **78**, pp. 531–88

Gyford, J. (1983), 'The new urban left: a local road to socialism', *New Society*, **64**, no. 1066, pp. 91–3

Gyford, J. (1984), *Local Politics in Britain*, London: Croom Helm

Habermas, J. (1975) and (1976), *Legitimation Crisis*, Boston: Beacon Press; London: Heinemann

Hakim, C. (1979), *Occupational Segregation*, Research Paper no. 9, London: Department of Employment

Hakim, C. (1982), 'The social consequences of high unemployment', *Journal of Social Policy*, **1**, pp. 433–67

Halevy, E. (1955), *The Growth of Philosophic Radicalism*, Boston: Beacon Press

Hall, S. (1984), 'Labour's love still lost', *New Socialist*

Halsey, A. H. (1985), 'Provincials and professionals: the British post-war sociologists', in M. Bulmer (ed.), *Essays on the History of British Sociological Research*, Cambridge: Cambridge University Press, pp. 151–64

Hamilton, R. F. (1965), 'The behaviour and values of skilled workers', in A. B. Shostack and W. Gomberg (eds), *Blue-Collar World*, Englewood Cliffs: Prentice-Hall

Hamnet, C. (1984), 'Housing the two nations: socio-tenurial polarization in England and Wales 1961–1981', *Urban Studies*, **43**, pp. 389–405

Handy, C. (1984), *The Future of Work*, Oxford: Blackwell

Harris, C. C. (1984a), 'Conceptualizing the place of redundant steelworkers in the class structure: of class and the market', Part One of a paper presented to the ESRC Seminar on Stratification, Cambridge

Harris, C. C. (1984b), 'Conceptualizing the place of redundant steelworkers in the class structure: "class", labour markets and "the social"', Part Two of a paper presented to the ESRC Seminar on Stratification, Cambridge

Harris, C. C., R. M. Lee and L. D. Morris (1985), 'Redundancy in steel: labour-market behaviour, local social networks and domestic organisation', in B. Roberts, R.Finnegan and D. Gallie (eds), *New Approaches to Economic Life*, Manchester: Manchester University Press

Hartley, A. (1975), 'Elie Halevy and England now', *Encounter*, **XLIV**, no. 1, pp. 40–6

Hayes, J. and P. Nutman (1981), *Understanding the Unemployed: the Psychological Effects of Unemployment*, London: Tavistock

Heath, A. (1976), *Rational Choice and Social Exchange*, Cambridge: The University Press

Heath, A. (1981), *Social Mobility*, London: Fontana

Heath, A. and N. Britten (1984), 'Women's jobs do make a difference', *Sociology*, **18**, pp. 475–90

Heath, A., R. Jowell and J. Curtice (1985), *How Britain Votes*, Oxford: Pergamon

Heller, A. (1974), *The Theory of Need in Marx*, London: Allison and Busby

Hennig, M. and A. Jardim (1979), *The Managerial Woman*, London: Pan

Henry, S. (1982), 'The working unemployed: perspectives of the informal economy and unemployment', *Sociological Review*, no. 30, pp. 460–77

Herzog, M. (1980), *From Hand to Mouth*, Harmondsworth: Penguin

Hill, S. (1981), *Competition and Control at Work*, London: Heinemann

Hinden, R. (1960), 'The lessons for Labour', in M. Abrams and R. Rose, *Must Labour Lose?*, London: Penguin

Hirsch, F. (1976) and (1978), *Social Limits to Growth*, Cambridge, Mass.: Harvard University Press; London: Routledge and Kegan Paul

Hirst, P. (1977), 'Economic classes and politics', in A. Hunt (ed.), *Class and Class Structure*, London: Lawrence and Wishart

Hobbes, T. (1949), *Leviathan*, London: Dent

Hobsbawm, E. J. (1959), *Social Bandits and Primitive Rebels*, Glencoe, Ill.: The Free Press

Hoggart, R. (1957), *The Uses of Literacy*, London: Chatto and Windus

Hoggart, R. (1960), 'Working-class attitudes', *New Left Review*, no. 1, pp. 26–30

Hoggart, R. (1970), *Speaking to Each Other*, London: Chatto and Windus

Humphries, J. (1980), 'Class struggle and the persistence of the working-class family', in A. H. Amsden (ed.), *The Economics of Women and Work*, Harmondsworth: Penguin

Hunt, J. (1982), 'A woman's place is in her union', in J. West (ed.), *Work, Women and the Labour Market*, London: Routledge and Kegan Paul

287

Hunt, P. (1980), *Gender and Class Consciousness*, London: Macmillan

Hutber, P. (1976), *The Decline and Fall of the Middle Class: and how it can fight back*, London: Associated Business Programmes

Jackson, B. (1968), *Working Class Community*, London: Routledge

Jahoda, M. (1982), *Employment and Unemployment: A Social-Psychological Analysis*, Cambridge: Cambridge University Press

Jowell, R. and S. Witherspoon, (eds) (1985), *British Social Attitudes: The 1985 Report*, Aldershot: Gower and SCPR

Kahn, H. R. (1964), *Repercussions of Redundancy*, London: Allen and Unwin

Kanter, R. (1977), *Men and Women of the Corporation*, New York: Basic Books

Kellner, P. (1985), 'Come back class-politics, all is forgiven', *New Statesman*, **110**, no. 2843: p. 9

Kerr, C. *et al.* (1960), *Industrialism and Industrial Man*, Cambridge, Mass.: Harvard University Press

Kerr, M. (1958), *People of Ship Street*, London: Routledge

Kets De Vries, M. (1977), 'The entrepreneurial personality: a person at the crossroads', *Journal of Management Studies*, **14**, pp. 34–57

Klein, J. (1965), *Samples from English Cultures*, two vols, London: Routledge and Kegan Paul

Kornblum, W. (1974), *Blue Collar Community*, Chicago: University of Chicago Press

Kumar, K. (1978), *Prophecy and Progress*, Harmondsworth: Penguin

Laing, D. (1971), *The Politics of the Family and Other Essays*, London: Penguin

Land, H. (1980), 'The family wage', *Feminist Review*, no. 6, pp. 55–77

Lane, R. E. (1962), *Political Ideology*, New York: Free Press

Leaver, G. (1985), 'Some aspects of the relation between employment, domestic organisation activity and consumption', unpublished M.Sc. MS. University College Swansea

Leavis, F. R. (1932), 'Under Which King, Bezonian?', *Scrutiny*, **I**, no. 3, p. 205–14

Leavis, F. R. (1972), *Nor Shall My Sword: Discourses on Pluralism, Comparison and Social Hope*, London: Chatto and Windus

Leavis, F. R. and D. Thompson (1933), *Culture and Environment*, London: Chatto and Windus

Lee, R. M. (1983a), 'The job-search activity of unemployed redundant steelworkers', unpublished working paper, University College Swansea

Lee, R. M. (1983b), 'The job-acquisition behaviour of redundant steelworkers', unpublished working paper, University College Swansea

Lee, R. M. (1983c), 'Survey of redundant steelworkers: selected results from waves 1 and 2', unpublished working paper, University College Swansea

Lee, R. M. (1985), 'Redundancy, labour market and informal relations', *Sociological Review*, **33**, no. 3, pp. 469–94

Leggett, J. C. (1965), 'Sources and consequences of working-class consciousness', in A. B. Shostak and W. Gomberg (eds), *Blue-Collar World*, Englewood Cliffs: Prentice Hall

Leighton, P. (1983), *Contractual Arrangements in Selected Industries*, Research paper no. 39, London: Department of Employment

Levitas, R. (1986), *The Ideology of the New Right*, London: Polity Press

Leys, C. (1985), 'Thatcherism and British manufacturing: a question of hegemony', *New Left Review*, no. 151, pp. 5–25

Lichtman, R. (1975), 'Marx's theory of ideology', *Socialist Revolution*, 5, pp. 45–76

Lindsay, A. D. (1925), *Karl Marx's Capital: An Introductory Essay*, London: Oxford University Press

Lipsey, D. (1982), 'Labour's new (non-manual) breed of councillor', *Sunday Times*, 19.9.1982

Lockwood, D. (1956), 'Some remarks on "the social system"', *British Journal of Sociology*, 7, pp. 134–45

Lockwood, D. (1958), *The Blackcoated Worker*, London: Allen and Unwin

Lockwood, D. (1960), 'The new working class', *European Journal of Sociology*, 1, pp. 248–59

Lockwood, D. (1964), 'Social integration and system integration', in G. K. Zollschan and W. Hirsch (eds), *Exploration in Social Change*, Boston: Houghton Mifflin

Lockwood, D. (1966 and 1975), 'Sources of variation in working-class images of society', *Sociological Review*, 14, no. 3: pp. 244–67: reprinted in M. Bulmer (ed.), *Working-Class Images of Society*, London: Routledge and Kegan Paul

Lockwood, D. (1974), 'For T. H. Marshall', *Sociology*, 8, pp. 363–67

Lockwood, D. (1986), 'On the incongruity of power and status', in H. Strasser and R. W. Hodge (eds), *Status Inconsistency in Modern Societies*, Soscialwissenschaftliche Kooperative: Duisberg

Lockwood, D. (forthcoming), *Solidarity and Schism*

Lukacs, G. (1971), *History and Class Consciousness*, London: Merlin

Mackay, D. I., R. MacKay, P. McVean and R. Edwards (1980), *Redundancy and Displacement*, Research Paper no. 16, London: Department of Employment

Mackenzie, G. (1973), *The Aristocracy of Labour*, Cambridge: The University Press

Mackenzie, G. (1974), 'The "Affluent Worker" Study: an evaluation and critique', in F. Parkin (ed.), *The Social Analysis of Class Structure*, London: Tavistock

Mackenzie, G. (1977), 'The political economy of the American working class', *British Journal of Sociology*, 28, pp. 244–51

Mackie, L. and P. Patullo (1977), *Women at Work*, London: Tavistock

Macpherson, C. B. (1977), *The Political Theory of Possessive Individualism*, Oxford: The University Press

Macrae, N. (1976), 'The coming entrepreneurial revolution: a survey', *The Economist*, 261, pp. 41–65

Mallet, S. (1975), *The New Working Class*, Nottingham: Spokesman Books

Mandel, E. (1975), *Late Capitalism*, London: New Left Books

Mann, M. (1970 and 1982), 'The social cohesion of liberal democracy', *American Sociological Review*, **35**, pp. 423–38: reprinted in A. Giddens and D. Held (eds), *Classes, Power and Conflict*, London: Macmillan

Mann, M. (1978), *Consciousness and Action among the Western Working Class*, London: Macmillan

Marshall, G. (1982), *In Search of the Spirit of Capitalism*, London: Hutchinson

Marshall, G. (1983), 'Some remarks on the study of working class consciousness', *Politics and Society*, **12**, no. 3, pp. 263–301 and Chapter 4 of this volume

Marshall, G. (1984), 'On the sociology of women's unemployment, its neglect and significance', *Sociological Review*, **32**, pp. 234–59

Marshall, G. *et al.*, (1985), 'Class citizenship and distributional conflict in modern Britain', *British Journal of Sociology*, **36**, no. 2, pp. 259–84

Marshall, G. *et al.*, (1987), 'Distributional struggle and moral order in a market society', *Sociology*, **21**, no. 1, pp. 55–73

Marshall, G. *et al.*, (1988), *Social Class in Modern Britain*, London: Hutchinson

Marshall, J. (1984), *Women Managers*, Chichester: Wiley

Marshall, T. H. (1934), 'Social class: a preliminary analysis', reprinted in T. H. Marshall, *Citizenship and Social Class*, Cambridge: Cambridge University Press, 1950, pp. 86–113

Marshall, T. H. (1950), *Citizenship and Social Class*, Cambridge: Cambridge University Press

Martin, B. (1981), *A Sociology of Contemporary Cultural Change*, Oxford: Blackwell

Martin, J. and C. Roberts (1984), *Women and Employment: A Lifetime Perspective*, London: HMSO

Martin, R. and R. H. Fryer (1973), *Redundancy and Paternalist Capitalism*, London: George Allen and Unwin

Marwick, A. (1982), *British Society since 1945*, London: Penguin

Marx, K. (1906), *Capital: A Critical Analysis of Capitalist Production*, London: Swan Sonnenschein

Marx, K. (1965), *Early Writings*, T. B. Bottomore (trans. and ed.), New York: McGraw-Hill

Marx, K. (1967), *Capital, Vol. I,* London: Lawrence and Wishart

Marx. K. (1972), *Capital, Vol. III*, London: Lawrence and Wishart

Marx, K. (1973a), *Grundrisse*, Harmondsworth: Penguin

Marx, K. (1973b), *The Eighteenth Brumaire of Louis Bonaparte*, in D. Fernbach (ed.), *Surveys from Exile*, Harmondsworth: Penguin

Marx, K. and F. Engels (1950), *Selected Works, Vol. I*, Moscow: Foreign Languages Publishing House

Massey, D. (1984), *Spatial Divisions of Labour*, London: Macmillan

McHugh, J. (1979), 'The self-employed and the small independent entrepreneur', in R. King and N. Nugent (eds), *Respectable Rebels: Middle Class Campaigns in Britain in the 1970s*, London: Hodder and Stoughton

McKenzie, R. and A. Silver (1968), *Angels in Marble*, London: Heinemann

McLellan, D. (1971), *The Thought of Karl Marx: An Introduction*, London: Macmillan

Merton, R. K. (1957), *Social Theory and Social Structure*, Glencoe, Ill.: Free Press

Meszaros, I. (1970), *Marx's Theory of Alienation*, London: Merlin Press

Miliband, R. (1969), *The State in Capitalist Society*, London: Weidenfeld and Nicholson

Miliband, R. (1977), *Marxism and Politics*, Oxford: Oxford University Press

Mishan, E. J. (1974), 'The new inflation', *Encounter*, **XLII**, no. 5: pp. 12–24

Mishan, E. J. (1976), 'On the road to repression and control', *Encounter*, **XLVII**, no. 1, pp. 5–17

Missiakoulis, N., R. E. Pahl and P. Taylor-Gooby (1986), 'Households, work and politics: some implications of the divisions of labour in formal and informal production', *International Journal of Sociology and Social Policy*, **6**, no. 3.

Mitchell, J. (1971), *Woman's Estate*, London: Penguin

Moore, R. S. 1975), 'Religion as a source of variation in working-class images of society', in M. Bulmer (ed.), *Working Class Images of Society*, London: Routledge and Kegan Paul

Moorehouse, H. F. (1978), 'The Marxist theory of the labour aristocracy', *Social History*, **3**, pp. 61–82

Morgan, K. (1983), 'Restructuring steel', *International Journal of Urban and Regional Research*, **7**, no. iii, pp. 175–201

Morris, L. D. (1984), 'Patterns of social activity and post-redundancy labour market experience', *Sociology*, **18**, no. 3, pp. 339–52

Mount, F. (1982), *The Subversive Family*, London: Counterpoint

Murgatroyd, L. (1984), 'Gender and occupational stratification', in L. Murgatroyd *et al*. (eds), *Localities, Class and Gender*, London: Pion

Nairn, T. (1964), 'Anatomy of the Labour Party', *New Left Review*, no. 27, pp. 38–65, and no. 28, pp. 33–62

Nairn, T. (1964), 'The English working class', *New Left Review*, no. 24, pp. 43–57

Nairn, T. (1977), *The Break-Up of Britain: Crisis and Neo-Nationalism*, London: New Left Books

Newby, H. (1979), *The Deferential Worker*, Harmondsworth: Penguin

Newby, H. (1981), *The State of Social Stratification Research in Britain*, London: Social Science Research Council

Nichols, T. and P. Armstrong (1976), *Workers Divided*, London: Fontana

Nichols, T. and H. Beynon (1977), *Living with Capitalism*, London: Routledge and Kegan Paul

Noble, T. (1985), 'Inflation and earnings relativities in Britain after 1970', *British Journal of Sociology*, **XXXVI**, no. 2, pp. 238–58

Norris, G. M. (1978), 'Unemployment, subemployment and personal characteristics', *Sociological Review*, **26**, pp. 89–108 and 327–47

Oakley, A. (1982), *Subject Women*, London: Fontana

O'Conner, J. (1973), *The Fiscal Crisis of the State*, London: St James

Offe, C. (1976), *Industry and Inequality*, London: Edward Arnold

Ollman, B. (1971), *Alienation: Marx's Conception of Man in Capitalist Society*, Cambridge: Cambridge University Press

Ollman, B. (1972), 'Towards class consciousness next time: Marx and the working class', *Politics and Society*, **3**, pp. 1–24

O'Malley, J. (ed.), (1970), *Marx's Critique of Hegel's Philosophy of Right*, Cambridge: Cambridge University Press

OPCS (1981), *Labour Force Survey 1981*, London, HMSO

Pahl, R. E. (1984), *Divisions of Labour*, Oxford: Blackwell

Pahl, R. E. and C. D. Wallace (1985), 'Household work strategies in an economic recession', in N. Redclift and E. Mingione, *Beyond Employment*, Oxford: Blackwell

Parkin, F. (1967), 'Working class conservatism: a theory of political deviance', *British Journal of Sociology*, **18**, pp. 280–90

Parkin, F. (1972), *Class Inequality and Political Order*, London: Paladin

Parkin, F. (1979), *Marxism and Class Theory: A Bourgeois Critique*, London: Tavistock Publications

Parsons, T. (1935), 'The place of ultimate values in sociological theory', *International Journal of Ethics*, **45**, no. 3, pp. 282–316

Parsons, T. (1937), *The Structure of Social Action*, New York and London: McGraw-Hill

Parsons, T. (1949), *Essays in Sociological Theory: Pure and Applied*, Glencoe, Ill.: Free Press

Platt, J. (1971), 'Variations in answers to different questions on perceptions of class', *Sociological Review*, **19**, pp. 409–19

Pollert, A. (1981), *Girls, Wives, Factory Lives*, London: Macmillan

Popper, K. (1945), *The Open Society and Its Enemies*, London, RKP

Popper, K. (1957), *The Poverty of Historicism*, London: RKP

Porter, M. (1978), 'Worlds apart: the class consciousness of working class women', *Women's Studies International Quarterly*, **1**, pp. 175–88

Porter, M. (1983), *Home, Work and Class Consciousness*, Manchester: Manchester University Press

Poulantzas, N. (1973) and (1978a), *Political Power and Social Classes*, London: New Left Books; and London: Verso

Poulantzas, N. (1974), *Fascism and Dictatorship*, London: New Left Books

Poulantzas, N. (1978b), 'The new petty bourgeoisie', in A. Hunt (ed.), *Class and Class Structure*, London: Lawrence and Wishart

Poulantzas, N. (1979), *Classes in Contemporary Capitalism*, London: Verso

Prandy, K. (1979), 'Alienation and interests in the analysis of social cognitions', *British Journal of Sociology*, **30**, no. 4: pp. 442–74

Price, J. (1985), 'Abortion and the right to life', *The Free Nation*

Price, R. and G. Bain (1976), 'Union growth revisited: 1948–1974 in perspective', *British Journal of Industrial Relations*, **XIV**, no. 3: pp. 339–55

Purcell, K. (1978), 'Working women, women's work and the occupational sociology of being a woman', *Women's Studies International Quarterly*, **1**, pp. 153–63

Purcell, K. (1979), 'Militancy and acquiescence amongst women workers', in S. Burman (ed.), *Fit Work for Women*, London: Croom Helm

Rex, J. (1964), *Key Problems in Sociological Theory*, London: Routledge and Kegan Paul

Richardson, G. (1985), 'Employment in the public and private sectors 1978 to 1984', *Economic Trends*, no. 377, London: HMSO

Roberts, B. *et al.* (eds), (1985), *New Approaches to Economic Life: Economic Restructuring, Unemployment and the Social Division of Labour*, Manchester: Manchester University Press

Roberts, E. (1985), 'The family' in J. Benson (ed.), *The Working Class in England 1875–1914*, London: Croom Helm

Roberts, K. *et al.* (1977), *The Fragmentary Class Structure*, London: Heinemann

Roberts, R. (1971), *The Classic Slum*, Manchester: University of Manchester Press

Robinson, W. S. (1950), 'Ecological correlations and the behaviour of individuals', *American Sociological Review*, **15**, pp. 351–7

Rodman, H. (1971), *Lower-Class Families*, New York: Oxford University Press

Rose, D. *et al.*, (1984), 'Economic restructuring: the British experience', *Annals of the AAPSS*, **475**, pp. 137–57

Rose, D. and G. Marshall (1986), 'Constructing the W(right) classes', *Sociology*, **20**, no. 3, pp. 440–55

Rose, G. (1981), *Hegel Contra Sociology*, London: Athlone

Rose, R. *et al.*, (1985), *Public Employment in Western Nations*, Cambridge: Cambridge University Press

Rose, R. and I. McAllister (1985), *From Closed Class to Open Elections: Britain in Flux*, London: Sage

Royal Commission on Income Distribution and Wealth (1979), *Report No. 8*, London: HMSO

Runciman, W. G. (1966), *Relative Deprivation and Social Justice*, London: Routledge and Kegan Paul

Ryder, A. J. (1967), *The German Revolution of 1918: A Study of German Socialism in War and Revolt*, Cambridge: The University Press

Sahlins, M. (1974), *Stone Age Economics*, London: Tavistock

Sarlvik, B. and I. Crewe (1983), *Decade of Dealignment*, Cambridge: Cambridge University Press

Saunders, P. (1981), *Social Theory and the Urban Question*, London: Hutchinson

Saunders, P. (1982), 'Beyond housing classes: the sociological significance of private property rights in the means of consumption', *Working Paper No. 33*, Urban and Regional Studies, University of Sussex

Scase, R. (1974), 'Conceptions of the class structure and political ideology:

some observations on attitudes in England and Sweden', in F. Parkin (ed.), *The Social Analysis of Class Structure*, London: Tavistock

Scase, R. and R. Goffee (1980), *The Real World of the Small Business Owner*, London: Croom Helm

Scase, R. and R. Goffee (1981), '"Traditional" petty bourgeois attitudes: the case of the self-employed craftsman', *Sociological Review*, **29**, no. 4, pp. 729–47

Scase, R. and R. Goffee (1982), *The Entrepreneurial Middle Class*, London: Croom Helm

Schlozman, K. L. and S. Verba (1979), *Injury to Insult: Unemployment, Class and Political Response*, Cambridge, Mass.: Harvard University Press

Schuman, H. and M. P. Johnson (1976), 'Attitudes and behaviour' in A. Inkeles *et al.* (eds), *Annual Review of Sociology*, Palo Alto, Calif.; Annual Reviews, **2**, pp. 161–207

Scruton, R. (1984), *The Meaning of Conservatism* (2nd edition), London: Macmillan

Seabrook, J. (1982), *Unemployment*, London: Quartet Books

Sewel, J. (1975), *Colliery Closure and Social Change*, Cardiff: University of Wales Press

Shapiro, R. (1985), 'Britain's sexual counter-revolutionaries', *Marxism Today*, **29**, no. 2, pp. 7–10

Shils, E. (1957), 'Daydreams and nightmares: reflections on the criticism of mass culture', *Sewanee Review*, **65**, no. 4, pp. 587–608

Shils, E. (1958), 'Ideology and civility', *Sewanee Review*, **66**, no. 1, pp. 450–80

Shils, E. (1960), 'Mass society and its culture', *Daedalus*, **89**, pp. 288 ff.

Shils, E. (1981), *Tradition*, Chicago: University of Chicago Press

Showler, B. and A. Sinfield (eds), *The Workless State*, Oxford: Martin Robertson

Silverstone, R. and A. Ward (eds), (1980), *Careers of Professional Women*, London: Croom Helm

Sinai, R. (1979), 'What ails us and why: on the roots of disaster and decay', *Encounter*, **LII**, no. 4, pp. 8–17

Sinfield, A. (1981), *What Unemployment Means*, Oxford: Martin Robertson

Stanworth, J. and J. Curran (1973), *Management Motivation in the Smaller Business*, Aldershot: Gower Press

Stanworth, M. (1984), 'Women and class analysis: a reply to Goldthorpe', *Sociology*, **18**, pp. 159–70

Stedman-Jones, G. (1969), 'The meaning of the student revolt', in A. Cockburn and R. Blackburn, *Student Power*, London: Penguin Books

Stedman-Jones, G. (1983), 'Poor laws and market forces', *New Statesman*, **105**, no. 2723, 27 May, pp. x–xiii

Stewart, A. and R. M. Blackburn (1975), 'The stability of structural inequality', *Sociological Review*, **23**, no. 3, pp. 481–508

Stewart, A., K. Prandy and R. M. Blackburn (1983), *White Collar Unionism*, London: Macmillan

Sweezy, P. M. (1949), *The Theory of Capitalist Development*, London: Dennis Dobson

Sweezy, P. M. (1974), 'Foreword', in H. Braverman, *Labor and Monopoly Capital*, New York: Monthly Review Press

Szreter, S. R. S. (1984), 'The genesis of the Registrar General's Social Classification of Occupations', *British Journal of Sociology*, **XXV**, no. 4, pp. 522–46

Taylor-Gooby, P. (1985), *Public Opinion, Ideology and State Welfare*, London: Routledge and Kegan Paul

Tebbitt, N. (1985), *Guardian*, 15 November 1985

Tebbitt, N. (1986), *Scotsman*, 10 April 1986

Thatcher, M. (1984a), West Midlands Rally, Hotel Metropole, National Exhibition Centre, Birmingham, 3 June 1984

Thatcher, M. (1984b), Speech to Small Business Bureau Annual Conference, Lake Side Country Club, Surrey

Thatcher, M. (1985), Speech to Conservative Central Council Meeting, Newcastle, 23 March 1985

Thomas, D. (1986), 'Asset sales fact sheet', *New Socialist*

Thompson, E. P. (1965), 'The peculiarities of the English', in R. Miliband and J. Saville (eds), *The Socialist Register*, London: Merlin Press

Thompson, E. P. (1967), 'Time, work-discipline, and industrial capitalism', *Past and Present*, no. 38, pp. 56–97

Toulmin, S. (1978), 'You Norman, me Saxon', *Encounter*, **LI**, no. 3, pp. 89–93

Townsend, P. (1979), *Poverty in the United Kingdom*, Harmondsworth: Penguin

Turner, J. H. and C. E. Starnes (1976), *Inequality: Privilege and Poverty in America*, Santa Monica, Calif.: Goodyear

Useem, M. (1983), 'Business and politics in the US and UK: the origins of heightened political activity of large corporations during the 1970s and early 1980s', *Theory and Society*, **12**, no. 3, pp. 281–308

Useem, M. (1984), *The Inner Circle: Large Corporations and the Rise of Business Political Activity in the USA and the UK*, Oxford: Oxford University Press

Wainwright, H. (1978), 'Women and the division of labour', in P. Abrams (ed.), *Work, Urbanism and Inequality: UK Society Today*, (1st edition), London: Weidenfeld and Nicolson

Wajcman, J. (1983), *Women in Control*, Milton Keynes: Open University Books

Walker, L. J. (ed.), (1975), *The Discourses of Niccolo Machiavelli*, London: Routledge and Kegan Paul

Wallace, C. D. (1985), 'Growing apart: unemployment polarization and family formation amongst young people', *Final Report to the Joseph Rowntree Memorial Trust*

Wallace, C. D. (1986), 'From girls and boys to women and men: the social reproduction of gender roles and the transition from school to

295

(un)employment', in L. Barker and S. Walker (eds), *School, Work and Unemployment*, Milton Keynes: Open University Press

Wallace, C. D. and R. E. Pahl (1986), 'Polarisation, unemployment and all forms of work', S. Allen *et al.*, *The Experience of Unemployment*, London: Macmillan

Webb, D. (1973), 'Research note: some reservations on the use of self-rated class', *Sociological Review*, **21**, pp. 321–30

Webb, M. (1982), 'The labour market' in I. Reid and E. Wormald (eds), *Sex Differences in Britain*, London: Grant McIntyre

Weber, M. (1968), *Economy and Society*, New York: Bedminster Press

Wedderburn, D. (1965), *Redundancy and the Railwaymen*, Cambridge: Cambridge University Press

West, J. (ed.) (1982), *Work, Women and the Labour Market*, London: Routledge and Kegan Paul

Westergaard, J. H. (1970), 'The rediscovery of the cash nexus', in R. Miliband and J. Saville (eds), *The Socialist Register*, London: Merlin Press

Westergaard, J. H. (1973), 'Sociology: the myth of classlessness', in R. Blackburn (ed.), *Ideology in Social Science*, London: Fontana

Westergaard, J. H. (1975), 'Radical class consciousness: a comment', in M. Bulmer (ed.), *Working Class Images of Society*, London: Routledge and Kegan Paul

Westergaard, J. and H. Resler (1976), *Class in a Capitalist Society*, Harmondsworth: Penguin

Westergaard, J., I. Noble and A. Walker (1985), 'From secure employment to labour market insecurity', in B. Roberts, R. Finnegan, and D. Gallie (eds), *New Approaches to Economic Life*, Manchester: Manchester University Press

Whelan, C. T. (1976), 'Orientations to work: some theoretical and methodological problems', *British Journal of Industrial Relations*, **14**, pp. 142–58

White, M. (1983), *Long-term Unemployment and Labour Markets*, London: Policy Studies Institute

Willener, A. (1975), 'Images, action "us and them"', in M. Bulmer (ed.), *Working Class Images of Society*, London: Routledge and Kegan Paul

Williams, G. A. (1960), 'The concept of "egemonia" in the thought of Antonio Gramsci: some notes and interpretations', *Journal of the History of Ideas*, **21**, pp. 586–99

Williams, R. (1958), *Culture and Society*, London: Chatto and Windus

Williams, R. (1962), *Communications*, London: Penguin

Williams, R. (1965), *The Long Revolution* (2nd edition), London: Penguin

Williams, R. (1973a), 'Base and superstructure in Marxist cultural theory', *New Left Review*, no. 82, pp. 3–16

Williams, R. (1973b), *The Country and the City*, London: Chatto and Windus

Williams, R. (1983), 'Problems of the coming period', *New Left Review*, no. 140, pp. 7–18

Williams, W. M. (1956), *The Sociology of an English Village*, London: Routledge

Willis, P. (1979), *Learning to Labour: How Working Class Kids Get Working Class Jobs*, Westmead, Hants: Saxon House

Wilson Report, The (1980), *Report of the Committee to Review the Functioning of Financial Institutions*, Cmnd. 7939, London: HMSO

Wollheim, R. (1961), *Socialism and Culture*, Fabian Tract 331, London: Fabian Society

Wood, S. *et al.* (1978), 'Approaches to the study of redundancy', *Industrial Relations Journal*, **8**, no. 4, pp. 19–27

Wood, S. (ed.), (1982), *The Degradation of Work?*, London: Hutchinson

Worsthorne, P. (1976), 'Of strong unions in weak societies', *Encounter*, **XLVI**, no. 1, pp. 22–8

Wright, E. O. (1976), 'Class boundaries in advanced capitalist societies', *New Left Review*, **98**, pp. 3–41

Wright, E. O. (1978) and (1979), *Class, Crisis and the State*, London: New Left Books, London: Verso

Wright, E. O. (1985), *Classes*, London: Verso Books

Wright, N. (1977), *Progress in Education*, London: Croom Helm

Wright, P. (1985), *On Living in an Old Country*, London: Verso Books

Young, M. and P. Willmott (1957), *Family and Kinship in East London*, London: RKP

Index